Julie Peakman is an historian and author. She is a Fellow of the Royal Historical Society and Honorary Fellow at Birkbeck College, University of London. She lives in London and on Leros.

'The best stories are the forgotten stories; the stories of battles that have been ignored and of ordinary men and women whose voices have never been heard. *Hitler's Island War* is both of these. Detailed, moving and authentic, this is a story that needs to be heard, both for its human aspect and for its strategic importance in the struggle for the Adriatic in World War II. This is required reading for military historians and for those who are fascinated by the experiences of ordinary soldiers at war, told with their own voices and through their own eyes.'

Paddy Ashdown, author of *Game of Spies*

'Julie Peakman's riveting tale of the battle for Leros during World War II combines a precise analysis of politics and strategy with a deft sensitivity to the traumatic experiences of those war-weary men who fought and died on that island. Through their letters, diaries and oral accounts, she provides a way for us to understand something of their fears, suffering, hopes, and, in the end, despair.'

Joanna Bourke, author of *The Story of Pain*

'Julie Peakman's deeply researched book is a vividly raw and personal story. She has made an essential – and unique – contribution to understanding those extraordinary events on an Aegean island in 1943.'

Nick Jellicoe, author of *Jutland: The Unfinished Battle*

HITLER'S ISLAND WAR

The Men Who Fought for Leros

Julie Peakman

BLOOMSBURY ACADEMIC
LONDON · NEW YORK · OXFORD · NEW DELHI · SYDNEY

BLOOMSBURY ACADEMIC
Bloomsbury Publishing Plc
50 Bedford Square, London, WC1B 3DP, UK
1385 Broadway, New York, NY 10018, USA

BLOOMSBURY, BLOOMSBURY ACADEMIC and the Diana
logo are trademarks of Bloomsbury Publishing Plc

First published in Great Britain by I.B. Tauris 2018
Paperback edition published by Bloomsbury Academic 2020

ISBN: HB: 978-1-7845-3268-0
PB: 978-1-3501-5637-1
ePDF: 978-1-7867-3299-6
eBook: 978-1-7867-2299-7

Typeset in Stone Serif by OKS Prepress Services, Chennai, India

To find out more about our authors and books visit
www.bloomsbury.com and sign up for our newsletters.

For Jad, with love

CONTENTS

ILLUSTRATIONS

Maps

Figures

All images are copyright of author except where indicated.

Plates

LIST OF ABBREVIATIONS

ADS	Advanced Dressing Station
BYMS	British Yard Mine Sweeper
GHQ	General Headquarters
GOS	Aegean Headquarters
HQ	Headquarters
HMG	Heavy Machine Gun
IWM	Imperial War Museum
LCM	Mechanised Landing Craft
LCT	Tank Landing Craft
LRDG	Long Range Desert Group
MEHQ	Middle East Headquarters
MO	Medical Officer
MTB	Motor Torpedo Launch Boat
MMS	Motor Minesweepers
NCO	Non-Commissioned Officer
PRO	Public Records Office
RAP	Regimental Aid Post
RIF	Royal Irish Fusiliers
SAS	Special Air Section
SOE	Special Operations Executive
SBS	Special Boat Squadron
TSMG	Thompson Sub-Machine Gun

PREFACE

I first landed in Leros in August 1975 at the age of 17. The Turks had invaded Greek Cyprus the previous year and war had ensued. The Greek junta had fallen at the same time, making a trip to Greece a more favourable prospect. I landed with a small knapsack, new Greek sandals, a sundress, suntan lotion and a sense of adventure. I had no idea that this would change my life. On first seeing Leros in 1975, I dreamt of having a place of my own on the island and I eventually bought a tiny run-down peasants' cottage in 2001. That was the beginning of my obsession with the subject of *Hitler's Island War*.

I think the feelings which induced me to write this book must always have been there at the back of my mind, ever since I walked into Leros's British war cemetery on my eighteenth birthday. I saw all these graves of young men, the same age as I was, with no life in front of them as I then hoped for. I knew nothing of the Battle of Leros then, nor what part it had played in the war, only that all these men had died fighting for an ideal of democracy which they held dear. The fact that I shared their ideal bridged the time and space now between us. These young men and others of their generation had died fighting for their country during the war (when my parents had still been teenagers themselves), and had made it possible for me to live my life as I was doing then. The memory of that birthday has always stayed with me.

I owe a great many things to a great many people in the writing of this book. I thank the Leros islanders who welcomed me to the island back in 1975. I particularly want to thank Nondas Kannis for helping us settle into our new home in 2001 and guiding us through much bureaucracy and looking after us for many years. Tassos Kanaris and Yannis Paraponiaris showed me great kindness over the years, sharing their unique collections of war memorabilia, allowing me access to photographic images, and photocopying articles for me. Their assistance was invaluable. Both these gentlemen have private war museums which, owing to their diligence over the years, incorporate war artefacts, articles and books. I also want to thank the many staff of various libraries and museums in both Greece and Britain; sources were gleaned from the Imperial War Museum, the British Library, The National Archives, King's College London, Royal Irish Fusiliers Museum Armagh, King's Own Regimental Museum, the Army Museum, as well as the Dodecanese Archives in Leros. Ben Fellows at the Army Museum and Amanda Mureno, previously at the Royal Irish Fusiliers Museum Armagh, deserve a special mention. My hearty thanks also go to Richard Hughes of the Imperial War Museum for obtaining permissions for me to use the photographs. Thanks also to Trustees of the Liddell Hart Centre for Military Archives for giving me permission to use quotes from their archival material.

I especially want to thank my good friend Sheila Lecoeur who read the whole manuscript and gave me sound suggestions. I also want to thank the Society of Authors who assisted me with a grant, and Iradj Bagherzade of I.B.Tauris for commissioning a book so close to my heart. I had been researching the project 15 years before I eventually took time out to write a proposal. I am grateful to history editor Joanna Godfrey for her kindness and patience as well as her succinct editing suggestions. Both went beyond their normal duties when my partner, Jad Adams, and I were caught up in a humanitarian crisis on Leros in summer 2015. I had to turn my attention from writing my book to helping the Syrian refugees coming into the islands in their thousands to escape the war. Not only were Iradj and Joanna totally understanding in granting me an extension on the delivery date, but they sent me large amounts of money to help buy food and clothes for very hungry people. Also thank you to all the lovely staff at I.B.Tauris for the whip-round for the refugees. My enormous gratitude is extended to all those wonderful loyal friends (and many friends of friends, and strangers) who donated to the cause and came through for a pack of unwieldy volunteers during that summer, shovelling money across the world to help people they would never meet. I was humbled to work alongside a sterling bunch of volunteers who became very close while working under such terrible conditions. Particular thanks to my good friend Anne Tsakiriou for her resilience and for helping me with two of the Greek interviews. The refugee crisis and the Battle of Leros came together for me at this point, most of the refugees trying to escape the war in Syria.

The people to whom I am most grateful of all are the soldiers who allowed me to interview them: all are listed in the bibliography. Trying to trace the soldiers, who were spread across the country, took a long time. I left messages on battalion websites, wrote to addresses which people had given me, chased them through letters in libraries or archival regimental magazines which carried their articles; some had heard of my search and made contact with me. I travelled the length of the country visiting these men with my tape recorder asking them questions that no-one had asked them before, some of them matter of fact, others deeply personal and emotional. How did you get water? What did the island smell like during the bombing? What did you do when your comrades got shot down before you? This was not always an easy process for them, as inevitably my questions brought back their memories of violent times. All of them were part of the military operation on Leros in 1943. Every one of them was a gentleman and courteous to a fault. All were more than willing to share their experiences and adventures with a person less than half their age. I cannot thank them enough for their valuable contribution to history. They shared not only their personal memories, but their diaries, log books, cartoon drawings and personal letters. I have donated the taped interviews and all the related information to the Imperial War Museum, London, with copies to the Leros Archives, in the hope it may be of use to future generations, and as a tribute to the brave men who helped defend the island against German invasion.

Some of the old military buildings are still standing: the Italian barracks, the radar wall, the lookout boxes, the tunnels of British HQ.

Some of the equipment from the period remains in small unofficial museums of local collectors on Leros. Anyone interested in the war and this period should come and experience the uniqueness of the beautiful island of Leros.

Jad Adams has been my soldier for more than three decades, always at my side in times of trauma, fighting in times of adversity and sharing in all the happinesses of our lives. He has always been there for me and we have shared a great many adventures over the years, exploring the world, meeting hundreds of interesting people and making some very special friends along the way. I dedicate this book to all those soldiers who died for us fighting for freedom in World War II, and all those volunteers working with refugees all over the world. They continue to give us hope. Lest we forget.

1

In the Beginning

If it were not for the bravery of the Greeks and their courage, the outcome of WWII would be undetermined.

Winston Churchill[1]

As the bullets whizzed past his ear, 21-year-old Lieutenant Ted Johnson remained quite still, crouching behind a large boulder. He was halfway up Appetici mountain on Leros, his sergeant lying next to him, killed by a single shot through the head. Half his men were below him, half above, the Germans were all around them. As he lay in the rubble of rocks and pebble, prickly gorse scratched his feet. The smell of sulphate filled the air after days of bombing overhead. Barely able to keep his eyes open after days of constant battle and no sleep, the only thing keeping him alert was the adrenalin pumping through his body, urged on by the amphetamine drugs given by the army to keep officers awake.

Ted recalled,

> We formed up a plan and did our best to take over and this was when Sergeant Caldwell was shot beside me. I hadn't had any previous battle experience at all. I had done lots of exercises and in theory I knew it all but I hadn't done any practical fighting before. I was completely in charge, a young chap with no experience supposed to recapture the situation. It wasn't on. My platoon was then probably about 25 men.

Surrounded by the enemy, Ted had no alternative but to surrender to save the lives of his men. For them the Battle for Leros was over. Ted and his men were taken to a German concentration camp as prisoners of war. While there, Ted received a letter from his mother. It had taken seven months to reach him. She had written it on 21 January 1944, but he only received it in August that year.

> My darling Wakes [as she called him],
>
> At last I can write to you after all this *awful* long and anxious time. Oh Wakes, dear you don't know what it means to me to know that you are *alive* and safe. It's a long time now since I got that awful telegram here telling me that you were missing. I guessed all along that it must be so, but of course when the wire came, it was just too awful. But Thank God all our prayers were answered, and last week I got another wire telling you were a Prisoner of War. It is awful for you darling child and I know how much you must hate it, but for me I am so overjoyed to know that you are alive that nothing else matters. I pray so hard that you will be cared for and not treated too badly, its just *awful* to think of you, and I can't do anything to help. Only this morning I got a letter from the W. O. [War Office] telling me where I could write, but until they send me a fixed camp address I can't send any parcels and that is so awful, because there must be so much you are wanting, I don't suppose you were able to collect up any of your little things, or were you? I was dying to write all last week but had to wait for this letter from the W.O. telling me where to write, *this* is evidently only temporary, and they will let me know your number and camp later, and then I can send you some composts.

This heart-rending letter is just one of the many sent by desperate mothers who had not known whether their sons were alive or dead.

The Battle of Leros in November 1943 was only a tiny part of the war, but it was significant in that this was the last island to crumble in the larger fight for the Dodecanese in Greece and, more significantly, the last territory which Hitler conquered and convincingly held. The Dodecanese campaign had been devised by Winston Churchill, then British prime minister (and in charge of the War Cabinet), who wanted to take possession of all of the islands occupied by the Italians.

Most of the men in this story started off with the best intentions of seeing the battle through, defeating the enemy and going home to their families. Instead most of them saw hunger, thirst, blood and guts, their comrades lying wounded or dead beside them. Many ended up as prisoners of war. Some managed to escape capture,

FIGURE 1.1   Letter to POW Ted Johnson from his mother, 21 June 1944

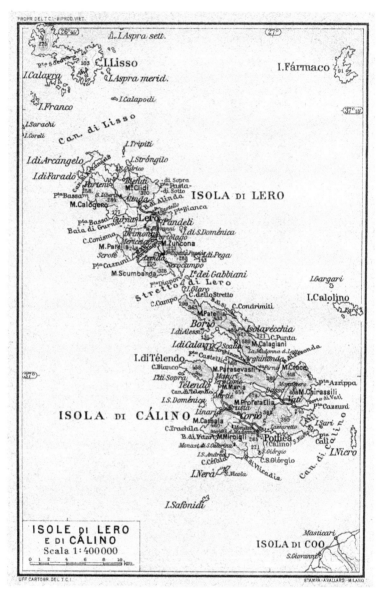

MAP 1   Italian map of Leros, 1929

but no-one managed to avoid the harsh realities of war. Death surrounded them. This is their story.

The Island of Leros

Leros is a small island, one of a group which make up the Dodecanese (literally meaning '12 islands'). Along with the other Dodecanese islands of Nisiros, Kos, Kasos, Patmos, Kalchi, Tilos, Simi, Stamplia, Lipsos, Scarpanto and Kalymnos (although Rhodes and Kastelorizo are also commonly included), it is situated near the Turkish coast, and was originally part of ancient Greece. The island is approximately 9 x 4 miles, covered in small bays and inlets all around the coast, pinched in at the centre with the bays of Gourna on the west side, and Alinda to the east, where its width narrows to a strip of about a mile covered in mountains, known as Rachi Ridge. To the north lies Blefuti and Palma Bay (Vaghia), to the south the main port of Portolago (now called Lakki) and, at the bottom, Xerocampus.

At various points on the island, mountains rise up to form rocky outlines against the sky. Much of this area remains uncultivated, the ground being too stony to work. Often the only buildings to be seen are churches perched on promontories and scattered among the whitewashed houses of the villages. The island is surrounded by pretty beaches and bays scattered along the coastlines. At the heart of the island lies Platanos, the main village (also then known as Leros town), overlooked by its stark windmills and medieval fortress built in 1309 by the Knights of St John of Jerusalem, one of the most prominent Roman Catholic military orders of its day. In Leros, the sun shines from around Easter time and a humid air breezes round the island. By October, the evenings become shorter and the rains begin to fall, often in huge torrents accompanied by thunder and sheet lightning that lights up the sky.

Leros has a long and chequered history of occupation and foreign invasion. For centuries the Dodecanese islands had been under the control of the Ottoman Empire, its grip only loosened with the outbreak of fighting between the Italians and Turks in the Libyan War in 1911. Italy began an offensive against the Turks with an attack on

Tripoli on 3 October 1911 and, during the conflict, Italian forces began to occupy the Dodecanese. By May, the Italians had taken over the islands of Calchi, Scarpento, Kasis, Misyros, Tilos, Kalymnos, Patmos and Leros with little opposition. With the signing of the Treaty of Ouchy (also known as the first Treaty of Lausanne) on 18 October 1912, the Italians agreed to return the Dodecanese to the Ottoman Empire. Unfortunately, the treaty's vague text allowed for Italy to continue to administer the islands, a fact which concerned both the British and French governments. The Dodecanese in effect remained under Italian military occupation, an important fact which was to affect the islands in World War II. Under the Treaty of London signed on 26 April 1915, the Italians were offered the Dodecanese as an incentive to join in the war on the side of the Allies in a secret pact between the Triple Entente (UK, France and Russia) and Italy. Turkey would eventually renounce all claims to these islands, in the Treaty of Lausanne ratified on 24 July 1923, thereby ending this war. Although the Italian annexation of the Dodecanese was formally recognised, the population was largely Greek. When World War II broke out, Leros and the rest of the Dodecanese islands were still under Italian control and it would not be until 1947 that the islands would become part of Greater Greece.

World War II

Britain and France officially declared war on Germany on 3 September 1939. Initially the Italians had remained neutral but, believing the Germans to be winning, on 10 June 1940 Prime Minister Benito Mussolini, Hitler's ally, declared war on Britain and France. Up until then, Greece had remained neutral, with a pledge by the British and French governments to maintain Greece's independence. However, this was to change when Mussolini's ambassador to Greece gave Greek Prime Minister Ioannis Metaxas an ultimatum: allow Axis forces to occupy strategic locations in Greece or face war. Metaxas refused outright and the date of 28 October 1940 became known as 'Oxi day', the day he said no to the Fascists' demands. It must be remembered, however, that the Dodecanese islands were a separate issue as they had long since been occupied by the Italians and were considered part of 'Little Italy' rather than part of Greater

Greece. This meant that the Axis powers held a distinct advantage over the Allies since they already had control over strategic points of the Mediterranean from the south as they planned to invade from the northern mainland of Greece.

The British began to be involved in Greece's affairs from 1941, when it became evident that the enemy was planning an invasion of the Greek mainland. In reaction to the country's crisis, a top delegation headed by British Foreign Secretary Anthony Eden was sent to Athens on 22 February. Eden offered to provide British support to oppose a German invasion. The Greeks accepted the offer, and the British army and air force began to move into Greece on 4 March 1941. In order to marshal their defences, the British Royal Navy was allowed to use the ports of Piraeus in Athens and Souda Bay in northwest Crete.

In a heroic effort on the part of the small Greek army in October 1940 and again in March 1941, Greece managed to fight off the Italian invasion on the Greek border with Albania. Disaster came, however, when a new front was created on 6 April 1941, with the German invasion of Greece via Bulgaria. Although the Greek army had been reinforced by limited Allied forces in anticipation of the German invasion, no further Allied help was forthcoming. The Greek army was outflanked and Greece had no option but to surrender. From ensuing events, it was clear that the Allies, under pressure in North Africa, were unable to provide sufficient forces to protect Greece, and by the end of April the Germans had taken Athens and the rest of the mainland. America would join the war in December 1941, but considered all efforts in the Aegean a liability from the start. The German army reached Athens on 27 April, and with the taking of Greece's capital city went the hope of keeping Greece out of the war.

Middle East Command had already been established in Cairo in June 1939, prior to the outbreak of World War II, intended to act as the base for the British Army Command set up to oversee operations of the land forces and co-ordinate the naval and air commands to defend British interests in the Middle East and eastern Mediterranean. Its purpose was to provide a centralised command structure during time of war in the Mediterranean and Middle East areas. The main naval control over the Mediterranean was located at Alexandria, Egypt. Up until then, the Royal Navy had controlled the eastern Mediterranean. As a result, maritime communications between Italy and its islands were impeded due to constant sweeps of the Aegean by British cruisers and destroyers. Italian supplies of food and equipment were restricted and little could get through. Attempts were made to supply by air and submarine, but these were inadequate. The last supplies from Italy to the Dodecanese using the Corinth Canal route came on a small steamer, *Tarquinia*, which arrived in Leros on 28 October 1941.[2] However, with Italians all over the mainland, supply routes continued via the Ionian islands.

The British had already attempted to take the island of Castelorizo (80 miles north of Rhodes and then still in Italian hands) in February 1941 in Operation Abstention, with the intention of neutralising Italian forces. The British Middle East Commandos landed on 25 February and took the island with little initial opposition. However, the Italians responded quickly, and the British failed to hold it. Due to the lack of naval and air support, withdrawal seemed the only option. This should have been a portent of things to come in the ensuing battle for the Dodecanese.

British forces had placed a garrison on Crete when the Italians had first attacked Greece on 28 October 1940 on 'Oxi day'. The Allies had watched as the Germans had subsequently invaded Greece in April 1941 in Operation Marita and took over much of the mainland, including Athens. Now, for Churchill, retaining a foothold in Crete was paramount as this was one of the most important strategic islands in the Mediterranean for both its naval and air force bases. Its airfields were of particular significance to both sides as without them bombers had to fly too long a distance to give adequate support. Whoever occupied the airbases essentially ruled the air. Churchill telegraphed the Chief of Imperial General Staff declaring, 'To lose Crete because we had not sufficient bulk of forces there would be a crime.'[3] In the meantime, evidently Hitler had his own plans; in his Directive 31, he stated, 'Crete [...] will be the operational base from which to carry on the air war in the Eastern Mediterranean, in co-ordination with the situation in North Africa.'[4] By May 1941, all eyes were focused on Crete.

Once Germany had gained the Greek mainland, the Allies were expecting an imminent air attack on the Greek islands. Along with Cretan civilians, they began making plans to defend Crete from a German invasion, including establishing thousands of troops on the island. Three thousand five hundred British soldiers were sent there, supplemented by Australians, New Zealanders – 27,000 in all. Greek batallions were also buttressing the numbers. However, with few British and no other support available to give air cover, food shortages were a problem and transport was inadequate.[5]

This was one of the first major errors that would affect ensuing battles in the Dodecanese. More Allied aircraft were needed on Crete for its defence, but the Allies were unwilling to commit planes which were needed elsewhere in the war. This lack of air cover would mean that the enemy would dominate the skies. Meanwhile, the Germans were secretly assembled in Bulgaria and Romania (now under German control) and flew out 10,000 paratroopers, and took 5,000–7,000 army troops by sea. On 19 May, after continual bombing by the Luftwaffe, the RAF withdrew, leaving the troops on Crete with no air cover for the first time in the war.

The Battle of Crete began on 20 May 1941 with an air invasion and the landing of German troops. At 8 a.m., hundreds of German paratroopers jumped out of dozens of Junkers Ju 52 aircraft and landed near Maleme airfield in western Crete and the town of Chania. Despite sustaining casualties, the Germans gained Maleme airfield, enabling them to land reinforcements and overwhelm the Allied positions on the north of the island. This was vital to the enemy war effort, as now they had an aircraft base and could give essential air cover to their troops to the detriment of the Allies. The Allied forces withdrew to the south coast where they were rescued by the Royal Navy, while others escaped with help from the Greek resistance forces or surrendered to the Germans. Crete came under German control on 1 June 1941.

The Battle of Crete was to prove disastrous for Britain in terms of both loss of morale and loss of airfields. When Crete fell, its airbases went with it. Since possession of the airbases on Crete, Rhodes and Kos (or lack of them) was to be instrumental in the larger fight for the Dodecanese, this was the first major blow struck against the future of the islands. The lack of air cover in the Dodecanese was to prove calamitous for soldiers fighting on the ground. Now, with Crete in enemy hands, a new tactic had to be found to dislodge the enemy.

Behind Enemy Lines

The formation of the Special Operations Executive (SOE) and its branches, the Special Air Service and the Special Boat Section (later the Special Boat Squadron or SBS), was a conscious effort to form a union of forces to create maximum havoc for the enemy at minimum cost in resources.[6] These developments played a significant part in the fighting in Greece and its islands from as early as 1940.

The SOE was initially an intelligence-gathering force, but one that would also conduct espionage, sabotage and reconnaissance behind enemy lines and offer support to any pockets of local resistance. Churchill's intention when he launched the SOE was to 'set Europe ablaze'. It was officially established by Minister of Economic Warfare Hugh Dalton on 22 July 1940 and would quickly be followed by the other groups focused on air and sea tactics.

Their methods were not to attack in force as an army unit, but to raid undetected as far as possible and lay bombs. Natural leaders of men emerged during these operations: David Stirling, David Sutherland, Anders Lassen and Captain George Jellicoe showed their grit and determination, earning the loyalty of their units. All of them already had excellent track records in the Middle East and would prove expert in the tasks of sabotage, fighting and rescuing in the Dodecanese islands. While the Special Air Service concentrated on flying men in and dropping them in parachutes behind enemy lines, the SBS did the same via sea transport, both having emerged from the SOE, the 'mother' group. The Special Boat Section was founded by 'A' Commando officer Captain Roger Courtney in July 1940 as part of the Special Air Service.[7] The SBS had originally been called the Folbots and attached to No. 8 Commando, men used to working in easily storable folding kayaks (folbots), but they changed their name to Layforce when the unit became attached to Middle East Command, the British Army command centre based in Egypt (otherwise known as MEHQ – Middle East Headquarters). They worked as small raiding groups, ten or so men to a boat, ferrying between islands, running recces to gather information, rescuing partisans or dropping off undercover agents. The task of these groups was to hinder the enemy by blowing up railways or aircraft bases. Most of the men were handpicked for the job, appraised for their level-headedness, determination and bravery. Typically they worked at night, often supported by the Levant Flotilla and the Royal Navy. They had good connections with the Greek resistance, a brotherhood of local Greek men fighting in the mountains in rough terrain; these men knew their localities, and some of them would act as guides and interpreters to British officers during raiding operations.

All three units – the SOE, the SAS and the SBS – were full of courageous young men eager to fulfil their duties using their own initiative. For the most part, they thought for themselves, could act quickly in response to enemy confrontation and were not averse to dangerous situations. Some of them did not take orders from authority easily, and many of them were foolhardy, but highly intelligent. David Stirling was one of the most important men in developing the Raiding Forces and inventing the rigorous training needed for action behind enemy lines. He was a quiet, thoughtful man, honest and courteous. Most of all he was respected by his men; his strong style of leadership and firm self-discipline motivated men to follow him, and inspired their loyalty and admiration. He had already gained a reputation for his successes in operations with the SAS.[8]

The men of the special forces had to go through rigorous training to ensure they were prepared to deal with anything the enemy might throw at them. Various 'top-secret training manuals' were written up as learning tools for officers on these special undercover operations and provided instructions on the tactics of guerrilla warfare: for example, what to do during the first 48 hours after arrival in the field; instructions on intelligence-gathering and planning; and how to establish cover and communications and methods of attack. The manuals suggested methods for educating civilians in passive resistance and simple sabotage, and ways of recruiting agents and informants. They also advised officers on codes and cyphers, secret inks, railway sabotage and training exercises to be undertaken. Essentially for anyone behind enemy lines, the booklets showed how the Germans operated – how German occupying forces maintained security, controlled civil populations and conducted searches, raids and interrogations. Counter-espionage methods and techniques for producing anti-German propaganda in occupied countries were helpfully laid out. Also included were details of the organisational structure of the Nazi Party, German police, German army, SS and Luftwaffe.[9]

Just as importantly, these secret SOE manuals contained a helpful list of the skills that might be necessary for those in active service, such as burglary and lock-picking – tips handy for men trying to gain access to locked buildings or attempting escape. Guidelines on 'passive resistance' explained everything from 'acts entailing virtually no risk' such as non-cooperation and making the lives of the enemy uncomfortable, to mass sabotage 'entailing considerable risk to person'.[10] Men in the field had to have a ready-made alternative life story for interrogators in case they were caught: they had to have prepared a fictional character with a complete historical familial background – a parallel to their real existence, a biography they could pull forth when placed under extreme pressure. Drugs were also a part of every SOE operator's kit and included an 'L' tablet, Benzedrine, and chloride of lime: The 'L' tablet came in a little rubber cover, and was a suicide pill. If the agent bit down on it, he would be dead in 15 seconds; Benzedrine was an amphetamine-type drug, given to help keep officers awake after hours of no sleep, which gave them a buzz of energy; and chloride of lime was used to purify water.[11]

These three groups – the Special Operations Executive (SOE), the Special Air Section (SAS) and the Special Boat Section (SBS) – along with their officers within the organisations were to become integral to warfare operations, the SBS being particularly important on the islands.

The Cretan Mission

One of those involved with Stirling's Raiding Forces was Lord Earl George Patrick John Rushworth Jellicoe. He had already had years of experience fighting in Tobruk and during the Rommel Raids. He had been educated at Trinity College, Cambridge, which had given him a grasp of ancient Greek. This was to serve him through quite a few escapades, despite surprising the local Greeks with the occasional archaic turn of phrase. He was a witty, jovial man and gained great respect from his fellow soldiers for his fearlessness. Jellicoe had already fought in the same unit as David Stirling in the Middle East 8 Commando and had impressed with his courage and the good rapport he had with his men. He had also made unsuccessful attempts to land in Crete in June 1941 and had served with 'L' Detachment (from April 1942) which was the core of the SAS.

Sometime in early 1942, Jellicoe went back to Cairo on sick leave where, by sheer chance, he ran into Stirling in a bar at Shepheard's hotel; 'much to my surprise he said he was looking for a second-in-command [of the SAS] and would I like to consider that. I said I would be delighted as long as my battalion would release me, and not altogether to my surprise my battalion had no qualms about releasing me.'[12] It was only now that the two men would get to know each other better. On the way back to the Middle East, they were on the same boat, but Stirling seldom emerged from his cabin except to play a game of chemin de fer and was nicknamed 'the Giant Sloth'. Jellicoe recalled, 'when I joined he asked me one of the things he would like me to do would be to keep a particular eye on, and get involved with, and help and advise on, matters relating to the free French unit squadron which had joined the SAS on the first of January 1942. This must have been about April [1942]. As a result of that I went on an operation to Heraklion', his mission to make a daring raid on German-held Crete with an attempt to blow up German aircraft and regain some of the lost ground for the Allies. On the night of 13 June 1942, a year after the Battle of Crete, Jellicoe used his special operations training to engage in a hit-and-run raid on Heraklion airfield. He was one of a group of men led by Georges Bergé Jacques Sibard (who had been a seaman with the French navy) and also comprising Sergeant Jacques Mouhot, 17-year-old Pierre Leostic and Lieutenant Kostis Petrakis of the Hellenic Army.[13] The Frenchmen were all members of the Free French parachutists who had joined the SAS at Kabrit. Each man carried a 30-kg pack containing food rations, explosives, detonators and 25 plastic bombs. For weapons they each had a Beretta machine gun, a Colt 45, a dagger, a map and compass, and a couple of hand grenades. Together, Jellicoe and his accomplices succeeded in blowing up the Cretan airfields. Although this was considered to be a major military success with more than 20 aircraft destroyed, in terms of loss of men it was disastrous – all Jellicoe's friends were captured or shot and he was the only one to escape.

At this stage, another man had joined the SBS, a previous fellow member of No. 8 Commando with Jellicoe – David George Carr Sutherland, whom Jellicoe already knew. He was to become a leading figure in the Dodecanese campaign, and was proving to be a valiant SBS member. Eton-educated, trained at Sandhurst and commissioned into the Black Watch, he had also served in Tobruk and had been with Stirling's 1st SAS Regiment in the Western Desert. Sutherland was on Crete at exactly the same time as Jellicoe on another operation elsewhere on the island, focused on blowing up another airport, his target at Tymbaki. Sutherland had aborted his mission as there had been no aircraft present – they had been moved – so he had gone to the rendezvous to await being picked up off the island. He was completely unaware of Jellicoe's presence on Crete, and their meeting is indicative of the louche attitude taken by Jellicoe. Sutherland recalled,

> One morning, with a spectacular dawn and the rippling sea below, I saw a lone figure approaching. He was wearing Khaki shorts and shirt, and had a jaunty way of walking. I held him in my binoculars and could not believe my eyes: it was George Jellicoe. I walked down the track to meet him. He was one of the sole survivors of a group of four French SAS who had landed from the Greek submarine the *Triton* on 10th June, paddled ashore and destroyed 21 aircraft at Heraklion airfield.[14]

Jellicoe and Sutherland ended up spending a flea-bitten night in a cave together awaiting rescue.

The next plan formulated for the SBS was for an attack on enemy airfields on Rhodes, then in Italian hands. The raiding force was to consist of only eight men, two guides and two interpreters while the Italian garrison was about 30,000 strong. Sutherland volunteered for the job in what was to become known as Operation Anglo in September 1942. Along with Marine John Duggan, he attacked

Rhodes with the SBS, this time destroying two airfields. Once again the mission had ended with the capture or death of many of the finest SBS operators, with only Duggan and Sutherland managing to escape. Sutherland said of the event, 'Operation Anglo was one of the most hair-raising experiences imaginable. It was also a voyage of self-discovery. I learned that if one keeps one's head and nerve and uses the ground properly it was possible to survive in an enemy-infested country.'[15] This was to stand him in good stead for the future operations in the Aegean. However, because of the heavy losses, Stirling was obliged to reorganise the SAS, which he now divided into four sections: the French and Greek Squadrons, the 1st SAS Regiment and the Special Boat Section.

The Free French Forces were already risking their lives, along with some of the Greek population, including Green Navy officers and the Sacred Brigade – the last two mainly consisting of a group of partisans hiding in the mountains of the islands, and various fishermen recruited to help the SBS. Since Greek paper money was virtually worthless due to racing inflation, the main currency used by the SBS to pay the Greeks assisting was either barter, or the gold sovereign – the equivalent of £5. About two million sovereigns were brought in by various British agencies for use as bribery and for the employment of local Greeks. One of the men employed by the British agents in the Dodecanese was Nikos Pyrovolikos who had been working in covert operations with the SBS during the war since 1941 transporting signallers and agents between the Dodecanese islands, Turkey and Cyprus. He worked with a group of other Greek civilians using a private boat, under the direction of a British officer of the SBS.[16] The English officer paid him a wage in gold sovereigns and brought him supplies; every 15 days the English officer came and filled the boat up with everything they needed for the trips: food, biscuits, chocolate and other provisions. Pyrovolikos was only one of many Greek locals employed by the Royal Navy in the service of the British government throughout the war.

By 1943, a complete overhaul of the special operations organisations was again necessary, not least because David Stirling had been capture by the Germans on 23 January while on a raiding mission in the North African desert. He was now incarcerated in

Colditz. Unfortunately, all the information on past and future raids lay in Stirling's head and no paperwork was available for the guidance of those who remained. They were left to pick up the pieces as best they could and plan the way forward. In response, Jellicoe stepped forward to take up command of the Special Boat Service.

The fact that Stirling was now out of action, together with the loss of many SBS agents killed or captured on various raids, meant that restructuring was once again essential and a more effective grouping was necessary. Sutherland recalled,

> The Special Raiding Squadron was given a war establishment of 230 officers, non-commissioned officers and men to include full operational planning, training and administrative back-up. The core of the unit consisted of three Operational Detachments of 60 men, based on five patrols, ten strong, with a Headquarters and signal element. The unit was formed on 1 April, All Fools' day, 1943 'As good a day as any', recalled George Jellicoe remarking as he took command.[17]

The SBS was renamed the Special Boat Squadron under the command of 24-year-old George Jellicoe.[18] Under his supervision, the SBS was about to be taken in another direction. Now divided into three units 'L', 'M' and 'S' (based on each commanding officer – Tom Langton, Fitzroy Hew Maclean and David Sutherland),[19] they would concentrate on the Aegean. The rest of the Raiding Forces under Paddy Mayne and the SAS went on to raid Sicily and Italy in July and September 1943. Jellicoe's force was to work with Christodoulos Tsigantes and the Greek Sacred Squadron (GSS). Tsigantes was a large, powerfully built bearded man, very intelligent and with a good sense of humour, and an ability to lead his men, personality traits which Jellicoe admired, and the two men became firm friends.[20] The Levant Schooner Flotilla (LSF) had been established by the Royal Navy with as many requisitioned local caiques, motorboats and high-speed launches as it could muster, and was called upon to transport the men between islands while they made recces, gathered information and made raids or rescues. Led by Lieutenant Commander Adrian C.C. Seligman, the flotilla had about ten boats in September 1943, each armed with 20-mm canons, Browning machine guns and Vickers light machine guns and operated with small crews, usually about five or six men.

One of the first jobs for Jellicoe was to prepare the men of the Raiding Forces for action. A training camp was set up in Athlit, south of Haifa, a place of beauty according to those who saw it. Sutherland described it: 'Picture a crescent-shaped beach about a mile across with a ruined Crusader castle at one end, the sea turning azure in the changing sunlight and the steep Carmel Hills behind. It was an ideal base and training for the kind of operations we expected to carry out.'[21] Gradually, the men began to build up their physical strength and endurance running mile after mile with heavy packs on their back. In between exercises, they played sports and swam. They were also taught boating, camouflage, map reading, hill climbing, musketry, signals and communication, parachuting, weapons and explosives. For pistol training they were sent on a course run by the highly skilled Leonard Hector Grant-Taylor. As an introduction he told the men, 'This is a school for murder, murder is my business. Not the vague shooting of people in combat, but the personal, individual killing of a man in cold blood. It's an art which you have to study, practise and perfect.'[22] Their dress included desert boots, Arab headdress, belt and holster pouches, rucksacks, knife string and rope, mosquito repellent, binoculars (three to a patrol) and a pair of wire cutters. Jellicoe had specifically requested a Danish man, Anders Lassen, to join his force, after seeing him working as a commanding officer under Stirling. Destined to be a hero, with his rakish good looks, blond hair and muscular body, he stood out as a natural-born killer. He was headstrong, deadly with weapons and would murder the enemy without compunction. Sutherland described him as a 'great outdoors' type who used a bow and arrow to kill a deer.[23] He obviously liked hunting, as Jellicoe had met him while shooting geese with Stirling in Keir, Scotland, had taken an instant liking to him and asked the chief of combined operations, General Robert Laycock, to send him over for deployment in the SBS. They were soon to be sent out on their first mission together.

With an increased deployment of more British liaison officers, by June 1943 a Greek underground army roughly 20,000 strong was mobilised. A series of highly effective raids was mounted on enemy lines throughout Greece, causing chaos and disruption to enemy action and employing German soldiers urgently needed in battles elsewhere. It was at this time that, according to Sutherland, the first SBS operation under Jellicoe's command was undertaken: the Cretan mission of 23 June 1943 named Operation Albumen. As Sutherland had been there before, he was given the job of overseeing the mission. Again the men were divided into three small patrols (in all, three officers over fourteen men and two guides), with each one targeting one of the three airfields. Ander Lassen took the usual hair-raising risks he was prone to, shooting four German sentries in the process of blowing up five aircraft. Similar success was had at Kastelli and Heraklion airfields. Sutherland said proudly, 'They were truly impressive and I have often thought how fortunate we were to have excellent officers and men in the SBS.' Although they had escaped alive, one man Kenneth Lamonby had been shot during the mission and died in Heraklion hospital. Twenty-five Cretans who helped them came off the island with them as they would certainly have been shot if captured. For now, though, the Special Boat Squadron were celebrating their success and were ready to take to the Dodecanese.

2

The Italian Capitulation

Look I am afraid I told a lie about having been parachute trained.
I've never dropped.

Julian Dobrski, SOE[1]

On the eve of the public announcement of the Italian capitulation, there was already a bleak outlook for Greece, despite the optimism of its people. *The Times* on 7 September 1943 reported from Smyrna on 'Destitute Athens'. 'According to reports reaching here, the morale of the Greek people, stiffened by the Allied victories and by the hope of an early deliverance, is higher than ever, but the physical strain resulting from the scarcity of food and other hardships is again becoming alarming, especially on the Greek mainland and on the islands nearest to Greece.' The black market was rife, 'prices have reached astronomical figures for meat and fuel'.[2] People were reduced to selling off their homes, furniture, jewellery and clothes in order to buy basic necessities. However, the most significant development in the war for the Greek islands was now about to take place.

The Italians had occupied and governed the Dodecanese islands since the Libyan War and had overseen their administration, despite the Greeks' yearning to become part of Greater Greece. In essence, during the early part of the war, the population had been under occupation by the Axis powers. But this was about to change when on 8 September 1943 Italy officially capitulated to the Allies.

Up until then, the Italians had been on the side of Germany. They had been content to be allied with Hitler so long as that seemed to be the winning side. However, Italy had suffered several setbacks following the Allied invasion of Sicily, and on 24 July 1943 the Fascist Grand Council voted no confidence in Mussolini and he was arrested. Marshall Pietro Badoglio replaced Mussolini as head of the Italian government and eventually signed an agreement with General Dwight D. Eisenhower, commander-in-chief of the Allied Forces, that Italian armed forces would immediately cease all hostile activity and withdraw from participation in the war. In reaction, the Germans took over in Greece and quickly moved forces to defend Italy, but it now looked as if there was a chink in their armour which could be exploited if the Allies could move their troops to the Dodecanese islands quickly enough. Despite its intention to remain neutral, on 13 October Italy would declare war on Germany.

With the public announcement of the capitulation, the race was on between Britain and Germany to see who could occupy the Dodecanese islands first. With Crete in German hands, it was now imperative for the Allies to ensure that Rhodes with its strategic airbase – as yet still in the hands of the Italians – came under Allied control. At this time, British aircraft were based in Cyprus over 360 miles away, reinforced by United States Ninth Air Force and two RAF bomber squadrons. British bombers only had the fuel capacity to fly to the Aegean and back, with no possibility of combat for any length of time, nor to be of any real use for defence purposes. The Allies desperately needed airbases from which to protect the islands, and Rhodes was the only major airbase in that area (Kos had only a small airstrip). Without air cover, enemy bombs could fall indiscriminately, and if Rhodes was lost, the Allies would effectively be without air cover.

The key players behind the scenes in Britain were General Maitland Wilson, commander-in-chief (known as 'Jumbo' Wilson because of his girth); Air Chief Marshal Sir William Sholto Douglas, air officer commanding Middle East Air Command; and Sir Henry Harwood in command of operation in the seas. The British did at least have permission from Turkey to dock their boats in its territorial waters during the day, despite Turkey being neutral. The British Raiding Forces already held a base at Bodrum, and the SBS and Allied caiques frequently used Turkish bays to avoid detection by enemy aircraft. However, by the middle of June 1943, it had become apparent that assault shipping, craft and air forces would not be available, and instead the naval force commander and staff were sent to Algiers to plan operations in the central Mediterranean.

The possibility of capturing Rhodes and subsequently opening up the Aegean for British occupation in Operation Accolade had been under active consideration at least since January 1943,[3] when Churchill had raised the subject at the Casablanca conference. His hopes were that the Allies could effectively have a fighting force in Greece and that the Italians would come on board to fight on the Allied side. He could then use the islands as bases to attack the German-occupied Balkans. He had been given the go-ahead by the Chiefs of Staff, although it was stressed that Britain would have to go it alone as the USA refused to become involved.

While the British were dithering, German troops had already made their move into Rhodes in January 1943, with two batteries of 88-mm guns to protect the airfields, a deployment which the Italians had allowed. From April onward, a German Panzergrenadier battalion began landing. Further reinforcements were made when three more batteries, technicians and gunnery experts landed and work began on concrete gun emplacements for defences. By the time General Kleeman landed at the end of June and formed the Sturmdivision with around 7,000 soldiers, all pretence of German officers' troops not taking over command of the island had been dropped.[4]

George Jellicoe had already been in communication with a secret agent of the SOE, Julian Dobrski, about the possibility of taking Rhodes in January 1943. Dobrski was a half-Polish, half-Italian count, going under the name of Major Dolbey, whom Jellicoe thought 'a very remarkable man'. According to Jellicoe, Dolbey had 'been involved in a major way with SOE in Cairo throughout the war', mainly while based at headquarters of Force 133 Cairo, Egypt.[5] Dolbey had sent Jellicoe a coded message about possible undercover operations in the Dodecanese. He wrote in their codenames 'from 'D/H 113' (Dobrski) to 'D/H 119' (Jellicoe), outlining the possibilities of an invasion of the island of Scarpanto (Karpathos) using it as a base to get to nearby Rhodes. 'Intelligence available points to 1000 Greek soldiers being on the island.' He added, 'It is thought by the DCO that we can bribe leading personalities [the Italian authorities] in Rhodes and get the island without firing a shot'. At the time, they were working with a Greek partisan called Odysseus.[6] Dolbey again wrote to Jellicoe, in a letter headed 'MOST SECRET' dated 8 April 1943, to inform him that the SOE were interacting closely with Greek agents who were trying to persuade Turkey to let them use its land. 'If George Petrides is in a position which will enable him to arrange transport to Bodrum [...] it should be possible to arrange communication for material, and maybe even for bodies, with the Turkish mainland.' But there was always a fear that there might be double agents in the fold.[7]

Churchill was eager to attack in the Dodecanese and, ever open to the use of caiques and small boats, sent a letter to General Ismay on 2 August 1943 suggesting,

> Can anything be done to find a modicum of assault shipping without compromising the main operation against Italy? It does not follow that troops can only be landed from armoured landing-craft. Provided they are to be helped by friends on shore, a different situation arises. Surely caiques and ships' boats can be used between ships and shore? I hope the Staffs will be able to stimulate action, which may gain immense prizes at little cost, though not at little risk.[8]

Churchill and Roosevelt attended the 'Quadrant' Conference in Quebec on 11–24 August, bringing Allied leaders together to discuss war operations. General Eisenhower was called upon to make up deficiencies in air cover, particularly in long-range fighters, but because of lack of manpower, any mass combined operation in the Dodecanese was vetoed by a decision of the Combined Chiefs of Staff.[9] They insisted that 'operations in the Balkan area will be limited to supplying Balkan guerrillas by air and sea transport, to minor Commando forces and to the bombing of strategic objectives.'[10] It was never envisioned, at least by the Americans, that resources for the Dodecanese campaign would be diverted from what was considered the more important aim of the invasion of Italy. There was not enough manpower and equipment available to invade both Italy and the Dodecanese. Main efforts had to be focused on Italy's defeat as one of the major players in the war. A memo was sent to Eisenhower and commanders-in-chief of the Middle East on 19 August which made the position clear:

It was never intended that the operations sanctions in C.O.S. (M.E.) [Chief of Staff Middle East] 400 should in anyway encroach upon the resources required for operations in the Central Mediterranean [...] Whilst adhering to this policy it was thought that advantage should be taken, within the resources that can be made available, of an opportunity to occupy either Crete or the islands of the Dodecanese in event of German withdrawal. We think it too early to discount entirely the possibility of a favorable opportunity occurring.[11]

In possession of most of the Allied military assets, America now had the upper hand in the decision-making process in the joint discussions between Britain and America.

On 31 August, the commanders-in-chief for the Middle East informed the Chiefs of Staff that the only operations that could be mounted from the Middle East in the Aegean were small-scale raids: sabotage, guerrilla operations by resistance groups and unopposed 'walk-ins' to areas evacuated by the enemy. The Allies wanted to bring Turkey into the war, and Churchill believed this was possible if the Allies occupied the Dodecanese. However, the whole project was ill-conceived from the beginning, as Long Range Desert Group (LRDG)'s second commanding officer David Lloyd Owen pointed out: 'It was tragically vague throughout and many fine lives were lost in a cause which few of us ever fully understood.'[12] While there had been talks about landings on Rhodes, Kos and Leros, Roosevelt and Eisenhower refused to divert any aircraft from the operations taking place in Sicily. Nevertheless, Churchill did not give up his larger plans for the Mediterranean front.

Since the arrest of Mussolini, Badoglio had been making overtures for peace, and discussions continued with the Allies until an agreement was made on the terms of surrender in Sicily. Italy would be treated fairly if all the Italian-held islands were handed over to the Allies, and its soldiers must surrender all their arms. As soon as the official surrender was announced on 8 September 1943, the British in Cairo radioed the Italian troops still on the Dodecanese islands, requesting they take sides with them – though it was not an easy task to suddenly change allegiance mid-war. Some Italian soldiers, such as the Siena Division on Crete, surrendered to the Germans without a fight. In other areas of Greece, the Italians quickly dispersed and the Germans were unable to round them up easily. Italian resistance to the Germans in the Ionian islands resulted in the notorious massacre of around 6,000 soldiers and many officers. Yet others escaped as quickly as they could to team up with the Greek resistance fighters.

The Italian surrender finally forced the Allies to act in the Dodecanese. Pushed by Churchill, General Sir Henry Maitland Wilson made preparations for landing on Rhodes as the main aim in the Dodecanese, with Kos targeted next as it had an airfield, and then Leros for its naval resources. Samos was considered to be of less importance, but nonetheless worthwhile as it had been under Italian control and could hopefully be easy to take over. However, the Germans had acted immediately by rolling out Operation Axis, with essentially the same aim as the British: to disable the Italian troops and take over the Italian-held areas of Greece. The Germans had already made preparations to take over the entire military administration of Greece and had deployed sufficient forces on the west coast of Greece, the Peloponnese, Melos, Crete, Scarpanto and Rhodes to ensure they retained control of these key positions. The Luftwaffe had gained the upper hand, with the airfields on Crete already under its control. Its next target was Cephalonia, which was overrun in seven days. Hitler ordered his troops to take no prisoners, and to shoot all resisting Italian soldiers, resulting in the death of over 4,000 of them. The islands of Karpathos, Siros, Andros, Tilos, Zea and Naxos all fell to the Germans. Despite Germany's strong position, its troops were now spread over a wide area of Greece. Many were kept busy trying to suppress partisan activities, their naval forces insufficient. Grand Admiral Dönitz presented a less-than-positive picture to Hitler of their defences becoming stretched: 'The position on the Balkans Peninsula is in danger from lack of forces. Maintenance of security in the Balkan rear area has become a difficult task.'[13]

Churchill admitted his own obsession with the Aegean, a passion which had been with him since World War I. He told General Maitland Wilson, 'When the tremendous events of the Italian surrender occurred, my mind turned to the Aegean islands, so long an object of strategic desire.' He believed that if the Allies won the Dodecanese islands, Turkey would abandon its neutrality and throw its weight behind the Allies; this would mean that the British could fly their aircraft and run their ships from Turkey and use it as a jumping-off base. He also thought that the surrendering Italians would now change sides and fight side-by-side with the Allies, thereby doubling his manpower, another incorrect assumption.

Nonetheless, he continued with his gamble, 'On September 9, I cabled from Washington to General Wilson, Commander-in-Chief of the Middle East, "This is the time to play high. Improvise and dare".'[14] The only force Wilson had available to him was 234th Brigade, which had been part of the hard-worn garrison of Malta. However, Roosevelt felt that it would take too much time and be a distraction from the war on other fronts. The final decision was approved by the Combined Chiefs of Staff at Washington on 10 September, which essentially allowed Churchill to move into the Dodecanese: 'The Combined Chiefs of Staff have taken note of the action the Commander-in-Chief Middle East is taking in respect of Rhodes and other islands in the Dodecanese. They approve this action, and are considering what further can be done.'[15] With the Germans soldiers already in occupation in Rhodes, the British leaders were aiming at a covert operation to disable enemy airbases.

Drop into Rhodes

Although the initial task of the SBS had been fighting behind enemy lines, their assignments shifted and they became responsible for taking over the Italian-occupied islands as bases for the Allies. It was at this stage that Jellicoe was called into action. He had been training in Athlit, near Haifa in Israel, but had gone up to Beirut to discuss business and to meet another officer and his girlfriend for dinner. He remembered,

> I went up to Beirut one day to talk to the submarine flotilla there, about using their submarines for attacks on Greek islands. That evening I was having dinner with a person whom I knew who had been in the SAS and his lady at the St George's Hotel when suddenly a military policeman arrived at my table, and asked me my name. He said he had just received a message from Raiding Force Head-Quarters [at Azzib, near Haifa], which was where we came under – we were stationed just north of Haifa. I was needed immediately so I drove back, or was driven back straight away that evening. There was a plane sent out from Cairo for me and I was to report to the aerodrome at the crack of dawn in full battle dress.[16]

He drove back to Athlit, and had a quick nap before setting off to the airport. Once in Cairo,

> I went straight to the Middle East HQ, and into a meeting which had been going on already for about half an hour with fairly senior officers. It took me a little time to know what it was all about. I learnt to my surprise that the armistice was coming into effect with Italy that evening [8 September], and they were very keen to get into contact with the Italian HQ in Rhodes which was under Admiral Inigo Campioni. They were proposing to send the fast patrol from Alexandria, but it was going to take two days.

Everything was taking too long and meanwhile British complacency was giving the Germans a head start.

Jellicoe was astounded that action had not been taken already and that little planning seemed to have been made for the taking of Rhodes much earlier. Leaders had known about the armistice several days before it was made public on 8 September, as it had been signed on 3 September. Jellicoe thought the committee was indecisive and noted with dissatisfaction that there was much wavering from the supposed decision-makers. There was a suggestion that a party of men should take a boat from Egypt, and proceed via Castelorizo but, as Jellicoe pointed out, it would take them days to arrive. While Admiral Campioni controlled the 35,000 Italians on Rhodes, there were already 5,000 Germans there commanded by General Kleemann, sent in earlier in anticipation of the Italian surrender. It was most important that Campioni be persuaded to hold out against the Germans until the Allies landed in force. If Rhodes was lost, Kos and Leros would be in greater danger. With access to such a close airbase, the enemy would have a serious advantage.

During the meeting, Jellicoe seized the moment.

> When all this dawned upon me, I just said I couldn't understand why on earth someone was not dropped in straight away that evening, and then they said, 'Would you care to be dropped in'. And I said, 'Yes certainly'. Then somebody across the table then said, 'Do you speak Italian?' And I said, 'No I don't'. And he said, 'Well, I happen to speak Italian as fluently as I speak English', and he then volunteered to come with me, and to supply a wireless operator, a man called Sergeant Kesterton, and I said, 'Fine.'[17]

Jellicoe and Dolbey lost no time in putting their plans into action for the drop into Rhodes, despite Dolbey being 42 years old at the time, compared with the sprightly 24-year-old Jellicoe. Along with Sergeant Kesterton, they took a Halifax bomber and prepared themselves for their parachute fall. If the drop was successful, the plan was that once Jellicoe and Dolbey had persuaded Admiral Campioni to surrender Rhodes to the British, the SBS officer J.T. Turnbull (who was overseeing the mission) would follow in to Rhodes in a high-speed launch to take up discussions with the Italians and offer some protection. Allied propaganda plans were afoot to drop leaflets and generally disrupt the Germans and encourage rebellion by the local Greeks. Dolbey wrote to their superiors, 'It is presumed that we could count on naval, military and air co-operation within the laid down objective.' Their presumptions, however, were incorrect. The response from their superior officers was made in a hastily scribbled pencil note indicating that little could be offered in way of support: 'very limited – only as stiffening at the best'.[18]

Their attempt to drop on the night of 8 September was aborted as the pilot couldn't find the island due to bad weather – the sky was full of mist. 'We flew up that evening at night [...] flew all around Southern Turkey but they never found Rhodes and they had to fly back.'[19] The lack of planning, and hastily made arrangements, led to an ineffective first run. 'I don't know how much warning the Middle East command had about the armistice, but it is quite extraordinary that one hasn't been given a little bit of a warning.'[20] Jellicoe said he would have planned it properly and taken his own wireless operator. The lack of any sort of preparation by the government for the eventuality of the Italian capitulation became all too obvious.

The following night of 9 September was more successful. Jellicoe and his colleagues had flown the three hours or more from Cairo, and by 10.40 p.m. they were over Rhodes, ready to be dropped. Jellicoe recalled, 'I always remember at the very last moment, before Dobrski was going to go out, the first person, he said, "Look I am afraid I told a lie about having been parachute trained. I've never dropped. If by any chance I hesitate, please give me a push". Well, he didn't need a push.'[21]

The strong wind blew them all off course and the three became divided as Dolbey's parachute took him further afield. Jellicoe remembered, 'Kesterton and I landed a bit further inland and were shot at a good deal on the way down. They don't hit you at night.' They had lost Dolbey. He had been whisked away with the wind. Untrained in parachuting and unable to control the angle he was coming in at, he hit the rough stony ground and broke his leg. The bone was sticking out through the skin in his thigh and he could not move. He was fortunate to hear soldiers nearby talking in Italian and called to them explaining he was a British officer and needed to be taken to their commanding officer.

Meanwhile Jellicoe had been picked up and taken to the Italian admiral, but the discussions did not go well. Jellicoe had hoped that he might be able to persuade Campioni to come on to the Allied side, but the Admiral feared for the lives of his men and fellow officers, and, with little in the way of Allied back-up on offer, there was small chance of any protection against the Germans. Campioni conveyed the unfortunate news that the Germans already held the airport. The island was divided, with the Germans in the centre and most of the Italian troops on the south side, with Campioni unable to contact them. The Germans had taken over all communications as well as the armed soldiers, and the airfields were already well guarded. Jellicoe had lost his radio in the drop so had no way of contacting his commander-in-chief, but Campioni allowed him to make contact with Allied HQ in Cairo in a coded radio message by way of Italian radio stations in Rhodes and Leros. Dolbey requested from the British HQ that 200 troops be parachuted into Rhodes immediately, reporting, 'We are rather worried as the situation requires immediate reaction.'[22] Jellicoe recalled, 'HQ could not promise to do much except to dispatch a brigade before six days, which was not enough for the Italian Admiral, although he remained polite and discussion continued.' [23] None of the reactions from HQ sounded positive. A handful of SBS men was the best Jellicoe could promise the admiral in the short-term, not enough to protect the Italian officers from the Germans. No doubt at the forefront of Campioni's mind were Hitler's orders to shoot all resisting Italian officers. Dolbey was taken to Simi and flown off to Cyprus where he could be looked after.

Jellicoe recalled, 'That was the last time I saw him until after the war, in Brussels quite a few years later.'[24] Jellicoe evidently admired Dolbey's courage, 'He is a very talented person, very brave too. I got to know him well after the war.'[25]

From the Italian point of view, while not unwilling to cooperate, with so many Germans on the ground and so few British to defend them, they had to be careful. Campioni was reluctant to take sides too quickly. He had met with General Kleeman the night before, when they had heard about the Italian capitulation. They had agreed on a truce, whereby both the Italians and the Germans should remain as they were in order to prevent further bloodshed. Although the Italians far outnumbered the Germans, the young storm troopers were highly motivated and in key positions.[26] In reality, the Germans were playing for time, waiting for additional troops to secure the airfields.

The only good news for Jellicoe was that the Italian garrison on Castelorizo had surrendered to the British on 8 September and was now in Allied hands. The only assistance to hand in the immediate vicinity was therefore from the men from LRDG, the SBS and the Greek Sacred Regiment on Castelorizo. Campioni, in fear for his and his men's lives, advised Jellicoe to leave immediately and placed an Italian armed torpedo boat at his disposal. He and Kesterton quickly made their way to Castelorizo, taking with them important information on mines in the area and an outline of Rhodes's defences, as well as 'two bottles of Rhodes wine and an excellent picnic basket'.[27]

With Rhodes about to fall into enemy hands, the small airfield of Kos and the naval base of Leros were now in dire need of protection, and their security depended on the SBS. General Wilson wrote in his despatches, 'At 17.15 on 11 September, information reached me that Campioni had lost heart, had refused permission for us to enter the island and did not wish to have any further dealings with us.'[28] Between 35,000 and 40,000 Italian soldiers surrendered to the Germans on Rhodes.[29] As one of the major staging posts in the Aegean, its possession by the Germans meant they now had control over its airfields. The dire effect of its loss was to become increasingly apparent as the days passed.

The Taking of Castelorizo, Kos and Leros

Jellicoe learned that the British had successfully landed on Castelorizo while he was still on Rhodes. Two motor launches had sailed from Haifa for Castelorizo on 9 September carrying a detachment of the SBS and the SAS.[30] Small patrols of the Raiding Forces accompanied by civil affairs officers had taken charge of the island, and extra troops were being brought in. The intention was to use the island as an advance base for penetrating the other Italian-held islands inside the Aegean.

Major David Sutherland was one of the men on the incoming crafts. He had had been in Haifa when given notice to move into the Dodecanese islands at midday on 9 September. He heard an excited message from the duty officer at Raiding Forces HQ in Azzib: 'The Italians have surrendered. Grab as many of your men as you can. Get them, weapons, and equipment on board a Motor Launch in Haifa harbour and occupy the island of Castelorizo as soon as possible.' He woke his assistant Captain Walter Milner-Barry, roused a dozen of his own men and another ten from 'M' Detachment and prepared to move out. Sutherland recalled, 'We piled everything we thought we would need, weapons, ammunition, cooking kit, blankets, etc. onto two 3 ton trucks and headed for Haifa harbour 20 miles away. The ML was fuelled, armed and ready for sea.'[31]

Sutherland and the rest of the squadron pulled into the bay of Castelorizo in two motorboats commanded by Lieutenant Commander Lesley Frank Ramseyer on the following day (10 September). It was just after midnight. A few shots were fired by the Italians, possibly due to a mistranslation of orders, but Sutherland sent a man in a folboat (a sort of folding kayak used by the SBS) to explain the situation, and a guide was sent out to lead them into port. By daybreak, Sutherland could see the crescent-shaped bay and the many little whitewashed houses built on the hills behind and was impressed by the sight. He was also gratified by the welcome of the locals:

> Our reception from the few people still living there was heart-warming. Bottles of liqueur which tasted like vintage port were produced. Now that we had arrived at last as liberators it was clear how much the bombastic Italians had ground down the poor long-suffering Greeks over the many years of unjust occupation of the Dodecanese.[32]

They found out only about 1,000 people were left as most of the Greek inhabitants had fled to the mainland; only a score of old people, a handful of fishermen and some children remained clinging on to their half-wrecked homes in distressful conditions of poverty and scarcity.[33] Walter Milner-Barry of the SBS wrote, 'They are desperately poor and look half-starved.'[34] Despite their abject poverty, the people of Castelorizo showed every hospitality. The Union Jack was hoisted up on the Castle.

After his lack of success in Rhodes, Jellicoe moved on as quickly as possible. He was about to meet up with his old friends from the SBS. 'I was sent back with Campioni's chief of staff [Colonel Fanetza] to Castelorizo, the most eastern island of the Dodecanese where I found that one of my squadrons under David Sutherland had occupied it with no resistance from the Italians at all.'[35] He found the SBS busy regrouping and landing equipment.[36] Sutherland remembers Jellicoe's arrival: 'I was enjoying a gin and tonic with Walter Milner-Barry in the Port Office when round the corner and into the harbour appeared an MTB [motor torpedo boat] flying the Italian flag, and on board was Jellicoe.' Nothing of any note took place en route except the disagreeable Colonel Fanetza missed his footing while alighting the boat and fell into the sea.[37] Naturally, everyone had a good laugh at his expense. On 13 September 1943, Castelorizo was formally liberated by the Allies, with the arrival of 350 men on the Greek destroyer *Koundouriotis* and the two French ships. The British officers, now reunited on Castelorizo, quickly congregated for a meeting to decide on their next moves.[38]

Plans were drawn up with the focus of moving on to Kos with back-up as quickly as possible, then to Leros to take up the surrender of the Italians. Protection of Kos's airfield and Leros's substantial navy base was imperative if the Allies were to have any hope of maintaining air cover. Jellicoe, along with Lieutenant Commander Ramseyer, Milner-Barry, Sutherland and about ten men in all from SBS 'S' Detachment sailed towards Kos on 13 September. Jellicoe remembered, 'There must have been an order from Cairo to move up to Kos and Leros as soon as we may, it must have been a day-and-a-half later or so [after arriving in Castelorizo], we left by the same fast MTB which the Italian had taken us to Castelorizo up to Kos with David Sutherland and some of his chaps. And we got to Kos in the morning.'[39] Sutherland was at first reticent:

> We did not know how we would be received, or if the Germans had forestalled us, or what the garrison would feel about our sudden arrival. But as we neared the harbour I could see lots of children looking at us, and as we ran through the narrow entrance a crowd was waiting for us on the quay. The enthusiasm and joy of the inhabitants was touching in its spontaneity. Grapes were showered by the Greeks on our patrols as they went ashore.[40]

Landing in the sunshine, they were greeted by civilians proffering wine and throwing flowers at the soldiers. After securing the 4,000-strong Italian garrison, Sutherland gathered his men and moved inland to take control of the airfield in Kos. That evening the Italian officers provided them with a splendid dinner of tagliatelle verde and some good wine. Jellicoe recalled, 'We were very well received by the Italians there.' The men were offered free haircuts and shaves by the locals. Jellicoe left Sutherland and his men there, 'and I went on with just two of my people, to Leros that afternoon, in this motor torpedo boat – it was extremely blowy'.[41]

A delighted General Maitland Wilson communicated to the Chiefs of General Staff the following day, 'We have occupied Castelorizo island, and have missions in Kos, Leros and Samos. A flight of spitfires will be established in Kos today, and an infantry garrison tonight by parachute. An infantry detachment is also proceeding to Leros.'[42] Two Spitfire squadrons and a squadron of the RAF regiment were established on Kos, where Sutherland's teams had secured the airbase. A Dakota aircraft accompanied by a flight of South African Spitfires dropped in 120 Allied parachutists from the 11th Parachute Battalion on Kos island that night of 13 September.[43] According to the newspapers, the islanders were delighted to see the British paratroopers landing on their islands. The *Daily Telegraph* reported, 'The noise of the transport places awoke the islanders who rushed to greet the sky invaders. At dawn a few hours later, the Luftwaffe tried to strike back at the airfield with low-flying strafing and bombing attacks by ME 109s and JU 88s.'[44]

Moving on to Leros, Jellicoe had no inkling of what he might find there, so was adjusting his plans as he went. His initial plan was to make contact with the Italian governor, Admiral Luigi Mascherpa, with the aim of getting him to surrender to the British. On arrival, he was pleased to find no opposition. 'The Italians on the whole were generally very helpful, perfectly friendly, not necessarily all that efficient. We got a very warm welcome from them.' As far as the civilians were concerned, he said, 'I supposed I was the first British officer there. But they were extremely friendly like they always were, the Greeks.'[45]

Admiral Mascherpa was much more cooperative than Campioni had been on Rhodes and showed Jellicoe round Leros island. It was no doubt easier for Mascherpa to hand over the island, as there were no Germans occupying as there had been in Rhodes (although the Germans had been in Leros in September prior to the surrender, a fact that was to give them an added advantage in that they had an understanding of the island's topography).[46] However, Mascherpa had already been contacted by Kleeman on Rhodes who had ordered him to surrender Leros to the Germans, which he did not do. The Germans had been planning to take Leros on 14 September, but had been delayed because their aircraft were tied up elsewhere, and German resources were now overstretched trying to maintain both Rhodes and Crete.

Fortunately for the Allies, Mascherpa was easily persuaded to come on to their side and to share information about Leros's defences and available equipment. The fact that many of the Italian officers on the island were old and had been sent to the islands in an undemanding post away from the action meant that, for the most part, they did not want to fight. To show his goodwill, Mascherpa provided Jellicoe with a lavish dinner in his honour. Jellicoe duly reported his success to his superior Colonel Turnbull, returned to Castelorizo and turned in for a well-deserved 14 hours' sleep.

A top secret telegram was sent to the commanders-in-chief from Chiefs-of-Staff Middle East on 15 September relaying a message from Eisenhower:

> We agree that with the resources at present at your disposal action you are taking in the Aegean to exploit Italy's capitulation is best possible. It is desirable on political ground that you should if operationally possible include some proportion of Greek troops in forces used for

occupation of the Dodecanese when opportunity occurs. We appreciate
that you would probably wish to support Greek rebels and encourage
civilian morale in Greece, by infiltration of small specialist units and by
bombing of particular targets. You will realise however that any such
action could only be carried out at present with resources at your
disposal but we understand that you are already proceeding with the
formation and training of these small specialist units in order to be
ready for any opportunity that arises.[47]

Churchill was pleased to hear that the troops' movement by sea
and air had begun on 15 September, and during the subsequent
weeks more would occupy different islands. Castelorizo, the British
garrison for strategic purposes, was hurriedly increased to some
1,300 British soldiers. Troops began to spread out to cover the
islands of Kos, Leros, Samos, Kalymnos, Symi and Stampalia.
Fairmile motor launches and caiques of the Levant Schooner Flotilla
were pulled in to help, overseen by Lieutenant Commander Adrian C.
C. Seligman.[48] Alongside the LRDG and the SBS were Macey's Raiders
(No. 8 Special Boat Commando).[49] During this phase, British naval
forces available for the operations consisted of six Fleet destroyers of
the 8th Destroyer Flotilla, two Hunt-class destroyers, 1st Submarine
Flotilla with six operational boats, 16 motor launches, four landing
craft fitted with anti-aircraft guns and eight RAF high-speed
launches.[50] They were busy transporting the British forces and supplies
to the nearby islands of Kos and Leros and intercepting enemy
shipping coming from Piraeus to the Dodecanese. The lack of Allied
aircraft in the area remained a major problem and Allied sea craft
bringing in supplies had to travel in open waters without protective air
cover for over 450 miles from the British bases at Alexandria, the naval
headquarters for the Dodecanese campaign.

Initially, the situation on Leros looked good. British reinforcements were landing to supplement the 5,000 Italians already on the
island, but only half of the Italians were armed. Six-inch battery
guns lined the top of the mountains, pointing out towards the
enemy; smaller guns were in line to defend the harbours and bays.
Meanwhile, now back on Leros, Jellicoe was enjoying himself.
'His jeep was a familiar sight all over the island and he seemed to bear
a charmed life.'[51] Sunderland had been sent on to Samos with his
group of SBS to be welcomed by the Italian authorities, who still held

the island, with dinner and wine – so far no Germans had reached Samos. A group of Royal West Kents soon arrived, leaving him free to go to Kalymnos and try and secure it. Again, it was still hoped that the Italians would cooperate and peacefully hand over these important strategic islands to the Allies. Over the next few days, the Allies began to build up their defences. Troops of the Durham Light Infantry were sent to Kos, the Royal Irish Fusiliers (RIF) went to Leros and the Royal West Kents were shipped to Samos. On 16 September, a further 1,500 British soldiers landed on Kos, joining the garrison of 3,000 Italians.

Small coasting vessels, sailing ships and launches were all pressed into service, and by the end of the month Kos, Leros and Samos were occupied with a battalion each, and detachments occupied a number of other islands. Unwilling to be overridden so easily, the Germans were quick to respond with heavy bombings. This was an easy job for the enemy given that the British had inadequate air cover and the US still refused to become involved. The Royal Navy made easy targets and both ships and troops had to lie low during the day when they could be easily spotted. The Germans had also mined the islands, making it increasingly dangerous for Allied ships to land troops, stores and equipment.

On 17 September, the British destroyers *Hurworth* and *Croome* landed a communications party of 300 troops, including A and B companies of Royal Irish Fusiliers 2nd Battalion, and plentiful stores safely on Leros.[52] That same day, a German counter-attack began with heavy air bombardment using Messerschmitt 109s and Junkers 88s (Ju 88s). After landing troops and stores at Leros on 18 September, 'Captain (D)' commanding the 8th Destroyer Flotilla sank two enemy merchant vessels and put the enemy's escort out of action.[53] Also on 18 September, HMS *Faulknor* and HMS *Eclipse* and the Royal Hellenic Navy's HHMS *Queen Olga,* which were on an anti-shipping sweep from Alexandria, sank a 3,000-ton and a 2,000 ton-merchant vessel and damaged their escorting craft at 1.15 a.m. just north of Stampalia (Astypalia, just below the west of Kos), their ship blowing up five minutes later.[54]

Despite the Royal Navy's admirable efforts, the lack of air cover was now becoming a significant problem for the Allies building

up Leros – especially since German-occupied Rhodes with its three aerodromes lay across the supply route. The German air force in the Aegean had long been weak, and, before it received reinforcements from the Italian and Russian fronts, successful anti-shipping sweeps were easily carried out in the southern Aegean and the Scarpanto Strait.[55] However, with Crete and Rhodes now in German hands, the odds were turning as the enemy sent every available aircraft to those islands in order to mount a campaign of insurmountable cover
· of the skies.

3

Troops to Leros

No one knew where we were going, but one man said it must be Leros from looking at the position of the stars. He was right. Next morning we went to Portolago in Leros, then the action really started.

John Norman Cowell, King's Own[1]

From mid-September, troops began pouring in to defend Leros and the surrounding islands from the expected German invasion. Most of the men were from the British 234th Infantry brigade led by Major General F.G.R. Brittorous. The unit had been formed especially for the operation, as the main British military force to capture and retain the Dodecanese islands. In the event, Brittorous proved ineffectual and was removed from post, to be replaced by Brigadier Robert Tilney. However, many thought Tilney a poor replacement as he was without sufficient infantry experience.

The ground troops arriving on Leros over the following months consisted of four main regiments: the 2nd Battalion of Royal Irish Fusiliers (also known as the Faughs), the 4th Battalion of the Royal East Kent regiment (known as the Buffs), the 1st Battalion of King's Own and the 1st Battalion of Queen's Own Royal West Kents.[2] The Durham Light Infantry went to Kos, the Royal West Kents to Samos (minus one company). During the first few weeks there was an outbreak of fever among the troops (probably malaria caught in Haifa and reaction to sand-fly bites) and some of the men fell ill. For the most part, though, men were finding themselves shelter, digging in and ensuring they had supplies of food and ammunition for their regiments.

Landing the Long Range Desert Group

Among the first to arrive on Leros was a squadron of the LRDG taken by the Greek destroyer *Queen Olga* from Haifa to Leros arriving the following day in the middle of an air raid.[3] Major Guy Prendergast had been promoted to lieutentant colonel and appointed commander of the LRDG, and Major Jake Easonsmith was appointed his deputy. Both were inclined to eschew publicity, an important trait given the activities of the LRDG were to be kept secret. David Lloyd Owen had been given command of the United Kingdom and Rhodesian 'B' Squadron. He said of his two colleagues, 'They were [...] to some degree reticent, under-demonstrative, dedicated to their duty and imbued wth a natural modesty that would have made it anathema to them to have received the plaudits of the public.'[4] Lloyd Owen himself was relaxed, with an amiable type of leadership which relied on persuasion and personal example. Normally immaculately dressed, he now had to scruff himself up a bit to fit in with his LRDG comrades. All three men had been sent to the Dodecanese to assist in taking over the islands. Part of their job was to watch German ships and air movements to try and weigh up German strength; the other was to command one of the toughest fighting forces on Leros.

The group had originally been called the Long Range Patrol, and was formed by Major Ralph A. Bagnold in Egypt in June 1940 mainly from New Zealander volunteers ('A' Squadron), but soon South Rhodesians and British volunteers joined them (forming 'B' Squadron), altogether around 350 men. They had warfare experience in the desert, and because of their skills they were selected to join the defence of the Aegean islands. They were given similar training in communications, self-sufficiency and survival techniques to the men in the other special forces and had a good working relationship with the Special Boat Squadron. Lloyd Owen recalled his time in May 1943 at the Cedars in Lebanon. The aim was to get his men as fit as possible including training in rock climbing and skiing.

> We made long and arduous marches carrying sixty and seventy pound packs; we passed nights out in the hard and cheerless snow; we struggled with teams of bucking, obstinate, hateful mules and sat daily

trying to master the intricacies of the Greek or German languages. And all the time we were getting fitter, and we became daily more able to traverse the mountains in fog, in cloud, in blizzard or under the fierce sun.[5]

Practice in parachuting, mountain climbing and abseiling was also part of their preparation. New equipment was especially made for them: insulated sleeping bags, specialised rucksacks, string vests, ski caps, solid reinforced boots and a choice of weapons. Their endurance of boiling hot days in the desert and freezing nights in the mountains in Lebanon ensured that the men in the LRDG came out fitter than any other unit.[6]

Their shooting skills had been honed to perfection. The men could strip down their guns with ease, cook rations, operate their new wireless sets and learnt to navigate their way around wherever they might find themselves. Radio operators were impressed with their issues of new packs of radio sets and miniature battery-charging engines. The sets were robust and simple to use and were the basis of the main communications between fighting units. Signal operators were highly trained and relied on sky wave signals or key operating. Codes were regularly changed so that communications would not be compromised. Radios could not be operated while moving: an operator had to set down and put up aerials and other equipment. Because of the need to keep up with essential information, the radio operator often had little sleep.

They started off with ten men to each patrol, which included an officer, a sergeant, one Royal Corps of Signals, two regimental signals and two general duty men, one of whom was trained as a medical orderly. Medical Officer (MO) with the LRDG, Captain R.P. 'Doc' Lawson recalled, on learning he was to be sent to the Aegean, 'What I had to do on the medical side was to find out the best way to change completely motorised patrols into small groups of mountaineers carrying everything they needed from the start to the finish of the objective.'[7] Food had to be chosen for its highest calorific value in the smallest volume and weight.

With the Germans now holding Crete, Rhodes and Scarpanto, the main aim of the LRDG was to harass the Germans in these areas.

MAP 2   Map of the Dodecanese Islands, 'Geographical Section, Chief
of Staff Map 1943'

A special directive was sent by Lieutenant General Anderson headed
'Most Secret and Officer Only' dated 11 September stating that
their 'most likely role will be to move into Kos and Samos, if the
situation permits, to stiffen resistance of the Italian garrisons and
local guerrillas to German control of the Islands. You may however,
be ordered to operate in Rhodes.'[8] However, the top commanders
of the operation showed very little understanding of what was
taking place on the ground, and this was to be a continual
problem throughout the Dodecanese campaign. Lloyd Owen
complained about the total lack of reliable information, calling it
'disgraceful'.[9]

Lloyd Owen and his squadron travelled from Haifa on a Greek sloop to Castelorizo, accompanied by a British and a French ship, sliding into the island on 13 September. The locals were ecstatic to see them. 'The narrow quayside was lined with cheering, rapturous Greeks waving little flags. Their genuine and spontaneous welcome did not make the task of unloading any easier.'[10] They had to offload 100 men, their equipment and three weeks of rations into smaller caiques and rowing boats. Many of the men then took the opportunity of a quick dip in the warm sea. Lloyd Owen and his officers were stationed in some small white houses near the harbour, and after informing Cairo of their arrival and enjoying a tasty evening meal and some local wine, fell asleep on their bedding rolls on the wooden floors.

The next morning the instructions came for them to move on to Leros. Lloyd Owen had no idea how the Italians in Leros might react. In fact, he should have been informed as Jellicoe had already received a welcome just a few days before, but it is evident this was not the case (this is one of the first indications that messages were either not getting through properly, or information was simply not being shared, a problem which would prove fatal later in Leros). Lloyd Owen recalled that the only message he received was a command, 'Long Range Desert Group Squadron will move at once to Leros to assist the Italian Garrison.' A further issue presented itself as he recalled: 'With only such scant information, and with none at all about how the Italian Garrison would receive us, I was also faced with the problem of how to get there.'[11]

Lloyd Owen decided to send Captain Alan Redfern ahead with a wireless set in a seaplane that Jellicoe had left behind. Lloyd Owen would follow on with the rest of B squadron when he heard how the land lay. As the seaplane was about to set off, manned by unwilling Italians, it crashed with Redfern on board and was put out of use. Lloyd Owen therefore had little option but to take as many men as possible and go over on the remaining Italian motor launch. This time he ensured they had a Royal Navy coxswain to navigate, a British engineer overseeing the engine room, and Lloyd Owen with a pistol in his own pocket overseeing the skipper – there was obviously still a lack of trust between the British and the Italians.

> It was a clear moonlit night as we sped past Rhodes. We could see fires burning. These were a result of a visit by the Royal Air Force an hour or two earlier; and later coming in behind us out of the moon we saw the big RAF transport planes which were to drop a company of our parachutes on the airfield at Kos.[12]

They were tired, wet and cold, unsure of what reception lay ahead.

When they reached Leros, they were met by Admiral Luigi Mascherpa who had been warned of their arrival. However, Lloyd Owen did not receive the welcome that Jellicoe had experienced. 'I can only describe his reception in the early light of dawn as frigid.'[13] Nonetheless, the admiral politely invited Lloyd Owen to lunch.

> I duly arrived at the time appointed and felt a tinge of embarrassment in my dirty clothes among so many gold-bespattered Italians who exuded perfume. But my embarrassment soon turned to resentment when I saw how those Fascist officers were living. We sat down to a five-course meal and drank finest wines and liqueurs from Italy out of golden goblets.

This was most distasteful to Lloyd Owen, having passed the starving Lerians outside, who had stopped him to beg for the leftovers. He showed his displeasure openly. He began to talk of defence plans against the German attack with the Italians who were obviously not pleased with this interference.

Luckily Lloyd Owen could relinquish his lead on defence; 'one morning I was woken with a message to say that three British destroyers were lying in the harbour. I went down to see what was going on, and on the quay I found a British Brigadier [Tilney] with his entire brigade. GHQ in Cairo must have forgotten to tell me about them!'[14] Such was the lack of communication on Leros from the beginning, even when the communications systems were still working.

The British still held on tentatively to Kos, which was now the Allies' only nearby airfield. Some LRDG were flown into Kos and were taken by destroyer to Leros, and smaller local crafts carried troops to Samos. A couple of 'A' Squadron patrols were despatched to the Cyclades, another to Simi, and others to various other islands. The intention was to spread Allied defences as far as possible and establish the islands as their territory before the Germans arrived to claim them. The LRDG was working hand-in-hand with the Special

Boat Squadron as they arranged themselves on various islands, all receiving a positive welcome from the local Greek communities. On Leros, their job would be to stand side-by-side with the Italian batteries to ensure they held their posts.

Faughs Follow In

The Royal Irish Fusiliers (Faughs) were the first large group of infantry to arrive on Leros. As military ground troops their immediate objective was to occupy the island and defend it from any possible attack. Lieutenant Edward 'Ted' Johnson was among those who arrived on 20 September. He had been picked out as officer material for the Royal Irish Fusiliers early on in his career and had been commissioned in June 1941. The Faughs had a fair amount of training in the Lebanon before they departed, somewhat similar to the LRDG and SBS, but not quite so strenuous. Ted recalled,

> Because the Battalion had been in Malta for such a long time as a garrison battalion, they were not trained operationally for anything other than defensive work. We needed to be trained to get into a more offensive spirit and to be able to operate in mountain districts. For instance, we trained loading equipment on to mules and living rough in the mountains. We then left here and came down to Palestine where we trained for combined operations but the first training was what we called dry-shod training. In other words, not on the sea or a lake but on dry land, landing craft represented by tapes. We learnt the principles of combined operation. From there we went down to Kabrit which was the home of the commandos at the time, where we operated on water with the Royal Navy and did attacks onto the opposite shore with proper landing craft. In other words, we worked as if we were going into proper action, with all the trimmings, the Navy and the water and so on.[15]

Ted Johnson had been with C Company Royal Irish Fusiliers in Palestine when he had heard the news of his posting. He recalled, 'I came back down to Haifa to find that two companies had already gone to Leros. My company, B, HQ and another company were detailed to go to Leros the following day [...] 'We embarked on two destroyers, HMS *Intrepid* and HMS *Echo*. I was on *Intrepid*.'[16] The journey was worse than they expected as the weather was poor, 'We ran into very heavy sea somewhere in the region of Rhodes, and

had a very rough time. All our weapons and the chaps themselves
were in pretty poor order because of the weather so it was probably
just as well we didn't have to fight our way onto the island.'[17] None of
the soldiers had been given any inkling of what was going on.

> We'd had no briefing about Leros. The first intimation we had that we
> were going to Leros was after we'd already left Haifa on the destroyer,
> officers were sent for and we were told by our second-in-command at
> the time who imparted the information to us that we were going to
> Leros and most people said, 'Where the hell's Leros? And what's Leros
> all about?' We had no briefing whatsoever on why we were going there
> or what we'd find when we got there. We had no battle plans.[18]

Neither had the soldiers been given any idea of what to expect
when they got there, whether they would leave the ship in full
battledress, or experience a peaceful arrival. This lack of information
is surprising given that both Jellicoe and Lloyd Owen had been
liaising with Mascherpa on Leros only days previously. The feeling of
trepidation among the troops as they sailed towards the island
was evident. Raymond Williams was on the ship with the Faughs and
remembered,

> Each man was keyed up and edgy at the thought of what lay ahead.
> No-one had much to say, but tensions and strain was registered in every
> face. The craft edged towards a concrete jetty and the atmosphere eased
> considerably when a couple of high-ranking Italian officers were spotted
> on the quayside, waiting for our arrival. With no sign of hostile troops
> around, it appeared that we were going to have things very much our
> own way.[19]

Ted recalled, 'We disembarked, the orders were to expect resistance
but it wasn't really known whether the Italian force on Leros were
going to be friendly or antagonistic so we were supposed to be
prepared to disembark in a warlike manner and virtually invade
the place.'[20]

Their commanding officer, Maurice French, and Intelligence
Officer Lieutenant Frank Smith had experienced a similar uncertainty
when landing in Leros a little ahead of Ted and his company.
On their approach Maurice French said to Lieutenant Smith, 'You
and I will go ashore, Smith [...] We don't want to look too frightening
and wear our steel helmets.' They had come into Portolago (Lakki) to

find the Italians lined up on the harbour with a band in full regalia to greet the British contingent. Frank recalled, 'As we steamed into harbour, we couldn't believe our eyes. The Italians were in magnificent array, with a band playing. Colonel French and I walked down the gangplank and went round the gunneries and looked over the gun emplacements, with great bonhomie and they [the Italians] opened bottles of vermouth.'[21] Ted and the rest of the Faughs could see French and Smith standing on the quayside looking relaxed. Ted recalled,

> They were there not in battle order, but normal short-sleeve order – not even wearing steel helmets so we were told there was no likelihood of enemy action so we just embarked in good order, as transport was available to take us away from the dock area. We were relieved that we didn't have to fight our way onto the ground because we'd had a pretty rough crossing that night.[22]

Those Italians who refused to stay as allies were taken off the island by destroyers.[23]

The advance party had already commandeered transport from the Italians and the Greeks. Some ordinary civilian-type lorries took them to the centre of the island where companies were allocated their positions. Ted Johnson recalled,

> I was allocated a platoon position by my company commander. Our position was in the region of 'Charing Cross', which is the road which goes through the centre of the island now – it's now a tarmac road but in those days was just a track. There was a crossing of two tracks on the western end of Meraviglia and that we called Charing Cross and we deployed initially somewhere in that area.[24]

The Faughs had headed towards the middle of the island around Mount Meraviglia where Fortress HQ had set up residence in the tunnels in the side of the mountain. It was not particularly high for a mountain, about 650 ft, just high enough to see the coast but for the lesser hills blocking the view. It gave a splendid view of the Crusaders Castle opposite on top of Castle Hill next to Mount Appetici across the valley below. Ted recalled,

> By then we knew the deployment of the other two battalions, we knew where they were. I remember taking my platoon on a route march up to the other end of the island. The idea of that was to familiarise us all

with the geographical layout of the island. This was up in the north. But we were also pretty heavily involved in unloading this supply ship, all hands were deployed on that. We tried to get the local Greeks involved but they weren't really the best of labour. And certainly when a raid developed at any time they disappeared with great speed.[25]

They dug slit trenches (holes in the ground big enough to give cover to one or a few men) and his three platoons lived in those for three or four days. 'We were very much under strength [...] maybe 60 chaps in all in our company. In a battalion there were four companies. Initially we weren't all in the same place; the other companies were in various other places.' [26]

Lieutenant Frank Smith's job was to liaise between the battalion and the brigadier along with Major Dixon the staff officer, Captain Craig, various intelligence officers and a crowd of signallers. He briefed them where they were to go and as to what was happening. At first, life was pleasant on the island. 'I went into a shop in Alinda Bay and bought a cigarette lighter, I bought a German make. The local population was very pro-British and they were pleased to see us take over from the Italians. They were very cooperative.' Frank had fond memories of sleeping out in the good weather. He camped under perfect sky under ideal conditions in September. As seen in the contrary feelings of Jellicoe and Lloyd Owen, there were obviously varying perceptions of how both the Italians and the civilians received the troops. Ted felt that neither were all that welcoming.

> My impression of the Italian army is that they were certainly not keen to see us. They had been living there for years beforehand and they had all their families there and they were really on a cushy number. I think they felt that by us coming onto the island, we were stirring it up, and there would be trouble eventually into which they would have to take part. I felt they did not want us to be there.[27]

Many of the soldiers were well settled in. Quite a few marriages had taken place between the Greek women and Italian soldiers. Occasionally, fracas developed with the locals.

> We had one incident of a fusilier being knifed in a pub one night. I didn't see it personally but we were told about it. One got the flavour that the Greeks weren't too happy to see us. We did our best to keep our

plans away from the Greeks we didn't want them involved from an operational point of view.[28]

Corporal Vic Kenchington was medical officer with the 2nd Royal Irish Fusiliers, who landed at the same time as Ted, having sailed on the other destroyer, the *Echo*, in the same fleet. He had also been with his unit in Lebanon, when he received his orders to go to Haifa. He remembered a good reception on Leros. 'It was lovely – there was no opposition there, the Italians were very friendly. We marched up to land between Alinda [and Gourna], to the narrow part of Leros, and stayed there for a few days.'[29] His impression of the greeting was fairly positive.

> The Germans beat us to Rhodes, so we went on to Leros. Kos got a lot of bombing. There were about 1,000 air raids on Leros. Colonel French [his commanding officer] moved us up to the hills to Charing Cross. There was a little house just below Charing Cross, which we used as an MI [military intelligence] room. Another house at the top, I used as billet along with another man.[30]

Fusilier Corporal Jack Harte came in on the ships with Vic Kenchington and Ted Johnson. He had the job as section leader of No. 9 platoon with Company A and was sent to Meraviglia equipped with one anti-tank gun, one Vickers HMG (heavy machine gun) and one Bren light machine gun, a few Lee Enfield rifles and a couple of hand grenades. Few rifle companies were available and most soldiers just had hand guns so it was fortunate that Jack had brought with him his illegal 9-mm Italian Beretta light machine gun, acquired while on special service in Sousse, Tunisia.[31] They dug in in an area where they could overlook Alinda as well as the harbour. Diet was frugal: 'we were not to taste bread, potatoes or fresh meat for the following two months, as we defended the island [...] Instead we lived off tinned stew, hard biscuits, bully beef – all in short supply.'[32]

The Fusiliers were worked hard and it is little wonder they were tired by the time the battle started. Jack Harte recalled, 'The work of building defences, laying mines, filling in crater, unloading cargo, arranging dropping zones, struggling in darkness across rough terrain to find containers, getting them away before daybreak, and finally standing to, all the while under constant bombing attack, contributed to us being dead on our feet the whole time.'[33] He used gelignite to blow a hole in the cliff so the men could shelter. Most of them were in slit trenches which provided little cover from the German bombing from Stuka 87 and 88s which went on all day relentlessly. Amphetamines were issued to the troops to help them stay awake. Shifts of two hours on, two hours off were all the sleep they could grab. 'The only thing keeping us going were the army-issued Benzedrine – better known as "Bennies" – and they didn't last long (hence the wartime song "Who put the Benzedrine in Mrs Murphy's Ovaltine!").'[34]

Charing Cross Headquarters lay halfway up Mount Meraviglia, with a good view of the Castle from the opposite side of the valley. Tunnels had been blasted through the mountain by the Italian officers, making the Headquarters a safe haven for the newly arrived British officers to run the foreseeable campaign. Each entrance was covered by camouflage netting with 'Leros town' (Platanos) below one entrance, and the other side overlooking Gourna and Portolago (Lakki). The tunnel (which still exists but is closed off) was five or six hundred feet long, and only the central part, from which two or three underground chambers opened out, was lit.[35] Trestle tables were used as desks for staff to plan on maps, and in another chamber, signallers were kept busy coding messages, deciphering and sending orders. The 'kitchen' consisted of a pit situated in the open on the Gourna side of the tunnel where two cooks heated up tinned bacon and sausages.

For the ordinary privates of the Royal Irish Fusiliers, life was tedious at first. Their job was to dig in, to create slit trenches and to maintain their defence positions. They 'stood to' between the hours of 4 a.m. and 5 p.m., but they had to be careful to avoid the German bombings while undertaking their routine duties. Bombing tended to happen throughout the day and cease at night. Twenty-four-year-old Fusilier Private Patrick 'Paddy' McCrystal was one of the men who were sent up to the mountains above Meraviglia. He had joined the RIF at 17, disguising his age, having already experienced a life of chores as part of a hard-working Irish family. He was therefore only too willing to accept responsibility and carry out his tasks as a true army man, although he was not convinced they had enough arms to protect themselves,

We had to do our duty, and look out for the enemy. They were expecting the Germans. They told us that the Germans were coming. We weren't there to defend the island, because all we had was a 303 rifle that we got on Leros. There was a couple of machine guns, right enough. But, that's all we had, a 303 rifle.[36]

For Paddy it was a boring time but he was stoic;

I was to sit looking out to the sea, up in the rocks. You could do nothing else. There was nothing to do on the island, you know. You would get up in the morning and wash your face. I had an old tin hat, one of the commanders had given it to us and I used that as a hand basin. The water came up by rations. I didn't get very much. The water was par-boiled with the heat.[37]

Thought turned to food, but even that was restricted. Also cooking or heating food was basic. 'We had very little [rations], just compound, you know. A wee tinnie, pint of milk, sugar and tea, all mixed up, a wee stove you put you pot on it, like boiling the kettle, you know. Charing Cross was the feeding point.'[38]

Different regiments of soldiers coming in at different times meant they did not form coherent units, which added to the confusion. Paddy recalled,

The battalion was scattered all over the place. Maybe about six or seven hundred all over the island. At first there was only the Irish Fusiliers, but then we were reinforced by the West Kents, and the Buffs, but we were the first ones in after the LRDG. There was only about two or three of us in Charing Cross, the others disappeared, I don't know where.[39]

Lack of information given to the men lower down the ranks simply added to their uncertainty.

Ships, Signals and Gun Batteries

Meanwhile, the Royal Navy were kept busy transporting troops, stores and equipment as well as targeting the enemy: On 20 September, HMS *Intrepid* and HMS *Echo* landed 600 personnel and stores from Haifa at Leros and sailed for Alexandria after dark. On the 22nd, HMS *Faulknor* and HMS *Eclipse* and HHMS *Queen Olga* landed 1,200 personnel and stores at Leros.[40] They sailed after dark with forces divided in case of enemy shipping sweeps. On the 23rd,

HMS *Eclipse* patrolled south of Scarpanto Straits and sank a merchant vessel close inshore under Cape Prasonisi at 1.30 a.m. and damaged an escorting destroyer which beached itself. The 8th Destroyer Fleet returned to Alexandria with 128 German POWs from Stampalia.[41]

A small group of early arrivals of King's Own boarded destroyers in Haifa and Alexandria and journeyed to the Dodecanese via Cyprus, skirting the Turkish coast. More of their troops would come in piecemeal on 5 and 12 November. During the 24-hour journey, the destroyers were almost continually bombed by the German air force, but fortunately no ships were sunk.[42] Sergeant Reg Neep was a signaller and had been among the first group of King's Own to land on Leros. He was responsible for laying the cables along the ground for the field telephones. He recalled his job: 'I was in the signals so was in charge of the signal unit [...] I was working below the Castle where the brigade was. A little unit, we had the communications system with the brigade headquarters and were forwarding that information to the various units. We were in a dig out, a shallow thing because the terrain wasn't easy for trenches, just rock.'[43] He would be there for a number of weeks suffering the enemy bombings. 'Our first 5 weeks on Leros were spent consolidating positions with some minimal back-up from naval guns, but the Germans air force with its nearby bases gradually gained complete air domination over the islands.'[44]

On Leros, the machine-gun batteries were manned by the Italians and some of the Fusiliers. These gunners manned the coastal defences using Bofors – anti-aircraft multi-purpose autocannons designed by the Swedish arms manufacturer AB Bofors in the 1930s. The Bofors was one of the most popular medium-weight anti-aircraft systems during World War II. A couple of troops of Bofors light anti-aircraft guns were brought in which could shoot 120 rounds a minute, but ammunition was short. Ted Johnson recalled,

> Because of the shallow water, we had to get our six Bofors brought in strapped to submarines – it was the only way to get them into port. Ammunition was dropped at night by Dakotas – that was how we were supplied. I was on Leros from the 19th September until the 11th November. During that time we were constantly being bombed by the Luftwaffe – Ju 87s and Ju 88s.[45]

The situation seemed covered in Leros, and the RAF had landed a squadron of South African fighters on Kos.

The *Daily Telegraph* for 23 September 1943 reported from Cairo (the report being a couple of days behind), 'Details released from here today disclose that the first British troops to land on the Dodecanese Islands of Kos and Leros, and the islands of Samos in the Aegean, were men of a parachute regiment dropped from British transport planes by the light of a full moon.'[46] The newspaper asserted that the 'combined operations which led to the capture of the islands were the fruit of a long planning and the training of troops in the Middle East for island garrison duties'. By 28 September, a secret telegram to the prime minister informed him, 'We hold Leros, with an Infantry Brigade Head Quarters and one Infantry Battalion (about 1000 men all told).'[47] However, action was not always going to go according to plan.

4

Digging In

We had no billets as such. There wasn't time for that. We just had foxholes and whatever we could find.

Sergeant George Hatcher, Royal West Kents

The month of September was a period of assembling forces for the defence of Leros and its surrounding islands. Following quickly on from the Faughs were B Company 2nd Battalion Queen's Own Royal West Kents sailing from Castelorizo to Leros on 18 September, some going on to Samos. As a military ground force, their tasks were similar to that of the Royal Irish Fusiliers: surveying the terrain, digging in and ensuring troops, supplies and equipment were in position. Further companies of Royal West Kents would arrive in dribs and drabs.

Among the new arrivals was 28-year-old Sergeant George Hatcher. He had arrived on Leros with some of the others from his regiment on a destroyer. 'We were on Castelorizo for a time until they wanted a bigger company [...] Once the Germans decided they wanted the Aegean islands, they decided we weren't enough in one company, so we were relieved by an Indian battalion, and we were sent to Leros to be attached to the Royal Irish Fusiliers.'[1] They arrived in Portolago but did not stay there. It was night-time and difficult for Hatcher to make out exactly where he was. Nor did he have much time to form an impression of the island. 'We spent the first night in a wooden hut. I think it was a tobacco shed or something of that nature. It wasn't in Lakki. I don't know where it was. And the next day we

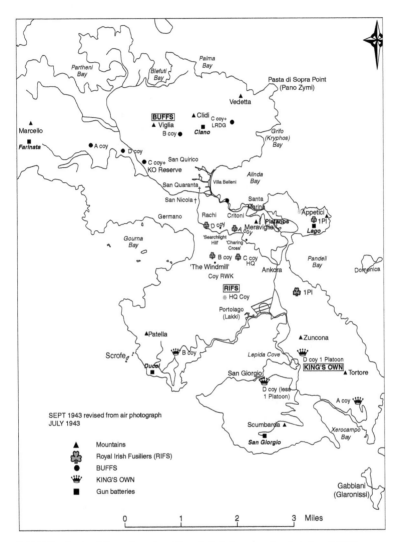

MAP 3   Leros Map showing Coastal defences, September 1943

were taken up into the hills, and put in our defence positions
because we knew the Germans were going to invade sooner or later.
We were to prepare positions on the hill.' This meant finding some
form of shelters and ensuring they had food and ammunition to
hand. The men were spread out around the sides of the hill, all placed
at various strategic points and had to make cover as best they

could out of rocks as it was too hard to dig trenches. 'It was a matter of building up rocks [...] Once the Germans landed, I didn't move a lot.'[2]

Lieutenant Clifford Clarke was in the same unit as Sergeant George Hatcher and they were great friends as well as comrades-in-arms. Clarke was a jovial man, his geniality encouraging his men forward. He had already seen action in Dunkirk in 1939, Malta in 1941 and had been in Egypt, Lebanon and Palestine preparing the assault on the Dodecanese, so was a seasoned officer. He explained, 'We trained until we had got everything defensively as we wanted it. Some Italian infantry said they were going to join us and we said no fear, we don't want you, but we did take the gunners. They are a very different breed, very good the Italian gunners.'[3] Initially they saw few other soldiers there. 'We were allocated the position we had to defend and we trained all over the place. I had a mobile platoon there. Their idea was that if anything was required I'd pull out of my positions and take my mobile platoon.'[4]

Opinions about the Italian soldiers varied, with some good reports, some bad. Unsurprisingly, most of the Italian soldiers were disillusioned, homesick and wanted to go back to Italy. The British had unwisely assumed it would be easy to move in and win them over, but many of them were unwilling to fight. Royal Irish Fusilier Private Paddy McCrystal recalled that the Italians covered their own posts and generally did not mix with his own unit.[5] As we have seen, though, some of the gunners did win praise. Private Sid Bowden with the Royal West Kents recalled, 'The Italians were very good, I will say that. They kept us with a bit of food, spaghetti, they brought some over to us. But they were singing all day long. I always remember one fellow said he was an opera singer not a soldier.'[6] There were about eight of them helping to defend the area where Sid was: 'We just passed and said hello and waved to one another. One day we did have a plane come into the bay and we, three of us, opened fire, then they stopped us from our headquarters they said we were giving our position away. It was all such a muddle.'[7] Some Italians showed friendship to the British soldiers, but not all the British men offered a reciprocal amicability. George Hatcher explained,

We got our water from a well, and the Italians were using the same well as us. One Italian, before the Germans invaded, was a barber and gave us haircuts. That's the only contact we had with them. We didn't mix with them at all. Oh they were all right. Some of our chaps took a dim view of them, ordered them about a bit, tried to show off a bit, the British soldiers. If they wanted to drink from the well, they pushed the Italians to one side, and would take their place, trying to show their authority.[8]

For many though, the Italians were not to be trusted at all. Lieutenant Clarke was particularly dismissive.

We never allowed any Italians to fight for us – no trust for the Italians. We knew if they'd let the Germans down, they'd let us down. They'd go with whoever was the more powerful. The Italians are generally not fighters at all, as a group, the same with their navy; they built fast ships so they could run away. They retreat very quickly. But they are capable of individual extreme heroism.[9]

By 21 September, 3,400 Allied personnel had landed on Leros, 2,830 by sea, along with 1,500 tons of stores and oil fuel and 15 Bofors guns. Unlike on Rhodes, the Italians' attitude was generally co-ooperative, though their fighting value was low. It was considered that even if Leros were reinforced by such British troops as were available, and Kos airfields developed and defended adequately, the Allies would not be in a secure position to continue operations in the Aegean until Rhodes was in their possession. Kos was important only in that it possessed an airfield from which single-fighter aircraft could operate over the Aegean and could attack Rhodes when the possibility arose. In comparison to Rhodes, the airfield at Antimachia was poor and it was never considered possible to hold the other islands long-term without recapturing Rhodes. Accordingly, on 22 September, the chiefs of staff's approval was obtained to mount Operation Accolade (the invasion of Rhodes and the Aegean) before the end of October with such forces as were available in the Middle East and could be spared from the central Mediterranean.[10]

Relaxation on Leros

Conditions on the island of Leros would prove to be difficult. At first the situation was controllable and the units that had moved in early (the Royal Irish Fusiliers, the SBS and the LRDG) even managed to experience some leisure time in Leros. When off-duty, some of the men took advantage of the hot sunny climate to swim in the sea, although this tended to be the officers rather than the lower ranks. Alinda Bay, with its pebbly beach and azure waters, was a popular bathing spot. Gourna Bay's sandy beach was also enjoyed as a swimming place, until an oil slick from a British submarine put people off and the British laid a minefield down there.[11]

Rumours reached the soldiers of brothels in Leros; two of these were in the southern areas of Temenia and Portolago (Lakki) – one was a large wooden hut which had been used by the Italian garrison as a brothel, but the women fled with the rest of the population once the bombing started. Another was identified by Lerian Dimitris Tsaloumas, then 22 years old. He recalled, 'There was a military brothel. It was in Crethoni. They had two barracks there. And there was one in Temenia in Lakki. They had two, for thousands of soldiers. This was for the Italians.'[12] Irish Fusilier Jack Harte also remembers an encounter with some local prostitutes. He had been with Corporal Jock McCullagh looking through his binoculars when he saw a group of local Greek women waving and beckoning to them to come and join them. It turned out this hut was a local brothel. Although they had no communal language except for 'jig-jig' which seemed to be universal, by actions of their bodies the women left them in no doubt as to what was on offer, but payment was required. They were willing to swap for food, but the men had not yet been given provisions.[13]

Officers were responsible for ensuring their men did not get venereal disease, as this put them out of action and was technically a court-martial offence. Lieutenant Richard Austin 'Jimmy' James was on Leros having come with his regiment of Royal West Kents as intelligence officer. He recalled the time when one of his men landed them both in trouble:

> Our medical officer came down to me and said, 'One of your soldiers has got VD', so I was a bit peeved about this because I said 'Don't talk nonsense. You know we have been confined to barracks in Haifa for months, and we have only been here a week. He can't possibly have got VD.' 'I am telling you, your man has got VD.' It was true and he was led off to hospital [...] It was a nuisance to me, because I had to go over to the adjutant to report it, as a soldier getting VD was a disciplinary offence, by putting himself out of action as a soldier.

He went over to see the adjutant, Mike Read, who told him to report to his commanding officer.

> So I went to see Colonel Tarleton who was a very war-weary experienced officer and he said to me – I thought I was in for trouble here and would get told off, 'Don't worry,' he said. 'Some men would put their penis where you and I wouldn't put the point of our umbrella.' What this chap had done, while we were unloading ammunition, he spotted the brothel in Leros port, Portolago, and he had nipped in there for horizontal refreshment for about four minutes and then joined the queue again, and that's when he got VD.[14]

At least one officer found time for a more protracted affair. A 20-year-old Maltese intelligence officer known as 'Grech' fell in love with one of the local women and had an affair with her over the few weeks he was stationed in Leros. Grech had been taken to the island to oversee the seaplane base and act as interpreter, arriving around 14 September.[15] He and his squadron leader had piloted a Supermarine Walrus, a British single-engine amphibious biplane reconnaissance aircraft which had landed them in Portolago. They were greeted with champagne and food and catered for by a group of good-looking young 'waitresses' who he found out were inhabitants of three *palazzini*, the brothels which had provided services for the Italian officers and non-commissioned officers. He was allocated a beautiful villa to himself, fully equipped and furnished.

> 'Next morning tea was brought in to me by one of the loveliest girls I had ever seen. She was dark, with flowing black hair, brown eyes and a tawny skin glowing with health and vitality. Slender arms emerged from the shoulders of a pale green dress that clung invitingly to full bosom and a willowy body.[16]

Her name was Maria and he was to pass the next few weeks in her arms. His villa was flattened by a bomb, but luckily Maria and he had moved the bed, his suitcase, a washing bowl, table, Primus stove and a small store of necessities into a cave for protection. The couple communicated in Italian and spent part of their days swimming naked in the sea. The young Maltese officer recalled, 'Maria in her birthday suit looked stunning, and I suppose that in those days I must have been a well-built lad. I think we genuinely delighted in each other and were truly happy for a while.' After the daily bombings, they foraged in the bombed-out homes for things which would make their life more comfortable in the cave: cushions, rugs, oil lamps, blankets, chairs. Other people came down and did the same.

The couple were visited by soldiers in need of items or information. Fellow officers Frank Ramseyer and Martin Solomon came to their cave asking for hardware, but Grech thought they were mainly after the expensive Italian wine and liquors left behind. The couple kept a fire blazing in front of the cave, made from broken wooden wreckage. 'It was a comfortable pause in both our lives, perhaps too comfortable [...] one evening as we watched the flashes and the necklaces of tracer weaving upwards into the northern sky, there came a moment when we both knew could not be long delayed.' Maria left for Xerocampus (at the southern tip of Leros) and Grech returned to his SBS command post. He was billeted in Alinda in what was called the 'Navy House' along with Stewart Macbeth, Dick Harden, Charlie Clynes, Max Bally (a Davis Cup tennis player, now an intelligence officer) and Hugh Stowell, officer of operations to Captain Baker, the senior British naval officer in the Aegean. They slept on bed rolls on the floor in any space they could find. Admiral Mascherpa had kindly lent them his personal chef, so they ate extremely well. One night they even had 'roast beef' on the menu – but when it turned out that the admiral's horse had gone missing, they realised it was not beef they had eaten.

Grech saw Maria once again when his superior officer David Sutherland had given him a day off and he drove down to the seaplane base from the officers' mess. In the doorway stood Maria and he was delighted to see her. 'I could hardly believe it! I had been down two or three times before, on jobs which had kept me too involved to do more than wave to her [...] and now here she was laughing and excited, with her arms around me, and her cheek against mine.' The couple eventually had to part as war took over the island.

The Sinking of HHMS *Queen Olga* and HMS *Intrepid*

The German counter-attack, when it came, was swift. General Lieutenant Friedrich-Wilhelm Müller, commander of the 22nd Infantry Division (Luftlande Air Landing Division), was given orders to take Kos and Leros on 23 September. The commander was purposeful, decisive and tenacious, and his team trained to an exacting standard. They had already conquered Crete and Kefalonia and were now intent on taking Kos, Leros and Samos. However, despite Müller's confidence, the understanding of the German position was not always positive and often conflicting. The German Admiral Lange who was commanding action in the Aegean as late as 18 September considered the Dodecanese a lost cause, even given that they held Crete and Rhodes. Admiral Ficke, chief of staff of Germany's Maritime Warfare Command, disagreed and thought that since the British had not landed in any strength, they had a good chance of succeeding in taking the Dodecanese. On 24 September, Grand Vernal Dönitz presented the Führer with a less-than-rosy picture of their situation in the Aegean and advised withdrawal. He told Hitler,

> The situation has changed. The Italian armed forces no longer exist and the position on the Balkan Peninsula is in danger for lack of sufficient forces. Maintenance of security in Balkan rear areas has become a difficult task […] Thus we shall lose, without a comparable strategic advantage, irreplaceable troops and material, which would be of decisive important for the defence of the continent.[17]

Hitler listened carefully, but was not to be moved. Instead, he stood his ground and said, 'Abandonment of the islands would create the most unfavourable impression. To avoid such a blow to our prestige we may even have to accept the loss of our troops and material. The supply of the islands must be assured by the [German] Air Force.'[18] With the Germans willing to throw their forces at the Dodecanese battle, the British soldiers were left with comparatively meagre resources.

While the British army was at the ready for any possible invasion of Leros, the Royal Navy was also playing its own important role in assisting the defence of the island. At night, they attacked enemy ships when they saw them, but the Germans retained air superiority during daylight hours. Allied air bombing targeted Rhodes, Crete and mainland Greece in an attempt to counter the multiplying strength of German air defence. By attacking Rhodes they hoped to prevent further supplies coming in and defend the other islands, including Leros. Churchill cabled Eisenhower requesting help declaring,

'Rhodes is the key both to the Eastern Mediterranean and the Aegean. It will be a great disaster if the Germans are able to consolidate there.'[19] Churchill was still hoping that the Allies might retake Rhodes at some point and thereby gain a foothold for Allied aircraft. He was given an armoured brigade and some landing craft, but there was too little assistance and it came far too late. Fifty Liberators of US Ninth Air Force dropped bombs on Eleusis in Greece and Maritza on Rhodes, slowing down the Luftwaffe's advance into Kos and Leros.[20]

Destroyers continued to transport troops to Leros. The *Faulknor*, an F-class destroyer flotilla, carried a maximum of 490 tons of fuel, giving her a range of 6,500 nautical miles.[21] This enabled her also to carry out patrols, sink several cargo ships and landing craft, and carry out bombardments of shore positions. HMS *Eclipse* was an E-class Destroyer of the Royal Navy also fitted with anti-aircraft guns and torpedoes. She shot down the SS *Gaetano Donizetti*, an Italian merchant ship captured by the Germans on 23 September. It sank in the Aegean Sea killing some 1,800 people on board – 220 German guards and crew and, unfortunately, 1,576 Italian prisoners of war. There were no survivors.

The Germans retaliated by bombing HHMS *Queen Olga* and HMS *Intrepid* in Portolago in Leros harbour on 26 September.[22] *Olga* sank immediately, killing six officers and 64 enlisted men. *Intrepid* was only damaged, but later that day another formation of enemy planes came over and the bombing tore a couple of holes in the side of her, causing danger of oil fire. Georgiou Papadopoulos was 16 years old at the time of the attack and remembers it vividly. He and his father had been working on a boat nearby about 500 m further down.

> It was 26 November, just after lunch about one o'clock. I was with my father on top of the boat. I remember a big noise. I still had the screwdriver in my hand. I was looking for my father and [...] nothing. I saw smoke where the big boat had been. I came down the step and many people were looking round. So many people were with only half an arm. A small boat picked the people up from the big boat and took them to the hospital in Lakki. The bombs had fallen on the other side of Lakki, they fell on the submarine factory. I came down from the boat looking for my father. I still had the screwdriver. I was asking, asking. They said, 'I never saw your father. He was probably hit.' I saw a lady,

I still remember her name, Crysanthou, 'Did you see my father?' I said.
'Don't worry, he was hit in the foot. He is OK in hospital.'

He went home to tell his mother. Next morning they went straight to the hospital and saw the same woman to whom he had spoken the day before. 'Her son was bad there. I saw my father. His leg had been sliced this way [he indicated sideways]. If this way, he would have no leg. He was taken to Alinda [Villa Bellini where there was a makeshift hospital].'[23]

Lieutenant Ted Johnson remembered the event well as it was his first contact with the Germans since he had arrived earlier that month.

A supply ship was sent in to us I don't know where it came from [...] it had to be unloaded pretty quickly because it was thought the Germans would react in a hostile manner against us pretty soon, and if they saw a supply ship in there, they would obviously attempt to sink the thing so it was a priority to get the ship unloaded. Well, we didn't succeed quickly enough. I think it was a Sunday morning a raid developed, and they did their best to hit this ship. Luckily, they missed it but they did sink HMS Intrepid at the time and the Greek destroyer Olga. They were both bombed and sunk.[24]

He also encountered his first fatality of the war. 'My first casualty on Leros was a Greek sailor who was killed on Olga. I helped pull him out of the water and he'd been down a bit of a time and that was a bit of a gruesome sight. I was 21.'

On the 27th at 2 a.m., Intrepid took a direct hit, capsized and sank, killing five men; ten were missing and three seriously wounded. The Germans brought out their antique and supposedly obsolete Ju 87 Stukas, which now had complete control of the airfields.[25] Among the dead of Intrepid were 19-year-old Able Seaman John Norman Green, 31-year-old Able Seaman Leslie J.S. Layton, 38-year-old Gunner George Edward Creasey, 45-year-old Chief Petty Officer Fred Pert and 35-year-old Ordinary Seaman Albert Edward Wright, all of the Royal Navy now buried in Leros cemetery.

Peter Colman was an ordinary seaman on the Intrepid when it went down. He remembered that Sunday as the German aircraft attacked the harbour in Portolago. His ship and the Queen Olga were engulfed in flames and sank with a large number of casualties.

During the day, work was carried out to make *Intrepid* seaworthy. The Captain, Commander Kit Kat, told us that he hoped to get our engines working and we would leave at a much reduced speed after dark. The Germans carried out another raid at about 4 p.m. *Intrepid* was seriously damaged and slowly started to sink, the Captain gave the order to abandon ship and I jumped into the sea. I was rescued fairly quickly by a local fishing boat, which had come out to help survivors. HMS *Intrepid* finally sank that night. We were more fortunate than the *Queen Olga*, I think we had 15 crew killed but I am not sure of the exact number.[26]

The survivors lived in damaged houses immediately after the sinking and Colman was included in a party that dug a large grave in the local cemetery. 'Another air raid occurred whilst we were doing this work. As soon as we had finished we were taken back into Portolago and did not see the funeral service of our shipmates.' A few days later, they were evacuated in a very small old merchant ship carrying Turkish markings.

One of the problems to become apparent in both the movement of shipping and the movement of troops on the ground was that of communication. Messaging was still undertaken by encrypted Morse code and was unreliable. Middle East Command would send messages to the islands and to the ships, but it was difficult to provide a clear picture from the ground of what was going on, even more difficult when under attack. Communications between the ships and the islands, and the ships and HQ were also often interrupted. At platoon level on the ground, military commanders relied on wires run overground or on runners and whistles.[27]

Enemy Bombings

By the end of September, the British were established in all of the Dodecanese islands except Rhodes; they held Kos, Leros, Simi, Samos, Stampalia and Ikaria. The Germans held Lemnos, Lesbos, Chios, the islands of the Sporades and the Cyclades (except for Ikaria), Kassos, Kythera and Anti-Kythera, together with Rhodes and Crete. The British continued to bring in troops. The month ended with German domination of the skies over the Aegean firmly established from airfields in Crete, Rhodes and the Greek mainland, giving the

Germans the ability to bomb Leros easily and neutralise Allied airfields in Kos. The relentlessness of the bombings inevitably affected the British troops. It not only made movement difficult, but it grated on the soldiers' nerves. Ted remembered,

> There was a continued raid situation going on for the next month; every day there were raids, whether heavy raids or minor raids. Nothing from the sea, all Luftwaffe. We knew we were getting no fighting air support because we were too far away from the nearest Royal Air Force base. Fighters couldn't reach us and even if they could, they couldn't stay long enough to help us in any way. They could just about get to Leros and have enough fuel to get back to Cyprus or wherever they'd come from. We did have at night supplies dropped by Dakotas. The Royal Navy were producing supplies for us initially. The RAF got involved a bit nearer the battle, the end of October, beginning of November time, and they dropped supplies at night. They dropped ammunition and company rations that sort of thing.[28]

Threat of air attack by day was the paramount consideration by the end of the month, when the first phase of operations came to a close.[29] Troops had occupied the island and been spread around the coast, mountains and pivotal places such as gun batteries. They had dug in or made shelters, and stocked up with food rations and weapons. Now, enemy raids became more frequent. 'One of my own platoon was killed by a bomb before the battle – Fusilier McConicky. He stopped one in a trench, a direct hit.'[30] Ted felt as though the pilots of the enemy aircraft were aiming directly at him on the ground.

> I remember one particular Stuka raid when I was in a position just before the battle. I can see the Stuka coming down to me now and it was the only time I prayed on Leros. I definitely prayed. I was in a slit trench and couldn't do anything about it and he was definitely coming towards [me]. Luckily the bomb didn't hit me directly but fell very close. I was showered with rubble and muck and stuff, but that's routine stuff really in the front line. You do accept it. It becomes run-of-the-mill stuff.[31]

Surface forces were now restricted to operating sweeps during the dark hours and retired to hiding places around the Turkish coast during the day.[32]

Over the weeks from 13 September, Allied aircraft defending Kos had suffered many losses from bombardment of the airfield and in air combat. The importance of keeping Leros and Kos was recognised by the Combined Chiefs of Staff who sent a message to Air Force Headquarters dated 1 October. They agreed on the desirability of capturing Rhodes but 'cannot accept prospect of withdrawal from Kos and Leros'. They believed the German air force to be

> badly stretched [...] nevertheless [we] do not consider area suitable under present conditions for employment of aircraft carrier [...] For assault on Rhodes it will be essential to provide short range fighter cover over beaches and this can only be done from Kos. We therefore consider it is now important to neutralise German Air Forces in Greece and the Aegean sufficiently to enable us to become firmly established in Kos and other Greek islands now held.[33]

Aircraft cover for the operation on Kos was completely inadequate and this element alone would have a serious effect on the British ability to defend the islands. Leros was twice raided and the Italian destroyer *Euro* was attacked by air in Partheni on 1 October.[34] Kos itself would soon be invaded and, if lost, with it would go the last hope of staging a frontal assault on Rhodes.[35]

5

Fall of Kos

If Cos falls we must expect early attack on other islands.

British Chief of Staff to Eisenhower[1]

At the end of September, David Sutherland of the Special Boat Squadron had been sent to Samos with 25 men with the intention of taking the island. The reception from the 1,500 Italian Blackshirts already on the island was far from welcoming. Their Fascist ideals were allied with those of the Axis, so they did not relish relinquishing themselves to a small group of British officers. Samos had been their headquarters, and as supporters of Mussolini under the command of Major General Mario Solderelli, they continued to stand firm against the Allies despite Italy's capitulation.

Eager to return to base himself, Sutherland was keen not to overstay his welcome on Samos. He was therefore pleased when a battalion of Royal West Kents arrived on 1 October, giving him the opportunity to leave for Kalymnos. At the time, Kalymnos happened to be the centre of the Dodecanese sponge fishing community. It was, and still is, a pretty island with a main harbour spotted with whitewashed houses clinging to the hillside overlooking the bay. Like Leros, it had been part of the Ottoman Empire and had then been taken over by the Italians. It was about 7 miles from Kos but only 1 mile from Leros at their nearest points, so any Germans encroaching into Kos or Kalymnos were a danger to Leros. One of the island's esteemed figures was a woman known as 'the Sponge Queen', Madame Vouvalis, who owned a huge sponge factory and ruled over the elite on the island. When Sutherland and Milner-Barry arrived on the island, she greeted them cordially and was a charming hostess, providing them with a magnificent dinner supplemented with a delicious wine she had dug up from her garden, having hidden it to protect it from the Italians. The following day Sutherland, Milner-Barry and Guy Prendergast popped over to the adjacent island of Leros for a meeting with Colonel Turnbull and Jellicoe to discuss operations, retuning to Kalymnos later that evening to share a memorable fish supper in a local taverna with Jellicoe and Lieutenant Commander Ramseyer of the Levant Schooner Flotilla.[2]

Lacking employment elsewhere, Jake Easonsmith, commanding the LRDG, and his fellow officer David Lloyd Owen had been sent over to Kalymnos with their patrols of LRDG men on 25 September and billeted together with men from the SBS overlooking the main town. Kalymnos had been designated the HQ of the Raiding Forces, and all its men had moved to the island awaiting further instructions. Commander Adrian Seligman of the Royal Navy also moved over to Kalymnos with his Levant Schooner Flotilla of five armed caiques. Little was happening on Leros – all the troops were doing was waiting for sightings of the enemy. Lloyd Owen recalled, 'It was clear there was no policy for the employment of the Long Range Desert Group or of George Jellicoe's Special Boat Service, which had been ordered to Leros.'[3]

Despite its likelihood, the attack on Kos had not been predicted. Sutherland said, 'At 2 a.m. on the morning of 3 October I was woken up by the sound of heavy fighting on Kos. My heart sank. This was the last thing we expected.'[4] Lloyd Owen and Easonsmith were staying together in the same house by the harbour in Kalymnos when they too were awoken by a tremendous noise coming from Kos. They realised something alarming was taking place. As they pulled themselves out of their sleep they stood and looked out from their vantage point on the balcony, watching aghast as the German invasion of Kos took place. Lloyd Owen recalled, 'We had slept on the balcony under mosquito nets, and we watched a fleet of all types of crafts moving in towards the east coast of Kos.'[5] Much to his annoyance, that evening he was ordered by his superior Guy Prendergast to take his men to Kos to see what they could do, but it was obviously too late, as he pointed out: 'It was very hard to see how about three hundred men, neither trained nor equipped for infantry fighting, could make much material difference where 2000 British infantry [on Kos] had already failed.'[6] He thought the order 'one of the most brainless and preposterous orders that I have ever heard'. Thankfully the orders were cancelled as Kos fell and the LRDG were ordered to evacuate to Leros. Lloyd Owen had little faith in any further instructions coming from his commanding officers – after all, he had been told there was no likelihood of a seaborne invasion of Kos, but this is exactly what had happened. Sixty-five British soldiers were killed and 1,388 men were taken prisoner in the Battle of Kos. The Italians fared much worse: 122 of their officers were shot and 3,145 Italian prisoners taken.

Jellicoe recalled the capture of Kos. 'I was in Kalymnos with David Sutherland and we saw what was going on and, as a result of that, one of our chaps, an agent of the SBS, Walter Milner-Barry, went over to the south coast of Kos. Thanks to him, after the fall of Kos quite a few people managed to escape. And that was what [...] three weeks before the attack on Leros.' Jellicoe knew it was pointless to send in his own men to do anything other than rescue the troops from Kos.

> I had very few of my SBS chaps there, there were much fewer SBS than there were the Long Range Desert Group. At the time, I had half a squadron under David Sutherland and I sent them off to Samos when I heard of this [...] I didn't think they would be able to play any useful part in the landing and I thought it was far better that they got off to Samos; and they managed to escape as a result of that.[7]

His men would be needed for skilful intelligence work, signals, strategic raids and rescue – it was the military ground forces which were intended for combat.

The German invasion, as they found out later, was led by a battalion of 65th Panzer Grenadier Regiment coming in by sea to meet up with the 16 Panzer Grenadiers who had landed further along the coast in the early hours of 3 October: a force of seven transports, two destroyers and seven landing craft, E-boats and caiques. Enemy dive-bombing raids followed on using 55 aircraft and lasting four hours, destroying an Italian gunboat, several smaller crafts and buildings and installations.[8] Lloyd Owen recalled, 'Any doubts that we had were soon dispelled by the smoke and flash of guns and the squadron aircraft, which were methodically destroying what little opposition there was.'[9] By 10.30 a.m. there were around 1,500 enemy troops ashore and communication with the island had ceased. Enemy parachutists were also dropped.[10] By the evening of 3 October, the German strength had been increased to an estimated 4,000 men. The Durham Light Infantry struggled valiantly to defend the island but were overcome.

A secret telegram on 3 October was sent to Eisenhower from British Chiefs of Staff: 'As long as enemy retains complete air superiority we cannot operate Hunt-class destroyers in area of operations. Enemy therefore has complete control of sea as well as of air in Aegean.'[11] While Eisenhower wanted to help, Air Chief Marshal Arthur Tedder (deputy supreme commander at Supreme Headquarters Allied Expeditionary Force under Eisenhower) was against taking air force resources away from the Italian campaign. General Maitland Wilson reported that German bombers were annihilating Leros and Kos, and Churchill once again called on Eisenhower for help. A report for Eisenhower from British commanders on the ground read,

> HQ troops Cos out of touch with Battalion HQ and two Companies [in] Cos Town. Enemy attacking port and Italians *not* fighting. Enemy have complete air and naval supremacy and prospects of holding Cos are slender. Loss of Cos would directly jeopardise security of grns [garrisons] of Leros and Samos total 234 brigade less one Battalion [...] Attacks of own Beaufighters today not successful but are attacking with 13 Wellingtons and Hudsons tonight. All available Beaufighters tomorrow being used for shipping strike.[12]

Eisenhower, recognising Churchill's anxiety, finally offered the air support so desperately needed and sent bombers and P-38s against Crete and other German-held airfields to try and prevent them reaching Kos.[13] As expected, further telegrams came in from Wilson requesting more immediate air and sea assistance. The response was that Allied Forces HQ were concerned about a continual drain on resources and could not justify such a commitment. Churchill was upset and wrote to Eisenhower stressing the vital importance of resources at this stage, that an operation against Rhodes was needed and might even persuade Turkey into the war.

We rely on you to defend this island to the utmost limit. Every measure is being taken to help you. Tell your men the eyes of the world are upon them. Tell the Italians that a terrible fate will befall them if they fall into the hands of the Hun. They will be shot in large numbers, including especially the Officers, and the rest taken not as prisoners of war, but as labour slaves to Germany.[14]

The Italian and British forces had effectively ceased organised resistance by 6 a.m. on 4 October and Kos was lost to the Germans.

While superior officers were ordering defence from their offices, the men on the ground were responding to the crisis as best they could and arranging to evacuate survivors. Captain Walter Milner-Barry slunk quietly into Kos with Lieutenant Alec McLeod of the Levant Schooner Flotilla and a small patrol of SBS at 3 a.m. on 4 October to try and find the Allied soldiers stuck in Kos. Firing could be heard in Kos town as more British troops sought escape. Many of the soldiers had already died in the fighting, but pockets of men were still stranded on the beaches. A bunch of Royal Air Force men were spotted, hauled into the motor launch and taken off in a caique.

Milner-Barry stayed behind with two other men, Lance Corporal Watson and Private Geddes, volunteering to help gather up more survivors. Milner-Barry was somewhat miffed that there had not been more volunteers, but of those who had remained he said, 'These two, though among the smallest, had more guts than the bigger chaps.'[15] Milner-Barry and his men went inland near a small wadi and spent the next few days continuing to collect escapees, mainly RAF men or Durham Light Infantry, and helping them get off the island. At the agreed rendezvous on the night of 7–8 October, the patrol boat returned to pick them up. According to Milner-Barry, at one stage a bunch of 'hysterical Italians', driven by German infantry into the wadi, attached themselves to the rescuers, thereby bringing attention to them all and resulting in the Germans mortaring their position.[16] Eventually, they managed to contact a launch to get the last men out to Turkey. In all, their brave actions had rescued 90 British soldiers, along with a large group of Italians POWs and a handful of Greek resistance fighters. They had spent ten days behind enemy lines using their wits and their own resources, supported by local Greeks bringing them food. Dressed only in their shorts and thin shirts, the men had struggled to keep warm by swapping sides, keeping one man in the middle to warm up while sleeping.

With Kos's fall went the only usable Allied-held airbase in the Dodecanese, thereby blasting any hope of future air action out of the sky. Journalist for the *Daily Telegraph* Leonard Marsland Gander recalled,

> The three landing strips in Kos were bombed into unserviceability. Incidentally we had no adequate radio warning system on the island. The Germans then mounted an overwhelming air and seaborne attack and overran the whole island in a few days. There were many thrilling escapes in small caiques. One man, of the Royal Irish Fusiliers, actually did a 'Channel' swim of over twenty miles to safety.[17]

The 1st Battalion of the Durham Light Infantry had done their best to hold off the enemy but it was an impossible task.

Eisenhower partially blamed the Italians for the loss of Kos, complaining, 'Kos with its airfields was lost; as a result it had been impossible to build up our garrisons with adequate weapons. This situation had been aggravated by the poor fighting spirit of the Italians and the inadequacy of their fixed defences and equipment.'[18]

The capture of Kos would have disastrous consequences for British operations in Leros. Surprised at the ease of their success, the Germans spread out to occupy other small islands On 7 October at dawn, 40 Germans soldiers landed in northeast Simi in Pedi Bay from a couple of caiques and a schooner. Anders Lassen spotted them and roared after them, throwing himself into the fray, supported by others from the SBS. Despite having contracted dysentery and suffering from a petrol burn in his leg, he managed to see them off. His bravery in the conflict earned him a second bar to his Military Cross. In revenge the following day, the Germans dropped tons of bombs on Simi town for two hours from Stuka planes, indiscriminately killing British and Italian soldiers and Greek civilians.[19] Deprived of air cover, the Allies were unlikely to be able to hold the other islands.

Evacuation to Leros

With only Kalymnos island standing between the Germans on Kos and the British on Leros, the soldiers on Kalymnos were ordered to evacuate to Leros carrying all the stores and troops on available crafts, arriving throughout the night. Lloyd Owen recalled, 'At nightfall on 4th October a fleet of curious little craft put out into the darkness and we sailed across to Leros.'[20] They unloaded all their stores as quickly as possible so the boats could go into hiding. Very soon they heard the drone of aeroplanes and the response from rattling anti-aircraft machine guns. Lloyd Owen recalled, 'Each time after the bombs had fallen there was that frightening silence, and a choking, dusty fog permeated the air.'[21]

Once on Leros, Lloyd Owen and his LRDG colleagues were placed under the command of the Royal Irish Fusiliers. The 'Raiding Forces' were made up of about 200 men from LRDG, 150 men from SBS and 30 commandos with Jellicoe in control and Prendergast as Second-in-Command. They had 40-mm Breda guns and five coastal defence batteries; each of the four 6-inch naval guns was Italian. Five LRDG patrols went to cover the gun battery positions to encourage the Italians to stay manning their posts. While their previous jobs had been to raid behind enemy lines, now they were to concentrate on putting their special skills into maintaining the defence of Leros.

Wilson, as Commander-in-Chief of Middle East operations, was reprimanded by Churchill in a telegram marked 'Personal and Most Secret' on 5 October.

> I do not understand why you have not reported the measures you are taking to rescue and support the garrison of Cos which is fighting in the Hills. No explanation had been furnished us why a seaborne attack by 7 transports escorted by only 3 destroyers encountered no opposition and was not effectively attacked when unloading or when returning either from the air or from the sea [...] What are you going to do now to resist the attack of Leros and Samos to which you refer as likely [...] Strong reinforcement in cruisers and destroyers have now been sent to you.[22]

The following day, Wilson reported to Churchill, 'Leros was heavily bombed again today. Concentration of shipping and landing craft in Piraeus indicates that attack on Leros may be expected shortly.'[23] As a precaution he had taken the measures of organising naval swoops, and submarine cover. The Allied air force concentrated on attacking airfields in enemy hands rather than defence of Leros or Kos. Wilson had planned for Wellingtons to attack Piraeus and B25s to attack

Rhodes and Crete the following day. The enemy had attempted to drop Piat mortars on Leros during the previous night but had been unsuccessful.

Churchill wrote to President Franklin Roosevelt on 7 October,

> I am much concerned about the situation developing in the Eastern Mediterranean. On the collapse of Italy we pushed small detachments from Egypt into several of the Greek islands, especially Cos, which has a landing ground, and Leros which is a fortified Italian naval base with powerful permanent batteries. We ran this risk in the hope that the Italian garrison which welcomed us would take part in the defence. This hope appears in vain, and Cos has already fallen, except for some of our troops fighting in the mountains. Leros may well share its fate.[24]

Churchill saw Rhodes as the key to the plan. 'Leros which for the moment we hold precariously, is an important naval fortress, and once we are ensconced in this area air and light naval forces would have a most fruitful part.'[25] Roosevelt was not impressed. His response was 'I am opposed to any diversion which will in Eisenhower's opinion jeopardise the security of his current situation in Italy.' He suggested the assault on Rhodes, which Wilson was planning for 23 October, should go ahead; but in the event, it never materialised. Roosevelt had still not sent the nine landing craft necessary for its operation. Churchill continued to press hard for some commitment from Roosevelt for reinforcements, but he was losing the battle. It was at this point that Hitler reinforced his troops in Italy, thereby tipping the balance against reinforcement for the Rhodes assault.

One of the most significant developments to emerge here is that Churchill was already thinking about the evacuation of Leros *even before* the German invasion of the island. Little has been mentioned by historians on this point, but it is apparent that this suggestion had filtered down through the ranks somehow; men reported in their interviews that they had heard about the possibility of an evacuation before the actual Battle of Leros had begun. In a letter to Roosevelt on 10 October, Churchill conceded that there was every possibility of losing Leros.

> I therefore propose to tell General Wilson that he is free, if he judges the position hopeless, to order the garrison to evacuate by night, taking with them all Italian officers and as many other of their Italians as possible and

destroying the guns and defences. The Italians cannot be relied upon to fight, and we have only 1200 men, quite insufficient to man even a small portion of the necessary batteries, let alone the perimeter.[26]

Churchill passed on the message to Field Marshal Harold Alexander, who was in command of the Mediterranean, stating,

You should now try to save what we can from this wreck [...] If there is no hope and nothing can be done you should consider with General Wilson, whether the garrison of Leros should not be evacuated to Turkey, or perhaps wangled along the coast after blowing up the batteries. Efforts must also be made to withdraw the Long Range Desert Groups who are on other islands. This would be much better than their being taken prisoners of war and the Italian officers executed.[27]

At this point he seems to have given up. In a despatch dated 14 October to General Wilson, he commented, 'I am very pleased with the way in which you used such poor bits and pieces as were left to you. *nil desperandum.*'[28] In his memoirs, years later, Churchill would write, 'As we strove to maintain our position in Leros the fate of our small force there was virtually sealed.' He recognised that the severe bombing attacks on Leros and Samos were a mere prelude to disaster. On the day of the fall of Kos on 3 October, Eisenhower had at last despatched two groups of long-range fighters to the Middle East as a temporary measure, but they were only present for a few days and withdrawn on 11 October. The fact there was no air support left Leros in a hopeless positon, a fact of which Churchill was painfully aware. 'The withdrawal of the fighters sealed the fate of Leros. The enemy could continue to build up his forces without serious interference, using dispersed groups of small crafts.'[29]

The message appears to have reached the troops on the ground. Some of the soldiers spoke of rumours flying around that they were going to be evacuated, which left them uncertain why they were fighting. How this matter became common knowledge among the troops is difficult to trace, but it may have been through the signallers, or from officers concerned for their men, or from SBS warning men to prepare themselves for the worst eventuality. The other possibility was that it came in with the Royal Irish Fusiliers. Those who had been left behind in Palestine in September were ultimately sailed to Leros from Alexandria on 14 October in HMS *Jervis*.

Only 30 minutes before they sailed, the captain had been told to stand by ready to evacuate Leros. This must have had a deflating effect on the incoming troops.[30]

Bombing attacks were carried out by the Germans every day, often 60 or more aircraft targeting the Leros coastal batteries. Both the batteries on Mount Marcello (northwest of the island) and on Mount Zuncona (east of Lakki) were put out on 8 and 9 October respectively.[31] While bombardments continued relentlessly, by day the soldiers waited in caves, in trenches or among the rocks, hiding against the air raids as best they could. At night, they waited to pick up the drops of supplies from Palestine or unloaded supplies at the dock in Lakki. The Royal Navy did its best to attack every night in the harbours of Kos and Kalymnos. There was no support at this stage from friendly aircraft, and the German Stukas ruled the air.

The enemy were inching into Kalymnos and it was only a matter of time before they took over the island. German craft were seen entering bays of Kalymnos on 10 October, and the next day shelling was apparent from coastal batteries aimed at Leros. Lieutenant Pavlides, a Greek soldier commissioned in the British army, volunteered to row across to Kalymnos to find out any news. He gathered what information he could and returned to report his findings to the British officers on Leros. A few days later Stan Eastwood of the LRDG, along with Sergeant R.D. Tant and Lieutenant Whitehead, encountered some Germans on Kalymnos. Eastwood and Tant were initially captured but managed to escape to Turkey, while Whitehead ran for it and swam out to sea; he later swam back inland and was sheltered by a local shepherd who clothed and fed him.

Despite Churchill's apparent concern about holding Leros, commanders-in-chief ordered the forces to hold Leros and Samos for as long as possible. Leros was reinforced with more troops, supplies, jeeps, trailers and guns, all brought in by destroyers, submarines and smaller craft. Other equipment was dropped in by parachutes: mortars, machine guns, ammunition and wireless equipment. Four hundred Buffs (Queen's Own Royal East Kents) and a battalion of King's Own joined the forces.

By 14 October the British had gained intelligence to suggest that the enemy was about to stage an invasion of Leros from Kos and Kalymnos with the 4,000 German troops already on the islands; extra ships and landing craft were to be sent by the enemy from Piraeus. British forces and air reconnaissance were therefore instructed to disrupt the arrival of the shipping and equipment and ordered to patrol and bomb the ports and harbours of Kos and Kalymnos islands. It was hoped that with a display of activity the enemy would believe that the British had more air and sea power than they actually had in the area.[32]

David Sutherland had moved back to Leros from Kalymnos with 'S' detachment on 15 October and was given the job of overseeing a garrison defence force manning roadblocks at night. He also took delivery of a consignment of jeeps and Bofors guns, all lathered in non-floating grease and lashed to the top of the boats' casing with steel wire. Men were busy ferrying stores around the island to wherever the troops were stationed. Lieutenant Commander Frank Ramseyer with the Royal Navy Volunteer Reserve ordered an Italian F-lighter armed with a 75-mm gun to be taken to Blefuti, where he thought the enemy was most likely to land. In fact, his assessment was correct, but by then the gun had been withdrawn to another position.[33]

As a distraction for the unit, Sutherland planned a celebration. He had been given the news that Lassen had been awarded his third Military Cross for his extraordinary bravery in fighting on Simi where he had been with 'M' detachment. Now back with 'S' unit in Leros, Sutherland asked one of the men, John Wilkinson, to mock up a medal using white paper, blue dye and two rosettes cut from silver foil. The unit gathered together to watch as Sutherland pinned this realistic-looking medal on Lassen's chest while a roar of approval went up from the troops.[34] However, the constant bombing was taking its toll on the men and Sutherland was no exception. He recalled,

> For me and all the SBS this was a terrifying and demoralising experience. RFHQ [Raiding Force Head Quarters] was in some buildings beside the water in Portolago Bay [Lakki]. One evening I was summonsed to a meeting out there. I did not notice a destroyer refuelling nearby. Suddenly, out of the blue, came the familiar shrieking sound of a Stuka on to its target. I threw myself full length, hugging the ground. The bomb landed fifty metres away with a massive explosion [...] The blast lifted me up and down like a sack of potatoes. From the top of my head to my boots I was covered in fine white dust, as if I had been

working in a flour mill. I got up badly shaken, looking like a ghost and
partially deaf.[35]

Standing nearby, Lloyd Owen noticed that Sutherland was covered in
blood, obviously injured but only superficially. Sutherland evidently
had a dreadful experience in Leros. 'For me at that time Leros was an
advanced form of hell. There were deep lines of exhaustion and
defeat on all our faces, and the whiff of disaster lying just ahead.
We were all demoralised by ceaseless bombing and the fact that the
enemy was calling all the shots.'[36] After his ordeal, Sutherland was
sent off to Samos for a rest. To lift his spirits, his boatman fed him
some fine tagliatelle with crayfish sauce; 'as you can imagine, with
this kind of treatment it did not take me long to recover and return to
the dreaded Leros.'[37]

Major Jake Easonsmith took over from Colonel Prendergast as
commanding officer of the LRDG on 18 October. This was a huge blow
for the LRDG, over whom Prendergast had presided for two-and-a-half
years. Prendergast was leaving because Colonel Turnbull had been
made head of the Raiding Force in the Aegean formed on 15 October
1943 and had specifically asked for him as his second-in-command.
Meanwhile, Lloyd Owen became second-in-command of the LRDG
under Easonsmith. They discussed the future of the LRDG with senior
officers of A and B Squadrons on 28 October. The New Zealand
government had already raised the idea of recalling the NZ Squadron,
since it had been committed to play a role in the Aegean without the
knowledge of the NZ government.[38] General Sir Henry Wilson believed
it was too short notice at this strategic operational stage of their
operations, so only part of A Squadron was withdrawn, leaving the rest
to take part. As he left for Cairo, Lloyd Owen took leave of his friend
Easonsmith just before the battle broke. 'I sensed it would be the last
time that I would see him. We talked about home and about his family,
to whom he was devoted; we talked about what we would do when the
war was over.'[39]

Danger at Sea

With 2,500 troops garrisoned there, Leros and Samos were heavily
dependent on the navy. The main operators at sea were destroyers,

motor launches and caiques, which were sailing around the islands dropping in forces and supplies. The navy's main aims were to destroy enemy shipping and prevent any landing craft coming near. In daylight, ships laid up in Turkish waters; since Turkey was neutral, the crew had to give the excuse of mechanical failure as the reason for travelling into Turkish waters. The Turkish officers would frequently come on board to 'inspect', but in reality for a hearty breakfast served up by the crew, including British marmalade.[40]

Vice-Admiral Algernon Willis took over from Admiral Cunningham as commander-in-chief of the Levant on 15 October and took control of the movements of ships at sea. Two days later, he sent a memo to his men outlining their position. With limited air cover available, naval forces were not properly protected and could not operate as easily as they wished. It was impossible to prevent the build-up of German forces on Rhodes, and his concerns were that the troops on Samos and Leros would not be delivered enough supplies and back-up troops. Although the navy did not have enough protection to operate in daylight, their presence was such that it gave the enemy concerns about launching an invasion.

Navy ships were making nightly sweeps of the seas surrounding Leros and nearby islands. HMSs *Phoebe*, *Faulknor* and *Fury* came from Alexandria on 15 October, and swept west of Leros and Kalymnos, but no enemy ships were sighted, so they withdrew north of Rhodes before dawn. At the same time, HMSs *Belvoir* and *Beaufort* swept east of Leros but saw nothing and laid up in Turkish waters. Near 1 a.m., an enemy convoy and two merchant vessels and two landing craft were located east of Naxos making for Kos. The Hunts tried to intercept, but were unsuccessful and could not find them, the convoy having escaped to the northwest. The Hunts swept the north coast of Amorgos before withdrawing south. On arrival at Beirut, HMS submarine *Severn* was recruited to carrying stores to Leros.[41]

However, the enemy were closing in. A report came in during the night of the 16/17 October that HMS *Hursley* and HHMS *Miaoulis* (the latter was under the command of the Royal Hellenic Navy who had saved the crew of the British destroyer HMS *Panther* on 10 October 1943) were searching the Kos area and the east side of Kalymnos. They set alight a small merchant ship in Port Vathi, sank an E-boat and a landing craft and set a sloop on fire in Port Akti in a spirited close-range action.[42] Captain Taprell Dorling with the Royal Navy described the event, 'It was 2 a.m. in brilliant moonlight that the two ships moved silently into a narrow cove fringed by steep tall cliffs. They sighted the two E-Boats lying close inshore. Opening fire at 600 yards they were soon hitting and the last they saw of the enemy crews was when they were hurriedly abandoning ship and scrambling ashore.'[43] They found a further three enemy vessels round the bay, which they hit. *Hursley* was hit in the fore mess deck, above the water line, but suffered no casualties. The Hunts joined 14th Destroyer Flotilla and laid up before dawn. HMS *Sirius* was hit by a bomb on the quarterdeck in a raid by Ju 88s at 6.30 p.m. and returned to Alexandria having lost 14 men with 30 wounded.[44]

Further ships, *Pathfinder*, *Eclipse* and *Beaufort*, were sent as reinforcements to assist in the bombing of Kos harbour. On the following night HMSs *Jervis* and *Penn* bombarded Port Kalymnos and set a merchant ship in the harbour on fire. This was evidently the second ship of the enemy convoy.[45] *Trooper* was sent to patrol east of Leros, where she struck a mine on 17 October. Various other destroyers were sent out, the navy giving as much cover as it could.

The loss of the Kos airfield, besides finally destroying hopes of fighter cover for surface forces, greatly increased the difficulties of supply as it prevented the passage and unloading of merchant ships and heavy lift ships which were urgently required to provide heavy artillery defences and to improve the transport situation in Leros. The navy was doing its best to give cover, deliver troops and put enemy shipping out of action. However, with the Germans now hiding in narrow bays all over Kalymnos, it was easy for them to focus on taking Leros, although the Royal Navy managed to take out an enemy troop convoy. While enemy destroyers were being damaged or taken out of action, the same was happening to the Allied ships. Mines would blow up HMSs *Hurworth* and *Eclipse* and HHMS *Adrias* with troops on board. *Adrias* was forced onto the beach at Turkey, *Rockwood* was put out by remote-controlled glider bombers, and *Carlisle* was hit and had to be towed into bay. Fortunately, Turkey did not object to the use of its territorial waters for maintaining destroyers in a position of comparative safety during the day.[46]

A clear route had been established by the British intelligence officers in Turkey and escape routes had been set up. Nikos Pyrovolikos, one of the Greek civilians working for the SBS, recalled, 'We were rescuing people all the time during the war. Taking people around. There were thousands of Italians on Kos, I don't know what happened to them. We took 50 Italians from Rhodes to Cyprus, a two-day trip. The rebels captured some Germans.'[47] He would also help transport some of the Jews from Mytelene (Lesbos) to Turkey when German atrocities against them began.

6

Making Preparations

We are still in plenty of trouble – but all is also still well.
Royal West Kents Lieutenant Jimmy James's letter to his mother

The soldiers on Leros were making mental preparations for the potential German invasion. They knew the enemy was creeping forward island by island. They had been told by their commanding officers that now Kos was in the hands of the enemy and the neighbouring island of Kalymnos was being overrun, there was every chance that Leros would be their next target. The troops wrote to their loved ones trying to put their emotions into words without causing too much anxiety back home. Second Lieutenant Richard 'Jimmy' James was with the 2nd Battalion Queen's Own Royal West Kents on Samos, about to be shipped off to Leros later that week. In a letter to his mother on 10 October, he wrote:

Dear Mum,

A letter sneaked through from dad this week – all is well and hope you are getting mine – although they may be very late. We are in a tight corner. Possibly the toughest spot I have been in this war. Forgive me if my letters are scarce but there isn't time. I think, no believe, we shall get through by God's help and our faith. And I wouldn't be anywhere else for the world. Because today I am just realising how utterly evil are the things we are fighting, how deep and horrible this has been the Axis's [Germany and Italy's] domination of Europe's soil. This is for us all a Holy War, and we must see it to an end. You have no idea what bravery has been performed by men and women during these years – with no reward but their own faith and knowledge of right. However dangerous and bleak it may be now for us, I am glad, more than glad, that we are with them as succour to their spirit. Pray for them: they make me ashamed of some of the people I have seen in the Middle East, and in England too. Today all my doubts are at an end – all things that have been done by the enemy since 1939 must be stopped once and for all.

As for me I keep very, very well and am as OK as anything. The weather is breaking and we have some rain for the first time. It always comes as a shock after so many months of utter dryness. The news all round remains good – And I hope gets better. At least we have the great satisfaction of knowing that Hitler must be a very worried man. Hope the nuts are good at home!

The looming danger was ever present and many of the men who had been on other islands were being sent to Leros to await the inevitable invasion, the enemy now less than a few miles away. The soldiers were writing what they thought might be their last letters home. A week later, on 17 October, Jimmy wrote again to his mother from Samos anticipating being shipped to Leros. He complained that he had had no mail for many days and was obviously disappointed at the lack of news from his family. In his letter, he could not help displaying his fears – possibly he was expressing his anxiety as a warning to his family – but at the same time he wanted to allay their worries for him. 'I expect you are being an old silly and have started worrying. I'm the only bloke who should be doing that. After all this time of not worrying at all over wine, women or wars – or money, men or manners, I'm not worrying now.' The weather had broken and 12 hours of continuous rain came down.[1]

Letters from loving mothers, wives, sisters and girlfriends kept many of the men comforted in these trying times. In return, many of the soldiers wanted to let their families know their situation. They knew letters would be censored if they disclosed their whereabouts (although many did not know where they were). Private Sid Bowden of the Royal West Kents wanted to give information to keep his mother to prevent her worrying, but even he did not know where he was. 'I had written to my mother and, in a roundabout way, I had told her where I was [...] no names, obviously. Actually, I didn't know I was on Leros really. I knew I was on a Greek island. When she hears on the radio that a famous Kentish regiment had been in action, she phoned the War Office because she hadn't heard from me. They told her she had a letter to say that as far as they knew, I wasn't on the casualty list. And I think that was when I was getting away.'[2]

Since letters from home were such an important part of the men's lives, delays between sending and receiving letters added to the anxiety. Clifford Clarke recalled,

> My wife and I used to write twice a week, and I used to write sometimes sixty pages but at times you couldn't post it for ages so you'd post the lot together. We numbered every one. My wife would get a dozen together. I have a whole box load I wrote to my parents. [He destroyed those written to his wife.] We had a code at the end of every letter, when I had moved anywhere – Give my love to Joan. Each name was a place where we could be. This was very wrong as here was I as an officer, censoring the men's letters, but my wife knew exactly where I was. If it was Mary, it was Egypt.[3]

Landing Reinforcements

During the last couple of weeks in October, more troops were delivered to Leros in a rush to prepare for the impending battle – more Royal West Kents were coming in from Samos and the Buffs were coming in from Palestine. The British authorities now had a good idea that the Germans would be focusing their attention on Leros rather than Samos, as it was nearer to islands they already held. While no-one knew exactly when or where the battle would start, everyone knew if would inevitably take place.

Lieutenant Jimmy James was only one of many reinforcements from the Queen's Own Royal West Kents who were hurriedly sent to Leros from Samos. He had no idea where he was being sent during that last week in October.[4] He recalled 'We didn't have much background [information]. We just had the posting that we were going out [...] I was with the battalion commander, a very likable man called Lieutenant Colonel Tarleton [Royal West Kent Regiment] on the *Frobisher*.' They were to be followed into Leros by the Royal East Kents (the Buffs) on 25 October and the King's Own on 5 and 12 November. All troops were now aware of imminent enemy attack.

Major Ewart William Tassell came in with the Royal East Kents (the Buffs):

We'd arrived with very little [...] no transport, no 3 inch mortars, none of the things you really want. But we'd got quite a nice bump of food [...] Quite a lot of people, some of the West Kents, Irish Fusiliers and so on. Odds and sods of them had turned up and they were there. They arrived before us, I think [...] We'd had all sorts of commander-in-chiefs with different ideas on how to defend an island. And eventually we found that they'd decided that strong points all round was the best way.[5]

The Major detected a problem from the start. 'We'd got very little ammunition. We'd had all this tush before. Hard to go on with nothing [...]We were right up here [Blefuti]. Germans hadn't landed at this stage. We were there for two or three days. Communication weren't so good really.'[6] Major Tassell had identified at least two of the many problems which would occur on Leros: that of too little ammunition, and that of poor communication.

Between their arrival on Leros on 25 October and 12 November when the battle began, the 4th Buffs steadily made preparations for the impending invasion. Because of the heavy and constant bombing during the daylight hours, work on the various defensive positions was normally carried out at night. Equipment was being dropped from Allied planes, only narrowly missing the troops below. Private Stanley Norman Froud of the Buffs recalled,

Two planes, DCs, came and, can you imagine, dropped stuff without parachutes, arms, ammunition, pup tents [a two-man tent used by the military ground troops] and all that? It came crashing down. We were all diving for cover. The stuff landed in awkward places and we had to run around and find it. Then we moved up, higher up into the hills. We dug a big slit trench, and we stayed there all day. We didn't know what we were doing it for, we weren't told anything, but an officer did come round and say to us that we had to stay at our posts [...] and die at our posts![7]

The Buffs were to spend most of their time defending the north of the island.

Most of the men had a mindset of self-survival – after food, their thoughts were on clothes, warmth, shelter and ammunition. Officers were billeted in houses allocated to them, but lower ranks had only an army ration blanket and slept out on the hard ground. Although Lieutenant Clarke was an officer, he was not stationed in the officers'

house but in the trenches on the mountain. His rank entitled him to a
sleeping bag and a batman. He recalled,

> You think about yourself. How you are going to keep warm. I had a very
> good batman, he dug me a trench with a cover over it. And I had a
> sleeping bag, I even had up photographs – photographs of myself and
> my wife, that sort of thing. When I went off with the group, I was
> thinking of coming back, so I left even my wonderful officer's overcoat
> (it annoyed me [to think of] some German wearing my overcoat).
> My batman was so good. He would put hot water out for me in the
> morning to wash and shave. He heated it somehow. As an officer, you
> never worried. Your batman did everything for you. An officer had to
> concentrate the whole time. He had my wireless set on his back – that is
> what a batman does. He was a fighting soldier as well.[8]

Food Rations

Most of the troops existed on army rations. Basic meals came from
tins: hot meat and vegetable stew or bully beef accompanied by
biscuits. Initially, there was plenty of food, and a fair supply of water,
though not for washing as water had to be carried up the hill and that
was an arduous task. Plates were therefore cleaned with dust and a
handkerchief.[9] Despite the basis of their rations being mainly tins,
some men were pleased with their rations. One of them was Reverend
Reginald Anwyl, the Catholic padre for the Royal Irish Fusiliers, who
had been shipped out to minister to the soldiers. Anwyl had become
an army chaplain in 1940 and was to provide spiritual sustenance to
the soldiers in his unit over the coming weeks. He was gratified to find
that he and the rest of the men could always eat satisfactorily. 'It was
very pleasant to find that HQ cooks had managed to turn out quite
an adequate dinner – not very difficult in these days of tins.'[10] One
man's rations would keep him going for 14 days, the most a man
could carry. Lieutenant Clifford Clarke said, 'We had plenty of
rations, they came in with the destroyers.' He recalled the kind of
things which were in their kit.

> We had combat rations, that was a box of stuff which had everything
> you wanted in it [...] That was really instigated by the Americans.
> It even had toilet paper in it. There were tins of meat and veg,
> toothpaste, everything you wanted, a bit more than survival rations, but

they always had chocolate and cigarettes [...] We got 50 cigs free, and 50 you could buy from the NAAFI [Navy, Army and Air Force Institutes] cheaply. As I didn't smoke at all, I always let my batman have them and so I was one of the few who never had any difficulty getting a batman.[11]

However, some of the smokers were disappointed because black marketeers working at the packing end back home had already stolen them. '[Some of] the chaps who did smoke opened theirs and found no cigarettes there. They were being loaded in England, and the stevedores would ease open and pinch the cigarettes. Can you imagine?'[12] Rations were limited, but Clifford Clarke developed a taste for the simple stuff. He reminisced, 'They give you your sweet tea, sergeant major's tea, you could stand your spoon up in it. A big bit of bread and a scamp of bully beef. I loved it. I still love bully beef. When you're hungry, you eat it and it tastes wonderful. It tastes better than caviar, I can tell you. I never minded. Food's always fine by me.' [13]

Senior officers fared better than lower ranks, as they had easier access to stores of gin, the fancier wines and the better food left over from the Italian stores. George Jellicoe recalled, 'There was no difficulty over food. We were supplied there. If we'd wanted food, if there was food available, they [the locals] would certainly have helped. That I'm sure is what was happening to begin with until the supply thing really got working. I was moving around a bit. I went to this island [Leros]; I also went up to Samos where I was extremely well received too.'[14]

Privates had to make do with the odd tot of rum ration or some pilfered whisky. Royal Irish Fusilier Jack Harte recalled how they came by extra provisions: occasionally when food trucks were distributing rations over the island, they took a sharp incline up a hill and slowed down, giving the more deprived soldiers an opportunity to offload a handful of goods. By this method, they occasionally found themselves in possession of a purloined tin of streaky bacon and a bottle of whisky, a welcome addition to the men's meagre rations.[15] Some of the soldiers managed to seek out the taverns in Leros, to the detriment of their duties. One private in Jack Harte's company slept through most of his duties, so he was given a reprimand; the private claimed he had sand-fly fever and malaria and was on quinine. Despite his supposed 'illnesses', Jack later found him in the local tavern, which opened at night after the bombings. The tavern had become an attraction for this young soldier, who 'always managed to down a skinful of cheap banana brandy'.[16] Others recalled the rough-and-ready wine bars, with a 'fiery raw brandy', probably Metaxa, and an unknown type of beer. Fighting broke out occasionally between the Irish and the Italians after a few drinks. One company rifleman, Fusilier Donnelly, was shot in the chest, ending up in Middle East base hospital.[17]

Medical orderly and stretcher-bearer for the Faughs, Vic Kenchington was in Leros for nearly three months, being among the first troops to arrive on the island. He remembers the food as being basic, but wholesome, 'We ate McConisky's stews, treacle puddings, biscuits, bully beef – tins of stuff. We had iron rations until the little NAAFI ship came. They gave us cigarettes. We laced the tea with rum at night. We got water from wells, had sterilising tablets.'[18] However, as the battle raged on, food became scarce. During the battle he recalled, 'We had five days with no sleep. We had no food. The organisation was finished as we were all cut off from each other and the information we were getting was very poor.'[19]

Reserve rations were taken up to the mountains to supply the men digging in on higher ground. The soldiers had the satisfying task of replenishing the food stocks of the civilians with supplies brought in from caiques from neutral Turkey. International law allowed Red Cross supplies to be brought over. Unfortunately the senior representative in the area was a pro-German Swede who gave false information, reporting that the Leros civilians' welfare was good and that he had found them 'well-fed and cheerful'. This meant that no food had been distributed to them, leaving them on the verge of starvation. In reality, on Leros the population was desperately short of food. Once the British arrived and understood the situation, they took over running about 1,500 tons of food a month under the Turkish Red Crescent, with whom they had better relations, with supplies paid for by the British government. The Turkish government added 500 tons of grain to the stock.[20]

Lerian Steve Bouris remembered receiving food from the British soldiers when he was a boy. He was about seven years old at the time and took water to the soldiers every morning in return for some biscuits. He also remembered about 300 metres of mines laid around the island, so they could not go fishing on the boats. Most of the civilians suffered because of the enemy bombing as it was so indiscriminate. Corporal Reg Neep recalled,

> Prior to when they were landing by sea or air they would saturate bombing for weeks [...] and because of the terrain on Leros, the civilian population were very vulnerable because of the little isolated hamlets which were an easy target for Stuka dive bombers so they had an awful time, the Greek population. Because the Germans didn't know whether we were in the hamlets or not, it was a really difficult situation for the local population.[21]

The best way for Lerians to counteract the lowering of morale as a result of the continual bombing was to celebrate. Royal Irish Fusilier Private Paddy McCrystal recalled, 'I saw a wedding one time, it lasted about three or four days, out in Alinda. They were celebrating, but I wasn't near them at all. That was just about the only people I did see.' [22]

Most of the soldiers did not have any interaction with civilians. Lieutenant Clifford Clarke recalled, 'We hardly came in contact with the people. A lot of them wanted to keep out of the way. We wanted to keep them safe if we could.'[23] He saw a few cattle on the hills but few living creatures. 'It seemed to me during the time we were there, the place had gone into hibernation. There had been trouble [under the Italians], they had stored up lots of stuff in their houses.'[24] Few animals were evident on the island. Sergeant George Hatcher recalled,

> The only thing I remember about the animals, they had a donkey that serviced the Italians. They were in a disused gun positions, and the donkey went to collect water from the well. It had a couple of jerrycans tied round the donkey's neck. Each time it came back to the gun positions, it had to go down the step, and every time it went down the steps, the jerrycans poured and the poor donkey fell over. And that happened every time; they never bothered to take the cans away before the donkey got to the step.[25]

Few Greek citizens remained on the island once the bombing started. Those villagers who had enough money or had relatives elsewhere had already left, either moving to the mainland or emigrating to America and Australia. Of the few hundred who remained, most took refuge in the caves around the coastal areas of the island. Some families sheltered there in the day during the bombing and returned to their own houses at night; others simply took their belongings and went to live in the caves. Many villagers were in caves around Portolago and Panageus.[26] Others started hiding in caves in Dromona and Kefela with about 20 or 30 people in each.[27] Every time the air raids started, church bells rang out to warn the local population to take cover. Thespina Taxhliambori, whose family had prospered under the Italians, was 19 years old when the Battle of Leros began. When the bombing started, the family left Leros as it was too dangerous to stay. They sailed at night for Lipsos as there were no military there, and only returned to Leros once the battle was over.[28] Her father and brother were fishermen and so the family managed to survive.

While some of the islanders saved what they could from plundered Italian stores, most of the people in the islands were starving. Peter George Koulianus, 16 years old at the time, recalled, 'From the day of the surrender, the civilians had difficulty finding food. We went in search of stockpiles for the British [...] We looked for clothes, tinned goods, anything we could find.'[29] He and his brother found work with the British soldiers after the Royal Irish Fusiliers had arrived

> My brother was 16 years old; he got a job in Meraviglia in 'Charing Cross' and stayed there 40 days working in the kitchen. I left Dromona and went into the kitchen drinking tea with the British soldiers, and they got me in the trenches. My other brother Nicholas was a tailor and fixed the clothes of Sergeant Jack in return for wine. We were good friends with the British soldiers. Most of those I met were Irish Fusiliers.[30]

When the situation worsened in November, his mother made him give up the work.

> Bombs were dropping on Meraviglia [...] The families were left to go into caves in Dromona, a very bad atmosphere. There was not enough room for all the families, people were everywhere. We spent daytime in the cave, then went back to the house at night. Aircraft was flying over here from sun up to sunset.[31]

Maintaining the Garrison

Maintaining the garrison was becoming increasingly difficult, and by 18 October supplies were running low in Leros as passage for ships became increasingly hazardous and supplying by air near impossible. Yet hundreds of men were dependent on a smooth delivery of stocks of food, ammunition, medicine and equipment and somehow the Allies' navy and air force had to get provisions through. Although Samos was well stocked, only small quantities could be transported to Leros via caiques. A few supplies were delivered by air, but lack of Allied planes made this difficult.[32] British Beaufighters were brought in on occasion to protect Leros at night when troops were being unloaded, and America had allowed some of their aircraft to be used: B-25 Mitchell aircraft, twin-engine bombers equipped with cannon, inflicted enemy losses while escorted by Bristol-made Beaufighter aircraft, versatile aircraft used initially as night fighters, and later in maritime strike and ground-attack roles. The Allied pilots managed to damage four F-lighters and torpedoed a 600-ton merchant ship. This at least reduced the likelihood of the enemy invading Leros for the time being, and Allied naval forces could concentrate on reinforcement and supply during the dark period when there was no moon. During brighter moonlight, they became too easy a target for enemy bombers. These Allied planes carried out around 86 sorties between 16 October and 16 November.[33] Many of the attacks they made were on Antimachia in Kos, attempting to blow up German-held airstrips, but they also assisted in the seas around Leros when ships were unloading supplies. During this time, the Allies were heavily reliant on the Royal Navy for the conveyance of stores, troops and equipment. Their crews would try and deliver, but the task was arduous due to the continual enemy attacks by air. Senior British naval officer Aegean Acting Captain E.H.B. Baker did his utmost to avoid bombardment by varying the times of arrival and hurrying up the time of unloading.[34]

Reinforcements were landed on Leros by ship and submarine during the second half of October: 967 men, 545 tons of stores, 18 guns, 3 jeeps and 2 trailers. HMS *Dulverton* ran at least four trips delivering troops and equipment to Leros. Don Bush was on the ship. He had only been in the Royal Navy a couple of years before he was sent out to Leros, and later recalled,

> I was a gunnery radar rating, and what was rather interesting in those days, we wore telegraphists' badges because if you got captured they were afraid you were going to get tortured to find out about radar as it

was still in its early days. The Germans knew about it as they had it as
well, in different forms. The *Bismarck* had gunnery radar, that's why
their shooting was so good. Several German boats had some but they
were different to ours.[35]

He remembers his initial trip to the Aegean:

> The first one we went up on, you couldn't move during the day because
> you got bombed. We used to go into the Greek inlets, and you'd take
> out some bits of machinery and put it on deck [...] you'd say we've got
> 24 hours because Turkey was neutral [and they had to unload all the
> equipment and get out of the enemy's reach before dawn]. And then
> when the night came, you'd go off and do something else, look out for
> any German ships that were about and bombard.[36]

Don spent a lot of time aboard ship circulating round Kos and Leros
mainly at night. 'We were patrolling around looking for any ships.
The idea was to stop them landing on any of these islands as they had
already taken Kos, and so, it's so close, we thought they were going to
go into Leros.'[37] They had to return to Alexandria to refuel.

HMS *Dulverton* was also responsible for delivering troops on Leros.
Don recalled,

> We picked up troops in Haifa. It was a detachment – I couldn't tell you
> how many but when we got to Leros might be a hundred chaps, we were
> so crowded anyway. By this time we had four short of 200 crew on
> board. We took them up and they were rather disgruntled as we took
> the mess tables out [of the hold] and literally shoved them [the soldiers]
> down as fast as we could – and their kit after them – because we had to
> get out again before it got light. It was earlier in the night than dawn –
> we had to be well clear by dawn because the planes started and they
> bombed hell out of anyone who was around.[38]

Life on board had its downsides and there were difficulties for some
men as the rolling seas in bad weather took their toll, as Don Bush
outlined. 'People were seasick, so there was vomit everywhere. There
was a thing in the navy – they don't mind you vomiting – if you vomit
you clear it up yourself no matter how bad you are. I was lucky, I didn't
suffer seasickness.' All the portholes were clamped down, so the sailors
had no fresh air.[39] Life on board was grimly unhygienic.

> There were 100 men here in the mess. All the hammock bills were taken;
> there weren't enough, so people would sleep on the tables on the
> lockers, anywhere they could find a place to sleep. There was a

bathroom, one shower, there were four basins for 100 men, and we were lucky because some of the old destroyers didn't have a bathroom at all. They would go out in the break and have a hose down. We had a toilet, they call them 'heads'; in the navy [...] you'll see this grating by the bough strip and that where we used to go out and sit.[40]

There were also problems with keeping personal items dry when on board.

You had a kitbag and you had lockers which you sat on. You each had a locker. The only trouble is when you got a rough sea you got a lot of water in the mess deck, then the ship would roll and you would have about two foot of water which would go in your lockers and everything would be soaking wet.[41]

The Royal Navy continued to land stores and cause disruption to Kos and Kalymnos: 20 tons of stores were landed in Alinda Bay on Leros on 19 October by HMSs *Eclipse* and *Pathfinder*, which came in from Güvercinlik Bay. Petrol dumps in Kos harbour were blown up by HMS *Belvoir*, causing a large fire. HMSs *Phoebe* and *Fury* came from Alexandria and bombarded Port Kalymnos on the lookout for F-lighters; HMSs *Hurworth* and *Beaufort* bombarded Kos roads with a total of 300 rounds, although *Hurworth* was hit by an 88-mm shell and one of the crew was killed.[42] More stores were dropped off in Alinda on 20 October before moonrise at 7 p.m. by HMSs *Fury* and *Beaufort* before withdrawing south, causing damage to F-lighters round Kos and bombarding Kos roads.[43] HMSs *Faulknor* and *Petard* attempted to land more stores on 21 October but it was impossible to dock on account of the moon and flares, so they laid up in Turkish waters, where they were joined by HMS *Dulverton*.[44]

Ships always made trips to Leros at night, usually slipping into Alinda Bay in inky blackness and offloading men and equipment. Alinda faced Turkey, so it was the easiest bay to come into. Ships carrying jeeps, trailers and mountain guns were unloaded in total darkness as fast as possible, usually in less than an hour.[45] Consequently, crews managed very little sleep. This continual movement and build-up of troops, ammunition, food, jeeps, and equipment of all kinds was a major job for the British navy, but they were supported by motorboats, caiques and any other craft which could help. As one despatch mentioned, 'It was intended that once the buildup of Leros was complete, its maintenance would be undertaken by caiques from Samos and from the Turkish coast, and at the end of the month [October] all available caiques were collected at Smyrna, Kusadasi, and Bodrum.' Meanwhile a great effort was made to make Leros secure for the winter, and destroyers were not spared the task of running in troops and stores.[46] The *Dulverton* would make a second drop of troops to Leros with a number of Royal West Kents aboard, having to land quickly and draw well clear before dawn and the arrival of the bombers.

Submarines were called in to assist delivery to help speed up the conveyancing. Twelve guns arrived on Leros in the submarine HMS *Severn* on 22 October, a second batch arriving on 29 October.[47] With the Germans now in hiding in narrow bays all over Kalymnos, it was easy for them to focus on taking Leros, although the Royal Navy managed to take out an enemy troop convoy. Meanwhile Allied shipping was about to suffer major setbacks. HMSs *Jervis* and *Pathfinder* managed to land at Partheni in the north of the island at seven o'clock during the evening of 22 October, with Beaufighters maintaining fighter cover. The crew unloaded stores, including ten jeeps with trailers, the first time that jeeps were landed in Leros.[48] During the one-and-a-half hours it took to set ashore the equipment, as a distraction HMS *Hurworth*, a Hunt-class mine countermeasures vessel under Commander Royston Hollis Wright, and the Greek Hunt-class destroyer *Adrias* led by Commander Ioannis Toumbas swept into Kalymnos waters, but both hit mines at 10 p.m. *Adrias* was hit first and had her bow blown off, with 21 men killed and 30 wounded. *Hurworth* blew up hitting a mine while coming to her rescue, split in half and sank within 15 minutes with 143 men killed. It was a heavy loss of life, but *Adrias* picked up the 86 survivors including Commander Wright, and managed to hobble to the Turkish coast, the ship being beached at Gümüşlük.[49]

Disaster stuck with the sinking of HMS *Eclipse* around midnight on 23/24 October east of Kalymnos. The ship had hit a mine and went down within three minutes. It was carrying not only vital equipment and supplies for the garrison, but A Company and part of the HQ Company of the Buffs. Private Stanley 'Bill' Froud, 4th Buffs, was on board when the detonation hit the ship under her forward boiler room, setting the fuel tanks ablaze. She immediately took on a heavy list and broke in two, spilling burning fuel into the sea. Stan recalled,

> I was standing on deck with my best friend Jack [Hawkes] and the other boys [...] and that was it, I didn't know any more [...] I woke up and all I saw was flames in my eyes and everything was still. My legs were caught in the wires going round the boat [...] my back was towards the edge of the destroyer and as she turned I went down with her. Strangely, it felt kind of peaceful [...] then, I don't know if I kicked or what, but I came to the surface [...] about 100 yards from the destroyer. I saw her turn over and the screws were still going fast as she went down [...] speeding down.[50]

Of the 200 Buffs on board, 134 perished, along with another 119 naval personnel.[51] Around 100 men were picked up by an RAF air–sea rescue launch despatched from Leros. The *Petard* sailing with them picked up 42 survivors, and a motor launch from Leros picked up others. The *Petard* was unable to offload her own troops, so transferred them to the *Hursley* and *Aldenham* where they landed next day. The only crane (for hoisting equipment off ships) remaining in operation in Leros was bombed and put out of action. Stan was the only survivor of his close-knit group of friends, most of whom had served together since 1939. He now had to face an uncertain future among virtual strangers, a situation which no soldier relishes. 'When we got to Leros I was without my own A Company and all the boys and men I'd soldiered with before, and believe me you feel lonely and naked without the men that you could rely on.'[52] He felt vulnerable without his peers around him. 'You know the cooks and all that. By then I had done about five years and you had young soldiers coming in, and inexperienced officers. I knew by then you had to look after yourself, you didn't want be led into anything stupid.'[53]

Along with the troops, ammunition and supplies for the garrison had gone down. On board the *Eclipse* was Brigadier General George Davy, the director of military operations, Middle East, en route to inspecting the defences of Leros. Davy was amongst the survivors. He went on to become the commander of land gorces, Adriatic.[54] Some days later a bedraggled man claiming to be a survivor of the *Eclipse* staggered ashore at Xerocampus dressed only in his underpants in a state of complete exhaustion. At first the soldiers he encountered were suspicious, but Hugh Stewell was sent for and could identify him as Lieutenant Middleton of the Royal Navy.[55] In doing their job, the Royal Navy had incurred many losses: four submarines and six destroyers were sunk in the seas around Leros, and various ships very badly damaged.[56]

Further reinforcements were on their way from Alexandria on 25 October. HMSs *Faulknor*, *Belvoir* and *Beaufort* escorted by HMS *Phoebe* laid up in the Gulf of Kos overnight, and the following day they, along with HMSs *Hursley* and *Alderman*, carried out an anti-shipping sweep west of Leros and withdrew south. Three hundred and ten troops and 40 tons of equipment were landed by HMSs *Dulverton* and *Penn* and HHMS *Miaoulis*. The Italian cargo submarine *Zoea* landed 40 tons of stores and mail at Portolago.[57] Two officers and two crew were killed when a motor launch was bombed off Lipsi but 13 of her men were saved. Again in the dark of night, the Fifth Destroyer Flotilla Force arrived at Partheni letting off troops and stores at 2.10 a.m. on 27 October and quickly withdrew to Güvercinlik Bay, Turkey.[58] Another 129 troops, stores and 15 jeeps were dropped off in Alinda at midnight on 31 October by HMSs *Petard* and *Belvoir*, the ships holing up in Iassus Bay.[59]

Early on in the occupation, medication was limited to treating injuries or old diseases picked up in the desert. Lieutenant Clarke had caught malaria in Palestine and self-medicated: 'I used to have two water bottles. One full of water, and one full of rum. When I had the shivers, I took the rum, when I was perspiring I took the water. But is not conducive to active service. Couldn't go sick. Half the men went down with malaria, we got them right again with mefolquine that was just after they'd invented that; before, they had to have quinine.'[60] Private McCrystal recalled, 'The only tablets we got were malaria tablets. The only ones who were sick were the ones who were homesick.'[61] Only officers seem to have been supplied with Benzedrine, an 'upper' to keep them fully operational and able to give orders in the desperate times of no sleep in the middle of the battle. As the wounded grew in numbers, the skills of the medical corps were stretched to their limits.

During the last week of October there were clear indications of the mounting of a major enemy assault force gathering in Piraeus.

Enemy landing craft (13 60-ft powered lighters of the I-boat class) had arrived by rail from the north. Simultaneously a group of three escort vessels of the U-J type were sailed from Piraeus to the Cyclades. Sightings of the loading of several merchant vessels with munitions, guns and supplies suggested preparations for a follow-up convoy. The Allies guessed an assault was being prepared for either Samos or Leros.[62] Churchill wrote to Roosevelt on 23 October 1943, perhaps somewhat sardonically, given that he had asked so much and was given so little in way of reinforcement for Leros, 'You will, I am sure, share my relief that Leros has so far managed to hold out. "The dogs eat of the crumbs which fall from their masters' table".'[63]

At the end of October, Force 292 was abolished and HQ Aegean came directly under GHQ Middle East. Brigadier H.R. Hall temporarily took over from Major General F.G.R. Brittorous as general officer commanding in the Aegean, but would be replaced by Brigadier Robert Tilney by 5 November. Brittorous had been seen to be failing as a commander, overloading himself with detail instead of commanding. Lieutenant General Sir Desmond Anderson who commanded all army and air forces in the Aegean had visited Leros and recommended the garrison be increased to four battalions, one of which should be a machine-gun battalion. Reinforcement accordingly arrived: four Buffs on 25 October and one King's Own on 5 November.[64] After his visit to Leros, senior army staff officers from Middle East General Headquarters with three commanders-in-chief made the decision on 30 October to reinforce the island with an additional 1,200–1,300 extra troops, guns and equipment to enable a reasonable attempt at staving off an invasion. Destroyers, caiques and schooners delivered another 1,280 troops, 14 jeeps, a trailer and 180 tons of stores, with submarines delivering another 33 tons of stores.[65]

The constant bolstering of Leros was seen as necessary preparation in readiness for an enemy attack. Everyone was standing at the ready, waiting for the action to take place. Churchill noted expectantly on 27 October, 'We heard that four thousand German Alpine troops and many landing craft had reached Piraeus, apparently detained for Leros, and early in November reports of landing-craft movements portended attack.'[66] The battle was about to commence.

7

Waiting Under Bombs

I can see the Stuka coming down to me now and it was the only time I
prayed on Leros. I definitely prayed. I was in a slit trench and couldn't
do anything about it and he was definitely coming towards me.

Lieutenant Ted Johnson, Royal Irish Fusilier[1]

The first 11 days in November were a period of waiting – a lull before
the expected storm, although there were increasingly heavy air
attacks as a softening-up method by the enemy. With the Germans
now holding the neighbouring islands of Kos and Kalymnos, it was
only a matter of time before they invaded Leros. Reverend Reginald
Anwyl was aware that the bombing had become heavier but it did not
seem to put him off his food. He recalled, 'I learnt that I could surprise
myself by eating heartily even in the middle of a raid and worry lest
I dropped my mess-tin while running for cover.'[2] He was on the
island for over 40 days and had fallen into a routine. His mornings
started at dawn with the awful prolonged bombing and the almost
equally feared silences. He spent his time ministering to the Catholic
soldiers, hearing confessions and giving communion. He was honest
about his fears, but was rarely able to express them, as his job was to
keep up the morale of the men. 'I spoke thus until I wearied of the
need to talk bolder than I felt and I would return bodily and mentally
tired to await at the Regimental Aid Post (RAP) the blessed arrival
of sun-set and the few hours of rest.' The RAP was a front-line military
medical establishment incorporated into the infantry battalion
and used for the immediate treatment of battlefield casualties.

It was based in a small two-roomed house, one half for Military Intelligence and the other the living quarters for Anwyl and two doctors (one was 'Doc' Pickering).[3]

An Italian hospital existed in Portolago (Lakki), and another makeshift dressing station in Villa Bellini in Alinda. However, many of the injured men used their battalion headquarters as the first place to get emergency aid. Fusilier Lieutenant Ted Johnson recalled,

> There was a hospital in Alinda Bay but as far as we were concerned our battalion medical officer was based at Charing Cross. Any casualties suffered by companies were to get back to Charing Cross, not direct to the hospitals. It was up to the medical officers to decide if they were a hospital case. If there was, a field ambulance stationed somewhere would take them, he would then evaluate them to that, but our immediate line of communication was back to the regimental post.[4]

Most of the soldiers spent their time either in slit trenches or in caves, unable to move far because of the bombings. As a consequence of this hindrance, Reverend Anwyl would say Mass at 'stand-down' in the evenings in candlelight, and then only to a platoon of soldiers who were close by, as others were too far to reach, positioned in the mountains. Before the group turned in, the Fusiliers were usually visited by their mortar officer Jimmy Hoare or Terry Bourke, who were billeted close by. The officers had plenty of alcohol, which they had salvaged from the island's only hotel (Hotel Roma in Portolago), although they restricted themselves to a couple of drinks a night, conscious of the need to remain alert. There had been at least two instances among the officers on the island where drink had provided the final tipping point in a nervous breakdown. In order to alleviate the boredom, Anwyl and the doctors did crossword puzzles, but hardly any books were available.

At night-time, they did little in the way of ablutions except for cleaning their teeth, and everyone slept fully clad ready for action. Reverend Anwyl would bless the whole island at night as he gave the benediction on his own. He worried about 'the troops that I knew so well living like animals in the ground, the Greeks unable to live in their homes and forced to cower in the more desolate hills with their families.'[5]

At 9 a.m. on 11 November, Reverend Anwyl set out with his tin hat on his head, a large stick in his hand and binoculars round his neck.

After only a few hundred yards he had to take shelter. He finally reached C Company of the Royal Irish Fusiliers and arranged to say Mass with them that evening. As he made his way onwards, the bombers seemed uncertain where to bomb but they were coming down heavily so he took shelter in a cave. Quite sensibly, he reasoned, 'I don't like caves as shelters as I fear the double danger of the entrance being blocked and of death by blast should a bomb fall near the entrance.' He could feel the movement that the bombs made. 'We lay in a heap and the mad rush of air warned us that the bombs were close.'[6] Local Greeks were also in there. 'Next to me was a young Greek boy who had been working with the gunners: the poor lad was trembling and I found room for pity in the midst of my fear.' Eventually there was a lull in the bombings and he made his way over to B Company in their new position on the hillside. John Salter, captain and second-in-command of B Company, and Duffy, a platoon officer, shouted him over and he gave them Holy Communion. Bombing started up again as they lay in the trenches watching as the planes targeted Mount Meroviglia. A large piece of steel hit Reg's metal helmet, making a large dent in the side. Not wanting to hang around he hailed a passing jeep going towards Alinda, but the bombing had already done its damage. 'The road was in bad condition and marked by many craters.' Some bombs had hit the cemetery, and gravestones had been destroyed or scattered.

Intending to make his way to D Company, he alighted from the jeep at the foot of the castle. As he did, Ju 87 dive-bombers began to attack the castle itself. 'There seemed to be an endless stream of them as plane after plane hovered over the sky, slipped sideways and then hurtled down.' The Allies on the ground reacted with their own gunfire, 'Great gouts of flame shot skywards in rapid succession, followed by columns of thick black smoke and dust until it seemed that the hill itself was crumbling before my eyes under some giant's thunderbolts.'[7] He decided to make his way to the advanced dressing station and met Royal Engineer Major Murphy who invited him to lunch at his billet nearby. After lunch, he returned to the RAP just at dusk to bad news: 'Jack Barber, the Medical Officer to the Royal Irish Fusiliers, and Pickering told me that they had had few casualties but that a lad from C Company had just been killed.'

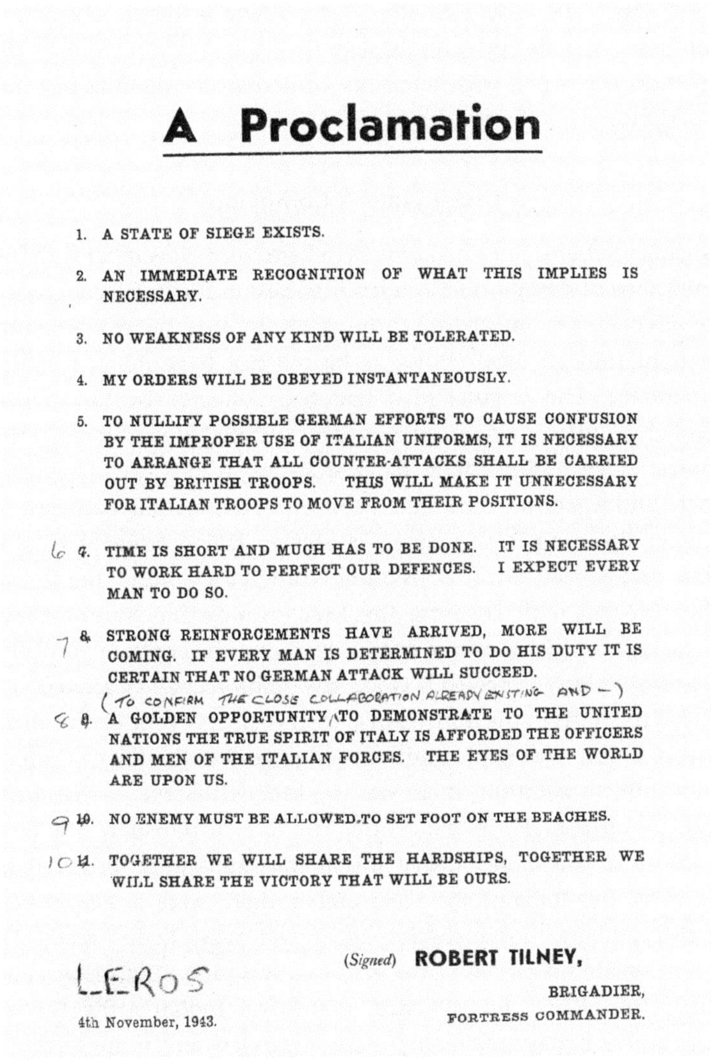

A Proclamation

1. A STATE OF SIEGE EXISTS.

2. AN IMMEDIATE RECOGNITION OF WHAT THIS IMPLIES IS NECESSARY.

3. NO WEAKNESS OF ANY KIND WILL BE TOLERATED.

4. MY ORDERS WILL BE OBEYED INSTANTANEOUSLY.

5. TO NULLIFY POSSIBLE GERMAN EFFORTS TO CAUSE CONFUSION BY THE IMPROPER USE OF ITALIAN UNIFORMS, IT IS NECESSARY TO ARRANGE THAT ALL COUNTER-ATTACKS SHALL BE CARRIED OUT BY BRITISH TROOPS.   THIS WILL MAKE IT UNNECESSARY FOR ITALIAN TROOPS TO MOVE FROM THEIR POSITIONS.

7. TIME IS SHORT AND MUCH HAS TO BE DONE.   IT IS NECESSARY TO WORK HARD TO PERFECT OUR DEFENCES.   I EXPECT EVERY MAN TO DO SO.

8. STRONG REINFORCEMENTS HAVE ARRIVED, MORE WILL BE COMING. IF EVERY MAN IS DETERMINED TO DO HIS DUTY IT IS CERTAIN THAT NO GERMAN ATTACK WILL SUCCEED.
(TO CONFIRM THE CLOSE COLLABORATION ALREADY EXISTING AND —)

9. A GOLDEN OPPORTUNITY TO DEMONSTRATE TO THE UNITED NATIONS THE TRUE SPIRIT OF ITALY IS AFFORDED THE OFFICERS AND MEN OF THE ITALIAN FORCES.   THE EYES OF THE WORLD ARE UPON US.

10. NO ENEMY MUST BE ALLOWED TO SET FOOT ON THE BEACHES.

11. TOGETHER WE WILL SHARE THE HARDSHIPS, TOGETHER WE WILL SHARE THE VICTORY THAT WILL BE OURS.

LEROS

4th November, 1943.

(*Signed*) **ROBERT TILNEY,**

BRIGADIER,
FORTRESS COMMANDER.

FIGURE 7.1   Proclamation from Brigadier Robert Tilney to the Leros troops, 4 November 1943

As the bombs rained down on the island, Reverend Anwyl would sing loudly to keep his spirits up as he strode across the mountains. His favourite hymn was 'We Stand for God and his Glory', which he could sing in Italian, cheering up the Italian troops as he went to give them Mass. 'The rocky formation of the island made the crashing of bombs reverberate and echo through the little hills and I foresaw the invasion beginning with ferocious bombing and shelling of every description while I was asleep!'[8]

Under Tilney's Command

Brigadier Robert Tilney had arrived in Leros on 5 November with full intentions of doing his best in his new post as fortress commander. He was commissioned to direct the pending battle, but not everyone thought him an ideal choice as he did not have much infantry experience. The original plan had been directed by Royal Irish Fusilier Maurice French; he had concentrated on protecting the central ridge of the island by positioning troops on Meraviglia, Rachi and Appertici, rather than scattering them along the coast to protect the island's shorelines. However, Tilney reorganised this plan and spread the troops more thinly all around the coast. The problem with covering the beaches was that Mount Clidi, Meraviglia and Racchi were not fortified and the central part of the island was less protected.[9] Once the reinforcements arrived, he placed the Buffs in the north, Royal Irish Fusiliers in the centre and a unit of Royal West Kents under the command of the King's Own in the south. In addition, there was the Mobile Reserve in the north and the fortress HQ in the centre. The lack of transport hindered mobility, and the only heavy anti-aircraft guns were those left in place by the Italians. By 5 November there were around 2,000 British soldiers (not including the Royal West Kents) ready for action, made up of 500 Royal Irish Fusiliers, 450 King's Own, 360 Buffs, 100 LRDG and SBS men, 100 Royal Indian Army Service Corps, plus battery regiments, signals, sappers and miners. About 2,000 Italians remained, but how many were effectively fighting is questionable.

Lack of coordination of the troops and of a proper workable defence strategy would inevitably affect the course of the battle, as Major Tassell surmised:

> When we got to this island [Leros], we found that the brigadier said, 'Oh no, there's a thin line right round the edges.' We hadn't got enough

troops to do that actually. I think what had happened – this is only hearsay – but I believe, that the two or three battalion commanders realised that the brigadier who was running the show then was no good and they'd turned him off [...] They decided the three of them, the commanders [commanding officers], would keep the forces intact and in their proper places, at the strong points and so on.[10]

They thought Tilney's idea of spreading the army round the coastal areas of the island instead of defending strategic points higher up would not work as there were not enough men to surround the island.

Most of the King's Own came in at Portolago on 5 and 12 November. Those who came in the early hours of 5 November were under the command of Lieutenant Colonel S.A.F.S. Egerton. Captain H.P.J.M. Burke had been on a course in the Middle East, but when he heard that the battalion was going into action, he quickly applied for permission to join them.[11] They spent the first night in Portolago until the evening of 7 November, when orders were received to move to a new position covering the beaches of Xerocampus in the south of the island, and platoon defensive posts were 'dug in'. The companies were strategically placed around the island: A Company commanded by Captain D.J.P. Thirkell-White was dug in around Xerocampus with Lieutenants Porte, Broster and Burgess second-in-command; B Company were in Mount Patella (the position of the Italian acoustic and optic detection net for the anti-aircraft warning); C Company were to move to the north of the island into the sector controlled by the Buffs. They formed part of the Mobile Reserves under the direct control of the brigadier. All the island transport consisting of about ten jeeps was allotted to this company; they were to report to the company every evening and remain until stand-down the following morning.[12] D Company occupied the high ground southwest of Lakki overlooking the bay. The King's Own signals platoon landed with HQ Company and joined Battalion Headquarters on 7 November. HQ Company was ordered to move to a new area on the high ground west of Portolago overlooking the bay, with a primary directive to counter-attack any enemy landing in that area. A RAP was established at their company headquarters. During the first two or three days the companies spent their time digging in, making slit trenches and collecting ammunition and stores from the quayside for distribution to companies. Line communication was established with all companies.[13]

Among the incoming troops during the early hours of 12 November was journalist Leonard Marsland Gander, one of the first independent witnesses to see what was going on in Leros. He was working as war correspondent for the *Daily Telegraph* and decided to go to Leros after attending a conference for war correspondents given at GHQ by Major General R. Scobie, chief of general staff to General Maitland Wilson, the commander-in-chief for the Middle East. Gander recalled,

> The General told us plainly that since he retook Kos the enemy had shown every intention of mounting an attack on Leros. 'We have built up to a considerable extent in Leros', he said, 'but it would be ideal and useless to pretend that the position is in any way secure. There is no longer any possibility of giving effective air cover in the area. Nevertheless, it is thought necessary to take a chance, and we intend to do all we can to hang on to both Leros and Samos'.[14]

As he crossed the sea, Gander had been concerned about the high possibility of being blown to bits by German bombers, 'The odds of it were extraordinarily high, but I had gone too far to draw back. The only thing to do was to "stiffen the sinews and summon up the blood".'[15] The German aircraft he believed, could cover the whole Aegean unchallenged, and bomb every British vessel in sight.

More often than not, soldiers were given very little information on their destination. Sid Bowden was a private in the 2nd Battalion, B Company, Royal West Kents and was just one of about 200 men of his company who got the call to be on the ready for moving out on 12 November. They had just got back to Egypt after a short trip to Castelorizo. Sid recalled,

> then the next thing we knew we were put on this destroyer. We had no idea where we were going. We knew we were going to marry up because the SAS were treating us to cigarettes and beer. They had already been up there a couple of times. But we landed on Leros, they laid the mess tables across the side of the ship [so the men could slide down them] because it was a death trap for destroyers in the harbour, and we just had to take our chance.[16]

On disembarkation, the men were warned to run for it, if attacks started. Everything seemed chaotic. 'The captain more or less told us if the air raids come, we should just go. That was how we got off.' He recalled going up a hill but had no idea where he was. 'This is where it's all vague to us. We were only privates, we were never told where we were going [...] We were digging in for two or three days, we got bombed several times when we got there.'[17] Lieutenant Colonel Tarleton, their commanding officer, had gone straight to HQ to request orders from Brigadier Tilney, then returned to Portolago to pick up his company and took them off to the stretch of the junction at 'Charing Cross'. A Company was to take the eastern side and coordinate their attack with C Company led by Major Read, who would attack from the south of Platanos.

Part of the Queen's Own Royal West Kents battalions were still in Samos on 11 November when they received orders that Leros was in danger of imminent attack and they should move to help with its defences. Lieutenant Peter Matthewman, the battalion intelligence officer, was informed by signal from Leros that the island was about to be invaded. British authorities had gleaned information from Allied air and sea craft who had seen the enemy gathering forces in Rhodes and Piraeus port in Athens; aerial photography and naval intelligence were crucial in relaying this information. Messages flew out to the Middle East and Turkey to inform those higher up, and requests were made to send any possible relief they could, especially troops. A battalion of Royal West Kents had to be pulled out of the mountains on Samos and transported to the port of embarkation; naval destroyers had to be called together to ensure protection.[18]

Lieutenant Richard 'Jimmy' James was still on Samos with the rest of his company of Royal West Kents when he heard the news and was most concerned about their situation.

> I know Colonel Tarleton thought the same, things became chaotic. It began to rain. We got moved down to the docks, we didn't go; then we got moved down and again and we didn't go, then on the third time we did go. So this was very bad for morale of the ordinary soldiers. They got confused and they'd got tired. They got woken up at night and told to move down to the docks, and then they went back not to their billets but to a temporary billet in the dockyards.

Finally, on 12 November, they sailed to Leros but it was a very hazardous journey, with German air attacks on the boats moving there.

To make matters worse, the battalion of Royal West Kents was being moved in piecemeal, which would add to their confusion once on Leros. 'One company, A Company I think it was, moved in earlier; B Company moved in later, and C Company and HQ Company moved in separately. So we didn't arrive there as a battalion.' [19]

As Lieutenant James pointed out,

> The Royal Navy had a very difficult task as they hadn't got air cover, and the Germans held Crete and the army had to get their ships through what was very hostile territory [...] the naval losses were very heavy. An awful lot of ships were lost. The Germans had by now got a 'magnetic' bomb which would hone in on a ship [...] We transferred to an Italian passenger boat [...] and it was a pretty dramatic incident because German planes were flying overheard [...] there were no British aircraft in sight, and we thought there might be bombing attacks.[20]

Although still young, Lieutenant James had a despondent feeling about their position in this part of the war. 'Don't forget most of the people there with me, and I myself, had now been in the war for four years and we were finally experienced on how things should be arranged. We were very aware that we were not in a very good and happy position, that the prospects were distinctly bad. The Turkish air bases had not been made available. There were no fighter aircraft acting as protection, and coming out of this position was not good. After that length of time in the war service – and my colonel partner had been in right from the very time of the Abyssinian crisis – we were feeling a reality about this.'[21]

Ocean Warfare

At the beginning of November, British agents reported they had seen the enemy undertaking landing practices in the Greek port of Lavrion on the tip of the Attiki Peninsula. In response, the Allies increased their stacking-up of troops and equipment in readiness for the oncoming invasion. Over the coming weeks the navy delivered hundreds of troops and tons of supplies as well as jeeps using the 5th and the 8th Destroyer Flotillas.[22] Allied bombardments of Kalymnos and Kos harbours and roads were carried out by destroyer forces under Commanding Officer Egan directing HMSs *Petard* and

Rockwood and ORP *Krakowiak*. Altogether they spent one-and-a-half hours close off Port Kalymnos and pumped 1,500 rounds of 4-inch into this small harbour.

Air reconnaissance photographs were taken to provide further evidence of enemy preparation; the images showed the enemy with nine landing craft and two escort vessels moving east arriving in stages until 10 November into the Kos/Kalymnos area, moving in daylight protected by air cover. British Beaufighters and Mitchells of 201 (Naval Cooperation) Group attacked the enemy by day, and destroyers sought craft out by night, but, because of the heavy enemy air cover and the navy's difficulty in spotting the enemy craft laying up camouflaged in small bays, these operations met with little success.

With the arrival of enemy reinforcements at Kos and Kalymnos on the night of 10/11 November, the German forces had four serviceable F-boats, 13 I-boats, five auxiliary naval craft and a number of armed caiques loaded with troops and equipment.[23] One report stated, 'The bulk of the enemy invasion flotilla having arrived at Port Kalymnos and Kos harbour, it was hoped that they would have to spend at least one night there fuelling and preparing to move up to the northern bays of Kalymnos, from which the invasion was expected to be launched.'[24] British attacks had caused delays to the plans for the German invasion and given a chance for Allied troops on the ground to organise themselves. The British Army Command was of the opinion that any invasion could be fought off. However, given the distance British destroyers had to go, to bases at Alexandria or Limassol, to refuel and obtain supplies, only a limited number could remain in the area. These were instructed to intercept at night and destroy the follow-up convoys.

Motor launches, motor torpedo boats and motor gunboats were under the command of the senior British naval officer in the Aegean. At night the motor launches carried out anti-invasion patrols, whilst the motor torpedo boats and motor gunboats were held at immediate notice in the harbour to act on enemy reports. Fuel stocks for coastal forces were established in Samos and in caiques, with small emergency stocks in Leros.[25]

Capture of British Minesweeper

Defences continued to be breached, causing damage to seafaring
vessels or sinking them, often with large loss of life and loss of
equipment. Worse still, if a ship was captured, it had the potential to
jeopardise the whole Aegean campaign as they carried the secret
codes books in order to make contact with other Allied ships. One
such security breach occurred on the eve of the Battle of Leros, with
the capture of British Yard Mine Sweeper (BYMS) 72, causing a great
deal of chaos for the ships and boats operating in the Dodecanese.[26]
The BYMS-72 had been one of two minesweepers (the other being
BYMS-73) which had arrived at Alinda at 01.00 on 11 November. The
army was desperate for extra troops and supplies, having lost both
with the sinking of HMS *Eclipse* less than a month earlier. BYMS-73
offloaded its equipment and moved off to take refuge in Güvercinlik
Bay, remaining there until nightfall. BYMS-72 remained at anchor
until early evening, when she parted company with her sister ship to
return to Alinda Bay so that the heavy cables for the Army Signal
Corps she was carrying could be offloaded. In early evening, as she
neared the bay within 3 miles of Leros, she was spotted and attacked
by the Luftwaffe. A 500-lb glider bomb struck the ship forward on the
port side, and the resulting explosion blasted the port 20-mm gun
and its platform into the sea, taking along the gunner who was
strapped to it and killing the other member of the gun crew.

Army personnel removed the bodies of the deceased and
transported the wounded crewmen to the makeshift hospital in
Villa Bellini in Alinda, while the ship discharged the cargo it carried.
While the commanding officer went ashore to receive orders from
Navy House, the crew remained aboard, hosing debris down from the
decks. After the coxswain had given everyone a fortifying round of
rum to enliven the spirits of the crew, the order came in that they
were to proceed to Portolago on the other side of the island for
repairs. Hugging the shoreline using only a small-scale chart (because
such charts cover a large area, they do not provide the detail needed
to navigate restricted waters), they sailed short-handed by the clear
starlit early morning. All her guns were now inoperative, and the
minesweeper was supposed to have been met at the entrance to

Portolago harbour by a motor launch that would guide her to a berth. However, the crew appear to have missed the turning and sailed on past the mouth of Portolago and on towards Kalymnos, where they were captured by the Germans. All the secret codes used by small sea-boats were aboard, which seriously compromised future operations, and which Vice-Admiral Commander-in-Chief A.U. Willis believed seriously hampered the Allied activities at sea.[27]

After this episode, two of the men, Leading Wireman Crichton and Stoker Yuill, escaped from Kalymnos. Their survival had been dependent on Greek locals who had risked their own lives to help them. A secret letter from Vice Admiral Dundas to the commander-in-chief in Alexandria written a month later commented, 'If they can be traced when Kalymnos is liberated, it is recommended that a suitable reward should be given to the Greek peasants who befriended these two ratings.' He too believed, 'All the confidential books must be considered compromised as already reported in my signal.'[28] Stoker S.A. Hudson of BYMS-72 was also found alive and well on a German hospital ship, *Gradisca*, when the British intercepted it. Crichton later gave an eyewitness account of the incident and described what had happened that night: The crew had arrived in Castelorizo on 8 November, hidden in Turkish waters for a couple of nights, then dropped soldiers off in Leros. They returned to deliver stores.

> We were bombed and damaged about three miles from Leros but managed to make our way in. We delivered our stores at a port on the east coast and were ordered out again to another anchorage on the west side of Leros [Portolago/Lakki]. We steamed for sixteen miles and were intercepted by ships which we thought were English. The ships told us to follow them in when they gathered around us and opened fire on us.[29]

They were surrounded by two E-boats, four large landing craft and three trawlers. They continued to attack until the ship caught fire and the captain told them to abandon ship. Crichton, Yuill and a third man managed to swim to Kalymnos, but the third man was shot through both knees. The men found a local Greek who looked after them, found them a small caique and took them to another island and then on to Turkey where they went to the British consul.

The reality of what had actually happened that night only came to light some years later, when one of the German officers aboard the enemy boat told the tale. The crew of the minesweeper had been intercepted by this public school-educated English-speaking young German officer, who had been in command of an E-boat patrolling to the east of Leros. It was he who had called out to them, saying it was a trap.

By sheer coincidence, one of the Allied officers, the Maltese officer known as Grech, had been in the Alinda area the night of the incident:

> We saw a glider bomber, easy recognizable by its red tail-light, pounce on a British Yard Mine Sweeper passing the entrance to the [Alinda] bay [...] The funnel and deck clutter aft took the full force of the explosion. They now called us to report the damage and request instructions. We signalled back telling the captain to make for Port Lakki round the northern end of the island. He would be met at the harbour entrance and piloted in.[30]

Grech drove his jeep at full speed to the seaplane base near Lakki on the other side of the island and, finding two fishermen on the quay, commandeered them to motor out to the harbour mouth a mile or so beyond. He could see that the BYMS had been badly damaged. He communicated the signal of the day to her and, when the correct response came back, signalled 'Follow me'; the BYMS swung round to follow him but a loudhailer cry came from another ship (that of the English-speaking German officer), 'It's a trap,' and to Grech's horror, the BYMS turned off, heading towards German-held Kalymnos. He flashed and flashed but to no avail. He realised the loudhailer warning had come from seaward. Years later he found out what had happened, by a surprising coincidence, when he met with a Captain Loetzmann who had been on the enemy E-boat. The German had been the man to call out on his loudhailer, 'Take no notice of that fool flashing, it's an Italian trap [...] follow me'[31] and so captured the boat.

The Eve of the Battle

In the early hours of 12 November, Jellicoe was still on Leros in command of the approximately 50-strong SBS force but recognised they were in difficulty. He sent about 30 of his best men including Anders Lassen, Jack Nicholson, Doug Wright, Dick Holmes and Porter

Jarrell off to Samos for safety so they could evacuate men from Leros if the need arose. It was imperative to avoid being captured and taken prisoner as this would take them out of the war and their skills were too valuable to lose. Sutherland had already left on 11 November under similar orders for evacuation. Jellicoe had told Sutherland, 'We know the Germans are going to attack Leros tomorrow. There is no point us both being here. I suggest you leave for Turkey tonight'; and so Sutherland made his getaway.[32] He found a small fishing boat in Pandeli and prepared to go to Turkey, taking with him Captain Chevalier, Lieutenant Casulli and eight SBS men. They sailed at about midnight – he had left just in time as the Germans were sailing towards Leros. Sutherland would spend the next year resting and skiing in the Lebanon Mountains.

The Germans on Kalymnos were only about a mile from Leros. They had built up substantial reinforcements on Kos and Kalymnos ready for the assault on Leros planned by Lieutenant General Müller for the night of 10/11 November.[33] In the event, it was put back a day because of inclement weather. In an attempt to soften up the opposition, enemy bombing was stepped up on 11 November, with 85 sorties taking place.[34] With their landing gear in position, the Germans were ready to mount Operation Typhoon (previously Operation Leopard; the name had been changed for security reasons). The leader of the assault, German General Friedrich-Wilhelm Müller, planned to begin the attack on the northeastern side of the island just above Alinda, called Griffo Bay (Kriphou), headlined by Pasta di Sotto. Another attack would be directed further north in Palma Bay (Vaghia). Here he aimed to capture Mount Clidi and the Ciano battery atop. Alinda was to be targeted second, bringing in landing equipment, anti-aircraft battery and heavy equipment. The third in line was to be Pandeli and the capture of Mount Appetici and Castle Hill Battery. Another landing was to be attempted in the Dromona/Gourna area on the west coast. Further plans were made for Ju 52s to drop a battalion of parachutists between 7 a.m. and 9 a.m. in the middle of the area between Alinda and Gourna, effectively splitting the island in two.[35] Whether this plan could be put into action was another matter. Although these exact details were as yet unknown to the Allies, the British were aware of mounting forces and enemy action pointing towards Leros.

Müller's intended assault force for the first attack consisted of three Panzer Grenadier battalions, one paratroop battalion and one company Brandenburger Küstenjäger Assault Engineers. These would be followed up with landing craft, anti-tank guns, various destroyers, minesweepers, torpedo boats and other craft.[36]

The British were aware of enemy movements: One British official report stated, 'During the night of 11/12 November, air reconnaissance showed considerable enemy movement of landing craft between Kos and Kalymnos, and it appeared that preparations to mount the assault on Leros were in train. The afternoon reconnaissance showed a concentration of landing craft in Kos harbour.'[37] Unfortunately, any Allied fleet of destroyers would be unable to reach the area until late on the night of the 12th/13th, so it was essential to conserve fuel; Captain (D), 8th Destroyer Flotilla's force, was therefore ordered to move to an anchorage nearer to Kos Channel and to send his two Hunts to attack any landing craft in Kos roads reported by air reconnaissance.[38]

On the eve of the battle, there were about 2,000 British and 5,000 Italian troops on Leros.[39] The British force comprised a battalion of Buffs in the north, the Royal Irish Fusiliers holding the centre and a battalion of King's Own covering the south around Xerocampus and Portolago (Lakki), with Major W.P.T. Tilly commanding Fortress Reserve. Various Queen's Own Royal West Kents would come in at different stages of the battle and fell in with the rest as and when they arrived.[40] Coastal defence had been entrusted to the Italians, but there was much doubt about their willingness to fight.[41] Men from the LRDG and SBS were scattered over the island, giving support to the Buffs in the north, and overseeing the Italians to ensure they held their battery positions. Indian Sappers and Miners, a frequently overlooked detachment in the battle, were doing much of the hard labour.[42]

There were some light and heavy anti-aircraft guns, but they were very old and worn. The only heavy artillery available was six 90/53-mm guns, which had hardly any ammunition. As for machine guns, the north had 12 to sweep the beaches, the centre had ten to cover beaches and Mount Rachi, and the south had eight to cover beaches. The fact that some of the radio equipment was ruined before the battle added to the problems. Lieutenant James said, 'A company of the Royal West Kents had their wireless sets flooded on their way to Leros from some mishap, so they were useless. Wireless command was very difficult, some companies had no communication at all. Most of the communication was undertaken by a runner.'[43] This lack of communication was to set them all on the path of confusion in the days to come.

At this stage, on 12 November 1943, the airfields on Rhodes and Kos were in the hands of the enemy and the Germans had complete control of the air. Leros had suffered over 1,000 air attacks in the previous six weeks and had been attacked from the air by Stuka dive-bombers and fighter bombers from dawn to dusk every day. Such saturation bombing was normal before an invasion, but was particularly distressing when support from the Allied air force was so limited most of the troops were unaware of any Allied air cover as their planes were rarely seen over Leros. Jake Easonsmith sent David Lloyd Owen a signal, 'the lack of RAF support was absolutely pitiful; ships sat around all day and Stukas just laughed at us.'[44] Allied destroyers went in search of German invasion fleets at night when bombing ceased, then withdrew at dawn. Lieutenant Jimmy James recalled the incessant bombing:

> It's very difficult to describe the overwhelming damage that the German aircraft could do; they could do just what they liked with no resistance. There was some Italian anti-aircraft fire, which was very courageous from them because the Germans would then try and eliminate them, but there was no aircraft at all. It has been said earlier that the British troops would never fight again without air cover. But they jolly well did in Leros.[45]

The futility of so little Allied air cover was not lost on the officers such as Lieutenant James:

> My own colonel thought from the start that without air cover the chance of getting a victory was very slight. It's possible I think, if there had been a determined counter-attack coordinated with some artillery support, as always in airborne and a sea landing, if we had struck within the first 48 hours we might have rebuffed the enemy; plus naval support which was splendid all the way through – they bombarded.[46]

8

The First Day of Battle

> We had never seen anything like it. We were scared stiff. It looked worse than it actually was, seeing all these paratroopers over your head.
>
> Sergeant George Hatcher, Royal West Kents[1]

On the morning of 12 November, the war correspondent for the *Daily Telegraph*, Leonard Marsland Gander, was awoken from his camp bed where he was sleeping in the same house as the officers in B Mess in Alinda.

> Somebody came clumping heavily up the bare staircase in heavily nailed boots and entered our room. He revealed himself as a little Cockney orderly, who spoke in a quiet, unhurried voice, half apologetic at disturbing out rest, and betraying not the slightest sign by his demeanour that anything unusual was afoot. 'The German invasion fleet has been sighted, sir', he remarked casually. It was so like a butler's entrance that I had expected him to add, 'Shall I show them up, sir?'[2]

A captain offered to take Gander and Crichton to HQ at Mount Meraviglia. This was Gander's introduction to the beginning of the Battle of Leros.[3] The invasion had begun.[4]

At 4.30 a.m., all men had been called to battle stations. Gander recalled, 'The melancholy clangour of the church bell struck on our ears with infinite pathos. I scoured the skies, and saw four specks resolve themselves into Stukas, our first aerial visitors of the day.'[5] They heard the explosions of Italian coastal guns announcing the beginnings of the battle. Gander looked at his watch – ten minutes past five at dawn. He recalled, as the planes flew into view,

'The Italian coastal batteries now opened up in earnest, their shells churning up the sea all around the invasion craft. I was standing beside a sturdy, sandy haired sergeant of the Royal Irish Fusiliers who was staring intently through glasses.' Francesco, one of the Italian gunners on Mount Meraviglia, opened fire as the four circling Stukas lined up to start bombing the Buffs in the north. He stood waiting for his moment. Gander watched the action: 'Then as the leading machine came into closer range he directed a stream of shells into its belly. The Stuka faltered, recovered, and then turned away towards Kos, leaving a long, thin, trail of black smoke. Francesco, hugely delighted, turned to me and grimaced his pleasure, his smooth olive face, square jawed, radiant.'[6] The planes now refocused on their new target – Francesco. More Stukas came in relays of fives, sixes and sevens, attacking batteries, bombing Scumbarda Heights, the mountain overlooking Xerocampus beaches.[7] According to Tilney, he had ordered the King's Own to move in from the beaches to the high ground in support of the gun positions on Mount Scumbarda.[8]

Gander was to iterate what many more would say in the years to come. 'It was an infuriating reflection that the Stuka dive-bomber was regarded in the RAF as obsolete. Yet here, because of a lack of fighter opposition, the enemy was preparing to use them again as in the battle of France.'[9] Two hundred and six German sorties were made that day, mainly by Ju 87s, and about 150 a day thereafter.[10] A small British bomber force flew over, consisting of seven Baltimores, three Hudsons and four Wellingtons, and bombed the enemy crafts although failing to manage a direct hit, but this disruption meant the enemy landing was delayed until 6 a.m.[11]

When the invasion started, some of the men did not realise it was happening. Reverend Anwyl woke slowly, only to notice the sound of gunfire was close at hand. 'I lay lazily trying to find a reason for it, since it was not Anti-Aircraft fire but from out 25 pounders. Officer Jack Barber was awake too and grumbled that this was a daft time to practise.'[12] It was at that moment that Jack's batman came in and said, 'They say that Jerry has landed at Alinda Bay, Sir.'[13] Both Anwyl and Jack Barber laughed as they had heard such rumours every morning. However, when Anwyl's batman came in and added his startling news that a large force of Germans was coming in at the most northern end of the island and was in action against the Buffs, they realised their worst fears were coming true; 'only a few had landed so far, he thought, but numerous invasion craft could be seen around the island.'[14]

German crafts of many types escorted by destroyers were standing off Leros on all sides. Allied guns were shooting at the nearest boats. Anwyl began Mass while the doctors set out the medical stores. He consecrated all the altar-breads, nearly 200 of them, and administered as many Holy Communions as he could to the soldiers. He started out for HQ after watching while the Italian naval guns fired shots at the enemy destroyers, but none were a hit. The British had 18 Bofors, but only six were allowed to fire at once, owing to the shortage of ammunition. The shell ration was often spent by noon, and by afternoon only automatic machine guns were available for firing at low-flying planes.

At the beginning of the invasion, Anwyl noticed, 'So far air attack had not commenced and there was an uncanny calm which gave an air of unreality to the whole business.'[15] Then suddenly swarms of dive-bombers approached the batteries that were firing on the destroyers and began relentlessly bombing them. Mortar crews were already in action, so Anwyl continued on his rounds of Holy Communion and began to climb Meroviglia Hill to HQ. He found Indian sappers and part of Company A; the rest were covering Alinda Bay. He gave out more Holy Communion to the Italian infantry whom he found in a cave unwilling to fight. Anwyl returned to the RAP. It seemed impossible that they could get their wounded to the advanced dressing station (ADS) which was north of them. He could see no British casualties but imagined there must be some amongst the Italian gunners on the hill. Stretcher-bearers were under constant bombing as they went out to pick up the injured. Michael Power was one of the first casualties to arrive, with a bad mortar wound to his stomach.

All British platoon commanders had their kit to hand, including their weapons and ammunition. Lieutenant Ted Johnson made a note of what he was carrying on the morning of 12 November 1943 as he prepared to go into battle: a 3.8 pistol and holster, two 69 grenades, two 36 grenades, 1 Italian grenade, a Verey pistol for shooting flares, three each of red and green cartridges, a knife in a sheath, a pair of pliers, a tin of bully beef, a ground sheet, 60 rounds of .38 ammunition, a compass in its pouch, a pair of binoculars in its case. This was standard uniform and equipment for any officer facing battle. Everything was strapped solidly to the waist belt, the ground sheet rolled and stuffed on the back of the belt. Braces were worn left and right to keep the weight on the shoulders.[16]

In its defensive position just before the battle, the platoon had eighteen rifles, five .303 Bren guns, a 2-inch mortar, a .45 Thompson Sub-Machine Gun (TSMG), 10,588 rounds of .303 ammunition, 1,220 rounds of TSMG ammunition, a .38 pistol plus 150 ammunition, 108 High Explosives Mortar bombs, an assortment of grenades, a smoke generator, two boxes of flares, 91 tins of bully, 5 tins of biscuits, 42 gallons of water, 21 emergency rations. There were also daily rations of large quantities of food and drink which each section had to provide for itself.[17]

Enemy Landing

Fifteen enemy landing craft, which were to form part of the eastern attack on Leros, had been sighted at 1.20 a.m. by reconnaissance Royal Air Force Wellington airplanes, but they were not identified as such by the commander-in-chief in the Levant Operations Room until it was too late.[18] Lieutenant J.G.G. Muir in charge of the Motor Torpedo Boat 307 force on its way to Leros from Castelorizo had heard there were two unknown destroyers off Kalymnos at 3.30 earlier that morning. An Allied motor torpedo boat force sailed at full speed from Alinda Bay at 4.45 a.m. to search for an enemy merchant ship reported four or five miles southeast of Leros. This was not found, but while sweeping northward the two destroyers were sighted off Pharmaconisi. However, these were mistaken for British destroyers.[19]

Only when the light was growing in the east of the island during the early hours of the morning was there a positive move by the Allies. Lieutenant Commander F.P. Monckton was on patrol at sea near Alinda in Motor Launch 456. At approximately 4 a.m., the crew sighted enemy forces 12 miles east of Leros proceeding north, and

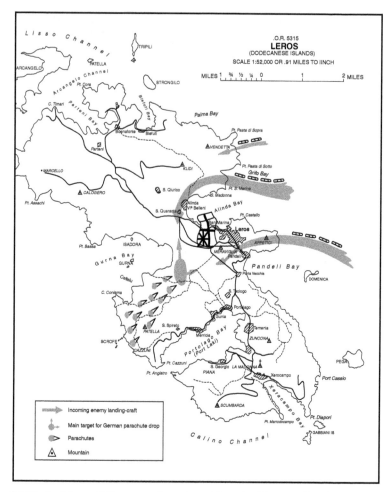

MAP 4   Map of German Invasion, Day 1: 'Geographical Section, Chief of Staff Map 1943'

although their findings were reported, there was an inexcusable failure to assist immediately and intercept the assault force; the motor launch was damaged as a result and had to return to Alinda.[20] The enemy were moving in, in two groups of seven and eight barges, but the Royal Navy were concerned about minefields in the area and did not want to interfere. It seems that, despite the delay because of the bad weather and Allied bombings which had attacked the

Germans' landing equipment, General Müller was determined to commence the attack on Leros without further delay.

The invasion started with the landing of the Küstenjäger assault troops on the northern part of island with Müller dividing his landing forces into various groups.[21] The first landings began at 6 a.m. and were made simultaneously between Palma Bay (Vaghia Bay) and at Grifo Bay (Kryphou; Κρυφού) in the northeast,[22] with around 500 German troops; (another landing would be made just around Pandeli at the base of Appetici in the centre of the island, with a smaller unit of about 120 men).[23] Altogether around 15 landing craft with about 40–50 German soldiers each attempted to land, some were sunk, but enough were left to unload the troops.[24]

The enemy took straight to the high ground between Palma and Grifo bays on Mounts Clidi and Vedetta while the Buffs and B Squadron of LRDG did their best to hold them down. They must have had a difficult ascent as the cliffs are steep and the terrain rocky. Enemy landings were attempted at Blefuti but were thwarted by shore batteries which sank one ferry lighter and two assault landing craft and forced a retreat. News had crackled back to HQ on the field telephone as to the state of the landings; as the five landing craft attempted to come in at Della Palma Bay and Pasta di Sopra point, Brigadier Tilney's response was 'Is anybody doing anything about it?'[25] In fact, the Allies were already opening up, with British 25-pounders and Bofors guns joining in with the Italian batteries along the coast firing at the landing crafts. Three of the landing craft were hit by Italian coastal guns and one sank, with survivors struggling to swim ashore at Strongilo inlet.

The one enemy company which had got ashore at Palma Bay was counter-attacked by Buffs D Company and destroyed. Major E.W. Tassell led the attack with Lieutenant E.J. Ransley. According to the *Historical Records of the Buffs 1919–1948*, 'Major Tassell had launched D Company against the enemy, and by noon after a fierce struggle in which the gallantry and fine leadership of Lieutenant E.J. Ransley was displayed, he had disposed of the Germans opposed to him.'[26] Reports varied as to how many German soldiers had made it ashore. According to Gander, about three or four hundred Germans were assembling in the Mount Vedetta (Vaghia) area.[27] Others suggest about 500 German troops came ashore at Palma Bay (Vaghia Bay) with 70 of them taken prisoner.[28]

A later Admiralty report suggested that the coastal battery gunners had opened fire too late as the Germans had approached the islands.[29] The incoming enemy started to gain Mount Clidi, taking over the Ciano Battery (also known as Point 320) at its summit, a fact of which Lieutenant Colonel Douglas Percy Iggulden, commanding officer of the Buffs, was unaware; due to communication breakdown, he had been at HQ between Partheni and Gourna trying to gain information, and only heard of the attack at 10 a.m. The battle for Clidi Heights (next to Vedetta) had started around sunrise on Monday 12 November 1943 and would last until 17 November.

The Fight for Clidi

Since Mount Clidi in the north was one of the most important features for defending the island, gaining control of its gun battery was imperative if the enemy were to be prevented from gaining ground. Don Coventry of the LRDG was there when the battle for Clidi Heights started. On his arrival in Leros, he and the rest of S1 Patrol had been sent to defend Mount Clidi, in support of the Italians manning the four 6-inch naval guns. The patrol was under Captain John Olivey, who had also temporarily left his group to report to HQ.[30] By 9 a.m. Mount Clidi was under serious threat from Germans climbing mountain surface rocks to gain footholds.

Up until then, enemy aircraft had not been present, but now they descended aiming at the gun batteries. Lance Corporal Coventry watched as eight Ju 88s attacked from the eastern side of the island and at least two of the Allied guns were bombed out of action. Although the first set of bombs missed them, as they took their second wave he realised he had to move quickly. 'I was watching through the binoculars and a bomb seemed to be coming straight down the lens. I shouted to Mackay [John Mackay] to take cover and we jumped over the dannet wire and slid down the slope into the cave where our wireless operators were.'[31] The bomb was a direct hit, chopping off the barrel of the gun they had been manning and setting fire to the magazine. With only four 6-inch naval batteries left, they watched as four German destroyers mounted a naval attack. Rifleman Oelofse, a Rhodesian, was killed in a direct hit from a mortar while in the forward trenches. The fight to defend Mount Clidi throughout the first day of the battle would take a combination of the LRDG, the Buffs, a unit of King's Own and a battery of four Italian 6-inch naval guns.

Italian gunners held the 6-inch coastal gun battery on the top of Clidi. Lionel Cowper of the King's Own, Major Tilly's deputy, was part of the counter-attack and recalled, 'Major Tilly's company of King's Own was hurried to the scene in jeeps [this was around 10 a.m.]. When it deployed to attack, the fire of its machine guns was smothered by that of the German mortars and the first effort was checked. The men rallied and gained a little ground, but in the confused fighting which followed they were slowly forced back westward.'[32] They were struggling, not only against numerical superiority on the ground, but also against persistent and almost unhindered enemy air attack.[33] Having gained ground, the Germans positioned themselves on high points with mortars and machine guns and continued to fight though the day.

An LRDG patrol also arrived about 10 a.m. to assist the Buffs. Their captain, J.R. Olivey, had returned from HQ and went to investigate. He recalled,

I took a walk down the trench to the North which had been severely bombed and was full of earth and stones. Troops were behind walls. On returning Lieutenant Browne and his platoon had disappeared. Corporal Coventry in a stone emplacement had heard nothing of this move. I noticed that the enemy were working round our left flank. The trench to the North which been captured, the occupants all killed.'[34]

King's Own Captain D. R. Humm, second-in-command to Major Tilly, was killed. By 5 p.m., the British troops had been pushed back to the Italian barracks.

Meanwhile, the Maltese seaplane officer 'Grech' had rushed from Navy House, where the officers were sleeping in Alinda, and took charge of a 'motley little gang' of two naval ratings, a REME (Royal Electrical and Mechanical Engineers) technician, two infantry men (one a corporal) and two Italians. They took up positions covering the road up to the main area where the Buffs were overlooking Partheni and Blefuti bays. All the island transport consisting of about ten jeeps had been allotted to the company (Mobile Reserves). Despite hard fighting, the enemy gained a footing on Mount Clidi.

Later that evening, Major Tilly ordered a counter-attack on Mount Clidi with the survivors of his company, and gruesome hand-to-hand fighting with the enemy took place.[35] The enemy was pushed down the forward slope, and in the course of the advance Major Tilly was wounded. Private Lemuel Bevan saw the counter-attack made by Major Tilly – he had been leading just three men.[36] With the arrival of enemy reinforcements, the company was forced back 30 yards before it could consolidate and hold on. When Lance Corporal J. Hall noticed that Major Tilly was not there, he went back – under close-range fire and within throwing distance of hand grenades – found his company commander and brought him back to safety.

During the fighting on Mount Clidi on 12 November, a bomb from a Stuka took out another naval gun. Andy Bennet was injured when gravel flew into his face and stomach while he was manning a Brenn gun with Don Coventry. He was replaced by Sergeant Cito Clader-Potts, and the fighting continued until dark, when hand-to-hand fighting again broke out. As grenades were tossed and guns fired, Clader-Potts was wounded in the leg by a grenade.

As the Germans moved up Clidi, the Buffs had insufficient troops to defend the area, and Mobile Fortress Reserve of King's Own were ordered to move up the feature, going through Buffs lines to launch a counter-attack. Lieutenant C.H.J. Morgan of Buffs recalled,

> Just before dark, a company of the King's Own who had been billeted in the vicinity of the main road leading to Leros (about four hundred yards forward of my Platoon's positions) came up through the company's positions en route to report to Commanding Officer of Buffs. This Company had been engaged with the Parachutists [that morning] and were by no means complete. On contacting the Commanding Officer, it was decided that they be attached to us. I therefore had about twelve King's Own attached to my Platoon. I was also ordered to keep a special watch on their Food and Ammo Store in their billeting area until they had sent a party· down to salvage the contents.

That first day many of the King's Own from C Company were killed or wounded on Clidi. Among them was Lemuel Bevan's friend Jimmy Riley, who had offered him his last cigarette, saying 'I shan't be needing it.' He was killed in action soon after.[37] At one stage they were running out of ammunition and Tommy Tressida was given the job of running back to the company store about a mile away from their position to pick up a box of grenades.[38]

With an order to evacuate Clidi, the unit withdrew to a ridge some 400 metres away. Little fighting ensued that night. In its new position the company was reinforced next day by a platoon of Buffs.[39] However, there are conflicting reports as to whether Mount Clidi was held by the Allies or not. One report says that by that first evening the Germans were 'in firm control of Clidi and the coastal battery on it'.[40] However, Private Bevan believes he remained on Clidi throughout the battle with four other men from King's Own and the position was never lost; the Allies had simply retreated about 30 yards and then regained the top.[41] The defence of Mount Clidi in the north of the island was vital if the enemy was to be prevented from moving inland. It also had a gun battery atop, which overlooked the bay, which was strategically important to halt further enemy troops and equipment from coming in. With many of the King's Own now dead, Bevan's small reformed platoon came under the command of the Buffs, who gave orders for them to hold the top and guard the guns. Bevan remembered spending the first night on the top of Clidi holding position and never left. He recalled, 'If you only knew how far it was that we were pushed back, it was nothing, just a few yards.'[42] This is supported by Cowper's statement, 'With the arrival of enemy reinforcements the company was forced back thirty yards before it could consolidate and hold on.'[43] Others report that Clidi was lost, then retaken, and that B Company Buffs with C Company King's Own retook Clidi. The LRDG reported, 'A counter attack on Clidi during the day was beaten off and it remained in enemy hands until retaken on the 14th';[44] this can be questioned in the light of Bevan and Cowper's evidence. Furthermore, according to a report for 12 November made by Greek Lieutenant Pavlides, 'Remnants of Italians GRN [garrison] and Long Range Desert Group maintained in position on top of Clidi and fired 6" guns at enemy on SW face Mount Vedetta.'[45] The first day, the Buffs had captured three German officers and 45 others. Since there were many attacks and counter-attacks with ground lost and gained, with much hand-to-hand fighting, it is reasonable to assume that certain points were held by the Germans and others by the British and Italians, with only a little ground between them.

Faughs Claim Appetici

While the enemy was landing in the north of the island in the early morning of 12 November, another 120 Germans had made a landing at the base of Mount Appetici and gained a foothold on the mountain in the centre of the island. They captured two of the four battery guns from the Italians on top of Castle Hill. The other two were still in action under the personal command of Capitano Nasti. However, the Italians appear to have abandoned the Castle as the Germans came nearer, as figures could be seen running down the hill. They were stopped in their tracks as the Irish Fusiliers came up to meet them, encouraging them back into positions.

By 9 a.m., under rather late orders, the men of Royal Irish Fusiliers Platoon 10 had moved up Appetici under command of Lieutenant West, supporting C Company with 2-inch mortars and small firearms.[46] In the face of the Royal Irish Fusiliers coming up the hill, the Italians turned back and joined them, helping them to recapture their position and the gun battery. Gander reported, 'What had happened was not, at that distance, very clear, expect that someone or something had put fresh heart into the Ities [sic], who were returning to their posts.'[47] Second Lieutenant R.J. Hilman was covering C Company with a Vickers machine gun firing from his position in Leros Castle.[48]

A leader of a platoon of C Company of Royal Irish Fusiliers on the first day of the invasion was 21-year-old Lieutenant Ted Johnson. He recalled,

> I was briefed at about nine o'clock that morning to do a counter-attack on Appetici because the Küstenjäger had occupied it. My company were the Mobile Reserve Company in the battalion. All the other companies were involved in their own little battles and the CO detailed my company to go and attack Appetici and try and take it back. This was my first proper action where live bullets were flying around. I had to get my chaps organised and go across. In theory I was supposed to meet an Italian officer who was going to brief me as to what the situation was up there. I don't know who he was as he didn't speak English, so that contact was useless because he couldn't communicate with me. So I had

to go forward myself with my runner and try and suss out what the situation was and what I would do about it [...] Appetici was the first day into the war. I ended that day up on Appetici in my own defensive positions. I'd got as far as I thought I could get over the top of Appetici and ended up on the reverse slope of it looking down on where I presumed the German force had retired to. We waited there for further orders. It was then down to my company commander to decide what I was to do next.[49]

For Ted, though, the situation was to worsen. Having got his troops up Appetici and overtaken a gun emplacement, as he was standing next to Lance Sergeant John Caldwell, his section commander, 'who was trying to get a sight of a target, [Caldwell] fell back. He was shot cleanly through the forehead and died instantly.'[50] This was Ted's first time in action and it must have been a terrible shock. Up until that point he had seen little of the enemy except in the air. 'My immediate reaction was to push on out of that unhealthy gun emplacement and take John Caldwell's section further down the slopes in the direction of the next gun emplacement with all weapons blazing.'[51] Fusilier Jack Harte believed, 'The actions of Johnson's platoon and others of "C" Company recapturing the summit and two gun emplacements, before orders were given to withdraw, was bravery of the highest order.'[52]

Stuka dive-bombers were continually bombing as they tried to regain their position on Castle Hill. Air attacks came from Ju 87s, and the Royal Irish Fusiliers were shot at by firearms from the German soldiers on the ground. Ferocious fighting ensued in which Lieutenant Hugh Gore-Booth was killed and was bravely carried back to HQ by Fusilier McKeever who was also wounded and under fire. Sergeant O'Connell was seriously wounded, later dying of his injuries. The officers later found out that it was a company of 120 German *Küsternjäger* firing at them.[53] Brandenburgers' *Küstenjäger* were coastal raiders, a crack team of German soldiers highly trained and skilled for special forces missions. They had landed at the base of Mount Appetici, climbed up the cliff and lay among the rocks shooting at them. By 10 a.m. gun positions were under the control of the Royal Irish Fusiliers and they had successfully prevented the capture of both Castle Hill and Mount Appetici.[54] Together the Italians and Royal Irish Fusiliers had fought back, retaking the gun batteries, and driven the enemy down the slopes but had not managed to push them back to the sea.[55] C Company reported that there were still about 70 enemy snipers pinned down on Mount Appetici.

At 10.45 a.m. Lieutenant Robert Austin Ardill led the Fusiliers of No. 9 Platoon, with Lieutenant Hillman in command, up to Leros Castle, carting Bren guns. They made it up the hill, a 500-ft climb, in 30 minutes. Two of their comrades made their escape under the constant bombardment, succumbing to shell shock, and deserted to a safer spot. Harte and his companion Jimmy Gollogher went in search of them and found them in the basement of an abandoned home near the town of Platanos. It was overrun with rats and the place stank. Harte had some sympathy, having fought next to one of them in Malta and seen him fight bravely. Gollogher was less gentle. 'Gollogher, a hard man, was completely intolerant of their actions. Unable to understand why they hadn't the guts or strong mentality that was the norm for him, he lost no time in branding them cowardly bastards.'[56] Harte and Gollogher did their utmost to persuade the men to return to their duties, but no amount of persuading would convince the men to return to their posts. They were beyond caring, their nerves completely shot.

Strangely, at 6.30 p.m. the order came through to Ted Johnson on Mount Appetici, instructing him to pull back his men to Fortress HQ at Meraviglia, leaving only one platoon to hold the position. This order made by Brigadier Tilney was completely in opposition to the one Maurice French (commanding officer of the Royal Irish Fusiliers, and their direct line of command) had given Ted Johnson. Ted recalled,

> Late that evening – and this is where the whole battle began to go wrong – the brigadier, not the commanding officer of the battalion, but the brigadier [Tilney], who was another step up, sent a message to Appetici, to my company commander, Major Ben Barrington. I didn't think much of Ben Barrington. Or Tilney for that matter. It is entirely wrong for a brigadier to order direct junior formation without referring to the commanding officer of those junior formations. No way should Tilney have sent a direct order for a company to withdraw. It should have been done through the company CO.[57]

The orders for C Company to withdraw from Appetici at this critical point would allow the Germans a free rein to take over. It remains unclear why this command should ever have been issued.

Obviously, there was a conflict of orders coming from Fortress HQ and Battalion HQ (the latter where Maurice French was stationed). Ted remarked sagely, 'I was beginning to realise that I was on my own in this battle.'[58] Meanwhile, the Italian commander had complained about being abandoned by the British and Lieutenant Johnson was given one platoon from C Company and ordered to go back up to Appetici again.

This constant change of orders is inconceivable in a well-planned battle. Taking men off positions they had fought hard to win, and then sending them back again, seems to have been a signature of Tilney's mishandling of his men. Not only did it needlessly wear them out, but it gave the enemy a chance to regain lost ground. Tilney had bypassed Maurice French in the chain of command, and only succeeded in adding to the confusion of the troops. Later that day, Tilney would plan for the rest of C Company of Royal Irish Fusiliers to join HQ King's Own on Rachi Ridge and tackle the parachutists who would soon land (see below), but the order appears never to have been given or had not got through. Instead they were simply resting over the hill. Neither Rachi Ridge nor Mount Appetici would have enough cover to combat the Germans properly.

At the same time that morning, round the other side of the island on the west coast, Corporal Vic Kenchington was with another group of Royal Irish Fusiliers busy trying to ward off an invasion coming in around Gourna.

> The first lot tried to come in at Gourna Bay and got a terrible beating. An hour later they came back. We had no air force. We couldn't move without getting bombed [...] We had a slit trench which was very well equipped about 4 or 5 feet deep with a false bottom. We unloaded a NAAFI ship and took all the goods into compound, but no NAAFI staff arrived so the brigadier told us to help ourselves. We had a large tin of sweet biscuits and some brandy [...] Corporal Roberts and Father Anwyl the Catholic padre was with us, all together in the slit trench.[59]

The padre visited all the wounded and gave those badly injured the last rites. The other person there was the MO, Captain Barber, who tended the wounded at the Regional Aid Post (RAP).

At this time, Kenchington was acting as an MO's orderly at an ADS. He remembered, 'We patched them up and took them down there.

Several got evacuated with the Royal Navy [...] There was also an ADS at Alinda [in Villa Bellini] covering the north side of the beach. When the Germans landed, that got cut off.' However, the Germans had failed to land on the west coast of the island. The Ducci Battery on Mount Cazzuni and the San Georgio Battery on Mount Scumbarda had successfully sent them scuttling. Meanwhile, A Company of Faughs had been using Vickers machine guns aimed at the enemy landing crafts in Alinda Bay.

German Parachutist Drop

At about 2 p.m. on 12 November, enemy fighter-bombers swept over the island from the southwest spraying machine-gun fire from the wings and pounding the rugged slopes of the mountains with high explosives. Right on their tail were 35 slower Ju 52s dropping the first lot of parachutists;[60] nearly 500 enemy paratroopers were dropped on Rachi Ridge, a high mountain ridge at the narrowest point of the island – the strip of land which lies between Gourna and Alinda bays. As the low-flying destroyer planes rounded upon the area at about 300 ft, they released their load of around 15 parachutists from each hatch.[61] The Leros drop was performed by 1st Battalion Fallschirmjäger Regiment 2 under Hauptmann (Captain) Martin Kühne (strength of the battalion: 470 paratroopers). One company of Brandenburgers would be dropped later as reinforcements.[62]

The sight was incredible. War correspondent Gander reported,

As I watched, fascinated, something white appeared under the fuselage of the leading machine. It bellied out into a great mushroom, beneath which the dark figure of the parachutist looked small and helpless. Then came another, and another, fifteen altogether, most with grey parachutes. The first man, who was probably the group leader, had touched the ground before the machine gunners on the sides of Meraviglia had recovered from the paralyzing shock of surprise. Then began a wild outburst of firing from the ground till the air was criss-crossed with red tracer dashes spurting from twenty directions.[63]

He added, 'The idea that the Germans would use parachutists was so remote from my thought that the happenings of the next few minutes had a supremely theatrical and dreamlike quality which almost obliterated the breath-taking surprise.'[64] To the east, twin-engine

German aircrafts splattered fire from machine guns and dropped anti-personnel bombs. Some of the parachutists caught in treetops and telegraph wires. Gander recalled, 'This was one of the occasions when all decent feelings of humanity are in most men swamped by the instinct of self-preservation. We thought of all those recklessly brave parachutists as vermin to be wiped out ruthlessly, instantly. I still fail to understand why it was not done, before they had time to reach their containers and equip themselves.'[65]

Reverend Reg Anwyl ministering to the Faughs was slower to recognise that parachutists had been dropped.

> I had scarcely realised that this was a parachute invasion but by now the planes were away and the small patch of level ground below me was filling up with the billowing parachutes of men and weapons that had been dropped. The paratroopers had been dropped from what looked like a suicidal height. I could see clearly the frenzied attempts of some of them to cut themselves loose and the fantastic movements of dead men carried away across rough grounds; some were still hanging from trees while others were still being pulled over walls and rocks beyond the landing ground.[66]

Reverend Anwyl made his way back to the RAP and watched through his binoculars as the two platoons of D Company of Royal Irish Fusiliers held their positions shooting at them; he believed they had little chance of doing anything except offering potshots as the floating images passed them by. The padre's time was filled with a rush of casualties. Fusilier Wall of Mortar Platoon was carried in with his foot smashed to a pulp. He had lost a great deal of blood, and the medical staff worked on him for four hours, Anwyl holding the bottles of plasma as there was no stand. The surgeon had decided to amputate when Doc Lawson of LRDG came in and helped take off the lower leg.[67]

Sergeant George Hatcher of the Royal West Kents was not in the exact vicinity of the paratroopers landing, but they were clearly visible to him.

> You imagined there were far more than there were, a load of them, pretty-coloured parachutes coming down. Because they were in a worse position than us, we could fire at them. We could shoot them down as they fell [...] we must have shot a hell of a lot. Not only our company, but everyone

was doing it. They were all having a go at it as they [the Germans] were
sitting ducks. It was frightening for them.

He and his fellow Fusiliers remained put, firing from where they were.
George and his men could not move as they were pinned to the
ground with fire from enemy planes shooting at everything that
moved on the ground. George said, 'You didn't dare show yourself.
They had no opposition, only from small arms that we had.'[68]

Enemy bombers were giving cover while their parachutists landed.
The Allied soldiers had to be watching out for machine-gun attacks
as well as small-arms fire. George recalled, 'The Luftwaffe was
terrible, they threw everything at us.' The men could do little to
retaliate. 'I remember one of our chaps was one of the first to be shot,
he was hit right between the eyes, I didn't see it, but I heard he was
one of the first casualties, hit from the German planes. Most of the
men didn't know much about it, until it was all over.' The casualties
were high and the experience nerve-wracking. At anytime a bullet
might hit its target. 'When the parachutes landed, you just kept firing
hoping you hit one of them, there were so many. One poor devil, he
got caught up in some telegraph wires – of course, everybody had a
go at him, which was a good thing as far as they were concerned
because it diverted the attention a lot more. He must have been very
well riddled by the time we had finished.' None of the men on the
ground had time to think about the men going down around them,
they just kept firing to try and hit as many parachutists as they
could before they hit the ground. 'You could see them landing. They
were some way away from us when they actually landed. Some
overstepped the mark and finished up in the sea. One plane went into
the sea.'[69]

Although many men on the ground had been unaware of an
incoming enemy parachute attack, others higher up the chain of
command knew all about it. A warning had already been sent the
previous day that German air troops were assembling in Athens.
Captain Saxton of the LRDG therefore had knowledge that a
parachute attack was about to take place.[70] His T Patrol and
Lieutenant Cross's T2 Patrol moved in from Alinda Bay to be joined
by a British patrol and some SBS troops to make up a 30-strong party
and were at the ready for action. Also involved in the conflict with

the parachutists were a company of Buffs, B Company Queen's Own Royal West Kents and A and D Company of Royal Irish Fusiliers.

Some platoons appear to have been totally surprised by the drop, with no information handed down the lines. Paddy McCrystal was dug in at the spot with the Royal Irish Fusiliers where the parachutists were coming down. He recalled,

> When the battle started I had just come from the hill you know, we weren't down at the sea. And the Jerries come behind us, where they dropped the paratroops. We didn't know that. It was no time at all, and we were surrounded. We had no chance. They come from sea and air. You could hear it, you know. The island was nearly impossible to land on. The paratroops, the sky was full of them.[71]

While the drop was taking place, Brigadier Tilney was in the HQ tunnel collecting as much information about the parachutists as possible – where they were and how many. The closeness of the fighting was gruesome, as Reg Neep testified. 'It is not a thing you talk about. We didn't have any heavy weapons but every soldier had a rifle or small arms so the paratroopers were very vulnerable when they were dropping by parachute in daylight so they lost an awful lot of men. The worst order you had to give in those circumstances was "fix bayonets", hand-to-hand stuff which is very unpleasant.'[72]

Some of the more deprived Lerians were able to take advantage of the tragedy. Peter George Koulianus, a young boy at the time, remembers the parachutists dropping down at the beginning of the battle.

> I was back at the house. I saw one aircraft going round and round. About 1.30 p.m., 30 or 40 paratroopers were dropped below Racchi. The winds pushed them up over the mountain, it was a rough area and shrapnel was exploding all over. Some of the parachutes did not open. The fighting went on for four or five days. We went to Racchi searching for food and found a dead soldier hanging from the tree. He had batons and machine guns and magazines. He must have been three days as there was a terrible smell. We pulled off his boots, washed them in the sea, and wore them.[73]

Most of the men took a stoical attitude towards their duties and simply followed orders, like Sergeant George Hatcher. 'We were at the opposite end of the island to the invasion; we were already in defensive positions so we were already under cover to a certain extent. Once we got used to the idea, we settled down and just pressed on with what we had trained to do. To start with, the invasion itself was very frightening but once we settled down, it is a question of carrying on as you were trained to do.'[74]

The Germans must have expected a high toll, their men being such an easy target drifting down from the skies as Reg Neep noted. 'The Germans troops suffered heavy losses, even greater than the British, especially the parachutists who were very vulnerable to rifle fire from the defenders as they dropped between the hills.' There was more close 'hand-to-hand' fighting as the opposing units came together, and Reg's small unit was devastated by the loss of officers and senior non-commissioned officers; only Reg and one other soldier survived. Due to the loss, Reg was promoted to acting sergeant in the field and carried out those duties during the Battle of Leros. Unfortunately, because there was no official confirmation of his field promotion, his officers being killed in the later stages of the battle, he did not receive pay or substantiation for this rank.[75]

The Germans were now regrouping and becoming a force to be reckoned with. Sightings had been made of surrendering Italians with their hands up, walking along the main road north of the island to Alinda Bay. Some Italians had been shot. Telecommunications were cut, and contact with the Buffs in the north was lost. German snipers then waited for the signal linesmen to approach to repair the cables and put them under fire. That afternoon however, the situation was to become even more fraught as fighting continued in other areas of the island, and those enemy parachutists who had survived began to link up with the German forces that had landed from the sea.

9

Central Collision

Some Germans staggered up the hill, and of course, you shot them. That wasn't the time to take prisoners, because they weren't giving up, they weren't surrendering or anything.

Royal West Kents commanding officer to Lieutenant John Browne[1]

In the centre of the island on Rachi Ridge, fierce fighting was taking place after the parachute drop during the afternoon of 12 November. Many Royal Irish Fusiliers and King's Own were killed in the fighting. Allied infantry was on the receiving end of intense mortar attacks, bombing and machine-gun fire as enemy flares directed Stukas to positions of the British soldiers on the ground.[2] Though both sides fought hard, the British were unable to dislodge the enemy. By 3 p.m., the enemy from the coastal landings had gained footholds in the north and east of the island while the parachute battalion who had landed in the neck were struggling to meet up with them.[3] The enemy were now above Gourna and Alinda, the areas either side of the island, effectively about to cut the island in two.

The positions were unclear to the British troops and no-one seemed to know what was going on. Sid Bowden of the Royal West Kents was somewhere behind a bay (probably above Pandeli or Vromolithos, east of Leros) at the time of the drop. He recalled,

When the paratroops came in, they came in more or less over us. They dropped in the middle of the island. That was a bit frightening. They glided in, you didn't hear 'em coming. They climbed down and my company was going in to attack the paratroops. But there was about

five of us left there to guard this small bay. One chap went off to find out
what was going on and never came back. He just said he was off, and
that was as far as we know. But the rumour was that he had swum over
to that small island [probably Agia Kyriaki], but whether that was true or
not, I don't know.[4]

Sid was ordered to stay put while the rest of his platoon were ordered
elsewhere. His small unit was not near enough to where the fighting
was taking place to be of any use. Sid remembered the strong smell of
cordite and believed he had a fortunate escape. 'I never actually saw
where the parachuters dropped but they said there was bodies all over
there. I was really one of the lucky ones.'[5]

The situation became more confusing and unsettling for Sid as
more men from his company were killed. 'After that, some more
people came down. I think it was some of the Buffs. I am not sure.
It was either Buffs or Irish Fusiliers. And told us we had got to join up
with them. We went on to another hill and took up position [...]
We were bombed several times.'[6] They had lost a lot of their own
officers and were placed under the command of other regiments. 'We
were with the Buffs, then we were with the Irish Fusiliers. We didn't
know who we were taking orders from really, half the time.' Sid did
not see much of the major fighting, as he recalled, 'The nearest
account of [seeing Germans] was snipers, once or twice but that's
about all. We didn't really go into any set attack as such. We seemed
to be wandering around doing nothing. Going from here and
then picking up stragglers.'[7] Sid was lucky to have escaped the worst
of the battle, yet his apparently aimless wanderings to and fro set a
pattern which many of the other men experienced that afternoon
and evening.

Combat on Rachi Ridge

Some of the worst fighting took place on Rachi Ridge during the
afternoon of 12 November. The ridge is the highest point running
north to south in the middle of the island at its smallest width. When
standing on the ridge, both Gourna and Alinda bays on the lower
coastal ground can be overlooked. Sergeant George Hatcher's platoon
officer had been ordered to remain in position, but his senior officer,
Lieutenant Clifford Clarke, had taken out a platoon of Royal West

Kents to lead a counter-attack on the ridge; Hatcher recalled, 'Clifford Clarke went out with his patrol, and he had a bit of a smacking up [...] Two of each platoon, about ten people, stayed behind and gave company fire [cover].'[8] Clifford Clarke recalled,

> When we got there we were given our various positions. I had a position which was extra to establishment Vickers machine guns which are much heavier than the normal Bren guns that you had as an infantry company. They were static and that was wonderful as it [the machine gun] was spraying bullets just where the paratroopers came down. Wonderful for us, but not for them. But we didn't really go to other positions. We knew every bit about our own positions and that is why, if things had gone properly, we ought easily to have been able to have dealt with these Germans who didn't know the country. You imagine the paratroopers, half of them shot on the way down, but they gradually built up.[9]

To Clarke it looked as if hundreds of parachutists had landed around the ridge area, but many were drifting down into the bay or the countryside which lay beyond it. Although it was a surprise too, he said,

> It was almost an admiration to see this thing, and somehow felt terribly tense, and so you started to fire at them as they were coming down, as you were taught to do. Quite clearly many were dead before they reached the ground. Others must have been wounded. And others weren't. So the idea of paratroopers, once you hit the ground, you get away from your parachute as fast as you can otherwise you are pulled away in the wind by it and dragged around. You then have to look round for your arms that, apart from side arms, come down separately and will hopefully be near you. If they are not, you have to find them, open them up and then disappear as quickly as you can to a rendezvous place where you all get together, and that is not always very easy, because plane's overshoot, some people come down in trees, all kinds of things. You can imagine the chaos.[10]

German casualty records state that 200 parachutists died before they landed, and another 100 or so sustained injuries as they fell, a loss of about 40 per cent of their paratroopers. By the same account, 450 parachutists made it to the ground alive (although the British soldiers fighting on the ground estimated the incoming number as much less), their aim to link up with the 500 or so who had come in by sea.

While the parachutists were gathering their force together, those German troops who had come ashore via landing craft to the north-east of the island were now making their way up the side of the Clidi mountain. Clifford Clarke was annoyed that things had been left. 'The time [to get cracking on them] was when they landed in the sea and started building up, then we should have [attacked them] [...] We didn't see any of them from the sea landing, because ours [our position] was more the parachute drop' (on Rachi Ridge).[11]

One major problem that was becoming increasingly obvious was that Brigadier Tilney was not maintaining proper communication with his commanding officers, nor following proper rules in the chain of command. Clifford Clarke recalled, 'I didn't really have contact with Percy Flood, my company commander who was away with the rest of the company [Captain Percy Flood was coming in from the Mount Germano area in the north].' The parachutists had evidently taken Clarke by surprise and it is clear that his superiors had not informed him of the drop even though it had been expected – another example of lack of communication. Clarke added, 'Tilney had difficulty keeping in touch with his battalion commanders. And the battalion commanders were coming backwards and forwards, not getting messages, doing things he countermanded, so lack of communication was a big problem.'[12]

George Jellicoe recalled not one but two landings of parachutists, but thinks the second lot came in the following morning.

> There were two major landings, and certainly in the first they had a lot of casualties because there was a good deal of wind. Some of them actually dropped in the sea. And of course, we did all we could. I had a very small body of chaps then, and theirs were very high-class parachutists. Very well trained and all the rest of it. In fact they had pretty heavy casualties but they played an important role.'[13]

Jellicoe was on the northern end of the island where some of the paratroopers landed. He remembered there were still around 200 surviving enemy parachutists left and they were regrouping.[14] He therefore issued orders to firearms teams to despatch themselves to various quarters to deal with them. He himself was at the forefront of the action. He recalled, 'We were stationed there all right [...] I had been asked to be there [...] that bit of the island, as you know, is really divided into three bits [north, centre and south] [...] and I and Sutherland had [had] the northern third of the island and it was there where the German parachutists landed [on Rachi Ridge and to its north]. There weren't a great many men on the ground at the time.'[15] Indeed, Sutherland had already left.

In the affray was 37-year-old Captain Alan Redfern acting as part of the combined LRDG/SBS Mobile Reserve Force. The force consisted of three officers and only 24 men, who were holding reserve Point 112, north of Gourna Bay, only a few hundred yards from the German parachutists. Other sections of the LRDG had gone to mop up any survivors from the first parachute drop, accompanied by 30 men from Jellicoe's SBS unit. Having heard nothing from HQ, Redfern had used his initiative to keep T2 Patrol at Point 112 whilst sending Y Patrol to the north of Point 64 (Germano), and leading T1 into the northeast side of the mountain. He was killed by enemy machine-gun fire at 3 p.m. on 12 September.[16] Of the death of Redfern, Lloyd Owen wrote, 'his loss was a great blow as he was a much liked and respected officer. He had done invaluable work with us.'[17]

Lieutenant Ted Johnson of the Royal Irish Fusiliers was still up Appetici having dealt with the incoming seaborne enemy who had climbed the mountain that morning. He was out of range of the paratroopers, but the landings had given him added apprehension.

> I was told later that they had landed and I thought, 'Oh yes something else we will have to deal with.' Initially I was told that parachutists had landed just inside Gourna Bay but I didn't know about various causalities. I only found out later what reaction had been taken to the parachutists and who'd been killed. Obviously, they [the British solders] initially did their best to shoot as many in the air as they could. But it is not easy to shoot somebody who is coming down on a parachute, waving about. You would think it would be fairly easy but it's amazing the number of chaps who got down quite safely, yet there was a fusillade of fire going up at them the whole time from various sources but many of them came down perfectly safe. In fact I believe most of the German parachutist casualties were from heavy landing on rock, not from being shot.[18]

The Royal Irish Fusiliers were now scattered about; Battalion HQ was on the north slope of Meraviglia; A Company were south of Alinda; B Company above Pandeli; C Company (Mobile Reserve) south of Meraviglia; and D Company scattered with a platoon on either side of Gourna Bay, with one platoon overlooking Alinda.

Enemy Snipers

As the Germans moved further inland, they took to hiding in ruined houses and behind rocks, taking cover where they could. From their hideouts, they started to take out any British soldiers on the move. LRDG commander Guy Prendergast went out on a reconnaissance to investigate the state of affairs and to see how many of the enemy were about. He crept round the lower ground around Platanos, keen to find out exactly how many of the enemy had made it that far down from the mountains and whether they had managed to link up with those on Castle Hill.[19] The small village square was lined with a few whitewashed buildings and he quickly found out that German snipers had secreted themselves inside, taking potshots at anyone walking through the cobble-lined street. As Prendergast neared Platanos square, he came face to face with a German soldier talking to two Greek women. Both he and the German fired, but escaped being hit by each other, and hastened out of sight as quickly as possible.

William Moss was amongst the men of the King's Own Royal Regiment who had moved from Mount Clidi to take part in the attack on the German parachutists earlier on Rachi. Now the enemy were moving inland from the mountains, some of them towards Alinda. He recalled that on 12 November,

> While on the way to attack an enemy position, we had to go in forward, suddenly our section came under small arms fire, which I presumed to be snipers. Paratroops had descended by now, and were getting organised, at about 2.50 pm this attack got more severe. We took up firing positions. Our weapons were hand grenades, one Bren Gun, one Boyes Anti-Tank Rifle and Tommy Guns and Lee Enfield Rifles. With us, at the time was Lieutenant Tiplady, I often wonder if he recovered – he ran into the fire and was wounded, he fell like a log.[20]

The situation became 'quite eerie; men were told to "take cover" and "keep a sharp look-out"'. Snipers were hiding behind walls, in bushes and blown-out houses, but there was no idea as to where to aim, or where they were. The Germans appeared to be well placed to take out the Allied soldiers as they came into view. Moss recalled,

We decided to make an attempt on this position, which we had previously been briefed on. It was a small hill, rising sharply. So we moved on slowly, and cautiously, when suddenly out of the blue came shots, from, I am not certain, a sniper, who was able to pick us off one by one. I was moving on steadily when our Corporal, named, Hicklin, got shot in his leg; that left myself to take command of the remainder of my section. We took up our positions again, for any attack, while doing so Private J Woodward, of Salford, was mortally wounded in his forehead, there was little we could do.

He gave the command for the remainder of his section to stay with him and await orders from their commanding officer.[21] At that moment Private Vines was wounded and he was left with only a handful of men: Private D. Hibbert, 'a very brave man indeed'; Private McDougal from Warrington; and Private H. Acton from Motor Transport Platoon. Moss decided they should make a run for it and break out. 'I gave the order to my Bren gunner to fire a few bursts of automatic fire, while the remainder of my Section returned to their own trenches on Mount Clidi under this covering fire. It was like an ambush, but luckily we got back safe and sound after losing some very brave pals of my section.' [22] Moss was ordered to take his section around the perimeter of Mount Clidi:

We had no sooner got dug in when the enemy attacked in force. We were taken prisoners, and searched, and our steel helmets were snatched from our heads. Then we got escorted back to the German positions, where my section was put in a pigsty on a lonely road running through the village. Time went by, when we had to form up in single file, and were made to carry mortar bombs for the enemy and now we were being treated as 'human shields' amidst the fire of our own troops.[23]

Moss and his companions were becoming increasingly nervous as they were shot at with rifle fire, small arms and Bren guns (presumably Allied fire) as they were forced to walk a couple of miles by their enemy escort. They meandered down a small path towards Alinda and ended up at the hospital in Alinda (Villa Bellini), now full of German troops carrying weapons. Alinda was being gradually infiltrated with enemy soldiers as they moved southwards to join up with their comrades who had landed on Appetici that morning. This gave them some respite, as Moss explains.

> Inside this hospital in the Bay of Alinda, we sheltered for a while tending to the wounded, and a surgeon was operating on a casualty on a table. A War Correspondent came up to me in a suit of brand new khaki, he looked like he had just come out of a tailor's shop. We were weary now, no food or drink. I decided to go to the door of this building, it was getting dark and very windy, in the near distance I could vaguely see the silhouettes of a few British Tommies, they were rushing towards the caves. I believe the War Correspondent was none other, but Marsland Gander.[24]

It was obvious there were not enough Germans around the hospital to patrol or keep track of prisoners, nor did they seem overly concerned to do so. Moss and his companion were about to make a run for it, and presumably Gander sauntered out at some stage too as he makes no mention of being captured.

At around 9 p.m., Moss heard a loud explosion from an Allied naval ship in the bay. Private Viner, of the Royal Welsh Fusiliers, then said to Moss,

> 'The next salvo and I'm away, how about you?' I answered, 'Yes, I'm off too.' The first salvo had scored a direct hit – it left a gaping hole in the side of this building. This is where the two of us made our dramatic escape once again. After a moment, we had gone just 50 to 100 yards, when a voice in the darkness shouted 'Halt! Who goes there?' A great relief seemed to come over me. 'Go to the front of the column!' When we reached the front we were escorted to a cave, where a Lieutenant Colonel, or maybe a higher ranking officer, gave us a good interrogation. 'What have you two been up to?', he said, but before I could speak he said, 'Stand to attention when you speak to me.' I was now the appointed spokesman, so I said, in a good military-like fashion, 'You will excuse me Sir, but we have just escaped, we were taken POW. Your patrol, or reinforcements, have just passed about 500 Germans.' 'Quartermaster,' he shouted, 'Give these men two blankets and some soup and put them up for the night.' We didn't get much sleep, but the rest did a world of good, thanks to this Officer.[25]

The enemy had quite quickly moved from their arrival point in the north to Alinda. Enemy snipers were intentionally picking off the officers, Lieutenant Jimmy James recalled.

> The attack on Alinda Bay was pretty awful. As the troops moved off they were all brought down by snipers, the officers were. If you were sensible, you wore as few badges of rank, as few indications you were an officer.

You wore battledress and carried a tommy gun or a rifle. They all got shot or wounded. A lot of casualties took place. The attack on Alinda Bay was incredible.[26]

Only three men returned from that platoon headed by Sergeant McKeown; Captain Bill Robinson heading Platoon 17 was killed, and Sergeant P. O'Connell took over, leading a pushback of several attacks during the night and next day. Lieutenant Prior was wounded and evacuated. All the wounded were taken to the RAP at 'Charing Cross' or to the naval hospital at Lakki.

Disorder and Confusion

As the afternoon of the 12th went by, the situation became increasingly muddled. Lieutenant Jimmy James recalled, 'Everything seemed to go wrong. Artillery didn't open up when infantry were advancing. One company didn't arrive, not because of their fault but inadequate orders. So, there was never a feeling of confidence that things were going well. My own colonel I know had all sorts of contradictory orders from the top.'[27] Communication broke down and there was no contact from the Buffs fighting in the north; the enemy (now occupying the middle part of the island around Alinda) had evidently spliced the telephone lines, effectively cutting off the north from the south. To counteract this, Tilney was planning on driving through the pinch between Alinda and Gourna and joining up with the Buffs in the north that evening. The Buffs had met with success, having retaken an Italian battery and had taken 150 German prisoners.

At 6 p.m. on 12 November, some reports suggest that after an attack on Quirico (the Italian battery on Mount Clidi) the enemy had gained possession, but a counter-attack had immediately been ordered. Tilney gave instructions for the Buffs to regain Mount Clidi overnight and move to Rachi Ridge to secure that area.[28] In order to dislodge the enemy paratroopers from their position on the neck, it was the brigadier's intention to counter-attack with two companies of Fusiliers and B Company, King's Own. The two companies of Fusiliers had already been fighting hard; to reorganise themselves and ensure their concentration in the dark proved difficult indeed. Of the three companies only one arrived at the rendezvous, so the operation had to be postponed. David Lloyd Owen was no longer on Leros, but keeping radio contact with the LRDG from a base in Turkey. According to his assessment, Mount Clidi's gun battery was temporarily lost on the 13th but regained the next day.[29]

The situation during the first afternoon was also confusing for the men of the King's Own in Xerocampus area in the south. The bay here is one long beach directly opposite Kalymnos, so there was every reason to suspect the invasion might come by the easiest route. The distance from the tip of Kalymnos and the edge of Leros near Xerocampus is just over a nautical mile, but it may have been thought too obvious an entrance by the enemy. The rocky mountain of Scumbarda looms over the right-hand side of the bay, and Allied gun emplacements were atop giving cover. At about 4 p.m., the King's Own received information from Battalion HQ that the position had deteriorated and that the company was to occupy the high ground above their position (up the mountain rather than down on the beaches) and if attacked to fight to the last man. Five hours later the company was ordered to return to its original position and to man the posts they had been covering before around the coast.[30] This movement had simply worn the men out for nothing. In any case, this was not where the main action was taking place.

The Germans had gained a hold on Appetici, and the Royal Irish Fusiliers were in trouble trying to defend the area between here and Meraviglia further down the mountain. Heavy fighting had taken place, with large numbers of casualties on both sides; the Royal Irish Fusiliers had lost an entire platoon, and the one still holding Leros Castle was in trouble. Nonetheless, they had success that day, having fought the enemy back up the slopes to retake Mount Appetici. Tilney was now to regroup, correlate the soldiers he had to hand and summon new strength. His plans were for a counter-attack on Rachi Ridge for the evening of the 12th using two companies of Royal Irish Fusiliers and B Company of King's Own. Now C Company was to be withdrawn from Appetici (having just won it that afternoon after a great ordeal) to join King's Own, the Reserves. Only one platoon was to be left on Appetici to hold it, an order not greeted warmly by the

Italians on the summit manning the gun battery. This was to prove a fatal mistake. During the night more German troops would be landed to strengthen the forces attacking Mount Appetici, and Appetici peak would be lost again.[31]

At 7 p.m. back at Fortress Headquarters that evening, Brigadier Tilney met with platoons from the King's Own and Royal Irish Fusiliers to plan a further night attack to dislodge the enemy from Rachi Ridge. Lieutenant Colonel Maurice French, commanding officer of the Royal Irish Fusiliers, was to lead two companies (less one platoon) of Royal Irish Fusiliers and two of King's Own. The attack was set for 11 p.m. but never took place, due to communication breakdown and problems organising the movement of troops – the King's Own experienced difficulties moving up from the south of the island quickly enough, and another company got totally lost in the dark. This failure gave the enemy a welcome opportunity to tighten their hold on Rachi Ridge, a position which had initially been quite shaky.

That night, Fortress HQ tunnel was packed to the brim with exhausted men trying to sleep, Marsland Gander among them. The floor was dirty with dust from a bomb explosion, and the smoke from the small bonfire inside left the place airless and insufferable. Gander went outside as his eyes were stinging, relieved to breathe the cool night air. News was floating round that the navy was coming in to protect the island with six destroyers and a cruiser. A sing-song broke out with 'Roll out the Barrel' and 'She'll be Coming Round the Mountain' harmonising round the mountains. It was not to be an easy night. Gander went in with the rest of them, trying to keep warm and sleep. 'I was weary from the strain and physical effort of the day and tried to lie down on the hillside to get some sleep, wrapping my wool-lined trench coat round. The loose stones made easily the most uncomfortable bed I have ever had.'[32] One sentry asked him if he wanted another blanket. The kindness, dogged determination and solidarity of the soldiers touched Gander. 'Selfless to a fault, brave as any knightly hero of antiquity, yet so unglamorous as to be practically unsung. I think of them always with emotion and pride when they came out of battle dirty, unshaven, their clothing torn and sometimes blood-stained, foul-mouthed, yet still game and good humoured.'[33]

Sinking of the *Dulverton*

At nightfall on 12 November, a southerly gale blew up which restricted the operation of light craft on both sides. HMSs *Faulknor*, *Beaufort*, *Dulverton* and *Echo* worked closely with the Greek destroyer HHMS *Pindos* and a flotilla of motor torpedo boats sweeping round Leros, Kalymnos and Levitha to prevent further enemy reinforcements reaching Leros, but found nothing. An urgent message was sent out for reinforcements to come from the neighbouring island of Samos where British troops were lying up, but there were no boats to bring the soldiers over. As the searchlight beam from Crusader Castle shone out to sea, two British destroyers came into silhouette against the sky. A spontaneous low cheer rose up from the camp at HQ. 'Good old Navy. They never let you down,' commented the Bren gunner. The destroyers began to bomb the German positions.

However, the excitement was cut short when HMS *Dulverton* was hit by a radio-controlled glider bomb in the early hours of 13 November, tearing away its bow and setting it on fire.[34] She had already made various trips to Leros transporting troops and supplies and this was her last ill-fated trip. At 1 a.m., an enemy plane could be seen circling around her. Orders came through to shoot down the plane as soon as it came in close. Don Bush, gunnery radar operator, was aboard on watch on the *Dulverton* that night.[35] He had been sitting on the high chair at the instruments panel and Stan Cowell came up to take his watch in the chair. He recalled, 'Suddenly there was a colossal explosion, the blast coming through from the Wireless Office, which was next door on the port side, the full blast hit poor Stan Cowell who was killed immediately.'[36] Luckily, Don had been on deck with 'Buck' Buckland, a New Zealand radar mechanic. 'Buckland and me, after being flung against the power panel, crawled out into what was left of the starboard passage, the door to aft at the brake of the forecastle being completely jammed and the forward end of the passage blazing furiously.' They managed to crawl through a split in the ship's side and swam away from the ship. From where they were floating, they could see the Turkish coast and German-occupied Kos. They turned to look at the ship; the bow section had broken away and was pointing skywards; the remainder of the ship was burning furiously.

The two men swam back towards the wreckage. They swam around the stern and found a number of men in the water and a large amount of fuel oil discharged from the leaning ship. 'There were small red lights fitted to our lifebelts, and thinking the higher the better, I clipped mine into my hair, which was covered in oil. This lifting pulled the battery out of its pouch and it fell into the water, and owing to the oil the light slipped off my hair. I watched the red light going down and down until it finally disappeared.'[37] They managed to climb onto a small raft which was picking up survivors. George Gorringe from the SBS was trying to help them and must have been in great pain as he had cracked his shoulder blade. All the while, the *Echo* and *Belvoir* were circling around protecting them as best they could, firing at enemy aircraft. Eventually, the men were transferred onto the *Echo* where they cleaned up, and were stitched and bandaged. Don Bush recalled,

> When we got a good number of chaps in, we went back to the *Echo* and we had to climb up these scrambling nets. Well you try, clambering up when you are cold when you are covered in oil. It's a very difficult job. But anyway I made it. We went in the mess deck and took off everything and chucked it [his clothing] down. I hung onto my belt with the money in. This chap's jumper went in the heap so I don't think he ever got his jumper back. The coxswain came and gave us a cup of rum. I went and had a shower. Then I found I was bleeding from all sorts of places and I had to go up to the sick bay. The doctor on the *Echo*, I was very grateful to him. The chap in front of me who was on the table, they were peeling the skin of his back, cos he had been either scolded or burned because he was a stoker – it was coming off in sheets.[38]

Survivors were transferred to a small caique and taken to Bodrum. After crossing the sea to the Turkish coast, the ship laid up in an inlet while the survivors took time out to bury their dead. Don recalled,

> There was one chap who kept yelling all night because he had lost his legs. [He died during the night.] They buried them over the side. I went to the funeral and all I had on was a towel round my waist, you see, absolutely starkers apart from this towel round my waist. We had the funeral and I was walking down the starboard passage and this

OFFICIAL ADMIRALTY COMMUNIQUE

The Board of Admiralty regrets to announce the following casualties sustained in HMS *Dulverton*, the loss of which has already been announced. Next of kin have been notified.

OFFICERS:	Missing Presumed Killed	- Commander S.A. BUSS, M.V.O., R.N. - Sub Lieutenant M.H. AGNEW, R.N. - Temp. Surgeon Lieutenant A.D. BONE, D.S.C., R.N.V.R.
	Wounded	- Lieutenant P. DOUGLAS, R.N. - Lieutenant Commander A.R.E. EVANS, R.N. - Lieutenant G.H.D. LEGARD, M.B.E., R.N.
RATINGS	Died of Wounds	- MAUNDERS Sidney - Stoker

Missing Presumed Killed -

ABBOTT Stanton G.	Able Seaman	LAW Cecil	Stoker 1st. Class
BARKER John	Telegraphist	LEWARNE Ernest J.	Ord. Seaman
BARKER Kenneth	Leading Coder	LEWIS John S.	Able Seaman
BARKER Thomas	Able Seaman	LUFF Frederick M.	P.O. Steward
BARLOW Jack	Able Seaman	LUMB William	Telegraphist
BIRKS Donald	E.R.A. 4	McCALLUM John Mc.L	Able Seaman
BURKE Thomas	Stoker P.O.	McCOY John H.	E.R.A. 5
CARDIN Kenneth	Able Seaman	McGHEE Thomas	Telegraphist
CARLTON Richard	Able Seaman	MARSHALL John	Stoker
CASSIDY Joseph	Able Seaman	MAYALL William H.	Ldg. Steward
CLARKE Albert A.	Signalman	MAYNE James A.	Ldg. Steward
CLIFFORD Leonard H.	Steward	MILTON Daniel J. K.	Stoker P.O.
COLLINS Edward C.N.	Yeoman of Signals	MOORE James R.	Stoker 1st Class
COWELL Edward S.	Able Seaman	MOSSMAN Charles	Able Seaman
CRACKNELL William J.	Able Seaman	MUNNINGS Russell C.	Able Seaman
DAVIES David G.	Stoker P.O.	O'DONNELL John	Ord. Seaman
DOLAN Charles	Able Seaman	PARSONS Leslie S.	Able Seaman
DRURY Leslie C.	Ldg. Cook (O)	PAYTER Arthur J.	Ord. Seaman
EVANS Joseph H.	Stoker 1st Class	PEDDER Donald F.	Ord. Seaman
EVERETT William F.	Ldg. Seaman	PENDERGAST Alex N.	Able Seaman
FIELD Norman	Coder	RICHARDSON Stanley N.	Telegraphist
GARLICK Sidney N.	Signalman	RING Leonard A.	Able Seaman
GODFREY James W.	P.O. Telegraphist	ROBINSON Harold	Stoker P.O.
GRAHAM Edward	P.O. Steward	SHARMAN Anthony N.	Able Seaman
GRIMBLEBY Clarence	Able Seaman	SHERBUT Harold	P.O.
HARRIS Albert G.	Able Seaman	SKINNER William F.	Able Seaman
HAYES Raymond S.M.	P.O. D.S.M.	SPAIN John	Ord. Seaman
HERLIHY Timothy	Able Seaman	STUART John	Able Seaman
HILTON Richard	Telegraphist	TELFORD George S.	Able Seaman
HOBBS Percival E.	P.O.	THOMPSON George	Able Seaman
HOGAN James	Able Seaman	TONNER James N.	Able Seaman
HOLMES David W.	Able Seaman	TURNER Alfred J.	Able Seaman
HOLZMAN Leonard	Ldg. Signalman	WELLS Sydney C.	Able Seaman
INMAN John A.	E.R.A. 5	WILKINSON Joseph S.	Ord. Seaman
JEREMIAH Thomas S.O.	Cook (S)	WOOD John R.	Ldg. Seaman
JONES Thomas	Stoker 1st. Class	WRIGHT Charles L.F.	P.O.
JUKES Edward G.	Telegraphist	WRIGHT Stanley A.	Ldg. Seaman

Sadly the 3 E.R.A.s listed here were reliefs for myself, Horace Parker and Stan Pennell. The relief for C.E.R.A. George Thorndycraft was a survivor.

FIGURE 9.1   Office Admiralty list of casualties of HMS *Dulverton*

Echo stoker came down and said, 'Hey mate is that all the kit you've got?' And I said 'yeah', so he said 'well hang on a minute' and he went down and came back with a pair of very tattered overalls, all split, and a pair of very old gym shoes and this was great. One moment you've got absolutely nothing and then this chap came and gave it to me.[39]

Don watched sadly as his deceased shipmates were buried at sea. The men aboard had to keep a low profile so as not to attract the attention of German planes; 'Only one man at a time was allowed up on deck for a call of nature, and in my case had to put an old scarf around my head to cover the bandages and look like a Turk.' After a few days, the group split into two on two Turkish caiques flying a Turkish flag hugging the coast travelling by daylight. There were plenty of German aircraft overhead, and the odd boat, but no-one stopped them. The survivors were taken to British-held Castelorizo, where they were kitted out with shorts and shirts. However, there was a nervous tension surrounding the troops already on the island – an imminent crisis was awaited. 'The troops here were Indians and were very nervous as they expected to be invaded any day.' For Don, though, his time in the Aegean was to be left behind him as a Lebanese schooner picked him up; the rest of the survivors were taken to Cyprus.

Six officers and 114 ratings had been evacuated from the *Dulverton*.[40] One hundred and nine men were rescued by HMS *Belvoir*, but 77 men including the captain were lost. Recovery of the ship was clearly impracticable, so the *Dulverton* had to be scuttled.[41]

10

And the Fight Goes On

Leros must be held at all costs.

Winston Churchill[1]

The next 48 hours were crucial to the way the battle would swing. At first light on 13 November came the return of enemy aircraft overhead, with 166 German sorties bombarding throughout the day.[2] Despite the high winds and squally seas, to the Allies' dismay between 6.30 and 7 a.m. that morning the sky was once again full of parachutists as another 200 crack German paratroopers were dropped from enemy aircraft.[3] These were the reserve parachute force 15 Fallschirm-Kompanie Branderburg paratroopers.[4] One lot of men was released in the sea by mistake and a Ju 52 was shot down. Another lot were dropped too low for their parachutes to open, as Gander described: 'One of the slow troop carriers, hit fair and square, went flaming down into Alinda Bay, a horrifying spectacle, with one solitary parachute visible dragging behind it, the doll-like figure still attached. Another JU flying lower and lower in distress dropped all its parachutists in the water where the silken chutes lingered for a short time like water lilies.'[5] Jellicoe, the SBS and the LRDG once again battled valiantly on Rachi Ridge to shoot down whoever they could from the second parachute drop and to keep those contained who reached the ground. Many of them were blown off-course by high winds. It was estimated that this time only about 12 of the parachutists were in fighting form by the time they landed; others had either been shot as they came down, were injured with broken bones, or fell to their death on the rocks.[6] It was estimated that there was a total of only about 1,000 German troops now on the island, yet the Allies consisted of many more, even if some of the Italians had shown an unwillingness to fight. The Germans should have been held off easily.

Appetici, Rachi Ridge and Clidi were key areas as the battle raged over the second and third days of fighting (13 and 14 November). Many of the men were given orders to attack, counter-attack or give cover around these focal points. More German troops had managed to land by sea in the early hours of the morning of the 13th, and once again enemy landing craft came in at Pasta di Sopra and Palma Bay in the north of the island. They had less luck when trying to land near Alinda: believing the British had been cleared, they attempted to come ashore but were unexpectedly bombarded by the Italian battery's Bofors guns. One landing craft was disabled and caught alight, whereupon tons of ammunition exploded. Gander watched fascinated at the awesome sight: 'After only a few minutes I saw a tiny tongue of flame licking round the stern. Clouds of black smoke developed and soon the whole vessel was a roaring furnace. Then it blew up with a mighty explosion showing that its chief cargo must have been ammunitions.'[7] About 200 German soldiers struggled to swim ashore towards Alinda. As the fighting continued, there was a build-up of Italian soldiers sheltering in hideouts trying to avoid capture by the Germans, as Major Tassell noticed. 'There were caves full of Italians who had given up. It was dreadful; you could smell this place miles away. The whole lot of them dumped there. I don't know what happened to them – I suppose they just petered out or something.'[8]

The enemy landing craft which had been seen off the previous day in Gourna on the western side of the island had repositioned and was coming in at Grifo Bay in the north, landing another 30 men.[9] Those who managed to get ashore worked their way from east of Mount Vedetta toward Rachi Ridge, but were hammered by British 25-pounders from San Giovanni. The German soldiers on Mount Vedetta managed to link up with the parachutists on Rachi Ridge, strengthening their hold. Allied forces managed to keep the enemy pinned down as they came ashore in more landing crafts further down on the central eastern coast in Alinda; many were hit by shells falling near Villa Bellini. The landing craft which had failed to get in at Palma Bay the previous day repositioned itself and at 6.30 a.m. managed to land troops at the base of Mount Appetici where they joined up with the rest of the Germans on the eastern slopes. Over the next couple of days, pockets of fighting were also concentrated on Appetici.

Brigadier Tilney had sent a message to Commander-in-Chief of Middle East Air Force, Air Marshal Sir Sholto Douglas again urgently requesting air cover.[10] Douglas replied he was doing his best with very limited resources, but there were problems: Leros was out of range of single-engine planes and at the extreme range of twin-engine fighters; the latter were unable to stay in the area to give cover for any length of time as they ran out of fuel. While 48 Beaufighters had made sorties over the island that day, continuous cover was impossible.[11] The navy, however, were still working hard to provide some protection. After bombing the enemy positions that night (13/14 November) the British ships *Faulknor*, *Beaufort* and *Pindos* had to leave Leros as they were running out of fuel, leaving behind *Echo* and *Belvoir* to continue the work.[12]

The 13th and 14th November (the second and third day of fighting) were the most chaotic of times for the soldiers. Conflicting reports, continual movement of troops and simultaneous battles add to the confusion. The three areas of the main fighting have therefore been separated below into into three sections covering the fighting of the 13th and 14th. 1) Castle Hill and Appetici; 2) Racchi Ridge and 3) Mount Clidi.

Fall of Castle Hill

Strategically situated on high ground overlooking Platanos, Castle Hill commands the centre of the island. The imposing Crusaders' Castle is situated on the side of Appetici overlooking the sea on one side and the valley above the small town of Platanos on the other. On the valley opposite, the soldiers could see Meraviglia. Over 13 and 14 November, Allied troops struggled to contain the enemy on its slopes. Lieutenant Ted Johnson and his platoon had successfully seen the enemy off the mountain on the first day of the battle, but had been withdrawn in the night, allowing enemy troops to scale its heights.

Ted recalled the terrible mix-up. 'We withdrew back to where we had started the battle from, back to our defensive possession, awaiting further orders. At some time during the night, we got the order to go back on Appetici. The order came to me in a very roundabout sort of way. Somebody had obviously realised we shouldn't have been taken off Appetici in the first place, so we were told to go back up there again.' Due to the mix-up, on the morning of 13 November at 4 a.m. Ted found himself once again trying to retake a mountain he had already had in his hands the previous day. He was now poised to recapture the gun battery on Castle Hill.[13] 'We got up there next morning round about dawn but in the meantime there was confusion. I was told to go to an RV [rendezvous] point to wait for another platoon to join up with me, and the company commander to go back up into Appetici. I got to this position, waited there for an hour or two and nothing was happening, no sign of the company commander, no sign of the other platoon.'[14] With his platoon sergeant, Sergeant Fitzgerald, Ted gathered the remainder of his men together and resumed defence positions below Mount Appetici, just above Leros town (Platanos), and waited for instructions. Lieutenant Johnson's men were tired of pointless wandering up and down mountains instead of being commanded to hold ground.[15] They were at least reinforced with mortars and small arms as they positioned themselves on the northeast slopes of Appetici's summit.

A counter-attack was now much more difficult, as during the night the Germans had brought in reinforcements and were now occupying the key positions on Appetici.[16] At about 11 a.m. on 13 November after a skirmish with the enemy, the Allies left holding the battery were forced to retreat. All four gun batteries were now under the control of the Germans, and a number of British and Italians had been taken prisoner including Lieutenant A. Woods commanding Platoon 15 and Ted's runner, Fusilier Roberts. Fusilier James McMaster had been blown up by a mortar bomb and killed earlier that morning; Lieutenant Armstrong, a South African commanding Platoon 14, was wounded and evacuated to Egypt.[17] B Company of Royal Irish Fusiliers had been unable to take part in the counter-attack as they were still busy defending their own area covering Pandeli. They were now in worse trouble as the Germans overlooked them from the gun battery of Appetici.

Brigadier Tilney seemed unaware of this problem until late afternoon on 13 November, when he met with Lieutenant Colonel Maurice French to see how the attack on Appetici had worked out over the last 12 hours. By nightfall a further counter-attack on Appetici was planned, although the plan was delayed until 2 a.m. because of confused orders and missing troops.[18] Naval bombing began at 1.30 a.m., used to 'soften up' the enemy prior to the planned attack on Appetici to follow at 2 a.m. *Echo* and *Belvoir* fired from Alinda Bay at Mount Appetici where the German position lay.[19]

On Appetici, on the third day of fighting in the early hours of 14 November, the delayed counter-attack took take place. The intention was that Lieutenant French would lead a company of Royal Irish Fusiliers and all available men from King's Own into battle to try and regain Appetici and recapture the gun battery. He was to work with the commanding officer of the King's Own battalion, Lieutenant Colonel Egerton, with Lieutenant Colonel French leading the way as he knew the terrain. The plan was for A and D companies of King's Own to approach under darkness, clear the feature after moonrise, and HQ Company would follow in to organise and hold position. A and D companies would then withdraw to Ankora (a spot where an anchor stands on the one main road coming up from Portolago) and be ready for the planned offensive on Rachi. According to Brigadier Tilney, he had not intended for Lieutenant Colonel French to lead the King's Own; he explained that just as the attack was due to start, Lieutenant Colonel Egerton 'had not got into touch with me, nor could he be found at his HQ or with his company commanders at RV with Colonel French for orders. Consequently I was forced to accept Colonel French's leadership of Colonel Egerton's battalion for the attack.'[20] Some reports state that B and C companies of Royal Irish Fusiliers were also to be involved in the counter-attack, but in the event were pulled out to go to Rachi Ridge to form an attack on the southwest side of Meraviglia.[21]

Just four hours earlier (10 p.m. on the 13th), a report had come through that the enemy was attacking Fortress HQ on Meraviglia, and all attention was diverted to it. Second Lieutenant Pavlides of LRDG stated, 'At 2200 hours enemy parachutists on Rachi attacked main Fortress HQ position [on Mount Meraviglia] from north-west using three inch mortar. Attack developed and seemed sufficiently threatening to the Fortress Commander to warrant alteration of plans.'[22] Tilney therefore ordered the withdrawal of HQ Company of King's Own and C Company of Royal Irish Fusiliers from the planned attack on Appetici to go and protect Fortress Headquarters.[23] This was to lead to further stress on Colonel French, now preparing to counter-attack on Appetici under-strength. One LRDG report insists that one of their officers was sent after French telling him to turn his force round and attack northwards. French informed the officer that this was impractical, but that he would send back HQ Company of King's Own.[24] Lieutenant Ted Johnson and the rest of C Company of Royal Irish Fusiliers were also ordered to return to HQ. The situation became further confused as two platoons had been withdrawn but had no instruction as to where to go.[25]

Consequently, at 2 a.m. on the third day of battle on 14 November, Lieutenant Colonel French began to lead his men into battle with fewer men than he expected, left with only parts of A and D companies of the King's Own. Effectively Lieutenant French was now left exposed, leading too few troops in a counter-attack, with no HQ Reserves and no signals to back him up. Furthermore, the attack was at night over terrain unfamiliar to all but himself, with most of the men in companies unknown to him. This went against all previous practice of officers leading their own companies, and against all established military rules that give a company cohesion.

With his liaison officer Lieutenant Robert Austin Ardill of Royal Irish Fusiliers and his personal orderly at his side, Colonel French grappled his way up the rocky mountain in the pitch black; they carefully made their way round boulders and gorse bushes which spiked bits of their bodies as the men brushed past. It was a laborious process and difficult to maintain direction in the dark. Two platoons got lost and were not seen again. Ardill recalled, 'The King's Own had disappeared. I only had my batman [...] Their officers had disappeared. The two companies which were supposed to have formed a pincer movement had vanished, failed in their mission and didn't re-appear.'[26] The men in the counter-attack were exposed as daylight broke, and the enemy spotted them. Suddenly a shot rang out: Ardill was hit, but not seriously. Lieutenant Colonel French was killed. Only one officer and 70 men came out of it alive.[27]

Lieutenant Colonel French was to be greatly missed not just by his own men but by his fellow officers. Brigadier Tilney recognised his reliance on French when he said, 'We lost the battle when we lost Maurice [French].'[28] He was not alone in recognising the talent and bravery of this experienced military officer. French had averaged about two hours sleep a night before his death. He might have suspected his time was closing, for he wrote to his wife on 12 October 1943, 'If anything should happen to me, remember that our separation is only temporary [...] It is cruelly hard that we should have been four and a half years apart, but the remaining separation will only be like a continuation of this and I will be close to you dearest Di – always.'[29]

The King's Own report written a year later gives one of the clearest accounts of the action on Appetici that night.[30]

During the early hours of 13th November the Company was ordered to move by Motor Transport to the anchor crossroads [Ankora] and take over a position from the Royal Irish Fusiliers. On arrival at the Anchor, guides were met and the company moved on foot to a position on the eastern slopes of Meraviglia covering Pandeli Bay; the position was taken over from 'C' Company of the Royal Irish Fusiliers. The same evening orders were received for the attack on Appetici. Orders for the attack were given out from Meraviglia in fading light. The force was to consist of 'A', 'D' and HQ Companies, 1/King's Own under the command of Lieutenant Colonel French Royal Irish Fusiliers. 'A' Company was to lead the attack and secure the searchlight and gun positions on the top of the feature. 'D' Company was to follow up on 'A' Company's left and 'mop up' the numerous caves and dugouts, while HQ Company was to form a semi-circle behind the attacking Companies and prevent the enemy from withdrawing from the feature. 'A' and 'D' Companies were to withdraw before dawn to the area of the Anchor Crossroads leaving HQ Company to hold the feature. The start line was the line of the Martello Towers and the Company was to cross the start line at 0001 hrs. Naval support was expected and this in fact caused the operation to be postponed for two hours. At about 2300 hrs the Company moved to the Anchor Crossroads where it was joined by 'D' and HQ Companies. The whole force then moved to the start line.

The assault on the German positions began at 0200 hrs on 14th November. The first gun position on Appetici was reached when the company came under heavy Machine Gun fire from the flanks, progress was slow; during the advance the coy commander was killed, the 2 i/c and two platoon commanders wounded. Just before dawn the German counter-attack came in and the company was driven back and finally forced to withdraw in the direction of the Anchor. After the withdrawal the situation rapidly deteriorated and confusing reports were received stating that Charing Cross was believed to be in German hands and that the road to Portolago was cut. Troops could be seen withdrawing from Meraviglia. It was not until later in the day that the situation became more stabilised and the remnants of the coy were once more reformed under Lieutenant Broster, the only surviving officer, and moved to occupy a defensive position in the area of the Anchor Crossroads.[31]

Although two platoons of Royal Irish Fusiliers had initially been ordered to Appetici to assist, this command had been inexplicably overridden in a message from Fortress HQ without Tilney's knowledge. Before Tilney could get them on the move again it was 4 a.m. and Appetici had fallen into enemy hands just before daylight.[32] As seen in some of the accounts of the fighting elsewhere, the revelations are frequently contradictory and full of confusion – hardly surprising in the middle of a war zone. Others give specific accounts of what was happening close at hand. According to some reports, B and C companies of the Faughs were to be involved but C Company had been withdrawn and B Company could not be extracted from Pandeli.

Colonel Cowper of King's Own was there on Appetici and gave his account of the action that night:

'A' Company was commanded by Captain D. J. P. Thirkell-White, Captain C. J. Blyth as his second-in-command. 'D' Company had to cover dark ground which abounded in caves, each one of which had to be assaulted separately, and platoons therefore were forced to act independently. Touch between the companies was soon lost. 'A' Company reached the first gun position, after which it came under heavy fire from the flanks, the company commander and two of the platoon commanders were killed. Blyth also was wounded and in great pain, but he continued to lead the company into the attack until he was again wounded in the neck and died on his way back to the regimental aid post. In spite of heavy machine-gun fire from the left flank, 'D' Company was able to gain ground and eventually, step by step, forced its way to the top of the slope where the situation was much confused. Here Major M. R. Lonsdale was wounded, Burke and Mathieson killed. Meanwhile the Germans launched an attack under cover of the fire of their mortars which threatened the safety of Fortress headquarters. 'A' Company was withdrawn from Mount Appetici. 'D' Company, with the Fusiliers, continued to hold the crest until well after dawn when, after heavy mortar fire, the Germans, 'every man a Tommy gunner,' attacked in their turn. They could not be held and the King's Own and Fusiliers were forced back down the hill amid showers of grenades.[33]

Fusilier Jack Harte was there with his platoon of Royal Irish Fusiliers, only about seven men in all on the crest of Appetici. The communication line had gone down sometime during the fighting of the previous day and it was only thanks to the LRDG getting through with support that they managed to find out what was going on.[34] That morning of 14 November, a couple of signallers, Alex McBride and Tommy Lloyd, managed to lay a line up to the castle. It was then that many of the Royal Irish Fusiliers learnt about the deaths of their comrades: Polly McIllwaine, Sergeant Caldwell, Sergeant Connell, 'Sab' McMaster, 'Gutrie Kane' and Lieutenant Gore-Booth, all killed.

Back on the Ridge

The fear of an attack on Battalion HQ on Meraviglia a few hours earlier turned out to be warranted. The Germans had in fact planned to take Searchlight Hill, just west of Meraviglia, in the early hours of the 14th. Enemy troops were coming towards Fortress Headquarters at 5 a.m. and King's Own HQ Company had been recalled from Appetici to defend Meraviglia. Jellicoe and the SBS fighting alongside LRDG were on Rachi Ridge from around 2 a.m. that night trying to halt any enemy progression pushing out.[35] Tilney ordered a renewed attack on Rachi using a company of King's Own and of Royal Irish Fusiliers to take place at 7.30 a.m. Once again the attack was delayed and only started at 9.30 a.m.[36] Simultaneously, B Company of Royal West Kents and C Company of Royal Irish Fusiliers would flank Rachi moving north on either side. King's Own Company were slow to follow up, trapped in light automatic fire from groups of enemy underground which had allowed C Company of Royal Irish Fusiliers to pass over them.[37]

Lieutenant Ted Johnson, having been withdrawn from Appetici, was in the middle of the attack on Meraviglia. He and his company had at least been given a hot meal before they received orders to start from the ground under the southwest side of Meraviglia. B and C companies were to join up to form one force and proceed north on Rachi.[38] It was a hair-raising experience as they had to cover open ground. Ted and his men made a dash for it, praying the enemy fire would miss them. They were being covered only by a pair of Allied Bofors guns the Light Aircraft Regiment was firing just over their heads aiming at the enemy. Ted admitted, 'I have never experienced it before, or since, and yet in more conventional battles elsewhere, gunner support a hundred-fold stronger than these Bofors was normal.'[39] They were about to make a hand-to-hand attack, so they fixed their bayonets while slowly walking towards the enemy, waiting for some of the men to catch up. Their officers' rifles were useless beyond ten yards, and the Thompson sub-machine guns were unreliable. All the time, Ted was conscious of the likelihood of being hit. 'I remember particularly in this attack being afraid of being hit in the eyes. I never gave a thought to the rest of my body, but even to this day I can remember being worried about my eyes, and every now and again cocking my steel helmet more forwards – not that this would have made the slightest difference.'[40] As they rounded the corner and charged, they were thankful to find the trenches empty. Ted had only seven men with him, among them Sergeant Wallace, Sergeant Fitzgerald and Corporal Byrne. He recalled, 'I did not know of any casualties at this stage but was well aware that the majority of the men with whom I had crossed the start line were not with me.'[41] His superior officer, Major Ben Barrington, eventually caught up with the rest of them, by which time they knew that the enemy lay in the mountain scrub just above them. They requested that King's Own move down the mountain from their position on Searchlight Hill towards them and they would try and meet the enemy in the middle, but they were unsure whether their message had got through as radio contact was unreliable. Ted therefore had had to go back to find out where the King's Own were and to arrange a relief force, which took two hours as the area was covered by enemy fire. He found their commanding officer, Lieutenant King, on the west slope of

Searchlight Hill and once Ted had explained the position of the Royal Irish Fusiliers, two King's Own platoons were sent to attack at dusk. Ted had had nothing to eat since very early that morning so was most grateful when Lieutenant King gave him half a tin of cold stew ('meat and veg'), 'the most wonderful thing I'd tasted for ages'.[42] Major Barrington had to be taken back to the cave at HQ after being hit by an exploding mortar bomb. Ted took over command of what remained of the company. He and his small unit bombarded the Germans, but there was still no sign of the King's Own. Unfortunately, Ted's unit was inadvertently bombarded from the Royal Navy in Alinda Bay as they were unaware of the friendly forces in that position.[43]

During this time, Lieutenant Captain Clarke had been on San Giovanni doing his best to give cover to the advancing King's Own and Royal Irish Fusiliers on Rachi Ridge. He had six Vickers and some Bren machine guns. 'I was feeling particularly bloody, but helped myself a bit by manning one of the Vickers and belting anything I could see. We got some grand shots.'[44] The enemy were using Verey lights and coloured smoke to signal to the bombers where to direct their bombs. Despite their efforts, the Royal Irish Fusiliers and King's Own were unable to dislodge the enemy from Rachi Ridge but did take 200 prisoners and inflicted many casualties.[45] Lieutenant Stokes and the remnants of his platoon went up to reinforce Lieutenant Clifford Clarke on San Giovanni during the evening of the 14th.

Since C Company of Royal Irish Fusiliers had not been followed up as they had expected, they withdrew to Searchlight Hill having been shot up. Sometime during the afternoon of the 14th, they got the order to prepare for extensive mortar bombing – a five-minute barrage entailing some 400 mortar shells of 10 lb each flung at the Germans. Mortar bombs rained down on the enemy targets at such a rapid pace that they overheated the mortar barrels. An attack was led by Major South who rounded up 40 to 50 Germans, all of them youths; they were shipped out on a naval vessel to the Middle East. Raymond Williams recalled that Christy Wall had his foot blown off during the skirmish, after a direct hit on the gunpit coping. 'It was a most distressing sight to see his foot missing from the ankle in an untidy mess of ragged trouser-end, flesh and blood, but he showed great courage through his ordeal. Our stretcher-bearers soon whipped him away for medical treatment, and all we could hope for him, was his immediate repatriation home.'[46] By now the Royal Irish Fusiliers were spread out all over the island.[47]

All day, Corporal Vic Kenchington had been rushing forward with his fellow stretcher-bearers picking up the injured, applying dressing where possible and injecting the wounded with morphine. By nightfall the gruesome task of digging graves for the dead had fallen to him. The lucky ones who had survived but were wounded were patched up and taken off the island in motor launches before dawn, when the bombs would start falling once more.

Clinging to Clidi

Various men from the LRDG had been in the Clidi area in the north of the island on the second day of fighting. Captain John Olivey was busy using hand grenades to flush out the enemy from caves, assisted by Corporal Coventry, Gunner Rupping and Rifleman van Heerden. Captain Olivey threw one with the pin still in, giving the Germans enough time to come out. 'They all put their hands up and looked surprised as I picked up the grenade. We had captured fifteen Germans in the cave and trooped them all to the top. Some of them were badly wounded and all were badly shaken. It was a good bit of work and we felt pleased with ourselves.'[48] Five men of King's Own were detailed to hold gun positions.

Fighting on Mount Clidi in the north continued throughout the second and third days of the battle.[49] By 6 p.m. on 13 November the Germans had captured the nearby Quirico feature (also known as Point 184) but would fail to hold on to it.[50] That night an attack was made on Quirico led by Lieutenant Geoffrey Hart of the Buffs and Sergeant Nolan leading Platoons 13 and 15. They had been ordered up the steep hill with no daylight reconnaissance. Both were hit as they cut their way through barbed wire and cleared the first trench. Sergeant Nolan was not seriously wounded but Lieutenant Hart was badly hit in the thigh and leg. He managed to roll down the hill and find an officer's driver to take him to HQ. The following morning of day three of the fighting (14th) at 7 a.m., disaster struck when navy signals went down, destroyed by an enemy attack. Only army cyphers were now available to signal the senior British naval officers on Leros. This added to an already chaotic situation. Meanwhile, Brigadier Tilney was making plans for the Buffs to attack from the north, but by the time the plans reached Colonel D.P. Iggulden, he and his men were already fighting on Mount Clidi at dawn on 14 November. With communication ineffective, Colonel Iggulden had taken the initiative, rallied his men and made a counter-attack to try and recapture the battery on Mount Clidi. Medic Ken Foley was injured on Clidi that day, later dying of his wounds. The LRDG moved back to reclaim the position they had previously held on Mount Clidi while all the time being subject to mortar and machine-gun fire. The Buffs moved off, leaving the LRDG to hold their position.[51]

The Luftwaffe made continual sorties dropping bombs, making holding the position even harder.[52] Lieutenant F.J. Belle, leading C Company, followed by Major Ernest Hole of Buffs, leading B Company, cleared Mount Clidi, taking 40 prisoners. Major Hole was later killed in action, aged 33; Lieutenant Belle would be wounded.[53] King's Own Major Gordon Hinshelwood Duxbury single-handedly bombed two enemy machine-gun posts before being killed. An officer of the battalion reported, 'Major Duxbury had gone forward alone and personally grenaded two enemy machine-gun posts, but was mortally wounded when going on to deal with a third post.' One of his regiment fighting in Leros said he had told him on the ship on the way out, 'Eastwood, the Bosche will never take me prisoner.'[54] Captain R.L.P. Maxwell was ordered to send out a patrol, which he led himself and was killed. All other officers of his company were killed. Evidently, signals were working again by 7.25 a.m., as a signal was sent, 'British troops have recaptured Clidi taking prisoners.'[55] C Company of King's Own and the Buffs had retaken Clidi (if indeed it had fallen), recaptured Quirico, caught 30 prisoners and established control of that part of the island.[56]

The Germans attack on Quirico was squashed by a counter-attack by C Company of Buffs under Major Vincent Bourne, which by midday had captured 70 of the enemy.[57] They continued to take out pockets of resistance, mainly coming from snipers in local houses, while moving towards Villa Bellini in Alinda. The hospital in the grounds of the Villa Bellini was now occupied by Germans.

By the end of day three (14 November), the Buffs, backed up by a handful of King's Own, controlled most of the north of the island having retaken Clidi and Quirico, although the Germans still held Mount Vedetta. C Company of Buffs were on lower slopes of Quirico pushing east towards Alinda. The King's Own and Royal Irish Fusiliers were holding positions on Rachi up on Searchlight Hill. Platoon 9 had been stubbornly holding out at Leros Castle.

Kampf Gruppe Müller, in a history of 22 Infantry, admitted on 14 November, 'it appeared to be almost impossible that we should ever win the battle. The destiny of the troops on Leros hung on a thin thread.'[58]

Days two and three of the battle had seen harsh hand-to-hand combat on Appetici, Clidi and Rachi Ridge. The enemy were now fanning out towards Platanos from Rachi, and Alinda from the Clidi area. Most of the men took a stoical attitude towards their duties and simply followed orders.

11

Tired, Hungry and Lost

So many lives lost, so many, what a waste [...] To die so young, I was only 20 years old when we arrived in Leros in '43. You, who are young, keep peace as a treasure, not war. Live long and happy, forgive me that I cry now, sorry, sorry.

Sergeant Reg Neep, King's Own[1]

The fourth day of fighting was to be the penultimate day of the battle as the situation became increasingly confused and the soldiers became more disorientated. Just past midnight in the early hours of 15 November, Irish Fusilier Jack Harte and a group of five men, including his sergeant, Smudge Smyth and Fusilier Jimmy Gollogher, were around the slopes of Appetici. They were exhausted, had not eaten for two days and had long since run out of water. They had been trapped up Mount Appetici since the enemy had brought in reinforcements the previous night. Now, surrounded by Germans, with no support, and running low on ammunition, they decided to go in search of provisions. Their previous meal had been on the evening of the 13th when a member of the LRDG had got through to them up the mountain with ten tins of McConachies stew.[2]

The night was moonless and misty, so at least there was some cover as they tripped their way over rocks down the mountainside. They could hear German voices nearby as they made for the road. It was a company of the enemy in hiding out of sight behind a 4-ft wall. Luckily, they heard friendly gunshots aimed at the Germans scaring them off – it had come from another group of Royal Irish Fusiliers who had had the same idea of going for provisions.

Together they managed to find some water and chocolate and planned to take them back to their men up near the Castle. It was about 4.30 a.m. as they made their way back up in the dark, but they were stopped at about 200 ft with fire coming at them in all directions. Harte used his Beretta to get out of the situation, but his small platoon was ripped to shreds, with Ryan catching shrapnel in his thigh and Brenna having his ankle torn by shrapnel.[3]

Battle Fatigue

Across the island the troops were now exhausted. LRDG reported, 'By this time all troops were very tired and suffering from lack of sleep and food coupled with almost continual and terrific bombing. No support could be given to the defenders by the Royal Air Force who could not operate fighters so far from their bases. Supplies were dropped on the island by night but sufficient quantities of sorely needed ammunition could not be provided by air.'[4] Reverend Reg Anwyl had been ministering to the shattered troops and remembered, 'I can see and recall first and foremost the incredible weariness which blanketed mind and body.'[5] Deserters were increasing, with men hiding out in ruined buildings, in the mountains or taking refuge in caves. One of the drivers moving the wounded deserted, so did the one sent to take his place.[6] The fear of getting blown up was justified, as Anwyl saw: 'The next driver was a very brave lad and made some very useful journeys before his jeep was blown up with him and a load of wounded on board.'[7] Generally, though, Anwyl says, 'It was cheering to see that few wounds were serious and to notice the courage of the men themselves.'[8] Bombing became so heavy that the men were trapped in their positions, either in caves or slit trenches. Anwyl sat on the floor, too tired to move, until his fear was succeeded by 'paralysis of the mind and atrophy of the emotions'.[9]

Sleep deprivation was becoming a big problem for the soldiers who had been fighting non-stop for three days, grabbing a couple of hours here and there as they could. Most of the British troops were experiencing battle fatigue. Private Paddy McCrystal recalled, 'Lucky if you got a day's rest. I didn't get no sleep for a month in Leros.'[10] For others the lack of knowledge of the terrain and lack of communication was frightening. Signals failed to work properly because of the mountains. Other lines of communications were severed as the enemy cut field cables that had been run on the ground. Messages failed to get through and nobody seemed to know what was happening in any area except their own. The last method of passing information, through runners and whistles, was becoming increasingly hopeless as men failed to get through enemy lines. Furthermore the battle lines were constantly changing.

Brigadier Tilney and the rest of the commanding officers were finding it impossible to give appropriate orders in scenes which were experiencing continual flux. Browne added, 'Fortress Head Quarters themselves had difficulty in keeping track of everybody and exercising effective control over their movements in a mobile situation when the line between ourselves and the enemy was constantly changing.'[11] Because of the poor physical condition of the majority of the soldiers and the continuous heavy bombing, the Allies would be unable to score decisively against the enemy during the day. Meanwhile, 170 German prisoners had been sent off to Samos during the previous night as another company of Royal West Kents landed. The Germans were, at the same time, bringing in important reinforcements at Alinda Bay. They were estimated at 1,000 fighting troops and had 88-mm guns, tractors and other heavy equipment.[12]

Food was running low for the men stuck up in the mountains, and the men became increasingly worn out as the battle raged on. Clifford Clarke recalled, 'The troops generally were getting pretty tired. They were on a battering day and night from the air. No-one could oppose them. We knew we were not going to get reinforcements, which meant we ought to have done something straight away [...] No rations were coming up [...]'[13] Despite trying to stay awake, after a couple of nights without sleep, most men began dropping off against their will. Clarke said, 'Sleep is odd, anyone can go one night without it, you can go two nights if you have sufficient impetus, danger, but with the great majority of people, the third night they will fall asleep.'[14]

The lack of ammunition became more apparent as it was spent in the fighting. Clarke recalled, 'I had plenty, but generally, especially those who had gone out, carrying what they wanted, were getting short of ammo.'[15] Major Ewart William Tassell with the Buffs recalled, 'We were carrying very little [...] [on the] scrounge really. There were no survival kits as I remember. Very little ammunition. Only what the troops could carry. Not much sleep, No. We were sleeping on the floor. We hadn't got anything, only what we stood up in and what we could carry.'[16] Lack of ammunition was a continuing problem. 'A great friend of mine, Captain [Jack] Green, who was then combined with the 3-inch mortar platoon, had arrived there with his rather depleted platoon. I think they had got mortars themselves, but no bombs.'[17]

Sometime on the 15th, during the day, all the troops moved off Rachi Ridge as the enemy had moved on further south and more protection was needed on Meraviglia. Private Peter Anthony Barham heard of the move, as he was in charge of signalling on Searchlight Hill. He recalled, 'I think the Germans had moved off too in the night. I think they were going to Mount Meraviglia – the main objective was where our headquarters was [...] We had an officer with us – Lieutenant Groom I think was his name. We landed up on a road where they supplied us with a meal [...] I should say there was about 300-odd, having a meal.'[18] Along the way, he managed to lose his company.

Unfortunately I wanted some water and they didn't have any there. I thought we had passed a pond with water a couple of hundred yards back. It wasn't accessible. By then, on the other side of the road there was some Greek people, and I said 'Water, water', or 'Aqua' whatever it was and they kindly produced – they filled up my water bottle.

By the time he had returned to his position, the rest of his company had gone. 'My wireless set was there, I'd left it there. I had no idea where they were going. So that was a bit awkward [...] I remember carting a great big box of these compo rations – quite heavy it was, on top of the wireless set and that. They'd issued us with battledress not long before.'[19]

He was left completely alone, not knowing what to do. 'I wandered down the road. I didn't know which way they had gone, and I eventually was getting a bit tired so I tried to go to sleep. People coming in, must have been company HQ or something, had to get out then. At that time the battle was over [...] All the stragglers, one lot going one way, one lot going the other, and another lot wanted to stay. We didn't know, we were all lost.'[20]

For Royal Irish Fusilier Ted Johnson, everything seemed in confusion: communications were patchy, orders were overridden by Tilney, who was not following the proper chain of command, and little progress was being made. On 15 November, Ted was fighting on Rachi Ridge with his platoon of Royal Irish Fusiliers. 'My right hand section was stopped almost immediately by enemy fire who had allowed the West Kents to pass over them. But my centre section with Sergeant Wallace made uninterrupted progress up the line of advance and Fusilier O'Neill with the left hand section also made good progress for about two hundred yards when he came under fire from a house ahead.'[21] At this stage he lost contact with Wallace. He could only see about 15 yards ahead because of the rocks and undergrowth.

Lieutenant Johnson recalled, 'At this stage of the fight I had managed somehow to scrounge some Benzedrine which kept me from succumbing to sleep, but my soldiers were by now very weary and, apart from the odd rum issue and much sweet tea taken during the hours of darkness back in our company positions, had nothing to sustain them from falling asleep wherever they lay down.'[22] The enemy was using coloured lights to indicate where the firing should be aimed, with great German swastika flags laid out on the ground to indicate their own positions.

Shell Shock and Death

The situation had become progressively worse as the battle raged on. Men's fear and concerns about their own survival grew, as did the decline in their physical condition. The continual bombing inevitably took its toll – not knowing where a bomb might drop was enough to shred most men's nerves. A number of them developed 'battle neurosis' referred to as being 'bomb-happy', as Raymond Williams recalled.

> These unfortunate individuals went to pieces the moment they heard the air-raid siren wailing the alert. The repeated dive-bombing of the past weeks had completely unnerved them. The worst cases were shipped back to the Middle East for medical treatment at Base-Hospital,

as their unstable behaviour under attack didn't help the rest of the garrison.[23]

Some of the officers were less sympathetic, mainly because they did not then know the medical condition of shell shock. Lieutenant Clifford Clarke recalled, 'One chap with shell shock in Leros, I thought he was just a coward. If I'd have known it was shell shock, I would have treated him more leniently. To us, he was letting us down.'[24] Fusilier Paddy McCrystal recalled, 'There was a lot of them that lost their heads when they came over, with the constant bombing. Shell shock. I couldn't tell you what happened. Most of them, they sent home.'[25]

Shell shock affected officers, not just the lower ranks, and some of the men were so badly affected by the bombings they could no longer fight. Ted Johnson recalled,

They couldn't take it. One or two officers as well, not just soldiers. They had to be evacuated as those sort of people become a liability. When we came to the eyeball-to-eyeball fight, there were even more people, it was discovered, who were not capable of taking it. By the time we got to Leros it was too late to sort out the bad ones. We had to try and soldier on with the material we had there. All one could do was to do the best by example, and hope the rest would follow you.[26]

Lack of leadership invariably created problems. Ted Johnson surmised,

If the officers don't behave properly you can't expect the men to behave properly. On another attack I was involved in, it was held up for an hour while a search was made for one young officer to control his platoon. He wasn't found, so alternative arrangement had to be made for the attack. There was no promotion in the field. If an officer was missing, the platoon sergeant would have to take over and do as best he could.[27]

Some soldiers failed to back the officers, as they were either too tired, too bedraggled or simply fearful for their lives and wanted to avoid getting shot. Ted led some men into battle only to find few of them had actually followed him.

I remember on one occasion I had an attack to do, I think it was on about the third or fourth day of the battle, I gave out my orders for what was to happen and, as it were, we went over the top to bag the thing. I looked round and there weren't many people with me. There were a lot of people who should have been close to me who weren't there anymore. That was a bit unnerving. But we got to the end of the thing, we managed to get through it. The morale of some of the chaps was definitely low because they had such a bad time in Malta.[28]

Other men showed extraordinary heroism. One man, Sergeant Doyle, crept round mines to rescue a Greek woman who had had her legs blown off, risking his own life. She was writhing in agony on the ground and could have set off a mine at any moment, but, with no thought except to save her, he went out to get talking to her, all the while trying to calm her. Fusilier Jack Harte recalled, 'As we watched in horror, there was little we could do, whether to stop him or to help the distraught woman. Any action could trigger a mine, making a bad situation worse.' Doyle inched his way towards her, made the nearest mine safe, then picked up her mangled body and took her to safety.[29]

As a medical orderly with the Royal Irish Fusiliers, Vic Kenchington helped tend the wounded and operated as a stretcher-bearer. 'Corporal Roberts and Fr Alwyl, the Catholic padre, were with us, all together in the slit trench. The padre visited all the wounded. He would give them the last rites. The other person there was the MO, Captain Barber – he tended the wounded at the RAP.' There was an ADS at Portolargo. 'We patched them up and took them down there. Several got evacuated with the Royal Navy. Another 25 of our regiment were injured enough to be evacuated. There was also an advanced dressing station at Alinda covering the north side of beach. When the Germans landed, that got cut off. We had five days with no sleep. We had no food.'[30]

One of the men in his unit was left for 36 hours before they found him.

We were told where he was and I went out to pick him up with two other stretcher-bearers. He was really badly injured, as he had been hit in the buttocks and legs. On seeing him, he kept asking could I please give him something to put him to sleep; all I could give him was five minims of morphine. I cut his clothes away, and the buttock wound was just a mass of maggots; he also had a compound fracture of his femur. I left the maggots and dressed his buttock wound with two shell dressings, put a dressing on his thigh, put him on the stretcher, tied a rifle sling on his ankle and to the handle of the stretcher. I gave him another shot of morphine, as we had a long walk back to the Military Intelligence room, as we were behind enemy lines, and had to make a devious route back.[31]

Captain Lawson, the MO for the LRDG, made an attempt at sanitation, and medical attention for the many in need. The bodies of those killed in the area were given a temporary burial in the bomb shelters and craters, and an aid post established.[32] Reverend Anwyl arranged the funerals after Mass in the evenings. Because of the bombing, digging graves for the dead had to be done after dark. Transport was limited and he had to wait for a jeep to come along 'and in the light of a bright moon, we buried those who died that day'.[33] But that was not always possible once the battle made serious headway. Then casualties grew dramatically.

Jack Barber ordered stretcher-bearers to follow the advancing troops. Men went in at different speeds and were bearing the brunt of the war differently. Reverend Anwyl noticed,

> The brave or foolhardy pressed forward like children going to the circus or a party, who were afraid to be late and so miss something. The majority moved on as one might expect, neither hurrying nor hanging back – these too were brave, but had no room for heroics. Finally there were a few who made strenuous efforts to fall to the rear without seeming to do so; they remained crouching or prostrate after a bomb burst, a little longer than was necessary, they stumbled rather obviously over the walls and sure enough, I saw those who had been leading one minute, bringing up the rear another. Let no-one scoff at these men – they too were brave or some of them at least, since their fear was greatest yet they too went forward.[34]

Deserters were becoming numerous as the hopelessness of the situation became increasingly evident. Anwyl recalled, 'Two stretcher-bearers refused point blank an order to go out on some mission because the bombing had increased.'[35] Some men were too tired to walk. Some of the officers, including Reverend Anwyl and Ted Johnson, were given more Benzedrine to help them stay awake. Reverend Anwyl found out the bad news of Lieutenant Colonel French's death. 'Bill Robertson was killed too. Terry Bourke, Tom Massey-Lynch, Prior and Mason came in wounded but not seriously'. Two more officers were killed, one being Hugh Gore-Booth, 'shy brilliant Hugh whom we had teased so much'.[36]

Major Ewart William Tassell was leading the Buffs in action when his sergeant major got hit. 'It was very difficult because we were bearing forward and he'd been hit in the stomach. We had two stretcher-bearers attached to the HQ medical team. So I said, "We'll try and take him forward" and they said, "Well, we don't really like to move him" and eventually we had to leave him behind which I didn't like much. But I believe he eventually got into this hospital.'[37] In most cases, there was little they could do for the wounded in the middle of the fighting, nor was there time to check if a man was dead or alive.

> We were moving all the time. Nothing like trench warfare, a very open business. For instance, I remember we came across all sorts of slit trenches which the Irish Fusiliers had dug and had been overrun and the trench had got two or three Irish men in there. I am afraid we didn't stop to see, because we'd got to keep going.[38]

Distressing sights of dead or dying men affected the remaining soldiers. A sickly aroma of fetid bodies filled the air. Some men were seen wandering around with bits of their body shot off desperately trying to find medical treatment. 'One particular instance I encountered was that of an Infantry Captain who had been blinded in the day's action, stumbling pitifully around like a lost child with a bloodstained dressing tied round his eyes.'[39]

Ted Johnson recalled that there was simply no time to deal with the bodies of his fellow soldiers.

> Many of the men who were killed were not moved until after the battle. They were left because you can't just stop and deal with a casualty. If you've got a job to do in the way of attacking a position, that is your primary job, and if someone is killed beside you, you have to leave them. When I did the first counter attack in Appetici with my platoon, one of my senior NCOs, a chap called Sergeant Caldwell, he was beside me. We'd got up to the first Italian gun position to try and observe what was further on where we had to go and he was shot through the head standing right behind me, and I couldn't do anything about it. I had to go on. I couldn't waste time with him unfortunately. Luckily he was killed outright so he wasn't just wounded. That shook me.[40]

Sergeant Caldwell's body was not dealt with until many days after the battle – he had no known grave, but he is now marked on the Athens war memorial. He had fallen in an Italian gun emplacement in a concrete bunker and must have been there for the next few days and somehow was not gathered up with the other bodies. Lieutenant Johnson recalled, 'I had two chaps in my platoon who have no known graves. Another chap killed up on Meraviglia, he was never recorded [...] We didn't do any of the burial at all. The Germans organised that at the end of the battle with Italian labour, I believe. We weren't involved.'[41]

As the bodies of soldiers piled up, everyone's main concern was keeping the Germans at bay, as Lieutenant Clifford Clarke recalled.

No-one cared about any bodies. You weren't starting digging them in or burying them. There was always a smell, and a smell of cordite and all the explosions. Don't forget they were shelling, there were bombs dropping. The bodies weren't rotting, they weren't rotting. They would have done eventually. You don't think about it. It's a job you've got to do there [...] You had to get used to it.[42]

Royal West Kents: Straight into Battle

The first call had been put out on 13 November for Queen's Own Royal West Kents to be sent to assist in the battle on Leros. Tilney had contacted GOC Aegean HQ asking them to send all available British reinforcements to Leros as soon as possible. Only six days earlier the island of Samos had been reinforced with 300 trained troops of the Greek Sacred Squadron.[43] Orders were finally given for the Battalion HQ, A and D companies (B Company was already on Leros fighting under Captain Percy Flood) to move towards the port of Pythagorian on Samos, with all their equipment ready to embark on two minesweepers and sail to Leros. The weather was so stormy, and the hour so late by the time they had got their equipment on board, the naval command gave them orders to unload as it would be impossible to deposit the troops on Leros and then reach Turkey that night. The soldiers had no alternative but to unload and return to their battle positions.[44] They would not come in until the following night of 14th/15th; the two remaining companies of Royal West Kents followed in landing in Portolago on 15/16 November.[45] One report stated 'The Royal West Kents came into the battle relatively fresh but unfortunately and unavoidably piecemeal.'[46] This meant that they did not have a concrete and solid unit under which to fight.

Lieutenant Clifford Clarke was already established in Leros when the rest of his battalion were moved in. 'The only reinforcements we eventually got were the rest of our battalion, the second battalion, who were at Samos and we put out a signal to get what help we could, and the rest of that battalion sailed down to us and met with disaster because by that time it was too late.'[47] It was a stressful crossing not simply because of the weather but because of the dangers of sailing when being preyed upon by enemy aircraft circling overhead. Sergeant George Hatcher had also come in early and was with Lieutenant Clarke with the arrival of the first small unit of Royal West Kents from Castelorizo. He too remembered when other members of their troops landed in the middle of the battle. 'About the second or third day, they brought the rest of our battalion from Samos. They landed in Alinda Bay, but of course by that time the Germans were very well entrenched and they got beat up pretty badly and that's where we lost most of our men.'[48] Other companies which had embarked on a journey to Leros were caught up in the storm and swept straight past the island, hiding in Turkish waters during the day and not arriving at Portolago (Lakki) until midnight of 14 November.[49] Peter Anthony Barham was with them. After a quick sleep and some breakfast, the soldiers were pushed straight into battle. 'We landed in Portolago. I think it was near Portolago [where we slept that night of 14th/15th]. We then had to go to a place where we formed up. We had breakfast.'[50] He recalled, 'I was attached to A Company which was about 90 men in the company, three battalions of about 30, at the headquarters.' '[...] I wasn't actually in the attacking as I was a signalman and I stayed at the top of the Searchlight Hill.'[51] Luckily for Barham he was in charge of communications he was not involved in direct fighting. However, because of the mountain ranges, signals could not always get through and communications were frequently lost.

Lieutenant Richard James of Queen's Own Royal Engineers had been on Samos when he got the call to bring his troops to Leros, the battle having already raged for three days. He recalled, 'It was a very hazardous journey. There was German air attacks, on the boats moving there.' Each company landed at a different time, leaving them at a disadvantage as they were no longer a coherent fighting unit. He recalled, 'The battalion arrived piecemeal on Leros. One company, A Company I think it was, had moved in earlier; B Company moved in later, and C Company and HQ Company moved in separately. So we didn't arrive there as a battalion.'[52] The troops coming in from Samos were in the unenviable position of coming straight into a battle. Lieutenant Richard James recalled,

> HMS *Frobisher* took us to Leros. Second-in-command was a chap called Fitz. He was a close friend of my elder brother's, also in the Royal Navy. We got into Leros and went to HQ and saw Fitz there. 'Whatever are you doing here?' [James asked]. We were in the final defence at Meraviglia in this 'Tom and Jerry' situation. 'I came out to help you out here,' [replied Fitz.] [...] We got the call to move down to new positions and left him where he was. I learnt later he'd been killed in the position we had left.[53]

Lieutenant James was immediately thrown into combat.

> Fighting began pretty furiously for about five days. I was with Colonel Tarleton. We went several times to island command [Headquarters] which was in the mountain in Meraviglia. It hasn't got very good memories for me. There was an attack launched along Alinda Bay. It was a very fierce and costly attack in terms of men. Every officer in the companies attacking was either hit or killed, except yours truly who was not hit. This was done largely by snipers.

He recalled one man, 'Drummer' Brown, who managed to get drunk every time he was out of sight of an officer. 'Three times when we were at the docks, he managed to get drink. Once I got him onto the ship sober, but then he got in with the sailors and got drunk with them.' Nonetheless Brown went on to excel in action. 'He and I set off to eliminate these snipers. We managed to achieve that and I am glad to say he got a military medal for it and that's why I won my Military Cross. It was a hell of a battle, we retreated up Meraviglia.'[54] Sometime later as the battle became more confused, Lieutenant James received orders to move south of Leros. 'We had orders to move off the Meraviglia heights right down the road to Portolago and up to the other side of Leros. By that time, there weren't many men still available. We were down to about 60 or something like that. Others were scattered in other places [...] Major Shore who was a splendid chap, he got shot on that road near the harbour.'[55]

John Browne recognised that the Royal West Kents were at a distinct disadvantage. 'With companies arriving unpredictably at different times and places, the battalion was never able to fight as a unit, and it was difficult to coordinate our activities with other units who had been engaged there since the battle started three days ago.'[56] Browne and his company came in on the destroyer HMS *Echo* arriving at Portolago at 4.30 a.m. on 15 November. He remembered how uncomfortable it was.

> An important factor in all our travels was the enormous weight of gear each man had to carry. There was no room to dump any of our kit on the deck of the *Echo*. It all had to remain lashed to us, otherwise it was sure to be lost. Each man – and his kit – spent the night wedged into any available space on deck. The speed at which we travelled kept the whole ship in constant vibration, and the noise made it impossible to speak.[57]

As Browne landed with his unit, before they could do anything else, they had to dig slit trenches to protect themselves from what would be a constant stream of overhead enemy aircraft. Two other companies of Royal West Kents were already dug in to the narrowest part of Rachi Ridge between Alinda and Gourna. Browne felt totally out of place. 'We were strangers, knowing nothing of the terrain, dazed and bewildered by the suddenness of recent events, and by lack of sleep.' The recently arrived Royal West Kents were tired as they had been travelling over two nights, and their arrival in the middle of the chaos left them stunned.

That night, HMSs *Echo* and *Belvoir* needed protection while transporting the troops. Assistance was requested from the navy who duly arrived at Alinda at dusk with HMSs *Penn*, *Aldenham* and *Blencathra*. They attacked the enemy positions from the sea, firing on three enemy caiques in the bay. HMS *Penn* searched for landing craft reported in Leros, while under repeated attack by enemy glider bombers, but failed to find any, yet bombarded Alinda for about 15 minutes. MTBs joined in patrols of the area with HMS *Echo* which had returned from Portolago, and attacked an enemy force approaching Alinda Bay, sinking a fighter and landing barges full of troops. HMSs *Echo* and *Belvoir* had been continuously shadowed and bombed round the north and west coast of Samos, so *Belvoir* took shelter on the Turkish coast, but *Echo* increased her speed and hurried on. The remainder of HQ Company, having been obliged to lay up in Turkish waters, arrived on the *Belvoir* during the night of the 15th. The troops were transferred on to MTBs and minesweepers.

Company D only made it later that evening after her destroyer had been damaged in a close miss and the troop had switched to a fleet of five MTBs and a minesweeper.[58] One official view reported, 'The success of the final attempt to reach Leros was due entirely to the calm efficiency of the Royal Navy and the speed with which they completed a very risky task,' one which John Browne and his comrades fully endorsed.[59]

War correspondent Gander watched as the troops disembarked from HMS *Echo* during the night of 15 November – 187 men shuttling off the ship.

> Rapidly, methodically, wooden chutes were run down over the ship's side on to the wharf. Then heavily burdened soldiers with packs, helmets, rifles and other weapons came sliding down on their rumps. They were so weighted down that many could not stagger to their feet, and the Italian dock labourers waiting had to help them up, to get each man out of the way of the next man slithering behind.[60]

They came off rapidly – speed was of the essence before the enemy could spot them. Boxes and boxes of ammunition came shooting down after them.

The destroyer was set to take Gander to Cairo that evening so he could get his story out. He was glad to be leaving the island but was concerned about getting bombed. Despite being continually shadowed during the night of 14/15 November and bombed from time to time by the enemy aircraft, HMSs *Penn* and *Echo* continued at the ready to intercept any possible enemy landings. However, the lack of radio communication in Leros meant that reports of enemy landing craft had to go through Alexandria and arrived too late for HMS *Penn* to prevent them.[61]

Another man from the Royal West Kents who came into the battle but never saw much action was Private Sid Bowden. He had also travelled across from Samos. 'I can remember a Corporal Martin. I've got a feeling he was in our company but there were different platoons, and our battalion arrived on the island about the third day. I think it was D Company that arrived on the third day and the other companies arrived on the fourth day. We were told they had arrived from Samos, but we didn't link up with any of them.'[62] He and his company had arrived in the middle of the battle but needed feeding before action. 'I can remember that clearly as we were quite hungry. We had had only the bits and pieces I had the first two days, then when we moved out, they took us to a cook house and we were issued with soup but there were snipers all round and we had to be a bit careful. That was our company headquarters. Halfway up the mountain. Bully beef and biscuits.'[63]

Sid Bowden ended up in hospital after his arm became infected shortly after he had arrived. 'After 3 days [...] I could hardly move my arm. It was all swollen up and I was sent to the hospital where they operated on it.'[64] He thought he was taken to Alinda to the makeshift hospital at Villa Bellini. The army doctors there did what they could; Bowden recalled, 'They operated on my hand. I was put on sedatives. Several nights they were evacuating the wounded from there. I remember when one of our lads came in. I think it was Bert Simpson, one of the West Kents. He died that night. I think he was one of the aircraft casualties as far as I knew. There was about six of us in the hospital, only army medical helping.' Private Bowden thought there were women acting as nurses helping in the hospitals, 'I don't know if it was the same hospital or what, but there was nuns down there attending the wounded. I don't know where it was. It was so vague at that time. It could have been a hospital in a different place, or it might have been a nunnery.' He was put under general anaesthetic and had a drip put into his hand to drain out the poison; 'it was up like a football. Some said I'd been bitten and others said I had a thorn. It was a bit painful.'[65]

By the time Sid Bowen was discharged from hospital with his arm bandaged up, the island was in chaos. He tried to get back to his own company, but by this time it was dark and everyone had dispersed.

> When they discharged me [...] I was just told to try and get back to my own company. And this was in the dark, in the evening. Anyhow, I met some Long Range Desert Group chaps who put me on the right track and told me where my company was, which I reported to the company HQ. I still had my hand all bandaged up. One of the officers said, well, I think the best thing that you can do is go down [...] I was put down in a small bay.[66]

He was put in an Italian gun position in a slit trench in the south and given a Bren gun and told to defend; they then brought him some food down. While Sid Bowden had been in hospital the battle had got underway.

The Enemy Closes In

At the beginning of day four of the fighting on 15 November there had been a plan. The newly arrived commanding officer of Queen's Own Royal West Kents, Lieutenant Colonel Ben Tarleton, went to Fortress Headquarters at 6.30 a.m. for a briefing with the brigadier. Tilney lay down the main objectives for the day: the first was for a northward attack on Rachi Ridge to be made by the weakened and exhausted King's Own from Searchlight Hill, invigorated by the newly arrived A Company Queen's Own Royal West Kents. This coupling was thrown into the battle rather haphazardly, since the units neither knew each other nor had trained together. Meanwhile D Company of Buffs were to continue clearing Germans from Alinda and San Nicola, along with whichever Royal West Kents were available. C Company of Queen's Own Royal West Kents and various Royal Irish Fusiliers, now weakened with fatigue, were ordered to attack Rachi and south of Alinda under Major Mike Read. Major Robert Butler briefed his men to come up on the other side of the ridge. King's Own and Royal Irish Fusiliers were to provide supporting cover with small-arms fire. Major Bill Shepherd with a composite of leftover men had orders to go to Agia Marina following C Company to mop up enemy resistance.

By 8.30 a.m. on the 15th, the Germans were well prepared and opened fire on A Company north of Searchlight Hill with all they had – sniper fire, mortars, dive-bombing Stukas. The noise was deafening as the bombs exploded all around. King's Own and Royal Irish Fusiliers had to withdraw to Searchlight Hill. Four men were killed, including Victor Hewitt and company Sergeant Major Frederick Spooner. It was only later that George Hatcher heard that his friends had been killed. 'I didn't know what the casualties were until I came out of the island. I heard Sergeant Major Spooner had been killed; he was one of the first to be killed. You only heard vaguely. You never heard anything official.'[67]

After the first attack, a second attack was quickly planned for Rachi Ridge to follow up at 2.30 that afternoon. Tilney was adding to the confusion as he continued to ignore the chain of command and had telephoned Lieutenant Johnson of the Irish Fusiliers at the Battery HQ of the Bofors and ordered that all available men should be collected and meet up with the commanding officer of the Royal West Kents at the fork in the roads south of Platanos. Lieutenant Colonel Tarleton of Royal West Kents went out in a jeep around 1.15 p.m. to round up the remnants of C Company and pull them together for the next attack. He found his men just south of Platanos. In the event, the attack was delayed as they had to wait for the exhausted men from the Royal Irish Fusiliers to join them. Those in the left flank had been ordered to move along the ridge about 600 yards inland, and the middle section were to be filled out by the reserve platoon. Meanwhile, at around 2 p.m., Lieutenant Austin Ardill had been waiting for Lieutenant Johnson with his platoon of Royal Irish Fusiliers, as he had been told by HQ that another platoon were coming down from the Windmill area to strengthen their force. Despite waiting 45 minutes, no-one turned up so the remaining 16 men made their way to rendezvous with the Royal West Kents as the brigadier had ordered. However, a new plan had been formed by the time he got there: the Royal West Kents were to take the ground lying between Meraviglia and Agia Marina. As fighting progressed, fewer and fewer men were left to make up platoons. The remaining soldiers were combining to form composite units, as many were left without leaders. While these groups of Royal West Kents were moving forward, C Company of Royal Irish Fusiliers were following on mopping up the straggling resistance.

Major Robert Butler was leading A Company of Royal West Kents on Rachi Ridge that day; his second-in-command, Captain William Grimshaw, was the only other officer available in his unit. Peter Anthony Barham recalled his Royal West Kents unit being taken to Rachi Ridge where they were supposed to attack. 'There was a German post at the end of Rachi Ridge and we were supposed to attack that via the mouth. I think they had been charged; I don't think they actually cleared the German position. We went there where they had parachuted. We went there till the 15th; they had

had time to settle in [...] Major Butler led the attack.'[68] As a signalman, Barham was not actually in the attack but stayed on the top of Searchlight Hill morsing out information. 'Major Butler was over A Company [...] I think Grimshaw was the second-in-command [...] He was the one who drew my attention, when I was on Searchlight Hill, to these bombs which had bounced over Mount Meraviglia. These bombs were going round and round and landing in the bay.'[69] Light machine guns were grouped along Searchlight Hill under Lieutenant Groom. The right flank of the platoon pushed on along the road hugging the coast of Alinda, lying in ditches as enemy planes hovered. Only the Italian anti-aircraft batteries were left to defend them. Platoon 13 lost its commander, when Lieutenant Jode, wounded, was replaced by Sergeant Wallington. Private F. White was also wounded. They continued under heavy sniper fire emanating from the houses occupied by Germans but cleared a path through Krethoni. Part of Platoon 14 led by Lieutenant R. Norris had gone astray and not been able to follow up as expected. They now moved forward for the attack. Only 60 men of B and C companies and Platoon 17 of D Company of Royal Irish Fusiliers were left to provide back-up to C Company Royal West Kents.[70] Captain J.W. Salter and Lieutenant J. Duffy of B Company turned up to assist, with another two officers and 19 men.

In the centre attack on Rachi from reserve platoon was Lieutenant John Browne leading the Royal West Kents, with Mike Read his commanding officer. The attack began at 3.30 p.m. on the 15th under a barrage of Stukas diving and aiming fire at the British soldiers. The enemy was on their right flank which the Royal West Kents had seemingly passed through. The middle and left flank made some headway. None of those following the Royal West Kents had actually made any contact with them. No-one could see further than 15 yards ahead as the rocks and growth blocked the view. During the advance, Read was wounded and could not move, but instructed his men to push on, with Eddie Newbald taking over as commanding officer. Men were spread out about 10 yards between them to reduce the risk of snipers or bombs hitting them.[71]

Two other companies were already situated in the narrowest part of the ridge between Alinda and Gourna. Browne's Platoon 15 was instructed to move up the only available road from Portolago to Platanos, where they could overlook Alinda Bay and ensure their comrades had arrived at their intended positions and achieved their objectives through the sightings of their Verey lights. Once they had signalled, Browne and his company were instructed to drive round the shore of Alinda Bay to the road junction near St Nicola Church and join up with D Company of Buffs fighting the enemy in San Nicola.[72] At around 4.15 p.m., Browne's platoon attained their objective, killing many of the enemy and taking 25 German prisoners. However, Browne was soon to become one of the casualties when he was shot in the chest. He recalled, 'Neither would cause any pain at the time, but the chest wound flattened me with a thump like the rap of a hammer, and left me gasping for breath, believing that my end had come. I had a crushing sense of how much of my twenty eight years of life had been wasted, and that, if there was any more of it, it must be better used.'[73]

These times of serious injury nearly always led to reflection for those soldiers it affected. Browne would muse, 'The awareness of time misused and opportunities thrown away has often recurred, but never so painfully sharp and bitter as it was then. This experience of serenity on one hand and waste on the other was my preview of heaven and hell.'[74] A couple of orderlies bandaged him up and took him to a nearby house, along with two other wounded, Private Chuter and Private Mountford. The Royal West Kents had captured two main areas (Point 100 and Point 36) but would be unable to hold them. They were being bombarded, realised they desperately needed back-up and sent a runner to send more men and Bren guns to assist. However, their commanding officer refused to protect their position and they were forced to withdraw to Searchlight Hill. The position was now left clear for the enemy to retake Points 100 and 36, and all those deaths and injuries appeared to be for nothing. Major Butler was incensed. He was wounded in his right leg, and Captain Grimshaw had been wounded in the wrist. Private Chuter was to die later in the hospital. Browne had gone back to take him some tomato juice when he found him. 'He was peaceful, and there had been no sound or sign of death. A regular soldier, 27 or 28 years old, he had been serving overseas for at least five years, cut off from family and

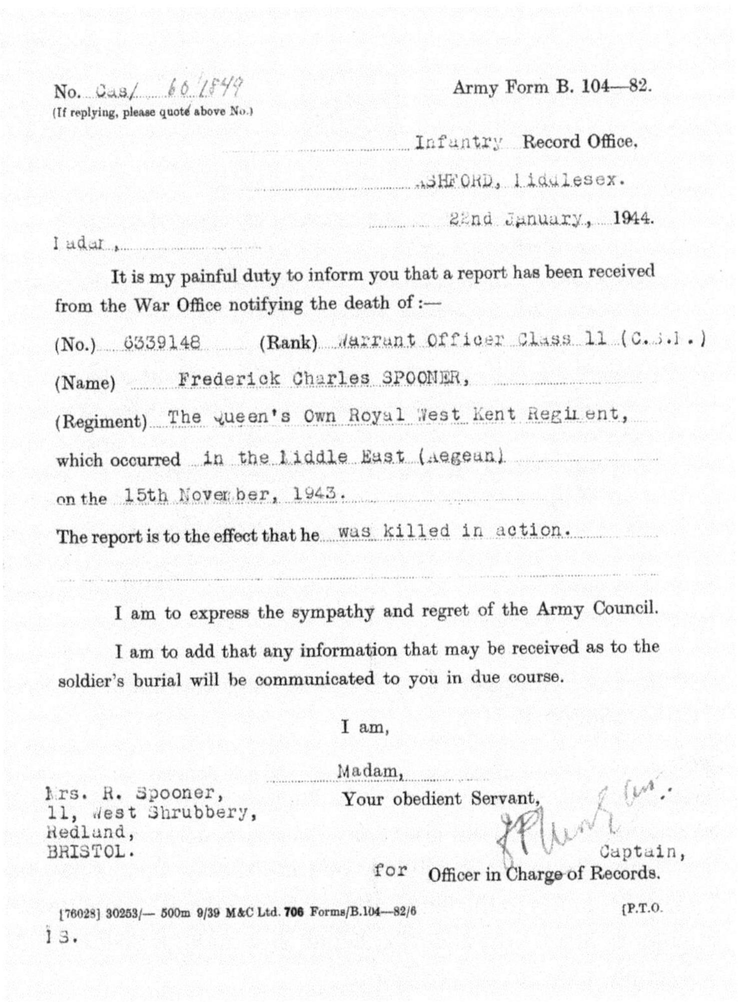

No. Cas/ 60/1849   Army Form B. 104—82.
(If replying, please quote above No.)

                                        Infantry   Record Office,

                                        ASHFORD, Middlesex.

                                        22nd January, 1944.

I adar ,

     It is my painful duty to inform you that a report has been received
from the War Office notifying the death of :—

(No.)   6339148   (Rank) Warrant Officer Class 11 (C.S.M.)

(Name)   Frederick Charles SPOONER,

(Regiment) The Queen's Own Royal West Kent Regiment,

which occurred in the Middle East (Aegean)

on the 15th November, 1943.

The report is to the effect that he was killed in action.

     I am to express the sympathy and regret of the Army Council.

     I am to add that any information that may be received as to the
soldier's burial will be communicated to you in due course.

            I am,

            Madam,

Mrs. R. Spooner,   Your obedient Servant,
11, West Shrubbery,
Redland,
BRISTOL.
                          Captain,
          for   Officer in Charge of Records.

[76028] 30253/— 500m 9/39 M&C Ltd. 706 Forms/B.104—82/6   [P.T.O.
13.

FIGURE 11.1 Notification of death of Sergeant Major Frederick
R. Charles Spooner

friends, patiently enduring the hardships and uncertainties of army
life, and earning the respect of his comrades.'[75]

    By 4 p.m., B Company of Royal West Kents and D Company of
Buffs had resumed their attack on San Nicola, but they made limited
progress so were relieved by the LRDG. They had been waiting for

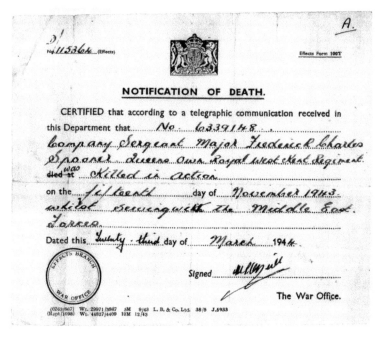

FIGURE 11.2 Notification of death of Sergeant Major Frederick R. Charles Spooner

Verey lights to let them know Rachi Ridge was in the hands of the British, but this signal did not come. Colonel Ben Tarleton suggested that at some point in the fighting, around the same time, Tilney had changed his orders to the Buffs and they were ordered to confine their activities to San Nicola and Villa Bellini area and not take Point 36. This simply added to the confusion.[76]

By about 7 p.m., many of the troops were dead or dispersed, but Captain Newbold pulled together C Company Queen's Own to pick up the wounded including Major Mike Read. Tarleton gave orders to Captain Donald Cropper to take charge of the defence positions. It was around 8 p.m., and he needed to speak with Brigadier Tilney directly, this being the only method to ensure clear communication with him. He took a jeep with his Intelligence Officer Lieutenant Jimmy James and met up with Lieutenants Groom and Norris who were also at Fortress HQ retelling the action which had taken place on

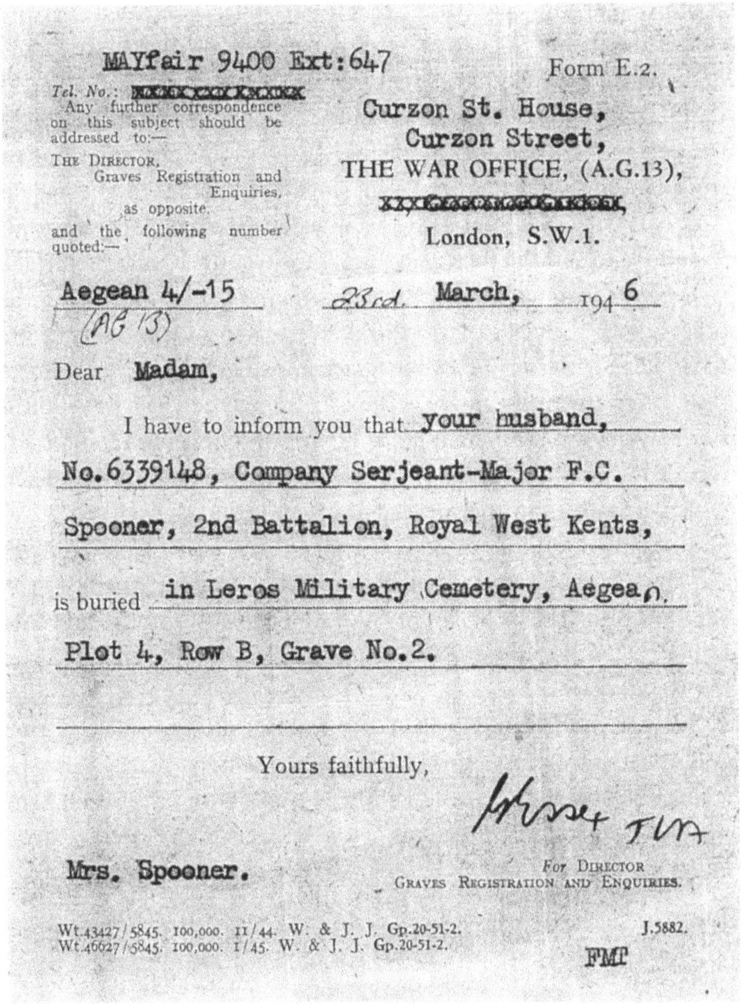

MAYfair 9400 Ext:647   Form E.2.

Tel. No.: ~~XXXXXXXXXX~~
Any further correspondence
on this subject should be   Curzon St. House,
addressed to:—   Curzon Street,
THE DIRECTOR,
Graves Registration and   THE WAR OFFICE, (A.G.13),
Enquiries,
as opposite.   ~~XXXXXXXXXXXXXX~~,
and the following number
quoted:—   London, S.W.1.

Aegean 4/-15   23rd March,   194 6
(AG 13)

Dear Madam,

        I have to inform you that your husband,

No.6339148, Company Serjeant-Major F.C.

Spooner, 2nd Battalion, Royal West Kents,

is buried   in Leros Military Cemetery, Aegean.

Plot 4, Row B, Grave No.2.

                    Yours faithfully,

Mrs. Spooner.   For DIRECTOR
                           GRAVES REGISTRATION AND ENQUIRIES.

Wt.43427/5845. 100,000. 11/44. W. & J. J. Gp.20-51-2.   J.5882.
Wt.46027/5845. 100,000. 1/45. W. & J. J. Gp.20-51-2.
                                                    FMT

FIGURE 11.3   War Office burial notification of Sergeant Major F.C.
Spooner, 23 March 1946

Rachi. At 8.30 p.m. Lieutenant Ardill and Lieutenant Duffy landed at
Captain Cropper's position with some men from Royal Irish Fusiliers.

By 9 p.m. the Germans were spotted on the road near Mount
Meraviglia. The Royal Irish Fusiliers in the area opened fire with Bren
guns but were forced to draw back up the slopes of the mountain.
Many of these casualties were caused by accurate bombing and

machine-gunning by the German aircraft. Confused fighting continued in many quarters after dark when two more companies of the Royal West Kent Regiment were put ashore from HMS *Belvoir* in Portolago Bay from Samos at around 11.30 p.m. They headed straight for Ankora led by Major G.V. Shaw. At the same time, the Germans were landing 280 men and some heavy weapons to the east of Appetici. This was to be the fatal batch of enemy coming into Platanos and skirting the village, moving towards HQ and Meraviglia.

Second Lieutenant Richard Austin 'Jimmy' James, the intelligence officer with Queen's Own Royal West Kents, was part of the reconnaissance group following up a company attack on Rachi Ridge, near Leros town. By now the houses lining the road were full of German snipers. Lieutenant James ran forward under fire and found a secure position from which the group could observe the attack. Then, with a private from the Intelligence Section, he cleared the houses and disposed of the snipers.[77] The enemy were flanking them. Captain Cropper ordered a withdrawal but was hit in the eye by shrapnel and had to make for the RAP but was captured en route. Captain C.M. Bernard was also wounded and had only about 12 men left standing.

The end of the day saw the British troops withdrawing from Rachi and Appetici and the Germans overrunning both points. By this time, soldiers of A and C companies of the Queen's Own Royal West Kents who had landed only the night before were nearly all dead.

12

Final Day of the Battle

We were coming up towards the Headquarters and there was a sort of scrapping, trying to go ahead but there was such little information as to what we had on either flank, we didn't really know.

Major Ewart William Tassell, Buffs[1]

The LRDG had been doing their utmost to halt the oncoming enemy. In the early hours of 16 November, reports came through that the Germans were moving down from Alinda towards them. Lieutenant Colonel Jake Easonsmith had gone with his LRDG unit towards Leros town (Platanos) to prevent the enemy coming further south but was caught by a sniper and killed instantly.[2] According to one of his men, he was 'brave, wise, with an uprightedness that shames lesser men' and was considered by many as the finest man to have ever served in the LRDG.[3] Guy Prendergast assumed his place as commanding officer of LRDG.

At the same time, the last reserve of Germans, an estimated 1,200 troops with heavy equipment and ammunition, were coming onto Appetici from a ferry lighter and four landing craft.[4] After hours of fighting, Platoon 9 of Royal Irish Fusiliers would be overrun at 4.14 that afternoon, and the Germans would gain Appetici and Castle Hill. The way was clear for the enemy to push forward to Mount Meraviglia through Platanos and make their way to Fortress Headquarters. From the other side of HQ, the German soldiers previously on Rachi had moved forward to the slopes of Meraviglia towards Leros town.[5] All the energy of the Allied troops on Meraviglia and in the surrounding area was diverted to the defence of Fortress HQ.

Germans on Meraviglia

The Royal West Kents congregated at Ankora (the Anchor feature at the crossroads in the middle of the island) at 1 a.m. that night as Lieutenant Colonel Ben Tarleton regrouped his battalion. He placed the newly arrived D Company under Major A.J.M. Flint in the Italian trenches east of Ankora junction and deployed some of the other men to cover the approach roads from the north. At 5.15 a.m. he heard that Lieutenant Richard Norris and most of his platoon had been killed while being pushed back towards Ankora. He also learned that Meraviglia was now coming under threat and took over Platoon 2 (a mortar platoon) to defend Fortress Headquarters. However, on telephoning Brigadier Tilney he was told not to worry and everything was under control. Evidently it was not, as shots continued to ring out around the Fortress HQ area.[6] Colonel Prendergast witnessed this from his position lying in a bombed-out Italian ack-ack position and watched as the enemy climbed up from Vromolithos. He soon found himself under mortar fire coming from the Castle area on the hill opposite. At the same time, six Stukas were roaming the island looking for targets, joined periodically by Ju 88s. 'I then went to the main HQ and told the brigadier that in my opinion it was essential immediately to stage a counter-attack on these troops to push them off Meraviglia feature.'[7] Tilney told him to return to his own HQ.

At 8 a.m. on 16 November, Tilney went to the LRDG HQ cave and said he was unable to stage a counter-attack and was going to evacuate, and advised that they should do the same. Lieutenant Mould and Lieutenant Prendergast therefore ordered their men to evacuate the caves as quickly as they could or they would be cut off. They grabbed water bottles, food, weapons and as much ammunition as they could carry and destroyed all secret cyphers.[8] The men smashed up all wireless sets so the enemy could not make use of them and made their way to a house in Portolago which they all knew. Not long afterwards (at about 8.25 a.m.) Tilney sent out an uncoded message to GHQ in Cairo informing them that HQ on Mount Meraviglia was being abandoned, that the troops were demoralised and the situation was hopeless.[9] He warned, 'If you reinforce Leros we can restore the situation. You Must, Repeat, Must provide air cover.

It is exhaustion we are fighting not numbers.'[10] Jellicoe received this despatch, along with the Buffs in the north of the island – but so did the thousands of German troops. Since all the British code papers for signal transmission had already been burnt in anticipation of the Germans' imminent arrival at headquarters, the signal had been sent out uncoded in plain English, allowing the Germans to intercept. This meant that the enemy now knew of the complete hopelessness of the Allied troops, which was just the fillip they needed for the last push. Müller immediately retransmitted it to his own troops to spur them on.[11] Even he was surprised by it.[12] Why Tilney would make such a terrible mistake was never answered. During the morning, some of the Royal Irish Fusiliers had received orders (from a source which has never been identified) to leave Meraviglia and move to Portolago (Lakki). Some, including Fusiliers Major William Shepherd and Adjutant Dougall, said the order came from Fortress HQ. Ted Johnson was unaware of the message, as he was still on the slopes of Meraviglia fighting all day while desperately trying to hold his position under constant fire defending HQ, a skirmish in which Captain John Salter would be wounded.

Lieutenant Colonel Tarleton of the Royal West Kents was unaware of the planned evacuation of Fortress HQ until a short while later, when Tilney caught up with him at Ankora and announced his plans for D Company of Royal West Kents to fight their way through the enemy lines and join up with the Buffs in the north attacking southeast towards Alinda. Tarleton had to explain to him that this would be impossible while the enemy held the slopes of Meraviglia and Appetici.[13] Luckily they were interrupted by Prendergast on the field telephone, who confirmed the situation, thereby saving the company from certain death. Back at Fortress Headquarters, he had managed to re-establish communication and was now in contact with the Buffs, the Royal West Kents and a unit of men in Portolago. He filled in the brigadier on everyone's various positions and Tilney requested that Prendergast hold HQ until he could get back.[14] Prendergast recalled, 'He told me to man the HQ cave and to run the battle to the best of my ability until he should return and again set up HQ there.'[15] Tilney returned that afternoon and Prendergast set out for Portolago with the intention of rallying some troops. However, once

Tilney was back at HQ on Meraviglia, events finally overtook him. 'I went far enough out of the western exit to draw Machine Gun fire to my raised hat. I endeavoured to look over the entrance to the summit towards east. As I did so, I saw a German standing over the top of me and Colonel Douglas Brown (artillery) who had followed [...] The HQ appeared completely trapped.' The brigadier gave orders for the white flag to be shown and surrendered the island to the enemy.

After 20 minutes, sensing a disaster, Prendergast had turned back from Portolago. He saw all the remaining British soldiers lined up in front of a bunch of German soldiers. He was surprised to see Tilney pull up beside him in a jeep, accompanied by Captain Baker and two German officers.[16] The damage had already been done and Fortress HQ was lost. Tilney was going to Portolago to request that Admiral Mascherpa surrender his Italian troops. Tilney had officially surrendered the island on 16 November at 5.30 p.m. when Brandenburgers had entered British Fortress Headquarters.[17]

Faughs Under Fire

Elsewhere on the island, men from other companies had had similar disastrous experiences on that final day. During the early hours of 16 November Mike Rochford, the battalion intelligence officer for the Faughs, had outlined the next move to Lieutenant Johnson and his men. An attack was to be made by the Buffs and Royal West Kents from north to south via Alinda to the Leros town area (this was fighting in the opposite direction to the previous days). Johnson and his men were to reinforce and give cover from higher ground up to the northeast of Meraviglia to reach their positions by 8 a.m. Once they had achieved their objective, they would join up with A Company commanded by Captain Archie Condey. The enemy were on the ground where the war cemetery is now situated in Krethoni, and heading south.

Ted and his unit never witnessed any attack from the Buffs and Royal West Kents, but nonetheless stood their ground on Meraviglia firing at the enemy until their ammunition was almost out. They eventually were shot into a standstill where machine-gun fire hit them from all angles on either side of the rocks where they hid.

The Germans had them covered and shouted instructions to surrender. Ted recalled, 'At about 10 a.m. the rocky position I was in, with about four others, of which Tom-Massey Lynch of A Company was one, became bracketed either side by sustained Spandau fire. We had exhausted all our ammunition and were hailed by our opponents to give up.'[18] Ted was feeling dizzy as his three days of Benzedrine were wearing off. Both men set about destroying the rest of the weapons to prevent them falling into enemy hands. They smashed their rifle-sights on the rocks in order to make their guns inoperable and stripped their one Bren gun of parts and hurled them into the rocks.

The pair were trapped on all sides, with Germans above and below them with only a handful of men to defend the ground. Ted said,

> My own company had been decimated, and I was meant to assist another company to make an attack [...] We were penned in by the Germans, who were at the bottom of the hill. We had come off the top of the hill at 8 a.m. to take up this position, but it was a stony outcrop with little cover, so our position was not too hot. We were down to five men: three soldiers, another officer and myself. We realised there was no point carrying on. We had no ammunition and no grenades left, so we destroyed our weapons, and walked down the hill with our arms up. The continued bombing and the incessant fighting over nearly five days had so reduced the fighting power of our forces that they were unable to continue.[19]

He recalled it was the hardest part of the battle. 'We had to raise a piece of white vest which somebody had produced from his pack, and when we were sure that no firing was coming in our direction we eased ourselves out of our rocky position and commenced the sad and shameful trek down the hill side to the point where we could see our captors.'[20] He picked up a greatcoat on his way down the hill, his self-preservation kicking in – the military coat, made of wool, would keep him warm and give him protection against the weather. It was the worst part for Ted. 'I have to say it was the most shameful moment of my life. The Germans were decent fighting soldiers – they were an elite unit of the regular army. The commanding officer said to us in English "Hard luck, good fight. Come and have a cup of coffee."'[21]

They were kept in a walled courtyard watched over by a German with a Schmeisser and some stick grenades. They were given no food but had as much water as they wanted. At 8 p.m., they were marched to Agia Marina and kept overnight in a building on the water's edge. Massey Lynch had managed to give his captors the slip and was nowhere to be seen.

Battling Buffs

Meanwhile, at dawn on 16 November, while the action was taking place on Meraviglia, the Buffs had been busy fighting in the north of the island. Together with B Company of Royal West Kents, they relieved the LRDG (who had taken over from them holding their positions during the night) and took up their previous posts around the San Nicola area. Captain Percy Flood, commanding officer of B Company Royal West Kents, could see no sign of the enemy as dawn broke, so he sent out Lieutenant Caller and Gordon Huckle on a recce.[22] The enemy appeared to have moved out of San Nicola during the night, unbeknown to the British, and had advanced towards Platanos.[23] B Company of Royal West Kents therefore decided to advance to Rachi Ridge, with D Company of Buffs taking the left flank.

Major Ewart Tassell of D Company Buffs recalled his orders.

> Because the divisional HQ was down in the south up on the high ground there, there was not much of the battalion [where we were], right in the top part [north]. We really don't know much about what was happening. Eventually I suppose the CO got information that things weren't going too well down in the south and he was told to proceed and engage with the enemy south [...] Then we marched off until we met some Germans, the first we'd met.[24]

By 10.30 a.m., Major Tassell had met up with Lieutenant Colonel Egerton of King's Own and CO Percy Flood of B Company of Royal West Kents at Searchlight Hill in the central part of the island. They had a quick discussion to ascertain the best action to undertake. Lieutenant Colonel Egerton reported to Captain Percy Flood that he would withdraw all troops from Rachi to meet up with Buffs in north and Flood's Company should cover them. Thus Major Tassell, Lieutenant Colonel Egerton and Captain Flood were making headway towards San Nicola.[25]

On returning to the Buffs HQ in the north at 1 p.m., Lieutenant Commander Ramseyer found Jellicoe preparing to go to Fortress HQ to get orders and find out what was happening. All communications were down. To get to Meraviglia HQ, Jellicoe would have to pass over enemy lines. Ramseyer drove him in a jeep as far as Navy House at the crossroads of San Nicola and San Quaranta, 'where I left them to make their own way by usual SBS methods of crawling under reeds, through hedges and around trees'.[26] Jellicoe managed to make his way past enemy lines to Fortress HQ to talk to Tilney and assess the situation; then returned the same way, back through enemy lines, to meet up with his men in the north and tell them what was happening. Major Ewart Tassell of D Company Buffs remembered the event: 'We were chasing these Germans going south because I had been told to report to the HQ down here. I was up there wondering, wishing I knew what was happening further south because I'd had no communication at all.'[27] He saw someone coming towards him.

It turned out to be George Jellicoe who had been wandering around. And so he talked to me and told me a little bit about what was happening. He had volunteered to go from Charing Cross [...] He comes up to see what was happening on the other side of the German line [...] He filled me in a little bit on what was happening down south – I had no idea what was happening – but, in fact of course, they were surrounded and almost at that time surrendering. Anyway, at the end of the enlightenment, he said, 'Well, I better get back' and he turned round and walked back to the Germans, just like that. Extraordinary bloke really.[28]

Still in the north, Ramseyer and Iggulden came across a group of soldiers walking up to Partheni away from the battle area. On being questioned they said they had orders to retire north; they had no arms and were exhausted and bedraggled. Driving their jeep further round, Ramseyer and Iggulden encountered a ruffled and irate Brigadier Tilney who stated he had given no such orders for withdrawal. He ordered the two men to round up all stragglers and take them under their own command with the Buffs. During the early afternoon, C Company Buffs were ordered to move towards Alinda and meet up with D Company Buffs. The King's Own commanding officer had ordered a withdrawal north (which was possibly where the men in Partheni had got their orders), but this was countermanded by Brigadier Tilney. While the Buffs thought they were doing well in the north, Iggulden (their commanding officer) must have sensed that the battle was not going well elsewhere – the centre particularly was under pressure. He ordered that someone should find a boat to ensure their escape if that time should come; Ramseyer recalled, 'Lieutenant E Percy and I jeeped to Partheni [...] A tug was instructed to have steam up by 1700 and lighters ready to tow; a caique, and two motor boats were prepared and sail craft checked over and placed with oars in them at what, we hoped, would prove strategic points round the harbour.'[29]

Various orders appear to have gone back and forth, but with communications going down, and groups of men reliant on runners and whistles, trying to keep information and orders up to the minute was near impossible. Mixed messages meant the soldiers were not coordinated in their movements. One example was that, to their utter amazement after finding themselves in the position of holding Rachi Ridge, D Company of Buffs and B Company of Royal West Kents and King's Own had received orders to move off it. Around 160 Royal West Kents (all that was left of them) were still under orders to move north to join up with the Buffs. During the repositioning, Major G.V. Shaw was mortally wounded.[30] Captain Pond and B Echelon met Colonel Iggulden to mount an attack on Rachi Ridge. This was the position they had held only that morning and had been commanded to abandon.

At this point, Tilney had withdrawn to Ankora and had given orders for Royal Irish Fusiliers (what was left of them) to march north and join up with the Buffs. It was hoped they could then attack southwards. Now 150 Buffs were moving towards Meraviglia, while 200 Royal West Kents were moving in the opposite direction – both out of contact with each other.[31]

Meanwhile, Colonel Tarleton, Royal West Kents, had sent out a platoon under Lieutenant J.A. Myers to find out the whereabouts of the Buffs. The news came back around 10 p.m. from second-in-command Major D.B. Pyke that all the troops together with Captain Pond and B Echelon of Royal West Kents had been recalled to Meraviglia.[32]

At this stage many of the men did not know that events had overtaken them and Tilney had handed over the island, for some of them went on fighting even after the surrender. Up on top of Mount

Clidi, they had been ordered to hold the position 'at all costs'. With communications down, they continued to fight. Five men from King's Own and LRDG led by Prendergast kept fighting and refused to give up well after the surrender.

For others, the hopelessness of the situation had become obvious. Private Stanley 'Bill' Froud, having already lost all his close companions before he had even landed when the *Eclipse* had gone down, was one of the few survivors of the battle. He had felt lost and helpless throughout the battle without the support of the men he had trained with beside him. Now he was desperate and felt the closeness of death.

> I know that near the end [...] a group of us, survivors from all sorts of units, we were taken up [...] to the top of a hill and were told we'd been ordered to gather together here and tomorrow we'd make a frontal charge and drive the Germans off the island. 'Oh my God,' I thought. 'This is the end of the line for me' [...]I knew if we tried that we'd all die.[33]

Luckily for Froud, when he awoke he heard it was all over. News of the surrender had taken time getting through. 'Our officer, Major Pyke, came up and said [...] "The brigadier's had to surrender." I didn't know if I was happy or sad or what. I wasn't worried, I'd gone past worrying by then.' Stan would end up in Stalag IVB as a POW.[34]

Colonel Cowper of the King's Own reported,

> On the 16th, 'A', 'B' and 'D' Companies having re-formed, the battalion concentrated for a final attack on the area [Meraviglia] occupied by brigade headquarters near [opposite] Appetici Hill, but before it could be launched news was received of the island's surrender. The total number of casualties is not known. Fifteen officers were killed; of those wounded, five were evacuated and three were included among the fifteen taken prisoner. Some sixty other ranks were killed and an unknown number wounded and prisoner.[35]

The withdrawal of Allied fighter planes had sealed the fate of Leros. With no air support and under heavy attack by enemy aircraft, the three battalions had fought for five days until they were exhausted and could fight no more.

Padre Taken POW

That same morning of the final day, 16 November, Reverend Anwyl and the hospital doctors were still tending the wounded. At about

9 a.m., Brigadier Tilney's message had come through to inform the Reverend and his unit that the battalion was retreating. Anwyl could see the troops moving towards the windmills to the west on the ridge facing the RAP where he was standing. The battalion's MO, Jack Barber, decided to join the troops, but the rest agreed to stay at the RAP as there were more wounded men who needed rescuing. Stretcher-bearers went out to pick up them up – 40 or 50 wounded came in for treatment over the next few hours. John Salter who had commanded B Company of Faughs almost from the start of the battle walked in on the arm of a stretcher-bearer with his face and body swollen. His jaw was shattered and torn, and blood was streaming from his mouth. Although he was evacuated to a German hospital by seaplane, they never saw him again. They later heard he had died from his injuries.[36]

By the end, there was relentless bombing of valleys and hills. Stores and ammunition supplies were going up in smoke, explosions were going off all around. Reverend Anwyl went outside to warn a signals officer about the Germans behind the RAP just as Major Shepherd, acting commanding officer, appeared; Anwyl noticed how he had aged over the last few days. 'He had become an incredibly weary old man.'[37] Mike Rochford also arrived, having been sent by the brigadier to find out where the battalions were – he had been out of touch with the rest of the forces for some time and Fortress HQ was under attack. Rochford intended to follow the Irish Fusiliers, who had gone off in the direction of the windmill. First Anwyl gave Rochford the sacraments, but could clearly see the man had no energy left: 'He could scarcely stand for weariness and looked near the end of his strength. However, he pulled himself together and seeing me looking sad said [. . .] "Don't worry about me, Father. I'm strengthened in soul by the sacraments and thank god I still have a drop of whisky!"'[38] He showed the little bottle and with a wave he was gone. He had a rifle but had lost his tin hat somewhere among the skirmishes.

Reverend Anwyl sat with the others and they chatted together 'almost cheerfully' talking of their chances of being taken prisoner and above all of the prospect of the chance to sleep.[39] Despite the distinctive Red Cross sign on the RAP, Anwyl was worried about the wounded if the Germans should come at night and possibly fling grenades. Both he and Dr Pickering agreed that they should give themselves up. 'We were already as good as prisoners and the sooner we were able to tell the Germans that there were no combatant troops in the area the better for all of us. I put on my clerical collar, bade the others stay inside and went out of the Regimental Aid Post standing in full view of anyone who wished to see me.'[40] He casually lit his pipe, put his hands in his pockets and stood as if he was quietly contemplating the sunset. 'In reality, my knees were knocking and I could scarcely find enough breath to draw my pipe.' He knew any nervous German might think him a threat and shoot him. At that moment, three Irish Fusiliers came running down from Meraviglia, but a burst of Spandau fire hit the rocks behind them, warning them to go no further. The Germans were unprepared to accept their surrender, which gave no comfort to Anwyl. The bullets hit two of the young soldiers, Fusilier Creighton and Fusilier Lawlor; a third man jumped into a shell-hole and crawled away. Anwyl grabbed a small red cross, and prepared to wave it at the Germans when Captain Mason came from his shelter to tell Anwyl that the wounded needed attention. However, one of the Germans emerged and beckoned Anwyl to go with him, taking him up the hill to a machine-gun post where one of the Germans could speak English. Anwyl told them that they were all protected personnel and he wanted to collect the wounded without interference.[41] The Germans let him go but warned them that they would be shot if they played any tricks. Back at the RAP, Anwyl and his group collected and looked after the wounded. After a few hours, they all rested on the floor, drank and smoked and gradually fell asleep wondering what would await them the next day.

The hopelessness of the situation is reflected in the *Historical Records of the Buffs*:

GHQ had by now realised the plight of the troops in Leros, and about 3.45pm., just as the enemy were once more converging on the summit of Mount Meraviglia from two sides, a message was received to say that evacuation was being arranged that night, seventeen caiques being available for this purpose. The chances of organising an embarkation and getting clear of the island in the face of enemy E boats and aircraft dropping flares were remote. By 5.30 pm., Brigade HQ, which had lost seven officers, was overrun by the enemy. Any lingering hope of co-ordinating the defence was now dissipated; the two halves of the garrison, consisting of depleted and exhausted units, were marching in opposite directions, separated by the width of the island and with no means of communication and no hope of making any further effective resistance.[42]

Approximately 3,200 British and 5,350 Italians were taken prisoner. The death toll had been 357 British soldiers, 157 drowned en route to Leros; of the German soldiers 162 were 'lost', 246 killed on the island and 659 killed at sea.[43]

In a telegram dated 17 November 1943, the commander-in-chief, General Wilson, wrote to Churchill,

Leros has fallen, after a very gallant struggle against overwhelming air attacks. It was a near thing between success and failure. Very little was needed to turn the scale in our favour and to bring off a triumph. Everything was done to evacuate the garrisons of the other Aegean islands and to rescue survivors from Leros [...] all would have been well if we had been able to take Rhodes.[44]

Churchill replied the following day, 'Like you, I feel this is a serious loss and reverse, and like you I feel I have been fighting with my hand tied behind my back.'[45] Having promised to commit his resources to Eisenhower, he had felt he had had no alternative but to submit to the US decisions not to send in reinforcements. Churchill acknowledged the gallant part played by the Greek navy throughout. For Churchill, Leros was a sad loss. On 21 November, he wrote to Anthony Eden, the foreign secretary, 'No attempts should be made to minimise the poignance of the loss of the Dodecanese, which we had a chance of getting so easily and at so little cost, and which we now lost after heavy expenditure.'[46] He contemplated that the British had probably downed 2,000 Germans on the way, but the enemy now held 3,000 POWs. He estimated the British losses to be about 5,000 men.[47]

The number of injured and dead became evident as the battle drew to a close. Paddy McCrystal recalled, 'The commanding officer. We called him Micky French. His brother, George was there. He was killed too [...] McCallister was one of those injured. Jesus wept. Matherson, O'Connell – the two brothers were sergeants. They were from round Dublin parts, from that part of the country.

They were killed.'[48] Paddy himself was hit in the head with a large piece of shrapnel, leaving a scar he would bear for the rest of his life. He ended up in the hospital in the POW camp for three or four months.[49] He realised that it was the end of the line for the British soldiers; 'We had done our duty, and the job was finished. I know exactly, the last job we had, the commanding officer – that wasn't French now – he says, if you can get away to the boats, get a boat, get away. Our time is coming, the Germans are coming, we had no chance, you know.'[50]

13

Surrender or Escape

You are now all prisoners. The G.O.C. [general officer commanding] has surrendered the Island. You will now march back to your billeting area where you will remain until the Germans collect you up probably some time early tomorrow morning.

Royal West Kents commanding officer to Lieutenant John Browne[1]

After the surrender, the position on the island was one of total bewilderment and confusion. Private Stanley Froud recalled that night,

The last few days had been so confusing that I can't remember much about them. I know that we were all gathered together, and we were all taken up into the hills. We were marching in single file and it was very dark. I could see the Long Range Desert Group men passing through us [...] When we got to the top of the hill we were told to lay down and rest, which we did, and we slept there all night. Next morning when we awoke, it was very eerie, it was very quiet, there wasn't a sound. I said to the man next to me, 'I don't know what's going on but it's too quiet.' Then an officer came up and told us the news that we'd surrendered. Before we got captured we were taken up in the hills and the officer said to us, 'Throw away all the bolts out of your rifles.' We said, 'What's that for?' he said 'I've got to tell you, they've captured the brigadier and the German general's shown him the troops that's landed, and they've got their big guns, 88s, and they could massacre the lot of us and so he's had to surrender.' We felt depressed. Anyway, the major said, 'Well, we're going to go down the hill. We've got to give ourselves up, but', he said, 'we'll all march down in orderly fashion, slope our arms and march down. We're still the British Army.'[2]

For the men who had fought so hard in the battle for Leros, to be told they had now lost was a hard blow. Reg Neep, a corporal of King's Own Regiment, recalled how he felt when he found out about the surrender; 'We thought we were winning and the Germans thought we were winning too, but our commanding officer, Brigadier Tilney, decided to surrender the island to avoid further loss of life, especially of the civilian population, allegedly [...]'[3] Peter Barham too remembered the eerie quietness. 'In the morning [of the 17th] of course, all quiet and sunshine, and you looked out over the sea, and you could see lots of landing craft coming in. They were obviously Germans so we must have surrendered, but we didn't get any messages to say that. We didn't know [what was happening].'[4] More of the enemy were coming in to take control of the island. 'They came up in Gourna Bay in the morning, I could see all these landing craft coming in. It was obviously all over [...] It was just one of those things. We had to hand in the rifle. I had already smashed up the wireless set.'[5] Many soldiers continued to follow original orders they had received earlier that day, unaware of the surrender. As news filtered through, men began to make their plans for a getaway. Understandably, many of them began to search for their own units or other survivors. Others ended up being taken to Portolago as POWs.

The Germans shot the Italian officers in Portolago (Lakki), in line with Hitler's order immediately after the Italians' capitulation that any Italians collaborating with the Allies should be shot as traitors. All Allied troops were ordered to withdraw to the port, and the men confined in a compound in the harbour. Lieutenant Ted Johnson was among some of the captured Royal Irish Fusiliers. He recalled that once all the captive soldiers were at Portolago, they were kept together, Italians (those who were left) and the British, all ranks together sleeping on the dusty floor. He tried to account for all his men in C Company.[6] Against the Geneva Convention, over the next two days some prisoners were forced to load two German gunboats with coal by hand-chain methods with wicker baskets.[7]

Problems arose with having so many men in one place, with no latrines, in the devastated buildings of Portolago. Reg Neep remembered the dire conditions at the end of the battle. 'Later all prisoners were marched round the bay to be interned in a large building without any "facilities" – tin helmets were found a useful "relief".' The men were reduced to urinating in their hats and putting it down a grating. In the heat, the foul smell was made worse than ever. A number of prisoners were now very weak from lack of food and water. The British MO examined these men and declared them unfit to travel. He protested to the senior German officer, gaining the soldiers a ladle of very watery and smelly boiled macaroni.[8] The Germans treated them reasonably well and gave them what was left of the rancid water and the sloppy food, which was eagerly received by the hungry men. Most of the British soldiers had not washed for days or weeks and there was no chance of that now. Reg recalled,

> The next day, we had another issue with food – rice and hard tack (biscuits). We were then marched to a German merchant ship and packed into the holds. Each hold measuring about 40 square feet, taking approximately 150 to 200 men. The holds were pitch black and filled to suffocation, each hold being subsequently battened down. When the ship got under way, conditions were so bad that men were panicking for lack of air so that after a few hours some hatches were partially opened to allow a little air in.[9]

Some of the men had been captured before the surrender. Jack Harte with the Royal Irish Fusiliers had spent all his days defending the Castle Hill position. He was one of the stoic Faughs of Platoon 9 who had held out on Appetici surrounded by the enemy halfway up the mountain – they were finally captured on 15 November. His realisation of the extent of the devastation now had time to sink in.

> For the rest of us, what followed was a harrowing experience. As we marched along somewhere in the vicinity of Appetici, the sight of dozens of Allied and Germans soldiers lying dead on the road and hillside was a stark reminder of the ferocity of the battle of Leros. At least I was alive. Absolutely sick with my lot, weary and worn out, I was pressed into handling the mutilated corpses that were strewn along the way.[10]

He covered the bodies with stones, laying their identification discs over the top in the hope they would receive a burial. Those who surrendered, like Jack, suffered guilt about being alive. Against all odds, they had survived when their friends had died. The images of

death and destruction would be imprinted on their mind for the rest
of their lives.

Tending the Wounded

The day after surrender, the platoon commander of Royal West Kents,
John Browne, found himself lying on a stretcher, with many others,
on the gravel drive leading to the makeshift hospital at Villa Bellini,
its façade broken by a jagged shell-hole at the first level. 'There were
many stretchers at the edge of the path and right round the house.
English doctors and orderlies walked up and down awaiting the
completion of preparations going on inside the house. German
soldiers walked about looking after their own wounded, greeting
their friends, and supervising the sorting of food and equipment.'[11]
Greek civilians were coming in: men, women, children and old
people, walking up the steps to the house to have their injuries
dressed. Browne's commanding officer, Mike Read, his arm in a sling,
appeared very shaken.

Browne and Platoon 15 had been captured after encountering a
group of Germans emerging from a house a few hundred yards away.
Browne had been shot in the chest. One of the Germans in a Red
Cross armband helped him to the makeshift hospital and sent a
stretcher for Private Mountford who had been injured in the last
throes of fighting. The following day Browne met up with Lieutenant
Crowder from the navy, who was now suffering from jaundice
(Crowder had been on Mount Meraviglia at the time of surrender
when the Germans overran HQ). Harold Price from Royal Artillery
was also with them in the hospital. He had hidden in the hills but had
gone in search of food, only to discover Germans on the caique he
was hoping to raid. They fed him and escorted him to hospital with
shrapnel in his back, which had gone septic. They soon met up with
Platoon 13 Commander Jode and Adjutant Donald Cropper, both
patients on the ground floor.[12]

A couple of days later, they were all moved into tents in the
grounds of the villa on the gravelled front, eight beds to each tent.
Bob and Joe, orderlies from Tyneside, dressed their wounds and
brought them food. Browne writes, 'Gradually, one after another,

we became well enough to get up and take our meals at a table outside the tent. The other tents were occupied by a number of Long Range Desert Group who, like Price, had grown tired of hiding and were admitted to the hospital, although they were not wounded.'[13] They did their best to find the men and bury the bodies under the direction of Padre Wright. The Germans did not interfere with their movements at all and the men were free to wander around.

News came in that any wounded now able to walk would be taken to Portolago in a truck and then transported to Athens. During the last days of the battle, the battalion medical post had been moved from 'Charing Cross' to the Italian hospital in Portolago under the Royal Irish Fusiliers regimental officer Captain J.M. Barber of the Royal Army Medical Corps. Wounded British and German soldiers were brought into one of the three wards and tended to by one of 12 men (mainly stretcher-bearers) working with the MO and Reverend Anwyl.[14] The most seriously wounded were evacuated by air or seaplane. Captain Barber was then sent to the medical set-up at Villa Bellini in Alinda with Corporals Roberts, Lynn, Whitbread and Kendrick, leaving Sergeant Philby to run the hospital in Portolago.

The British crew members injured in the glider bomb attack on the BYMS-72 before its capture on 11 November had also been taken to the makeshift army hospital at Leros, but had been moved inland once it was known that the German invasion was about to take place. Those who were able had walked to the Navy House and then on to the caves at the bottom of Searchlight Hill, where Italian ammunition was stored. They had remained in the caves, together with some German POWs, for three days. In late morning of their final day, one of them had ventured from their hiding place to use the latrines and hurried back with the news that the place was full of Germans. When enemy soldiers located the wounded within the cave, an injured German officer requested that the British be given good treatment because the German POWs had been well looked after. All the injured prisoners were loaded onto an old cargo ship, the British on deck and the Italians below. Upon arrival in Athens, the injured were transported to a hospital and, from there, by train and lorry to Germany.[15]

Those who were left, as their injuries healed, could wander around the island, and naturally they looked for methods of escape.

Round St Nicholas Bay in the north around Blefuti, escapes were being hastily arranged by a British naval officer. Those trying to escape hid in the little church keeping watch, waiting for him to return. Lieutenant Mike Rochford, Faughs intelligence officer, and Captain Greenwood were also assisting in organising the escapes. The church was occasionally searched by the Germans, and that night, and arriving too late, Jack Barber fell into their hands. The Germans fed him and escorted him back to the hospital. Officers were moved from the hospital to the house next door which was much more overcrowded.

The captives now at least had time to try and freshen up. Men shared shaving kits and grabbed whatever they could that might come in handy for later. Some of the men who had been in hospital had no clothes. The field ambulance officer whose job it was to find food and clothes for the men seemed oblivious to his responsibilities; according to John Browne he just sat and smoked his pipe all day. Thinking he would be better off seeking something to wear from other sources, Browne approached a German lieutenant who ordered a young private to go with them to the store house to obtain what they needed. On another occasion, they were given citronade and jam doughnuts when they went to try and obtain some boots. There were no boots to be had as 200 German soldiers had been shipwrecked a few days earlier, and demanded to be shod. However, Browne and his men were given six tins of meat. The soldiers serving them wrapped it all up in a map of the Aegean, whether as an aid to escape, or because he was unaware, they did not guess at.[16]

When the men were well enough to walk into Platanos, Browne and his companions met up with the Lerian civilians, most of whom were generous and friendly. They encountered a peasant who slapped a couple of packets of cigarettes into their hands. A woman hanging out of her window called to Browne and filled his haversack with tinned food, and loaves, 'crooning as she did so and stroking my head with her free hand'.[17] Such heroic acts did not go unrecognised by the soldiers. They knew that the Greeks helped them at risk to their own personal safety, as the Germans would have punished them for such transgressions. On their return journey, more people gave them loaves and other food and cigarettes.

Browne and a few others realised that they had to escape or they would be transported to German POW camps. They searched out a rowing boat in the cove of St Nicholas Bay and arranged to meet up with a few others, 11 men in all.[18] An Italian colonel joined them and uttered, 'I very frightened' – hardly surprising seeing as the Germans shot Italian officers as traitors, but he disappeared before they left the next night. They had some difficulty trying to persuade the skipper of the boat to take them as he was reluctant to go. Two young women carrying a bottle of brandy had been sent to distract the German lookouts. The men eventually managed to set the boat moving; most of those aboard were sick but they eventually landed on the Turkish coast, and then took a caique to Bodrum and Kusadasi, landing on 7 December.[19]

An Abortive Attempt

Reverend Anwyl had been ministering to troops when he heard of the surrender. He watched as parties of Buffs passed by singing 'There'll always be an England' and a lump came to his throat. Paddy Ardill and Tom West of the Fusiliers arrived at their station both determined to have a hearty breakfast before they went any further. Ardill stripped to wash and was surprised to discover three furrows in his chest and two more on his back, probably bullet grazes. Those who fought with him later agreed he deserved every medal he could receive. According to Anwyl, he was later awarded the Military Cross.[20] Ardill was determined to escape and was thinking of trying to swim to Turkey via one of the islands, so Reverend Anwyl gave him a life jacket he had found lying around. Anwyl then set about collecting the wounded on stretchers and carrying them to the makeshift hospital in Alinda as there was no transport. Villa Bellini was one great dressing station; although the building had been hit by shell fire, it was usable. Anwyl recalled, 'Wounded lay all around though small ships were taking lesser wounded Germans away – probably to Kos, where they had a hospital.'[21] Anwyl gave communion to the wounded. The Indian sappers helped dig the graves of the three young soldiers still unburied at the RAP. The Reverend then set off in the hope of obtaining permission for a regimental burial party, leaving Roche his batman to guard the stores and his personal kit.

In Portolago the Italian hospital – though a quarter of it had been ripped away – was in full operation, with surgeon Jack Barber working away on the wounded. The Italian naval chaplain had given out the sacraments, so Anwyl decided to wander back to the RAP. No one was stopping him and he was still able to move back and forth as he pleased between the hospital in Alinda and that in Portolago. Once back at the RAP, he found Roche and a couple of others with the Red Cross flag still flying. They decided to settle in for the night, covered the window with a blanket, lit an oil lamp against the dark and ate in relative quiet until they all fell asleep.[22] The next day Anwyl came round, cheering up the wounded. He had the foresight to fill a couple of water bottles with the remaining gin. He joined his comrades Terry Bourke, Jimmy Hoare and five other officers going to Portolago. Along the quayside, they found uninjured prisoners standing aimlessly around awaiting transport to wherever the Germans were going to take them. They had all made themselves at home: they lit fires, washed and shaved; some were playing cards 'as though they were a lot of scouts on a picnic'. [23] A few sat looking dispirited, 'sick at heart'.

One of the Greeks employed by the British came into the medical compound trying to find British officers to help them get off the island. One found his way to Anwyl; the Reverend recalled, 'He then informed me that a motor launch would come to St Nicholas Bay at or about midnight for a week beginning on the Thursday following, that he would be able to provide a limited supply of civilian clothing to enable a dozen of us to escape.'[24] The escapes would be made singularly at two-hour intervals. Anwyl confided in Jack Barber and their senior officer, Colonel May, who agreed to let them decide among themselves who would go, so long as there were enough medical staff left behind.[25]

A young Greek boy was used as a messenger between the intended escapees and those organising the getaway. He gave Anwyl a note, 'One can escape tonight – one only.' They tossed a coin to see which of them would go, and Anwyl won. Under the basket of tangerines left by the boy, they found an old coat and trousers. By this time

Anwyl had grown a beard and, once dressed in peasant clothes, with his hair suitably matted and generally dirtied up, he looked the part.[26] Usually, the medical facilities were unguarded and he easily found a gap in the wall and met up with the agent who had contacted him earlier. A small patrol of Germans on the way stood between him and his intended path, but they let him pass without incident. The guide took him to some cottages and handed him over to another guide with a miserable-looking horse. 'Apparently we were to go up the hills and, as we would be visible to the Germans, it was wise to look like two peasants going to scratch at their little plot of land'.[27] After some capers trying to mount the horse without success, it was decided that the Greek would take the horse and Anwyl walked. They arrived at St Nicholas Bay, and since the rendezvous was in full sight of the Germans, Anwyl was obliged to find a soft piece of ground hidden by bushes and settle in until nightfall. After some hours, he heard the Greek call out to him that he must make his way to the beach, where he would find a small chapel once used by fishermen, and there imitate the cry of a seagull. En route, Anwyl met another Greek and together they went into the chapel and waited.

> The furtive entrée of a few men did something to allay the suspense as it was clear from the manner of their coming that they too were escapees. Someone shone a torch for a second and in its light I was pleased to see khaki uniforms. Some of the new arrivals had blankets and we were able to cover the two small windows of the chapel and then introduce ourselves. Amongst the British were an officer and a private that I knew: there were two other British soldiers and three Greeks. To my great joy the officer told us definitely that a launch would enter the Bay at or about midnight and that he had been sent from Turkey to organise the escapes.[28]

Anwyl thought it foolhardy of the men who had already escaped to be returning to help them, but these men (the Special Boat Squadron) were committed to assisting escapees. The officer had some food on him and they sat in a circle sharing bully beef, a chicken, a few pounds of raisins and a small pack of biscuits. They smoked and chatted, dropping into hasty silence when they heard footsteps approach. It was more Greeks. 'By this time, we were thirteen in number and the tiny chapel seemed full of big men and tobacco smoke; much of the tobacco smoked was Greek or Italian and I found the aroma rather trying and longed for the time when we could go out.'[29]

After another long wait, the officer told them they were all moving to the beach and would wait at the water's edge as the German patrol came round to search the chapel on occasions in the night. First they had to clear up the mess they had made. 'We carefully swept together the cigarette ends and biscuit crumbs with our hands, took the blankets down and opened the windows. Then we moved slowly to the beach. Despite frantic attempts to be silent in our movements, we made between us a frightful noise as our heavy boots slithered over the sharp rocks.'[30] Jagged stones dug into the men's boots, which also made for an uncomfortable hideout as they waited for the launch. The officer mentioned that the motor launch had been expected two nights earlier but had not turned up, much to the concern of the men.

Anwyl only had on thin rags full of holes and soon the cold began to bite. Tension grew as they crouched near the beach in their uncomfortable hiding positions. 'It was only 10 p.m. when we moved to the beach and the minutes passed with agonising slowness. Often someone would ask the time from a soldier who had a watch with a luminous dial only to find that the hands of the watch had scarcely moved since the last time the same question had been asked.'[31] They patiently hunkered down straining their ears for the sound of the throb of the launch's engine. When at last it came, it was well past midnight. Anwyl recalls, 'I was so miserable that I could scarcely believe it possible that an end could ever come to my aches and when at last someone whispered excitedly that he heard the launch, my heart leapt for joy.'[32] One of the men whispered to him, 'God! Hot coffee in Turkey in a few hours'. But the sound came nearer and went away again. They got a tantalising glimpse of the vessel in silhouette before it disappeared. They all felt terrible. 'The cold now pervaded my whole body; in wretchedness and desperation, I flung myself full length on the sharp rocks and thereafter scarcely moved until at 4 o'clock, the officer said that we should disperse to our hiding places before dawn as it made it dangerous to be about.'[33] In the end, it all became too much for Anwyl and he returned to the depot to be taken prisoner of war.

A prison ship arrived to take on the walking wounded, and patients were being sent from Alinda hospital to Portolago to be taken aboard. Four trucks and ambulances loaded with 24 patients had already left that afternoon. Anwyl and his party were with the last eight patients coming from Alinda hospital, inadvertently late after their truck ran off the road and crashed into a ditch. They were so long delayed that they missed the ship, were turned round and sent back to Portolago hospital to put the patients to bed. It was not until 8 December that an Italian hospital ship would arrive to take them away. It was staffed by a German crew with British medical staff, and Captain Barber and Captain J.W. Hoare were also taken aboard. The German officer was very amenable and treated them well. As luck would have it, a day or so later the ship was intercepted by the Royal Navy and brought to Brindisi where all the British officers were rescued.

The Germans meanwhile piled their dead in the field alongside the garden of Villa Bellini using Italian labour and a mechanical drill to dig out the rock. The stench of the rotting bodies reached the sick. The Germans made darkly stained crosses embossed with gold letters for their dead. The English had only managed to rush together crosses from odd bits of packing cases and hastily scribbled the names of the fallen soldiers on them with indelible ink pens.

Lieutenant Clarke's Getaway

The day of the surrender was a day Lieutenant Clifford Clarke would never forget. He was with his men performing his duty as platoon commander of the Queen's Own and he remembered how he and his men had been on the mountains with the mobile platoon waiting to fight.

> When I heard, a runner came down from headquarters, and said the guys have surrendered. I said, 'Look, I don't believe it.' I thought he may have been at his rum. So I held him, and sent one of my senior NCOs to go out and check. I wasn't going to disperse 150 men with someone running down so I sent him to check. And he came back and said he's right. And that's when I said right, now we have all got to try and escape. I felt terrible about Tilney, I thought he's a traitor. We've got 150 men still ready to fight. We'd still got ammunition left. There were a lot [of Germans] about but we could have still done a lot of damage,

do something. I couldn't think of surrendering. It's just not what we were trained to do. That's when we went down to the harbour.'[34]

He watched sadly as his company commander, Flood, gave orders to his men. Clarke recalled, 'Percy Flood stood in front of the men and he said right, we now have to surrender, that's what the general said. Your duties are to give no more than rank, name and number. Your duty is to try and escape. He could have been shot. This was Percy.'[35]

Nothing could have been further from Clifford Clarke's mind than surrender. He reckoned he still had a chance of escape. 'The best thing was getting away. The escape. The worst thing, the one that really shook me, because I had never contemplated it, was the surrender. That really did [...] because I was not expecting it. As far as I could see, I was getting more powerful. I wasn't getting through to HQ what was happening as it was really chaotic.'[36] He was later to find out that the Germans nearly pulled off a huge deception when they radioed to Samos in the brigadier's name ordering them to send the Greek Sacred Squadron to Leros for assistance. They were boarding three destroyers before they realised it was an enemy lure, just in time to recall the troops and the destroyers.[37]

Clarke realised he would have to think quickly about his escape. He ordered his men to break up into small parties, to get food and water, to take to the hills and decide an escape plan. He knew he would be unable to take everyone with him, so was forced to select. The journey would be arduous and dangerous and he needed men he felt best equipped for the job if they were to have a chance of getting away successfully. He chose Lieutenant Stokes (Royal Irish Fusiliers, HQ Company) and the rest were Royal West Kent men: Colour Sergeants Hayward and Milton, Corporal Hunt, Private Moore (Clarke's batman) and Private Thompson (requested by Hayward).

Lieutenant Clarke's determination to escape was spurred on by the thought of his family. 'Uppermost in my mind was the thought of what would be the result of a "missing telegram" sent home.' He supposed his wife would manage, but not his parents. He also reckoned he 'was not built to be a POW. Anyway I was damned if I was going to finish the war that way.'[38] The first plan was to find some provisions. 'Our little party found a house with some stores, where we ate some bully and biscuits, and after putting either a tin of bully or M&V or a

packet of biscuits in each of our pockets, we moved off down towards
Portolago [Lakki]. We also took a greatcoat or blanket each.'[39]

Among Clarke's chosen men was his most trusted and respected
friend, Sergeant George Hatcher, on whom he knew he could rely.[40]
Hatcher recalled how they had lost everything they had brought
with them. 'We took all our kit with us. We lost that. Beat a hasty
retreat, in the end. I often wondered what happened to it,
private letters, and papers and things. The most exciting part was
the escape. I was with Clifford Clarke. Whatever happened to him,
happened to me.'[41]

Hatcher had been fighting alongside Clarke, his commanding
officer, during the surrender, and he also recalled that the men with
him thought the Allies were winning. 'We weren't actually pulled
out. We realised ourselves, we thought we were doing all right [...]
Someone said, the CO has surrendered. So the first thing we thought
we had better get away. We had to think about our own skins, we
didn't want to be taken prisoner.' They made their way to the docks
in Portolago (Lakki), where lots of men were milling around.
'Everyone had the same idea, get to the port, and get away. Hoping
they were going to find some boats. Of course, the bombers had
destroyed most of the boats. Then we came across this pile of
collapsed canvas boats. I don't know what they were used for, or what
they were intended for, there was a pile of them. We decided to have
a go at one of those.'[42]

Once in Portolago, they had to move carefully in case any
Germans were patrolling the vicinity, although all seemed clear. They
found two Indian Royal Engineers in the harbour, who had three
collapsible boats. Clarke had been a Royal Engineer, so he knew they
could be fixed. 'They got them, fitted them up. They hadn't got any
oars but we found something.'[43] He noticed that while they had the
two Royal Engineers helping to erect their boat, the other two were
erected by ordinary soldiers.

> They hadn't got engineers with them and they didn't do it properly, it
> collapsed in the harbour and they all fell in. I think some were drowned.
> The next lot got as far as the end of the point, we heard lots of machine-
> gun fire and searchlight going round, so what happened to them – we
> assumed they were shot up. So we set off. We eventually got through

the boom. We knew darn well we could get to Lipsi [one of the nearby islands to Leros about twenty miles or so from the Turkish coast]. I had just remembered the map and compass, the rest hadn't but I'd still got mine. I said there's no way we'll get to Lipsi before daylight; if so we'll be shot out of the sky. So we've got to pull into this ledge, pull the boat up and wait until the next night, which we did.[44]

Hatcher recalled, 'There was another chap, who was an officer who we didn't know at all [Major Barnet]. He came along [while they were still on Leros] and asked if he could go, and he turned out to be some official who had been on the island before and knew a good deal about it [...] He came too – there were about ten of us altogether'.[45] Indeed, the boat they found would only take about nine or ten men in all. The company sergeant was sent off to get some water but he never came back. Lieutenant Clarke said, 'I don't like to belittle him but he wasn't too keen on coming, and I wonder if he just disappeared, but I didn't say.'[46] In any case, they could delay no longer – they had waited all day until dusk and had to be clear of the harbour by the time the moon came up. Hatcher recalled,

It was a moonlit night and once the moon got up, it would be too light to get away. In the end we had to leave him. He was obviously taken prisoner, we scouted around and found a couple of oars and some bits of wood and we paddled away not knowing where we were going. This queer officer [Major Barnet] who came with us said he knew where we could go [...] We will make for Lipsi the other end of the island from where we were. We rowed all night and paddled all night and finished up on a rock at the end of Leros. So we holed up there for the rest of the next day 'cause we knew the Germans would be out looking for us. We hid the boat up and took cover in the rocks, watching the plane go backwards and forwards looking for any survivors.[47]

Clarke remembered the journey all too well. 'What a night! It was terribly hard work rowing. We worked in two shifts of twenty minutes each on four oars, the "off duty" shift using pieces of wood. There was no let-up at all; there couldn't be. We had to make that rock by dawn.'[48] As dawn broke on 17 November, they realised they had the whole day to spend on this cold rock about 100 yards square just off Leros to the north, with Lipsi in sight. The men were ravenous and thirsty after the night's hard rowing. They wolfed down the two tins of bully beef, a tin of meat and veg, a tin of cheese a few packets of biscuits, but had only one-and-a-half litres of water between them all. They passed the water round in a mug. Lieutenant Clarke said, 'We put this [water] round, each had a sip each until in the end there was dust. No-one took gulps.'[49]

Meanwhile Clarke was having a recurrence of the malaria he had caught in the Middle East and was feeling decidedly ill. 'When I was shivering I sat on the edge of the boat or stood in the sun with a blanket round me, and when I was sweating I spent the time bathing my face in the pools of sea water amidst the rocks. It was the lack of water that worried me most, as I had been drinking quarts every day.'[50] The group of men had another snack at midday and another gulp of water. At four o'clock they finished off what was left of the food with another mouthful of water each. They set off once again as soon as it was getting dark – about 5.30 p.m. in Leros in November. Clarke recalled, 'Then we launched the boat the next night, and luckily I had a compass. I was doing the navigating. And I made Stokes be the one in charge of the rowing. One of the Indian engineers – they spoke English – said "I have got too tired." He couldn't row anymore. Later I got in touch with Stokes to thank him. He was very good indeed.'[51] Luckily the remaining few had the strength to carry on.

After about seven hours, Lipsi loomed in silhouette in front of them. Hatcher recalled,

> We went out on the wide open sea, and were wide open for any attack. As we were rowing we suddenly saw a small German convoy going into the harbour. We all had to sit and hold our breath and stop rowing, and hope that they didn't see us, and they didn't; anyway, we got to Lipsi and eventually made our way. This officer bloke said he knew someone on the island so he went out looking for them.[52]

As soon as they had landed, Major Barnet went off to find his Greek contact, although the rest of the group were still unsure who the officer was. Barnet had obviously found them a safe haven, as a Greek family kindly looked after them for a couple of nights. Lieutenant Clarke recalled, 'What a welcome! They jumped around us, shook hands, almost kissed us, I think a few of them did.' They were carrying with them wine, water, bread and raisins. 'We fell upon the water first, and a steady gurgling sound was coming from eight throats (Barnet and Hunt had already been attended to) for many minutes. The wine and then the food.'[53] They collapsed the boat and camouflaged it.

Lieutenant Clarke was most impressed with the hospitality of the local Greeks on Lipsi.

> When we got there, they were wonderful. They turned themselves out [of their house for us]; in this house, that served as their home, there was a raised platform at the end where the whole family slept, then there was the rest of the place. We didn't differentiate. We put all the men – there was only ten of us – the men, the other ranks, they went on the platform, and the three officers went on the floor, a bit separate. We saw alongside the door there a bundle of rags, we wondered what it was. It turned out to be granny.[54]

They cooked on the fire at the end of the room and there was hardly any furniture, just an old stool. Hanging from the roof were bunches of dried herbs. The next morning, they laid on items for washing, 'There were two bowls and two of the family details to each, one held a jug of rinsing water, and the other the soap and a towel. We went through the ordeal in twos, all getting the same attention, until we were all done.'[55]

Hatcher also recalled the locals with great warmth. 'They were lovely old people. How he [Barnet] had known them I don't know. Anyway, we bedded down for the night in the one-room cottage, we all shared a bed.' The following morning they got up and were given breakfast when they suddenly heard gunfire. 'Someone came running up said the Germans were coming to the harbour to find any British people who had escaped, so we had to drop our breakfast quickly and run to the hills.'[56] Once the Germans had left, the family called out to them in their hiding places and brought them fruit and raisins. George Hatcher recalled, 'We disappeared up there into the hills for a couple of days and we were eventually taken away by Greek caiques, and again I think it was due to the influence of this officer bloke.'[57] Lieutenant Clarke recognised how dangerous it had been for the family: 'very generous people [...] they risked their own lives, feeding us in the bushes when the Germans came through. They'd have been shot out of hand [...] When it comes to military aid of civil power it was amazing.'[58]

Major Barnet had found a boatman who agreed to take them in a caique to Turkey. However, the Germans had scuppered all the small boats, so the journey arranged with the local Greek was now impossible. The party had three options. One was to beat up the Fascists on the island and take their caique, an action about which Corporal Hunt was most enthusiastic. However, this would have put their helpful Greek family in jeopardy and, as Lieutenant Clarke said, 'after what they had done and risked for us, we felt we would not let them in for this.'[59] This suggestion was therefore abandoned. The second option was to try and make Turkey in their folding boat, but it was about 20 or 30 miles away and there was every likelihood they would get spotted out in the open sea in daylight. The third option was that, since the local Greek who had helped them was a British agent, take up his suggestion to wait it out as he knew that the SBS were patrolling the islands trying to get people off. He felt certain they would return in a couple of nights with a motorboat. That night they slept under the olive trees and waited.

The men knew they must make their move from Lipsi as soon as possible. By the next day (19 November), word was out that there were ten British escapees on the island and visitors appeared throughout the day bringing food, wine, blankets and pillows. The soldiers realised this was probably all the peasants possessed and were most grateful. Their Greek agent came to see them and told them it was too dangerous to remain in the same area, as everyone on the island knew their whereabouts, and they must move to the other side of the island where the caique would come to pick them up. A two-mile stumble in the dark across stony ground followed, where they bedded down near the coast. Luckily, the SBS were actively researching for any escapees and they were also trawling the island looking for them. Lieutenant Clarke said, 'Major Barnet [of the Raiding Forces] had been dropped behind the lines with pockets full of sovereigns [independent men from Raiding Forces were given sovereigns to pay the locals], that sort of thing. So he wanted to escape, and he knew how to contact the SBS.'[60] They were woken just after midnight by Major Barnet telling them the caique had arrived. On board were a Royal Navy officer, a few ratings and a Greek liaison officer. Lieutenant Clarke said, 'I will never forget that journey. It was pouring with rain, freezing cold and very rough. We rolled and dipped, and every big wave sent a sheet of water right over the boat.

We were all on the one small deck on which there was no shelter at all, trying to crouch under a couple of old tarpaulins. I, and I think most of the others, were absolutely soaked through.'[61]

They finally arrived in a tiny cove on the Turkish coast, only to get shot at by the Turkish guards. One of the party was shot through the hand. The naval lieutenant was irate and began waving his fists at the Turks; he rowed a small boat ashore to sort out the problem. The rest of the party did not see him for hours while they waited – he had had to traipse five miles to meet with the local military commander to account for them all. The commander was most apologetic and came aboard with his officers to apologise to the man they had shot. Everyone became very friendly, and what could have been a tragedy, turned out well. For Sergeant George Hatcher, the escape was a daring adventure. He recalled, 'You took everything in your stride while it was happening, just thinking of yourselves. It was more exciting afterwards, [when you think] what you'd let yourself in for.'[62]

14

The Rescue Parties

Well, look here. There must be hundreds of British soldiers still at large.
Someone ought go back and organise their escape.

George Jellicoe, SBS

The LRDG and the SBS were trained for rescue and escape activity and
took immediate action to leave the island. None of them had any
thought of surrendering, nor did they necessarily believe what they
were being told about the surrender. In any case, they were already
planning their getaway. Colonel Guy Prendergast went to search for
the remainder of his men and was thankful to bump into Dick
Croucher and Ron Tinker who informed him that the MO, Richard
Lawson, was leading a group of their men off to Mount Patella, west
of Lakki. Patella had been the telecommunications centre of the
Italians, called 'FAM-DICAT' because it housed both the coastal front
command and the land anti-aircraft defence command. This was the
place the navy had told the men to assemble and from where they
would try and pick them up should the island fall. However, this area
was now heavily populated with Germans, so Prendergast and his
party joined up with Captain Craig, the brigade intelligence officer,
and a private from the King's Own Regiment and decided to make
their way to a cave east of Mount Tortore (Tourtouras). This was on
the other side of Portolago on the Xerocampus side.

In an attempt to scavenge some provisions and pick up more men,
Prendergast went to Mount Scumbarda where he found Private
Lennox, who had been searching for an escape boat. The two men

cobbled together rucksacks, rations and blankets, but were caught by a group of Italians who came into the cave threatening them with revolvers and a tommy gun. Ushered into the underground control room for the coastal gun, they were surprised to find themselves in front of a group of drunken Italians. They decided to make a run for it, managed to escape and found their way back to the cave at Mount Tortore where they caught up with Captains Croucher, Tinker and Craig and the private from the King's Own. Three of their party tried to swim to Kalymnos via two smaller islands[1] but were dashed by the high seas and had to return. Rations were becoming seriously depleted, and desperation was setting in. The colonel decided to go to Xerocampus to try and find food and a sound boat, but all the ones he found had holes in them. Eventually he went back to meet up with the others where they told him they had seen a craft coming in near the previously agreed rendezvous. They decided to signal and were picked up by the RAF Air Sea Rescue launch on 22 November.[2] They would later meet up with Jellicoe and Lieutenant Commander Ramseyer of Levant Schooner Flotilla in Bodrum.

Another party with Second Lieutenant R.E. White and four others (the men Prendergast had been looking for) baled a small rowing boat that had been sunk at Xerocampus bay and made a perilous journey to join the others who had escaped to Turkey. Small groups continued to escape up to a fortnight after surrender. The *London Gazette* reported:

> After its fall on 16th November, evacuation of such troops as could be got out of Leros was conducted by Lieutenant-Commander L. F. Ramseyer from a caique, he himself having escaped from Leros by caique 12 hours after its surrender. He began to conduct the evacuation of troops out of Leros by naval craft, R.A.F. high speed launches and any other crafts soldiers could lay their hands on. SBS patrols began landing to pick up any British troops still at liberty.[3]

A Royal Air Force launch evacuated the LRDG patrols from Seriphos, and Levant Schooner No. 2 successfully picked up the LRDG left in Mykonos.[4] Escapees from Leros found their way south in a variety of craft, including two Italian F-lighters, one towing an LCM (mechanised landing craft), two LCTs (tank landing crafts), an Italian tug towing a MMS (motor minesweeper), various minesweepers and coastal craft, all of which arrived in Levant ports by 2 December. Lieutenant Stowell took an F-lighter from Leros on 15 November with 177 German prisoners on board, reaching Haifa via Samos on 25 November.

Jellicoe Sails Out

As soon as he realised Tilney had surrendered, George Jellicoe set about contacting all the men who had been manning the northern gun posts to let them know. In two available jeeps, he rounded up his own men – in all about 25 of them, including T1 and T2 Patrol. They took possession of an Italian caique and a small motorboat in Partheni and sailed straight to a small island 'north of Leros' where they hid during daylight. They managed to get to Turkey the next night, where they joined an old minesweeper and made the three-day voyage down the Turkish coast to Haifa.

Jellicoe had been in the north of the island with Brigadier Tilney and Lieutenant Colonel Iggulden of the Buffs at two o'clock that afternoon of 16 November when an attack south had been ordered.[5] He had searched for the remaining men in the area and made them into a coherent group. Along with Sergeant Workman and Corporal Dryden, Jellicoe returned to HQ to get a clearer picture of what was going on. He recalled:

> I always remember that on the last day I got a message from Brigadier Tilney saying would I report to his HQ. And that was in the afternoon, I think. It was impossible to get through, it meant getting pretty well through the German lines so I had a sergeant with me. We waited until it got dark and then got through. And then had quite a stiff climb up. And I always remember that because there were a lot of people just lying around [...] our chaps [...] which we were holding, and I walked up with them. The sergeant and I knew the HQ well because that's where I had seen the Italians the very first time I had met up with them.[6]

It was dark as they climbed Meraviglia toward HQ and he expected to meet up with Brigadier Tilney. He was horrified that the first person he ran into was a German colonel standing just behind Tilney in the opening to the HQ tunnel. Jellicoe remembered, 'Tilney said, "Terribly sorry George, but when I sent for you I didn't know I was going to be captured." And then he said, "Incidentally, a friend of yours, Alan Phipps, is missing. I don't know if you can do anything to locate him because I don't know what has happened to him."' Jellicoe didn't know him well. 'He was in the navy [...] I didn't know him until I met him in Leros [...] army wireless wasn't all that good at long range, and in the navy he had better wireless communication. He was sent up to Leros very early after its capture to take charge of the communications between Leros and Alexandria and Cairo [British Middle East HQ] and I got to know him there. In fact, I had known his father.'[7] Eric Phipps had been the ambassador in Berlin, and Jellicoe had spent a long time in 1936 in Palestine where he came to know him.

Uppermost in Jellicoe's mind was trying to get as many of his men off the island as he could. He explained to General Müller that his men would only surrender if he personally informed them.

> I said, 'Look, I have some chaps' [...] I think I probably exaggerated the number [...] they were all by themselves up in the north of the island [...] 'I would suspect that they have no idea about the surrender, and I think it would be a very good thing if I were to inform them of that.' I think the Germans went along with that [...] I remember walking, must have been quite a way from Alinda, up in the dark, and a lot of Germans were coming the other way, a real problem.[8]

Jellicoe was impressed with the general's behaviour; Müller agreed that if Jellicoe gave his promise of return and surrender, he would let him go to his men.[9]

As he walked back to find his group, all the time Jellicoe was searching for Phipps but he failed to find him. 'I went to look on the plateau there. I couldn't find him. I was very glad that I had done that because I had morphine on me.'[10] He was able to inject two or three soldiers, both British and German who were badly wounded and in pain, before reporting back to General Müller. Since he had given his word Jellicoe felt obliged to return, but audaciously he again persuaded Müller to let him go, telling him he needed to persuade the rest of the British soldiers to surrender. This time he did not give his word and felt at liberty to find any means possible to effect his escape, taking with him as many men as he could find. He was later to discover Alan Phipps had been killed in action engaging a couple of Germans attacking the Fortress HQ. He was later buried in Leros cemetery.[11]

Jellicoe was driving around with Captain H.W. Blyth in a couple of jeeps they had found in Alinda and came across about 25 men of the LRDG and other SBS men they had met on the way; 'I got to our people. By then I decided if it was at all possible to get away from the island that night we should do so. We went up to the bay in the north. We were lucky we found a boat, lying there which we just pinched and we sailed before first light, or just as it was dawning, to the island to the north.'[12] The remaining men from LRDG and SBS found an Italian caique in the early hours of the 17th and a small motorboat and made off to Lipsi from Partheni.

> We lay up all day there and we sailed across to the Turkish coast the next night. I then sailed up the following night to Samos where our chaps were – mainly the Sacred Squadron were there. And I got one or two of my chaps to go back to Leros with their boat and they evacuated quite a lot more in the following nights, going back more than once or twice. Other people were getting people away too, the Greeks were helping.[13]

As soon as Jellicoe landed in Turkey, he was ordered to go straight to Churchill to report on events. Jellicoe recalled,

> I went back up to Ankora and almost as I arrived there, there was a message saying I was wanted back in Cairo. And I got the train down to the south and then got flown down to Cairo […] There was a car waiting for me at the airport, and I found myself driving out toward the pyramids; and suddenly the car turned off to the right to a rather fine house, and they said this is where Winston Churchill is staying after the Tehran conference. He is having some time in Cairo and you are to report to him. I went straight up to his room, it was after lunch, he was in bed; and rather typically for him, he didn't mind how senior or junior people were but he wanted to know what had gone wrong in the Dodecanese campaign. I told him what had gone wrong. Plenty of things had gone wrong.[14]

He spent around half an hour with Churchill debating the lack of foresight, planning, and all the tactical errors and failures which had occurred. Jellicoe had to respond truthfully that the airfields should have been captured at the onset before embarking on the campaign.

Raiding Forces to the Rescue

A couple of unsung heroes in the rescuing parties were Ashley Martin Greenwood of the LRDG[15] and Lieutenant Ramseyer of the Levant Schooner Flotilla, who risked their lives returning to Leros to evacuate the soldiers. On reaching Turkey, Jellicoe had suggested that someone should go back and rescue those left on Leros, and Greenwood volunteered to accompany Ramseyer (Jellicoe had to go back and report to HQ Cairo). They readied themselves for their return to Leros to pick up any men still at liberty. At one o'clock in the morning on 21 November, they pulled into St Nicholas Bay with a Greek agent known as 'S'. The St Nicholas chapel was decided on as a rendezvous where any escapees would gather, and S and Greenwood parted company, agreeing to meet up later. Since the northern parts of the island were remote, Greenwood called out to any British soldiers who might be hiding. At 4 a.m. he called in on a Greek's house to ask if they had seen any British soldiers around. Although he was offered a drink, they could not give him any news. He found some men on the gun batteries and told them to go to the chapel and wait for him. After collecting more men, that night he returned to the chapel and met up with S who had found some more men in need of rescue – a few Greeks and a couple of British soldiers. They waited for the return of the high-speed launch for six nights but saw nothing, while the number of British potential escapees rose to 15. Greenwood decided to go looking for a method of escape – accompanying a Lerian man herding his animals – disguised as a local. By the eighth day he was joined by Peter Mould of LRDG whom they had sprung from the hospital. Mould had a bad dose of dysentery and was still in uniform. Since wounded prisoners from Alinda hospital were allowed to walk all over the island, they covered him in bandages and dressed him in peasant clothes to make him look like a civilian casualty.[16] The lack of German interest in seeking out any remaining British stragglers is surprising given the fight they had put up. They seemed reluctant to leave the main roads, and did not seem bothered about capturing escapees.

S and Greenwood managed to secure a rowing boat found in St Nicholas Bay, but both were recaptured when searching for food, after an informer had given out the information that the chapel was being used as their meeting place. Somehow they managed to warn the others waiting for them, and a Greek known as 'Z' took them to Blefuti Bay to arrange more boats, but they were stopped by a sentry. Z quickly distracted the guards by offering them some mandarins, while the rest of the party managed to get away. All the boats they found had holes in them, but with the help of local Lerians they managed to patch them up so they seemed seaworthy. They stole some German blankets and at 6 p.m. set out for Lipsi, landing around 9.30. To their surprise, they found other escapees were already there, and were greeted by a voice, 'Hello boys. Come right in!'[17]

Sid Bowden and Don Bush managed to escape by rowing a boat to Turkey with a small group of LRDG, two Royal Engineers, an Indian and an Italian soldier. They were recovered by a schooner and taken to Alexandria.[18] Sid explained,

> It was the fifth day, we had an Indian with us [and some] Long Range Desert Group chaps. There were remnants of everybody, more or less. We was going to re-form to go into a counter-attack when an officer came down from the hill and told us the island was surrendered. I think it was a Long Range Desert Group officer [Greenwood]. It was somebody who knew more what was going on than we did. We sat around and six of us got together and said well, the port's there now, there are some folding boats down there. How about us trying to get away.

In the dark, they made their way towards the port and opened out some Canadian folding boats. 'So we set off; across the bay to us was a tug, and I think it was the tug that pulled the beam across at nights, and that was getting up steam. We could see there was people in there. We just rowed off and kept rowing all night.'[19] Others were trying to get away at the time as he saw a tug further on. 'I've got a feeling it was one of our captains, Captain Clarke – they got away.' They rowed and rowed and by late morning finally arrived in a bay.[20]

Sid's companion Navy Radar Operator Don Bush recalled,

> In the evenings, I'd say we left there about seven o'clock. What we did was used our steel helmets as oars and paddles. One bailed out while the others paddled. We were heading to Turkey. We just said Turkey's over that way. That is more or less all we could do really. We had no compass. No, we couldn't see Turkey as it was dark. I knew there was

German torpedo boats searching. We did see several of them but they missed us [...] one plane came and had a look at us in plain daylight, just swooped down, but didn't attack us or anything.[21]

From there they were taken on a destroyer down to Bodrum and put onto a tank landing craft to await transport to take them back to Egypt.

Some of the men who had been taken prisoner managed to get away in the confusion. Vic Kenchington, MO with the Royal Irish Fusiliers, remembered,

We were taken prisoner but after two days decided to leave. There were four of us: an SBS marine, Long Range Desert Group 'Chalky' James White, Irish Fusilier Ryan and myself. We left after two days and went to Alinda. We found a boat which didn't leak and a couple of oars and left the island. We could hear engine noises from Portolago so went north 3 or 4 miles from Turkey. We had hardly any food left, just a few tangerines, some hard tack chocolate, a bottle of water and some cigarettes – we shared the cigarettes, we shared it all. We finished up with blistered hands. After about 22 hours, we got to Turkey and got interned. Gareth Evans, one of the British consuls there, got us out and took us to Bodrum. There were a lot of naval ships. We went back to Palestine on a boat, then back to Egypt. There were just 27 left of our battalion.[22]

He recalled, 'We surrendered the island to the Germans to save lives, as we had no supplies, and everyone was made POWs.'[23]

Other small bunches of men were pulling together to get off the island. Lieutenant Gordon Huckle, Coy Sergeant Major Greenyer and Private Crowhurst managed to obtain a small leaky caique from some helpful Greek locals in Gourna. At midnight on the 17th they rowed to the north tip of Leros and were picked up by motor launch within a mile of the Turkish coast.[24] Captain P.R.H. Turner and Lance Corporal Honey raided what food they could find and hid up until nightfall. Although caught by a German soldier on patrol in Alinda, they pretended they were Greek locals and were let off. They discovered Italians mending a caique trying to escape and convinced them to take them along, landing at Bodrum on 20 November. Sixteen other men of the Queen's Own Royal West Kents got away.[25]

Not all of the intended escapes were successful. John Olivey of the LRDG was on Clidi with a six-inch battery gun in the north of the island and refused to surrender, continuing to fight along with many of the rest of the LRDG men. He ordered his corporals to gather their men and, as quietly and quickly as possible, to move to the north of the island onto rocky terrain. He stayed behind to hold the Ciano Battery on Mount Clidi, but on hearing some Germans coming toward his position driving sheep, he assumed the position of a dead body. He waited in hiding until darkness came, then decided to return to the fort to try and blow up a large naval gun to the east, which, although he had laid charges on it earlier, he could not light as he had no matches on him. To his surprise, two Germans had settled into the fort who mistook him for one of their officers. Forced to shoot them both, he attracted the unwanted attention of other enemy soldiers and hastened down the rocky valley. Passing three groups of about ten enemy soldiers, he managed to find his way down the mountain, throwing stones to distract them and then hiding behind the rocks. Slowly, he made his way to the rendezvous he had given his patrol. By the time he reached the appointed spot, it was daylight and he was hungry, thirsty and tired. He could find no water where he had left them, so went on to the Italian barracks where he uncovered some bacon fat, bread and water. He finally found an empty house where the bed proved to be too much to resist and he put down his head and fell asleep. He awoke to find two German soldiers standing at the bottom of his bed. He recalled, 'By 8 a.m., it was clear from the singing of German songs from the village and from the large number of enemy seaplanes in the bay that the island had surrendered.'[26] They took him off in a jeep to the dock where the prisoners were being held. After a couple more abortive attempts to escape, he was shipped back to Athens with the other POWs – around 20 other officers and 1,500 other ranks; Doc Lawson and an English padre were also on board. Olivey would be awarded the Military Cross for his actions in Leros, the citation reading 'Captain Olivey was himself still firing a Bren gun and throwing grenades thirteen hours after the island surrendered. Throughout the battle he showed no thought for his own safety and at times fired heavy coastal guns over open sight against the advancing enemy. This was despite persistent bombing attacks on a very large scale.'[27]

Others trying to escape by small boats did not make it. Major Ewart Tassell of D Company Buffs had identified a boat earlier, just in case he needed it for an escape, but he was too far away from it when the time came.

> Up on the coast where we were stationed [Blefuti], this was before the invasion, there was a shed not far from the beach [...] I had vaguely thought there is a half-decent boat there. I had done a bit of sailing so I knew what I was looking for. I thought if the worst comes to the worst, I might want this boat. Well I did want it, but I could not get at it because I was miles away by the time we had surrender to the Germans. I was dumped down in the bottom somewhere [Lakki] and eventually joined up with a few more of the two or three officers who were left, including Commanding Officer Iggulden. 'Oh,' he said, 'I am so pleased to see you. I thought we had lost you' – because I hadn't seen them, you see. I had been detached from HQ for some time. And from there, we were crammed into an ex-Italian destroyer, stuffed into the forecastle, this wretched thing – which I didn't like at all. I'm not very good at being [cooped up] [...] this Italian destroyer dumped us in Athens somewhere. From there it took us three months to arrive in Germany as POWs.[28]

He blamed his capture on the fact that they had been given no information; the first he knew the island had surrendered was through a German broadcast, 'a chap with a loudspeaker'. He instructed everyone to surrender. 'That was all right but knowing the Germans don't always speak the truth, we didn't take too much notice of that.'[29]

Of the 123 LRDG troopers on the island at the time of surrender, 70 escaped; the rest were missing or had been taken prisoner. Among the dead was their charismatic leader, Commanding Officer Jake Easonsmith. He had been shot down by a sniper when leading his men through Platanos where the Germans were hiding in half-ruined buildings. He was buried in Leros cemetery along with J.T. Bowler, S. Federman, K. Foley, P. Wheeldon, H.L. Mallett, L. Oelofse, A.J. Penhall and Alan Redfern. Kenneth Probert, one of the many soldiers captured, stated that a British submarine took officers away before capture, leaving those left behind to serve in POW camps in Germany.[30] In all, the Raiding Forces managed to get over 1,000 men off the island. Many escaped to Bodrum and made their way back to Palestine. This was the last operation that the New Zealand squadron of the LRDG would participate in and the troops would be disbanded on 31 December 1943.

Many men escaped to small islands nearby and were sheltered by Greeks, then moved on to Turkey. Of the Buffs, Major Read, Lieutenant Tillard and six other ranks escaped, 24 were killed, 59 wounded, 14 missing in action. Iggulden was captured and taken as a POW.[31] Of the King's Own the battalion lost 15 officers, 8 wounded, 60 other ranks killed, an unknown number of others wounded. Only one officer and 57 other ranks got to Palestine.[32]

Of the four companies who had fought on Leros, fewer than 250 survivors got away.[33] Jellicoe got out more than 20 SBS and others in a caique from Pandeli; LRDG Guy Prendergast escaped, but John Olivey was captured. For those who escaped, Captain Clarke's comment summed up the feeling. 'It was just that we were in the right place at the right time. We were lucky really.'[34] For those who were caught, although the possibility of being killed was now less likely, there was still a voyage into the unknown awaiting them as prisoners of war. The Allied forces remaining in Samos, consisting of 220 British troops and 380 of the Greek Sacred Squadron, were all evacuated on the night of 20 November, along with 8,300 Italian troops, and civilians. Most were sent by train to Syria.

15

Prisoners of War

Telegram to Lieutenant Ted Johnson's mother

What Ted Johnson's mother must have felt at the time she read this telegram can only be imagined. For many mothers, telegrams were the bearers of the terrible news that their sons were missing in action, possibly dead. Their heartbreak would only be relieved with news of their son's survival or their ultimate arrival on their doorstep long afterwards. Ted's mother was one of the fortunate ones as she was to see him once again. For others, the loss was permanent.

After their capture in Leros, all soldiers had been ordered to assemble in Portolago (Lakki). Those who could took off to one of the small bays and tried to escape the island to Turkey; those who remained were to become prisoners of war. The British prisoners numbered approximately 200 officers and 3,000 men of other rankings. The Italians numbered 350 officers and 5,000 other rankings.[1] Reports were heard of the cruel treatment of the Italians by the Germans. The story has long circulated in Leros that at least one boat full of Italian officers that had set out from Pandeli was intentionally scuppered by German fire coming from the shore.

Lieutenant Richard 'Jimmy' James was to end up in a German prison camp. He had known George Jellicoe well and, looking back on his capture, regretted that he had not managed to meet up with him as he realised that Jellicoe would have helped him escape. Both had been fighting in Leros at the same time in different areas of the island and their paths had not crossed.

> Jellicoe was in charge of Special Boat Service out there [...] I had no contact with him in Leros. I wish I had done he might have got me off it! That's the most annoying part of it, if we had only had proper warning that the thing had been surrendered, we could have perhaps made contact with the Special Boat Service. One or two people who were further over, at Portolargo, they managed to get off there. Two or three men got across to Turkey in very grave conditions. Sergeant Major S.W.J. Greenyer, he got over there [...] Got hold of a boat and got over there by using his hands. Sergeant Greenyer was a very determined man.[2]

The fact that they were given no information about the surrender left Lieutenant James and his men with little opportunity to get off the island. 'There were opportunities to escape, and officers elsewhere on the island did manage to get away. We did not know anything had happened until suddenly at dawn on 17 November, no aircraft came over, and we gathered then that fighting was over. Of course, our chance of making escape was highly ridiculous.'[3] It was too late for Lieutenant James and his men. James also knew Lieutenant Clifford Clarke well. 'We both got commissions in the same regiments, the Royal West Kents. We then spent the next 43 years together. His company commander was Captain Percy Flood. We knew each other on a daily basis for the next four years.'[4]

Unfortunately, Lieutenant James did not make the escape journey with Lieutenant Clarke's party, but Clarke held him in high esteem. Years later, he recalled James: 'He is a very fine chap. He was with us on Leros, but he was captured. He was given the rough treatment, when he went to Athens, the SS saw them and – he is a highly educated chap [...] He was pulled out, they said he was a spy. They took him to Berlin. They chucked him in the cells. He was interrogated for weeks and weeks.'[5] Because he was an intelligence officer, the Germans targeted Lieutenant James for special treatment, dragging him out of his cell at all hours, depriving him of sleep and interrogating him in an attempt to extract information from him. He suffered punitive spells of solitary confinement but gave away nothing except his name, rank and number.[6]

Another of the POWs rounded up at the harbour was Royal Irish Fusiliers Liaison Officer Frank Smith.[7] He only heard about the surrender much later in the evening of the 16th and found himself among other soldiers streaming down the hillside through the minefields making their way to Leros town. Here he was relieved to find a few other battalion officers, among them John Penny and Bob Ambrose. 'Whilst conferring on the best policy to adopt – if any at all, as we were all so completely weary and fatigued'[8] – they did take a moment to ponder the possibility of escape, but had no success in finding a boat. Frank bunked down for the night in Tom West's old Platoon Headquarters.

The day after the surrender, Frank Smith did not wake up until 11 a.m., he was so exhausted from the previous days' fighting. This was typical of every single one of those who had been engaged in the battle. Yet despite being prisoners, the men seemed to have considerable opportunity for movement. When Frank got up, he took off to Meraviglia in a jeep in an attempt to retrieve his kit and some food from the HQ Tunnel where he had been stationed. Germans were everywhere. Nonetheless, he managed to find a well-stocked cookhouse and they ate a breakfast of bacon, sausages and biscuits. Three Germans nearby appeared not to be interested in his activities, but were more focused on having a good breakfast. They had lit candles, put on a gramophone record and were sitting sharing a bottle of wine and some chocolate. 'They returned my greeting of "Morgen", with indifference, asked my rank, and promptly offered the last half bottle of the General's wine.'[9] He returned to 'the boys' with his acquisitions of a new pipe, a blanket and some shaving accessories. He had also managed to pick up some tea and cigarettes.

The POWs had little option but to interact with their captors. One of the German officers they nicknamed 'D'Arcy' because he was trying to perfect his English; another whom they called 'Natze' talked of Leros, the war in general and the future prospects for Germany. Food was more easily provided for the officers than lower ranks; when Lieutenant Frank Smith asked for food, he was given a couple of tins and tobacco. He and his comrades had fresh sardines for breakfast and a good dinner of stew, potatoes and carrots or bread and Italian bully beef. But one of the biggest problems was boredom – after all that fighting and stress, living on one's nerves, they now had nothing to do. Frank and his fellow officers were housed together in one building. They hardly ever got out of the house, and became restless being penned in all day, so they asked for an escort for a walk and went as far as 'A' mess where the other soldiers had been staying. There had been thorough looting there and Frank only managed to salvage a tie and some braces. They all slept on the floor.[10]

Officers were eventually segregated after about four days of hanging around in Portolago and put on a destroyer in a hold with the hatch bolted shut until they got to Piraeus. The air was putrid. Some of the British prisoners had already been taken off on two Italian destroyers on 19 November. Major Bill Shepherd (Royal Irish Fusiliers) was one of them and had been two days living on the quayside in Portolago awaiting the Italian seaplane to take them to Athens. 'Officers and seniors NCOs were issued with two small tins of meat, a few hard biscuits and taken on board a filthy ex-Italian Destroyer for a night's journey to Piraeus [...] During the night German naval officers had the British officers taken to their quarters saying they did not know officers were being carried on board.'[11] Sergeant James Mulhern of the Royal Irish Fusiliers played the pipes to cheer them up.[12] Others were taken on 20 November on a German naval vessel. Many of them had on only what they were wearing. In some cases this was summer dress, khaki shorts and shirts, and clothes intended for good weather. Invariably, they would feel the chill in the days to come.

Leros to Athens

The rest of the rounded-up British POWs prepared for their move off the island on the morning of 21 November with no breakfast, just nibbling on a few dry biscuits. The officers were invited to have a drink with their captors. As Frank Smith stood on the quayside with four other senior officers, he watched sadly as British soldiers, now POWs, boarded the German ship to take them to Piraeus, leaving at 1 p.m. Again, most of the men were put in the hold. Conditions on board were rank, and the troops became increasingly irritable, as one Irish Fusilier explained. 'Five days in a cramped stinking POW ship and tempers suffered. The amount of people who should have done this, that, and the other, increased hourly.'[13] The soldiers were squashed into the hold, and were plunged into darkness as the hatch was closed, each man struggling to find a small space to rest. The stench was horrendous, the unwashed bodies smelling of putrid sweat. The heat climbed, and no air was coming in. Men were urinating in their helmets, and the overpowering smell of ammonia led to retching. They cracked open the hatch and called to the guards to let six of them out at a time for some air, and to empty their helmets. Men were allowed out a few at a time then placed back in the hold.

During the voyage, they were all worried about the possibility of surface attack. With 2,300 prisoners aboard, including Italian officers, the ship was badly overcrowded and Frank was concerned that it might roll over as they moved off from Portolago. He was squashed together with nine other officers on a small winch platform, lucky enough to be on the surface. Although they attempted to sleep in their greatcoats with a blanket apiece, it was difficult as it was cold and stormy, and many of the men were seasick.

Feeding the men on board was a major problem and for the most part they ate only cheese and biscuits, or bread and bully beef, distributed by Frank with a couple of his sergeants. The lower-ranking privates had a worse time of it as always. Fusilier Paddy McCrystal recalled, 'We went to the bottom of the ship. They gave us a few tins of corned beef, wee small things, about 2 oz something like that, 80 per cent salt. We had it for about four days. And that didn't last long, we were not long getting through that.'[14] Meanwhile officers made hot tea on the steam pipes of the ship. Sugar and coffee were pilfered from the Germans.[15]

The dishevelled troops arrived in Piraeus, Athens's main harbour, about 11 a.m. the following day. On disembarking they were heartened to see hundreds of Greek people lining the street, cheering. For more than one soldier, it felt like the march through Athens was more of a victory march than one of defeat as young women and girls threw kisses, and children threw apples, oranges and cigarettes for them. Women were in tears as POWs threw their cap badges for them to catch. All the troops purposefully sang and gave Victory signs in response to the photographers and officials, mainly to show they were not subdued. One fusilier remembered:

From Piraeus dock through the streets of Athens, to our temporary home in a disused and absolutely bare factory on the outskirts of Athens gave me my first insight into 'Occupied Europe'. What an insight! The people of Athens, half-starved, did all they could to cheer us up, including throwing apples, fruit and what food they had, to us. It was at this point that the brutality of the Germans to people in occupied countries became apparent. Our escort used their butts and bayonets, and the motor-cycle patrols ran on the pavement in an endeavour to run people down.[16]

All the prisoners were amassed by two o'clock and started marching through the streets of Athens for about three-and-a-half hours (some say it was much longer). Piper Major Mulhern was again to offer sustenance to the flagging spirits of the captives, as he piped a stirring march to lift their morale, much to the consternation of the German guards.[17] Fusiliers McEntaggart and Duggan recalled,

On reaching Athens we were forced to march around the streets of the city, for propaganda purposes, while the German newsreel men took photos of us. When they started doing that we gave the 'V' sign, just to show that we were not downhearted. This so annoyed the Huns that they kept us marching around Athens for ten hours [probably much less than this], and any of the inhabitants who tried to give us food or water were driven away by our guards.[18]

Lieutenant Clarke (who had escaped) was worried his wife would see the photographs of the march. 'My wife didn't know where I was, she saw a picture in the paper of the Royal West Kent prisoners being marched through Athens, and she didn't know I wasn't one, and she said, "Clifford won't like that."'[19] The Greek civilians, in spite of their poverty, attempted to show solidarity. Reg Neep said of the march through Athens from Piraeus, 'I always remember one lady was carrying a young child in her arms and she put her hand out with a crust of bread in it and she was really rifle-butted severely away from us.'[20] The troops finally arrived at their camp about 5.30 p.m. very tired but they all had to sleep on the floor.[21]

For some of the men, it was at this stage that they realised the enormity of their situation, and experienced the sunken feeling of the vanquished. Major Tassell of the Buffs recalled:

You know what you get [...] when you are suddenly defeated. You live on your nerves for a while, and it suddenly comes down [...] The first

I remember in Athens is a sort of – what hell it was – they penned us up. I wanted to escape. Next door, with us, was a whole lot of Italian prisoners and I can remember these chaps could sing. They were all singing this marvellous classical stuff. From there I tried to get out on the roof of the shed, but couldn't manage it.'[22]

The officers and other ranks were separated again in Athens, and grouped together in rank (as they had been before they left the island). The lower ranks were poorly treated, as Privates McEntaggart and Duggan remembered. They were put in a disused aircraft factory, where 'we began to know the meaning of starvation, as our rations were very small. The factory was in a filthy state and the floor was covered in oil. The only bedding we got was one blanket each.'[23] They stayed in the factory for about a month. Reg Neep recalled, 'We became desperately hungry. Mid-morning the next day, we were issued with a ladle of macaroni and later that day we were given 10 oz. of bread plus $\frac{1}{2}$ oz. of margarine each.' For the next ten days they remained on the concrete floor, their daily food rations the same. The lack of privacy for the POWs was part of the humiliation process. Reg Neep recalled while in Athens there was no toilet provision. 'The civilian population was still working there, we were in a very distressed situation because there were no toilet facilities and it ended up in the middle of the road. They built toilets with a long pole for people to squat on, which was open to the public so the population was walking past us as we had to do our toiletries.'[24] By now it was early December, the weather cold and abysmal.

German guards were the remnants of their army – old, bedraggled or very young, with buttons missing from their coats – and were not very good at keeping watch over their prisoners.

During his stay near Athens, Reg Neep met a sympathetic German guard, a Canadian who had been on holiday in Germany when hostilities broke out. Unfortunately having a German-sounding name, this youth found himself forcibly conscripted into the German army on non-combative duties. He had been robbed of his papers and passport and made to stay. He gave the British POWs the current war news (as told by the German propaganda machine). Contact with the British NCOs was also made by a member of the Greek underground who had more factual reports of the state of the war in Europe. Food continued to be meagre, water was severely rationed, but they obtained a little protein when Red Cross parcels were distributed – 12 men to share a parcel of Horlicks tablets, cocoa and tins of rice and concentrated chicken jelly.[25]

The officers obviously had a slightly better time of it, as Liaison Officer Frank Smith recalled. He met up with Tom Lynch, Austin Ardill, West, Penney and some of the rest of his company, as well as Paddy Slanley. There were, at least, washing facilities which Frank took advantage of, sluicing himself down, changing his clothes and rinsing out his dirty laundry. Dinner consisted of potato stew plus one loaf of black bread for five men per 24 hours, so they were very glad of their small reserves. He chatted to the other men, sharing their escape experience, drank Ovaltine, ate margarine and jam (augmented by their bread and sugar) and welcomed a Red Cross parcel which arrived that evening with 30 cigarettes and a small bar of chocolate.[26] The Red Cross continued to call in occasionally to give the men Horlicks, chocolate and more cigarettes.[27] There was a roll call every day after a breakfast of bread and jam.

On 24 November, Frank wrote, 'Wash and shave followed by bed repairing and spring-cleaning of household.' He had wounded his hand, which was dressed by a German MO. Although he called it 'insipid', he ate better than the lower ranks, with macaroni cheese, 'flavoured by ourselves with salt and /or sugar, augmented by bread and sugar. 5 cigarettes. Made large drinking mug from jam tin.' Some of the men even made rice pudding. During the rainy evening, they watched a concert given by an Italian band.[28] Frank seems to have been given a considerable amount of freedom as he was even taken out by his German guard D'Arcy for a drive through Athens to the Acropolis, and was shown all around the Parthenon and other temples by a tourist guide. He noted in his log book, 'Talk and drive back by 1545 hrs.'[29] News filtered down to them about the fate of the other soldiers who had not made it. On 27 November, Frank was told of the death of John Salter whom he had dropped off in hospital in Leros. Such unwelcome information could only have further choked the men, many of them still in their twenties. Frank was only 28 years old himself.

Those captives in the LRDG did not stay POWs for long and managed to escape during the march through Athens. Paddy McCrystal watched them as they lost themselves in the mass of people.

> We were marching up to Athens through the main streets. There was a crowd of Long Range Desert Group. They were near the back. I looked round and the next thing I see, I was on my own. The boys had gone into the crowd and scattered out. I was all by myself and I was wondering what am I going to do? Am I going to stay with this crowd or am I going to go out [try and escape] as I couldn't get the food down on account they had greasy food in Greece. The Long Range Desert Group boys got away. They mixed with the crowd. They disappeared. I was on my own. I was walking up and down. I could have done the same but I couldn't be doing with the food. I don't know whether I was right or wrong.[30]

As the dark enveloped the crowd, it became easier to slip away. Guards were by now unevenly spaced and the streets had grown narrower and dim. Some of the German soldiers gave chase when the odd prisoner escaped but rarely followed much further than the first couple of streets, then resumed their place at the side of the POWs. Captain John Olivey who had been fighting on Leros with the LRDG was one of the plucky ones. He had nipped down a side street, and although he was followed for a while, he hid behind a wall until the guard gave up the chase and rejoined the group. Two Greek women followed him and took him to a safe house belonging to a tinsmith and his Maltese wife who provided him with some civilian clothes. That night he ate a family meal with them, later sharing their only room where they all slept.

He was shifted between safe houses, and watched helplessly as his rescuers were paid in gold sovereigns – as the months crept by, he realised that he was worth some money to those housing him and they were reluctant to let him go too quickly. Olivey eventually managed to get a message to his superior David Lloyd Owen on 30 January 1944 to send rescue and get him out. After threatening to break free from his safe haven, he was taken to Turkey with another 90 refugees, landing in Cairo on 25 April 1944 – he had been travelling or hiding for over five months.

Cattle Trucks to Moosburg

The Germans began to move British and Italian soldiers out of Greece on 3 December, transporting them to German camps on cattle trains. Reg Neep recalled,

> After thirteen days on this site [the disused factory] we were marched back through Athens and to the railway terminus. We were split into groups of forty, each with four guards, each group into a closed goods wagon 8 or 9 ft. wide, 1/3 of the space for the forty prisoners and the 2/3rds for the 4 guards. There were small grills one in each corner for ventilation and a thin layer of straw on the floor. The sliding doors were then chained shut, about 30 wagons in all.[31]

Each wagon had only a bale of straw and one or two buckets for 30 or 40 men. Some of the men had chronic diarrhoea, making the confined space even more intolerable. Frank Smith recalled, 'Five of the forty had dysentery and the odour from our little bucket, coupled with the remaining odour of our predecessors made fresh air a rationed commodity.' The door opened on the fourth day and the men crashed out to greet the rush of sunlight and fresh air, but only five minutes' break was allowed a day. Conditions in the train wagons were dire, Frank Smith recorded in his log book. 'It was bitterly cold. 1 loaf of bread and 2 tins of bully per man for four days. Allowed out for 5 mins relief. Through Yugoslavia, beautiful scenery.'[32] Six days later it was snowing and they had run out of water. There was a small amount of beef and bully left but they were fast running out of food.

Some of the men held in the central section of the train ended up much worse off as they were let out less frequently. Paddy McCrystal was in the central wagon,

> There were thirty people in a wagon, and we were in there for about fourteen days. We went through Greece right down to Bulgaria, Hungary, Austria. They let us out maybe for ten minutes for a walk. We were in the centre, we were right unlucky. Every time we missed it [being let out of the wagon]. They started at the beginning and let half of them out. Then they started at the back the next day. And sometimes they missed us. We got out a couple of times, but not as often as the boys in the front or the back. Conditions were unbearable. I remember pulling into Sofia, and the air raid went [...] We got the smell of it.[33]

The train travelled north towards a mid-European winter. The men were still only dressed or partially dressed in tropical kit, and huddled together to keep from freezing. Reg Neep recalled, 'On the third day with only two stops for physical relief, we were shunted into a siding at Sofia, Bulgaria where we had our first food for three days, a bowl of soup and a slice of black bread.' They went on to Salonika, Yugoslavia, with many stops to allow troop trains and armaments to pass and occasional stops to allow repairs to the track, which had been blown up by the resistance bands.[34] 'It was so cold now that there were ice flows on the river, the coldness was also aggravated by dysentery affecting some of the prisoners, plus very active lice. Medical help was refused by the guards.'[35] When they reached Bucharest, prisoners in the worst condition were examined by a German MO and taken to hospital (they assumed). On the eleventh day of this journey, they reached Vienna, with snow everywhere and no food for two days. 'The next day we had a bowl of "skilly" and the following day a cup of water. We were now so weak and exhausted that we didn't know what day it was.'[36]

A few of the POWs on the wagon trains managed to make daring escapes, then had to cross unknown terrain for months before they could get home. In one wagon, among the prisoners were Sergeants Cone and Baxter Frieney and Fusiliers Dalton and 'Skin' (the Cook) Kelly of the Royal Irish Fusiliers, as well as men from LRDG, Royal Signals, Artillery and Engineers, all 40 of them crowded in. They managed to dig a hole in the floor of the wagon with a knife that 'Skin' Kelly had kept hidden. Most of the prisoners thought it not worth risking their lives, but a dozen of them wanted to give it a try. They sorted themselves into three groups and plotted their escape route. The plan was that each group would drop through the floor of the train at half-hour intervals to give each of them the best chance of not being spotted. They then drew lots as to which group went first and who got the map or compass: Sergeant Cone's group (with Fusilier Dalton and one of the Long Range Desert Group) drew first drop and the map; another group made up of an LRDG man and a gunner of the Royal Artillery drew second place and got the compass; and the third group, Sergeant Jimmy Semple and his friend, got the last drop and no aid to direction. They were on their own.

The actual action of dropping through the floor not knowing what would happen was terrifying, one of them recalled, 'The wheels were making sparks fly from the track, and I felt a fear clutch at my heart. How in God's name would I get on the track?'[37] The train slowed down to 10–15 mph and the first group had to go. 'By this time our spirits were quite boisterous and we were full of confidence. Though God knows why. It was our intention to try and reach the Albanian coast, with possible help from the Yugoslav guerrillas,'[38] but then nerves got to them. The first group dropped, they all held their breath and waited. 'A whisper, then a soft moan, followed by a scream and we knew fear of the worst magnitude.'[39] They all expected to see a headless body, but all the groups dropped out safely. Others who escaped included four non-commissioned officers of Royal Irish Fusiliers, Company Sergeant Majors Finch, Herbert Dawson and Finnley and Sergeant Walsh. That was only the beginning of a long arduous journey through the mountains. Jimmy Semple and his companion were lucky in that they encountered some guerrillas who helped them get back to safety. Those who remained in the trains went on to the camps.

Another escapee, Gunner Ron Hill of the LRDG, had been sent from Leros on a night raid to Levitha. After being captured, he was placed in a POW cage with other prisoners in Athens and then onto the cattle train. He and his companion, Trooper Jim Patch, managed to escape through the ventilation space on the wagon, dropping from the train onto the track into a pitch-black wet night. He recalls as he was lying on the ballast recovering from the fall (his parachute training had come in handy), watching as the rear light of the train grew smaller and smaller as the train raced away into the distance and disappeared round the bend. 'A feeling of utter loneliness came over me and I asked myself whatever I was doing in the middle of occupied Europe when everyone I knew and all the comforts of food and shelter were on the train.'[40] He pulled himself round after meeting up with Jim Patch who had leapt from the train with him. Although they had jumped carrying their provisions – the remains of a Red Cross parcel given to them in Athens – the wheels had run over the small blanket, which was now full of holes. Hill had twisted his muscle on jumping and had a nasty open wound in his leg. At first, they walked by night, but because it was so difficult decided to walk by day keeping a keen lookout for anyone else. Inadvertently, they ended up climbing one of the highest mountains in the region, Solunska Glava (Salonika Head), with little land in sight, just clouds stretching out in front of them. Disillusioned, they there decided to make their way to the nearest village and seek help. They managed to fill their water bottles and moved on. One man who waved them away trying to warn them of Bulgarian soldiers nearby was later shot, a fact they only found out 25 years later when they returned to the village. Most of the POWs, however, remained on the cattle wagon and were to see out the next 18 months or so incarcerated in German prison camps.

16

The German POW Camps

It was an extremely cold camp exposed to the bitter winds from the East, and for several days there was no form of heating at all, no wood to burn and the huts were running with condensation which formed into icicles.

Royal West Kents Sergeant Reg Neep[1]

The captive British soldiers from Leros arrived by train in Moosburg in Bavaria after about 14 days spent in freezing cattle trucks, having covered a distance of 1,400 miles. They arrived 'filthy, lousy, weak, hungry and cold'.[2] Reg Neep recalled, 'We were then marched a few miles to the POW Camp Stalag VIIA,' a transit camp holding military and political prisoners of many nations, with each in a separate compound. The soldiers were inspected by the camp medical officers, then showered with disinfectant, their hair cut to the scalp and all of them given metal identity tags. They were then allocated to their accommodation and taken to wooden huts with three-tiered bunks where they collapsed totally exhausted.

Ted Johnson had been transported by train and remembered the journey all too well. 'We travelled through Salonika, Yugoslavia, Bulgaria and Austria (Vienna), on to Stalag VIIA at Moosburg [...] We were all cold, as we were still in our tropical uniforms, and it was winter in northern Europe. Food and drink consisted of loaves of bread chucked into the trucks, and ersatz coffee. In Moosburg we met prisoners from all over the world, but it was only a transit camp for us.'[3] Ted recorded in his log book that he arrived on 15 December 1943.

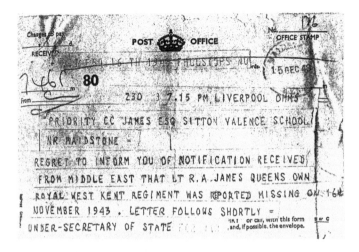

FIGURE 16.1 Photocopy of the telegram from the War Office to Richard James's family informing them he is missing, 15 December 1943

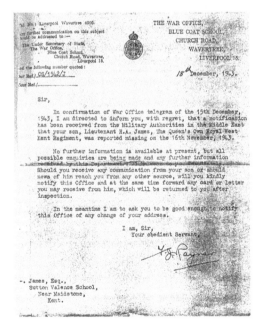

FIGURE 16.2 Photocopy of the letter from the War Office to Richard James's family informing them he is missing, 18 December 1943

The POW camp at Moosburg was Germany's biggest wartime prison camp; it covered 86 acres and held around 18,000 prisoners. Most POWs went through it at some point, as it was the main processing camp. It had originally been built to house the 10,000 Polish prisoners from the German offensive in September 1939 but had long outgrown its capacity.

Ted was moved on to Stalag IIIA at Luckenwalde, an interrogation camp for officers, 32 miles from Berlin. 'We arrived on Christmas Day 1943. I was put in solitary confinement for 14 days with no interrogation. I was eventually taken from my cell in the middle of the night. The interrogator knew more than I did about why we were there. They thought it was a ridiculous operation.'[4] Intelligence Officer Lieutenant Richard James was also interrogated in Luckenwalde, but because they suspected his position as an intelligence officer, he was subject to greater mistreatment. He was also held in solitary confinement in a cell and put on a diet of four small potatoes and a bowl of soup, whittling him down to six-and-a-half stone. They pulled him out every so often for further questioning.[5] Back in Liverpool, his family were anxiously awaiting news of his whereabouts. They knew about the fall of Leros but heard no more until 15 December, when they received a heart-stopping telegram, 'Regret to inform you of notification received from Middle East that Lieutenant R. A. James Queens Own Royal West Kent Regiment was reported missing on 16th November 1943.'[6] A letter came through a few days later on 18 December adding, 'No further information is available at present, but all possible enquiries are being made and any further information received from this department will be sent to you immediately.' The authorities requested that the family should inform them if they received a card or letter from him and send it on to them for 'inspection'.

By late 1943 some 15,000 Italian military internees arrived, though most of them were quickly dispersed to other camps. The British captives from Leros were at the top of the pecking order along with any Americans the enemy had picked up, with the Italians lower down and the Russians at the bottom of the heap. The camps were supposed to be run in accordance with the guidelines of the Geneva Convention and the Hague Regulations, and were inspected by the International

Committee of the Red Cross, but differentials in the treatment of the prisoners were apparent. The Germans were particularly nasty to the Italians who were starving; when they were reduced to searching the swill bins for something to eat, the Germans guards chased them away. The Russian POWs were treated even worse and were in a dreadful state when they joined the camp on 7 March. Frank Smith thought them 'pitiful specimens' in various states of malnutrition. Reg Neep also noticed that the Russian prisoners received fewer rations and no food parcels. He remembered one incident in their neighbouring compound; 'One night a guard dog was released into the Russian compound where it attacked the prisoners, but they retaliated by killing the dog. It was then skinned and eaten raw, the skin and bones being then thrown back over the wire.'[7]

Leros Interns

After his interrogation, Ted was sent to Oflag VIIIF, a special camp for officers at Marisch-Trübau, Czechoslovakia, arriving on 16 January 1944. The camp contained mostly British officers captured in North Africa and the Greek islands, around 2,000 in all, but there were also some Greek, French and American POWs. 'Food was scarce in the camp, but the heating wasn't too bad that first winter,' Ted reported. 'The Red Cross were tremendous. We were meant to receive a Red Cross parcel once a week, but this didn't always occur due to the bombing.' A Red Cross food parcel usually contained 16 items and a piece of soap. Eleven essential items were included: 2 oz of sugar, a 4-oz slab of sugar, a tin of Nestlés milk, 8 oz of margarine, 16 oz of meat and veg, 8 oz of jam, 8 oz of biscuits, 4 oz of chocolate, 10 oz of eat rolls, a tin of veg, 3 oz of cheese; and five of any of the following: a tin of egg flakes, 8 oz of bacon, a 4-oz tin of cocoa, a tin of salmon, a 12-oz tin of herrings, a tin of mustard, a 12-oz tin of bully beef, a fruit pudding, a tin of compressed oats, a tin of Marmite cubes, a tin of pepper, a pack of dried fruit, 50 cigarettes, or 2 oz of tobacco.

One of the luxuries was hearing news from outside the camp. One source was a radio the officers had managed to salvage and kept hidden from the German guards. Every evening, Ted and his fellow officers managed to pick up the BBC news, known as 'The Canary'.

A couple of men acted as lookouts to avoid detection by the guards. 'Only a handful of people controlled the radio. No one else knew where it was hidden. I didn't know. The Germans knew we were getting the news though.'[8] When a new prisoner arrived, there was always a concern that he might be a stool pigeon. He was therefore treated with suspicion until the rest of the men knew him to be trustworthy. The new arrivals would be vetted by the other prisoners – questions were asked relating to home and training in an attempt to catch them out. Some were uncovered as spies, mainly Germans who had been educated in Britain and had acquired convincing British accents. According to Ted, 'There were cases in other camps of these people being killed, but not in my camp (to my knowledge).'[9]

The camps were usually made up of a series of log huts, one or two storeys high, in an asphalted compound surrounded with barbed wire. The officers were given quarters of identical size, furnished with a table, chairs and wooden bunks. Rooms were intended for four men but often had three times that number. The lower ranks were squashed into dormitories. Fusilier Paddy McCrystal shared with many other men. 'When we got to the prison camps, they put us into big brown rooms, about 25 to a room, they gave us bunks, sleeping on a double, up and down [...] I went to VIIA and stayed there for about a month and they sorted us all out to different camps. Most of the Irish Fusiliers landed up in Stalag IVB [about 5 miles northeast of Mühlberg] and we stayed there for a few months, then went to Stalag IVF.'[10] The lower ranks again were the worst off food-wise. Paddy recalled, 'We got very very little. Brown bread, 50 grams of it. We got soup, I don't know what sort it was, just flavoured, like water. There was nothing in it. All it did was fill you full of wind.' Daily food rations were one slice of black bread, 2 oz of margarine and a spoonful of jam every other day, and occasionally some beet sugar, a mug of acorn coffee and a bowl of a soup concoction, very watery, per day.[11]

Private Lemuel Bevan was transferred to Stalag XIA, which was very crowded, and some men had to sleep on the stone floors with no blankets or pillows. The luckier ones got a two- or three-tiered bug-ridden bunk, but everyone tried to avoid the bottom bunk. During the night men urinated over the side rather than lose their spot.[12] The latrines were not merely unsavoury but positively dangerous.

They consisted of a trench with a pole to hang on to, but it was slippery. Bevan recalled, 'If they fell off, they fell in and drowned in it.'[13] He only had one shower in his two years in the camp. He received half a Red Cross parcel for Christmas, but after being without decent food for so long, the rich ingredients made him sick.

Reg Neep was most grateful when he received an unexpected boost to his rations, 'a lovely surprise', he recalled. 'On December 21st, each POW received a Canadian Red Cross parcel, a red letter day! Each parcel contained a tin of sardines, a small tin of spam, 12 oz of corned beef, a packet of crackers, 4 oz of cheese, butter and 4 oz of coffee, powdered milk, sugar and raising and a bar of chocolate. What a morale booster, but no more were issued during our stay in this Stalag. Our daily exercise was limited to a 50 yard stretch outside the hut, but with plenty of armed guards with Alsatian dogs.'[14]

After 12 days at Stalag V11A, Reg and some other prisoners were marched to the railway and the dreaded cattle trucks. 'Once more, no food or water during the three day journey to Kaisersteinbruck where we disembarked and were marched six miles to Stalag XV11A, 16 miles to the South East of Vienna. This was to be our home for another twelve months or so, housed in wooden huts with the familiar three tiered bunks. A week after our arrival, we were again issued with a Red Cross parcel (one between thirteen men).'[15] The 'skilly' rations of cabbage water for the British were served from a guard's hut in a tower high up in the middle of the compound. Shortly after his arrival, Reg was on duty there mixing the sauerkraut when a Russian youth got over the wire and entered the tower for food but was caught by one of the guards who rifle-butted him down the concrete steps, injuring the youth badly. Reg then impulsively knocked the guard down the same steps, rendering him unconscious. As a consequence, Reg was put into solitary confinement for 14 days, where he spent his 21st birthday.[16]

After their capture and transportation on the cattle wagons, at the end of December Fusiliers McEntaggart and Duggan found themselves in Stalag IVB. McEntaggart tells of the monotony of the camps and the terrible quantity and quality of food. After six o'clock roll call, they had breakfast, which consisted of black coffee.

'The morning was spent taking exercise as best you could within the camp and at 1200 hours we were paraded for dinner. Barley or turnip soup was all we got; at least that is what it was called but it never seemed to have either barley or turnip in it.'[17] Twice a week they were given a few potatoes. At 2 p.m. they were given more black coffee and a small ration of bread. 'If it had not been for the Red Cross food parcels few of us would have survived, and it is to them that we owe our lives.'[18]

Quick decisions had to be made as a soldier's immediate future often depended on it. Any soldier below the rank of corporal was sent to do hard labour in working parties outside the camp. McEnggart avoided this by 'promoting' himself to corporal, but Duggan ended up doing hard labour in Leipzig. He describes his time as quite different from those at the camp.

> After leaving Stalag IVB, I was one of the working party sent to Leipzig to help clear up the rubble and mess caused by our air raids. We also had to repair the roads. After four months on this work I was sent to Stalag IIIA which was somewhere north of Berlin. Here, Irishmen serving in the Allied Forces were being collected with the idea of making us join the 'Free British Corps'.

Duggan's accommodation was much worse than his friend's, with about 250 men to each barrack room with only straw to sleep on. The food situation was also dire. 'On the day of our arrival we got no food, and the next day only coffee and a loaf of bread between twelve men.'[19] Incredibly, the Germans set about trying to force them to fight on their side; the most serious repercussion if they refused was that the Red Cross parcels were stopped. The Germans then tried to make them wear civilian clothes but they refused as this would mean that they could be conscripted into the German army. 'This failure annoyed the Germans very much and resulted in our being made to work twelve hours a day and given very little to eat.'[20] POWs 'disappeared' while Duggan was in Stalag 3A. 'One man called Graham, who was in the Australian Forces, was working on a farm with me. One day the guard thought he was not working hard enough so he was taken away. The next time I saw him he was lying dead on a table in the Stalag.'[21] Duggan did not see him die but presumed his death had been caused by the guards. As heavy bombing increased from the Allies, the food situation grew worse as the Red Cross could no longer get through.

Privates were used as forced labour either filling roads, reconstructing buildings, working in oil refineries or forced down mines, although this was against the Geneva Convention. Many of the POWs would try their hand at sabotage during their shifts. Usually they had to work 12 hours a day, six days a week. Reg Neep remembered,

> British privates and lance corporals were sent out of the camps to work on farms etc. and were paid 5 shillings per week. They had no choice, but they fared slightly better for food on the farms than the basic camp ration. Russian prisoners died by the thousands as they had no supplements to their poor camp rations. Mass graves were dug at the rear of the camp, and bodies were carried from the morgue each day. We estimated that each mass grave held 4,000 bodies and during this winter, the third grave was opened.[22]

Making the Best of It

As Christmas loomed, everyone's thoughts turned to home. To be away from family and loved ones was bad enough, but they also had to contend with the poor living conditions and meagre provisions. It was particularly difficult on Christmas Day, but the men were making the best they could of a dire situation. Everyone was pooling rations making cakes, puddings and pies in preparation.[23] They managed to make cheese and fish pies, and even an orange pudding.[24] They created Christmas decorations and shared their food to put on a large spread. Frank Smith won a Canadian Parcel which helped no end. He recalled, 'On Christmas day we had a hearty breakfast of porridge, bacon and fried bread, issued with beer. They had soup hors d'oeuvres, steak and kidney pie followed by Christmas pudding, cheese and biscuits. Too full for words.'[25] There was a church service and carols and they even made a cake with icing for New Year.

Lieutenant Ted Johnson was in particularly low spirits; when a fellow officer wished him 'Merry Christmas', he nearly answered, 'What's merry about it?', but he soon rallied. The officers' rooms acted as a duty room for the company so they had to show willing, made a brew, made porridge with biscuits at 9 a.m. and opened a tin of sardines. They went to church at 11 a.m. and sang carols: 'Hark the Herald Angels Sing', 'While Shepherds Watched', and 'O Come, All Ye Faithful'. Ted recorded that he 'ate a very good lunch of pea soup, bully and a brew' after which he started to feel better – the Christmas

FIGURE 16.3   Cartoon from Ted Johnson's POW log book

FIGURE 16.4   Images from Ted Johnson's log book

spirit was infectious despite the lack of alcohol. He wrote to his mum and watched the snow fall outside. At 6 p.m., the officers all sat down to enjoy the Christmas dinner they had prepared, made up of a hearty helping of German stew followed by a huge pudding, topped with a

FIGURE 16.5   Images from Ted Johnson's log book

rich chocolate sauce. 'This was the first meal I couldn't finish since being captured. Everybody was out for the count after supper for a while.'[26] On New Year's Eve, they all went to 'The Rum Pot', a makeshift recreation room, for evening entertainment of singing and music. It was so crowded that Ted and his chums went back to his room, made a cocoa brew and ate all his biscuits. Frank Smith remembered that they were given some beer and played 'Auld Lang Syne' on the harmonium.[27]

Entertainment was one of the central points that made life more bearable at the officers' POW camp. The men created their own diversions. They often held concerts, or sang accompanied by a guitar, banjo or harmonica.[28] In April 1944, for example, the Tommy Sampson Band played 'soft shoe shuffle' and Maurice Butler gave an 'Emergency Symphony Concert' of Mendelssohn's 3rd with a 16-piece orchestra which Frank thought was 'very good'.[29] The more thespian-inclined of the soldiers put on plays. Ted listed the shows performed in the barn from January to April including *Blythe Spirit*, *Lady from Abroad*, *Hollywood Cavalade*, *The Corn is Green*, *Dancing over Europe*, *The Taming of the Shrew*, *School for Scandal* and *Gaslight*. In May, because of the cold and lack of adequate food, performances were suspended and no big shows were put on after *Aladdin* at Christmas 1944. An open room for sports such as table tennis, boxing, football and badminton kept them physically active, while a series of well-organised lectures kept them intellectually stimulated. Anyone with any knowledge about an interesting subject would be invited to speak; for example Bill Bowel gave a talk on 'Cricket, Fielding in Australia'. Other topics covered were The Beveridge Plan, Forestry, Modern Music, Greece, The Making of Disney's *Fantasia* and The English Political Scene.

Letters from home began to arrive from around January 1944. They were a vital part of men's lives, and hearing from family made for a happier day. Ted kept a tally of all his mail incoming and outgoing during his time in the camps throughout 1944 and 1945. Because of censorship, there were limitations as to what they could tell their families, and what their families could tell them. As a result, most of the information was dull and routine, making for boring news, but nonetheless eagerly pored over by the men.

Lieutenant Gordon Emeric Horner recalled, 'You found after a while there was nothing new people could say in a letter, but, by God, you fell into the dumps if you did not get one.'[30] Letters from home often came with extra gifts. Along with the two letters Frank Smith received from his mother and his sister on 14 January were parcels full of raisins, apple pudding, chocolate pudding and some apricots.[31] Some letters were unintentionally amusing and kept the soldiers entertained. One fond and very young wife innocently wrote to her husband, 'Now, darling, you must start planning what we shall do on our first night home.' Another newly married wife wrote to her husband, 'I have now got seven American officers billeted at our house. I didn't want them, but the poor dears were so far from home and so lonely. So I am making them comfortable in the way you used to say only I could make a man comfortable. For I do feel I want to do my bit, and give them what little I have left to make them happy.' Another letter, 'You always wanted to travel, dear; and now at last you have your wish.'[32] For the most part, letters from family cheered the men and gave them familial security.

Bob King was a 3-inch mortar officer with the King's Own.[33] He too was to suffer the indignities of a German prison camp, which followed much the same trajectory as the experiences of Frank Smith and Ted Johnson. He was also sent to the initial clearing camp Stalag VIIA in Moosburg and then on to Oflag VIIIF. 'It was comparative luxury, a former Czech military academy, centrally heated and the accommodation was bearable. We slept in two tier bunks around a room with central tables. We also had lockers. The bunks were slatted with loose slats. Occasionally we had to donate one of these for shoring up a tunnel being dug as an escape route.'[34] He thought the camp highly organised, with a camp 'university' with the possibility of studying virtually anything a person wanted to: languages, history, literature and maths. There was a surfeit of lawyers in the camp: of 2,000 officers, 100 were lawyers. Their resourcefulness was such that they ran courses for those studying for the Bar and solicitors' examinations, and even made arrangements for examination papers to be sent over via the Red Cross. This was encouraged by the Germans, who had a vested interest in seeing their prisoners occupied in subjects other than escaping.

Spot checks were increasingly made as the Germans' position in the war grew worse. Normally, the POWs were counted twice a day, but they found ways to disrupt the counting methods. Bob King recalled,

> The count would take place on the ground floor. At each end of the building was a staircase leading to the second floor and to the cellar. After the count had started the first three in the line would nip down into the cellar and attach themselves at the other end. The Germans would then find that they had three more than they should have. They would start the count again. The three at the end would then slip back again. This meant they would be three less than there should be.[35]

Whether the Germans cottoned on to the trick, they never knew. It was easy enough to make them irate and trigger-happy. One Indian officer was shot dead crossing the tripwire laid inside the perimeter fence while trying to retrieve a deck tennis quoit.

Routine and Boredom in Oflags

The days were long and ran into one another. Boredom was a problem and meals were a central part of the day. In Oflag VIIIF, the men would wake around 7.45 a.m., with the bugle roll call at 8.15 a.m. when the men were counted. After the parade, they returned to their bunk to tidy up and prepare a scanty breakfast ready for the arrival of tea at 9 a.m. Ted reported, 'Tempers were usually short at this hour so silence reigns at the table except for the odd remark answered by an unintelligible grunt.'[36] Normally breakfast was a mug of tea and two slices of bread, butter and jam, or porridge or some soaked prunes, depending on how the food parcel was spinning out. After breakfast, the men would wash and shave and go for a walk around the camp. Hot showers were something of a luxury as Frank Smith exclaimed in his log book, 'Hot shower – marvellous – removed fortnight's filth.'[37] The more men who went out for a chat, the better chance that the orderly would sweep out the room. At 11 a.m., a man might be lucky enough to collect mail from the Red Cross store.

Some men would go to the library that the prisoners had set up, others would do laundry if the water was working. The library contained over 6,000 books provided by the Red Cross. Basketball, softball, football, badminton, cricket or quoits were played if the weather was good. Sometimes the air raid warning would go, which set everyone on edge. If any noise was heard which suggested aircraft or bombs, men would dart to take cover in the huts (although these

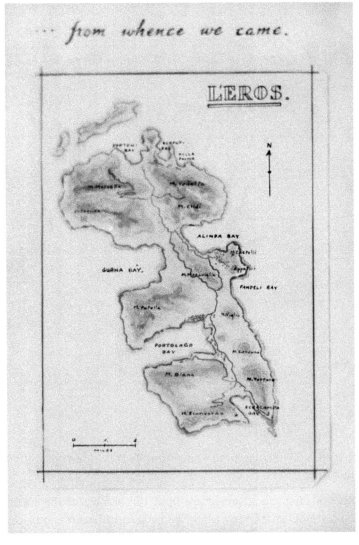

FIGURE 16.6   Frank Smith's map of Leros

FIGURE 16.7   Image from Frank Smith's POW log book cartoons, 'Rumours'

did not offer much protection from the bombs). If the situation looked problematic, Ted would go back to his room and place his photograph frame in his pocket, and his small silver spoon which he valued about all else, put on his coat and hat and have his emergency

FIGURE 16.8 Images from Frank Smith's POW log book cartoons, 'Famous Words' and 'Bird Fanciers'

pack ready, then sit back and watch things develop. At the end of the war, the men boxed up all the books and sent them to a boys' club in London which they founded.[38]

Men would mend watches, play poker or bridge, and make household items (Frank Smith made a photo frame).[39] They would go for walks in the snow to occupy themselves and to collect wood to keep themselves warm. In the evenings they would have casino nights with gambling, Aunt Sally side shows, darts, horse racing, a fortune teller and bagpipes. Bets among the men as to how the war was faring were common. If a show was running, they would go and see it at around 3.30 p.m. and it would last until roll call. Afterwards, they would wash and brush up for the evening, although as Ted Johnson said, 'Why, heaven knows, as one wasn't going anywhere.' Roll call was at 5.45 p.m. to be counted. Supper was usually taken at 6.30, usually a cooked dish with some bread and jam. The cooked dish was 'a meal which everyone looks forward to, although it was usually over within ten minutes' – variously potatoes and stew, rissoles and mash, cottage pie, fish pie, or bacon and sausage pie of meat and veg from tins.[40] During the evening, they would again chat, read or write.

FIGURE 16.9   Images from Frank Smith's POW log book cartoons
'It happened one evening'

Usually the men went to bed about 10 p.m., making sure everything
was in position in case the warning system went off in the night. Ted
kept his photograph and silver spoon in his coat pocket.

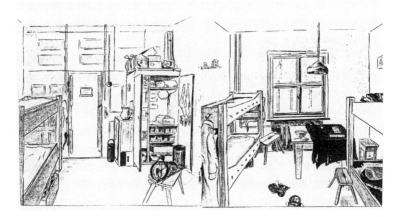

FIGURE 16.10   Frank Smith's drawing of the inside of his POW camp

News was papered onto a wall, creating a 'wall newspaper' to keep the men informed of any current events; this included any news gleaned from German guards or from 'other sources' via the prisoners. Maps would be hung up next to the item dotted with pins to show the progress of the Allies.[41] The guards offered no objection, most of them apprehensive about the outcome of the war and unwilling to upset the men they were overseeing. The camp regulations allowed typewriting but did not allow duplicating.

As time went on, the hygiene and medical situation worsened for the POWs. Because of the lack of food, many of them weakened and were unable to fight off diseases. At the end of January 1944, typhus broke out in Reg Neep's camp. British POWs were inoculated, but not the Russians, so many died.[42] British POWs who died were buried in the local churchyard. 'We thought that it was a form of intimidation that the bodies were always removed from the morgue to mass graves or churchyard whilst we were queuing for our daily "skilly" ration, however we gradually became hardened, even to this.'[43] Escape committees were formed, to which all proposals had to be submitted, and, if accepted, the suggestion went on the waiting list. Many unsuccessful attempts were made, mainly due to the British camp being encircled by prison compounds of other nations, as the British were thought most likely to try and escape. Ted Johnson said, 'I didn't attempt to escape. The escape committee in the camp vetted all plans.

If a man had a cast iron plan and a good reason, then it would be approved. Some escapes were only for Intelligence Officers, so they could take back information to the War Office.'[44]

Those in Frank Smith's camp were warned in March 1944 to prepare to move. They had no fuel left, little food and it was icy cold. Some of the men stayed in bed in an effort to keep warm. On 14 March they were shoved into a truck, boots and braces removed and given some bread and half a tin of beef. They moved off squashed into a confined space in a very crowded truck. They were kept on the move to Regensburg where they took a train through Dresden, ploughing through virgin white snow to Königselt and onwards. The conditions were once again cramped and the men's bodies buffeted all night long with the mess tin falling over. They were occasionally let out to relieve themselves, to the sight of glorious scenery – hills, woods, mountain, farms, rivers covered in snow. Through Bloxdorf, a walk to VIIIF, then on to Marisch-Trübau, 'The party begins. Forms had to be filled in – it was a resemblance of school days meeting old faces.'[45] Frank met up with Ted Johnson and John Penney.

Many of the prisoners were moved from the officers' camp at Marisch-Trübau and put into cattle trucks for a three-day journey to Oflag 79 about three miles from Brunswick. Ted Johnson arrived on 4 May 1944 and recalled, 'At the beginning of the journey we were handcuffed. The handcuffs were hopeless and archaic, so were easy to remove. At the end of the journey we handed them to our escort – he was not amused.'[46] The constant round of new prisoners at least brought some news of the outside world, reviving the spirits of the interns.[47] The guards were mostly disinterested older or disabled men who wanted an easy life, so allowed certain minor transgressions to pass which previously might have been punished. The guards were also conscious that they might be denounced in a few months if liberation came, as looked more and more likely. Ted recalled, 'There were guards who only had one arm, and those who only had one eye. They were very old, and their clothes were poor quality. We felt sorry for them, especially during the winter of 1944/5, which was very cold.' At least much-needed items came through for him, to help with daily life and hygiene. In December 1944, Ted made a list of the items he received from the Red Cross for Christmas, which included a shirt, pyjamas, towel, socks, bag, handkerchiefs, blades, brushes, tooth-paste, pencils, soap, five files, chocolate, ointment, laces, boot polish, mending, comb, sponge and bag.

On 6 June 1944, the second front opened up in France and all privileges ceased. All POWs wondered if the end of the war was in sight. Reg Neep recalled, 'There was tremendous excitement at the news of the second front, but at noon that day, we were all ordered out of the huts, the guards went in and sabotaged all our carefully reserved food items, this was to stop food being saved for escape attempts.'[48] The men had a scheduled visit from a Red Cross team at this time (after the Russians had been forced to clean up the camp), but the Red Cross officials did not speak to any of the POWs, so they could not make any complaints. Scrutiny from the guards became more intense, and random searches were taking place. Reg listened to the news on their knocked-up wireless system; 'We only listened in for a very limited time and only in fairly "safe" periods and it was apparent that the Russian Army were advancing more quickly than the Allies [the British and Americans], and were only 120 miles away, near Budapest.'[49]

The men's situation worsened as the war continued. Bob King found his days increasingly bleak. In particular, they were down to half a Red Cross parcel a week and all of them were incredibly hungry.

> We would become obsessed with anything to do with food. It was not unusual for someone to be unable to sleep at night because he could not get his mind off, say, a bacon sandwich. Lectures started about food. An officer called Acton who was a fellow of the Institute of British Bakers and who had been employed by Cadbury gave us exotic recipes. I returned home with twenty-seven recipes for everything from Rum Babas to Chung Wings. Those who had been in the wine trade took orders for post-war deliveries, South African fruit farmers promised deliveries of tropical fruits. It was a world of fantasy.[50]

Social distinctions became evident as food was bartered for – orderlies bartered for officers' marmalade, and offered their coffee in exchange for officers' tea. Despite the lack of food, some thought the need for cigarettes was even more important. Lieutenant Gordon Horner recalled, 'The richest man in the camp was the man with the most cigarettes. I have seen a tin of bully beef newly arrived in a Red Cross parcel, go for 10 fags when cigarettes were scarce. When they were more plentiful, a tin of bully would fetch 50.' If no food was to be had, £1 could be made for a single smoke. Payment was by cheque sketched on a piece of a paper drawn on the buyer's bank or by IOUs.[51]

With rations drastically reduced, the men were living off a few boiled potatoes and watery soup, supplemented with stew only twice a week. German supply lines had broken down and Red Cross parcels had stopped coming through. So hungry were they that food was constantly on their minds. Men's war diaries are full of lists of food, what they had to eat, what the Red Cross brought them, what they cooked and what they missed. Weight loss was rapid – some lost up to four stone. Activities ceased as no-one had the energy to do anything but lie in bed.

Allied bombs intended for enemy targets inadvertently fell in, or near, the camp. One night all the huts' heating facilities and windows were blown out. Ted recorded raids on Brunswick on 24 August 1944, which saw the camp hit; three people were killed outright, eight severely wounded and evacuated to the main hospital, another six wounded and admitted to the camp hospital, and 25 'walking wounded'. The roof was taken off one of the huts, and the water mains were broken in a couple of the others. Electric cables went down all over the camp. Bob King also remembered the bombing. 'At about 11 o'clock in the morning eleven bombs hit the camp. Fortunately for us we had taken refuge in the cellars. None of the buildings was seriously hit but the cookhouse was demolished. Electricity and water was cut off and the drainage system was smashed. There were forty POW casualties, three fatal. The Germans suffered more heavily.'[52]

The Long March to Liberation

Prisoners were being shuffled about from camp to camp to keep them out of reach of the Russian army which was moving closer and closer. Reg Neep and his POW companions were among those rounded up for a freezing journey over open country – they trekked for miles, were put on trains and marched again, their destination unknown to them. He recalled, 'On 14th February [1945], it was announced that we were to be moved again as the Russians had advanced 300 miles in just a few days and that we were to be marched west about 25 miles to entrain again at Bautzen.' They were allowed only a stop of five minutes every hour tramping through heavy snow. 'We were marshalled into a long column for the trek with many guards on either side of the POWs. We were very apprehensive wearing as many clothes as we could get hold of as we set off in the middle of a snow blizzard, several hundred men using only minor roads or across open country, and we heard distant sounds of gunfire from the East.'[53] Marched hundreds of miles in the bitter cold, they were starving and becoming emaciated.

> When on the march, if a clamp of beet or turnip or swede was seen in the fields, everyone rushed to uncover the vegetables before the guards rifle-butted us away, sometimes opening fire with their rifles, but even the gunfire did not deter the scramble for food. The daily five minute halts now stretched to ten minutes or fifteen minutes or even longer as we got progressively weaker, some of the guards appeared to look at us sympathetically, but were scared of showing this.[54]

One night in early March was significant in Reg's survival; 'After another twenty-five mile forced march, we were put into a very large barn for the night.' They decided to escape, digging with spoons below the wall of the barn and after some hours, and thoroughly exhausted, they broke through the wall of the barn, only to find themselves in a smaller barn for the night with two guards patrolling outside. This was an unsuccessful escape attempt, but in any case, they were in no fit state to cope with freedom. However, in the loft of the barn, they found a rabbit hutch with a very large angora rabbit (obviously the farmhouse pet) inside. After a considerable struggle by the three men, all of them in a weakened state, they managed to kill the rabbit. It was then skinned and the meat divided into three portions, and because there were no fires allowed, eaten raw over the next few days, the bones sucked for a few weeks after. Reg believes eating this rabbit saved his life. They eventually arrived at a camp for political prisoners, and were put in a compound there, but there were others there in an even worse physical condition. These were concentration camp prisoners on one of the notorious 'death marches'. Reg recalled, 'They were all wearing striped clothing and we realised with horror that these were the Jewish prisoners and that this was the Nordhaussen Concentration Camp. There was a very sinister atmosphere and we were very thankful to be moved on again the following day, but the memory of those unfortunate Jews stayed with us.'[55]

Some of the guards deserted when they had heard that the American army was fast approaching and were worried about their possible fate if the POWs were released. A group of POWs including Reg decided to take advantage of the reduction in guards and attempted to escape, as the remaining guards were becoming nervous and agitated and their future actions were uncertain. While the guards were collecting their food ration and also being distracted by another group of prisoners, Reg's group slipped away and made their way to the nearest houses to steal some food. Walking westward, they came across a disused quarry where they made a biscuit concoction on a wood fire in a ruined hut, with the flour and milk they had stolen. The following day they were approaching a village which was under shellfire. They were ecstatic to see the American 'spearhead group', consisting of a US jeep, gun carriers and armoured cars, entering the village from the other direction. The Americans halted, identified the group of POWs and issued them with some food ('K' rations) plus small arms and advised the POWs to hold the village until their main force arrived a few hours later.[56] Reg and his group bedded down in a barn with blankets and the following day made their way to Halberstadt where they obtained transport to Hildesheim airfield. Deep craters pitted the runways where it had been heavily bombed. They hitched a ride on a returning army supply plane, a Dakota, which crossed over the holes with some difficulty, and flew to Belgium. From Brussels there was a special unit for the repatriation of servicemen, and the group were flown by the Royal Air Force to a reception unit in the south of England. After a medical examination and the normal debriefing process, Reg was given a travel warrant to his home town, and proceeded to Carlisle where he spent the next six weeks on special leave. His only memento of his experience as a POW is the metal identity tag he wore and a letter from a former employer received at Stalag XVIIA.

Fusilier Paddy McCrystal's final days of captivity were also harrowing. 'The last 21 days of the war, I was in a confined cell and we were getting bread and water only every three days. Not a solid meal in three days. I never saw anybody, I never spoke to anybody. The only communication I made with anyone was the day before I got out.'

He managed to make contact through the paper-thin walls with a pilot who had been shot down. He remembered, 'He said, "The war is over. You needn't worry,"' It was the last town the Germans had captured.'[57]

On the evening of 11 April 1945, the POWs in Ted Johnson's camp could hear the fighting approaching. They could hear the guns. Shells were dropping all night and no-one slept. Bombs fell on the camp, causing some casualties, mostly German. The next morning, on 12 April 1945 at 9 a.m., they were liberated by two Americans in a jeep with a French foreign worker from US 9th Army. Ted recalled,

> One jeep with three soldiers drove up to the gates. The guards were packed and ready to go. There was a fantastic atmosphere when we were liberated. I went out in search of food, and came back with a loaf of bread and a Luger pistol. I ate the whole loaf in one go. I had one hell of a bellyache. Some of the other camps nearby were in a very bad state. As officers, we didn't have to work. The troops did, and these chaps who were in a bad state were the priority for repatriation. We spent another week in the camp before it was our turn.[58]

Some men openly wept.[59] The Germans seemed happy enough to surrender, as Ted Johnson recalled. 'All goons [Germans] were rounded up without a shot being fired and marched away, they looked just as happy as we did.' Rations came pouring in all afternoon. 'Everybody was bubbling over with goodwill and happiness that night, and no wonder.'

Lieutenant Horner, who had been in the Oflag since 1942 after being captured in Italy, describes the scene: 'About nine o'clock in the morning I was roused by a commotion went out to see what it was, and found the whole camp in pandemonium.'[60] The camp went mad, with soldiers dancing, jumping and shouting. Others looked dazed. Everyone was overjoyed to watch the surrender of the camp commandant. The German officers threw their guns into a pond to avoid having to hand them over.

On 14 April, the men could openly listen to the BBC news. The following news bulletin came over the waves: 'Allies have captured Brunswick. Five miles from the town, a POW camp of over two thousand officers and four hundred other ranks has been overrun. No names have been received, but next of kin are being informed as soon as possible. The name of the camp is Oflag 79.'[61]

The liberated had to hang around for a while for planes to pick them up and take them home. Not until 23 April were the planes seen flying over. Bob King remembered, 'Looking out of the window I could see the sky full of Dakotas circling the adjoining airport. We collected our few belongings and rushed outside. There we lined up in groups of twenty and were told that we would be flown to Brussels where we would spend the night.'[62] An officer asked him, 'Would you rather have tea now or go to England?' The return home was magical. 'It was the most beautiful spring evening with a slight mist. As we flew across the Channel there appeared a few horizontal lines, as if in a Scarfe drawing, then revealed for what they were: The White Cliffs of Dover.'[63]

Ted Johnson was flown to Brussels in a Dakota, decontaminated (in case of lice) and given a new set of clothes. 'We didn't have such a bad problem with lice in the officers' camp, as we had access to running water.' From Brussels he was flown to near Aylesbury, then taken to Waddesdon Manor where he was debriefed. 'I was given leave, which was extended until I was told to come back. I ended up writing to the War Office saying that I needed some money – could I come back? I was sent on a European POW resettlement course in Dunbar. While I was on the course, the atomic bomb was dropped on Nagasaki. After this I was sent back to my old battalion, which was reforming, and was then sent to Palestine.' He added, 'I was promoted in the field on Leros to Captain. However, the submarine carrying the confirmation back to Beirut was sunk in the Aegean. I wasn't aware of this until I was released, and discovered that I was only being paid as a Lieutenant, so I was receiving less money than I thought I was!'[64]

Duggan was eventually liberated by the Russians. He left the camp with a paratrooper and an American soldier and together they headed for the Elbe, which they swam across and met up with the Americans on the other side. They were taken to Torgau, a town on the banks of the Elbe in Saxony, and finally came to the 25th Holding Battalion and met up with his friend McEntaggart. For the men who had survived the battle of Leros and the German prison camps, it was finally the end of their suffering.

17

Aftermath Considerations

What the public will want to know is who planned expeditions against islands which could not be effectually reinforced by sea or protected from the air? Under whose direction were the forces in Leros and Samos kept in their hopeless position after Cos had proved a failure and the air-support it might have rendered was not forthcoming?

The Spectator, 19 November, 1943[1]

Private Sid Bowden's view was echoed by many as he mused on the enterprise of the Leros campaign: 'One big cock-up, right from beginning to end. We didn't know where we were going. They didn't tell us. It was just a muddle-up because nobody knew what was going on.'[2] Adding to his comrade's sentiments, Acting Sergeant George Hatcher in Second Battalion Queen's Own Royal West Kents remarked,

It should never have been. They should have known before it started. We understood Churchill's idea was to go up to the Balkans and invade that way. We all knew he should never have gone that way because it was impossible to get air cover. There is no aerodrome nearby for fighters to operate from. Once we were there, we were stuck. The Germans could come and do as they liked with us. There was no anti-aircraft weapons. We were sitting ducks, we didn't dare move.[3]

The Spectator for 19 November 1943 gave an equally scathing verdict on the Aegean events in an editorial entitled, 'The Sacrifice of Leros':

Public opinion will not be satisfied until the whole question of Cos, Leros and Samos has been cleared up. After days of heroic resistance in which 3,000 British troops and 5,000 Italians received and deserved public admiration for holding on against perpetually reinforced German troops and mass bombing-attacks against which there was virtually no protection, we now learn that the inevitable has happened – that the garrison has been overwhelmed and the island lost [...] And incidentally it might be asked, from whom in Whitehall emanates the lame and preposterous argument that the effect of the diversion of German effort needed to recapture Leros may prove equal to that caused by our fight for Greece and Crete? The expedition to Greece was a delaying action directed against the victorious Germans in the moment of Greece's extreme agony – a moment when the holding up of the enemy was of vital consequence for all military operations in the East. The recent ill-judged expeditions to the Aegean were undertaken when we have overwhelming superiority in the Mediterranean and when adventures of this kind should be undertaken in sufficient force or not at all. To adopt the course taken was to make a present to the enemy of gallant troops and the prestige of a local victory which they so badly need. The least that can be done now is to give a full explanation of the planning and conduct of these ill-conceived and ill-supported operations.[4]

While there was an obvious eagerness on Churchill's part to commence with a campaign in the Dodecanese, some people thought it had been unwise to go in without a clear strategy. George Jellicoe certainly thought there was a lack of clear planning for the enterprise:

I think there was inadequate preparation. What was absolutely essential was to capture and hold the three airfields on Rhodes because without them, we had no air cover [...] It was quite extraordinary [...] You know he [Churchill] was a tremendous enthusiast for opening a third front but with short notice and with no proper preparation, it was not likely to be a success.[5]

The extent of the damage became evident in the minutes of a meeting of the Chiefs of Staff on 24 November 1943. Churchill believed that in Leros the British 'lost 5000 first-class troops, with four cruisers and seven destroyers sunk or damaged'.[6] One hundred and eighty-three British and Commonwealth soldiers lie in Leros cemetery, and 135 (mainly Buffs) drowned in the sinking of the *Eclipse*. The Germans suffered around 1,109 casualties out of their 4,500 troops.[7] One source reckons out of 525 Italian officers on Leros about 50 died in combat, and about 440 were shot by Germans.[8]

According to another source, the Italian navy lost 2,500 men at Leros; 1,100 Germans were killed, 4,800 British lost (3,200 became POWs).[9] Of the 33 destroyers (7 Greek) and 6 cruisers in the Aegean, 6 destroyers were sunk and 4 were damaged, and 4 cruisers were damaged. Two submarines and ten small coastal craft and minesweepers were sunk. Of the 288 British aircraft which flew 3,746 sorties, 113 were lost. For those who had fought in the Battle of Leros, their time as prisoner of war would begin after the surrender of Leros to the Germans by Brigadier Tilney. After the German takeover, both Admiral Mascherpa, who had commanded Leros, and Admiral Ignio Camponi, who had commanded Rhodes, were executed as traitors at Parma on 23 May 1944.[10]

Undoubtedly the lack of air cover was a major factor in the failure to win the battle for Leros. The commander-in-chief of the Levant remarked,

> We failed because we were unable to establish airfields in the area of operations. The enemy's command of the air enabled him [the enemy] to limit the operations and impair the efficiency of land, sea and air forces that by picking his time he could deploy his comparatively small forces with decisive results.[11]

The failure to save airbases in Crete, Rhodes or Kos was a disaster ensuring the enemy's complete domination of the air. The continual bombing had an undeniable demoralising effect on the troops as they failed to see any British aircraft in the sky, nor could they move easily without being bombed or shot at from the air. Had more aircraft been made available, especially modern long-range fighters, the troops on the ground might have had more chance of success. However, the Germans diverted more of their resources to the operation.[12] The temporary Allied assistance given as Kos was falling came far too late and was not enough. The withdrawal of the American fighters essentially sealed the fate of Leros. The distance from the Allied airbases 450 miles away in Alexandria and Cyprus made it impossible for them to provide any realistic continual air cover. Even when fighter cover was available, long gaps of time were inevitable, as British fighters usually had to return to base after the first attack owing to shortage of fuel, and it took anything up to three hours for relief to arrive. Because of lack of air cover, the navy came under threat. They also had further problems as Allied destroyers were limited to two nights in the Aegean at the most, after which they had to return to refuel. It was impracticable to base small seacraft on Castelorizo or any of the Aegean islands owing to continual enemy air attacks which were very accurate by day.[13] This was to have serious adverse consequences on operations of the forces on the ground.[14]

There is no doubt that the factor most often referred to by the fighting men on the ground was the complete lack of Allied air cover and the inability to stem the enemy aircraft, with continual bombing causing morale to sink. Clifford Clarke blamed both lack of air cover and lack of adequate reinforcement: 'We could have dealt with it, and were dealing with it, and could have handled it if it hadn't gone on too long, because we had no chance of reinforcements at all, and no air cover whereas they did. That was the disaster really.'[15] This was partly the result of Eisenhower's refusal to give the Allies cover, but also of the loss of Allied-held airfields in Crete, Rhodes and Kos which could have been held with more resources. The constant daily bombardments from enemy planes were overwhelming not simply in terms of destruction but in pinning the soldiers to the ground. For any success, it was essential to get hold of and keep at least one of the large airfields, which the Allies failed to do.

However, lack of air cover, while an overriding factor, was only one of a multitude of reasons for the failure to hold Leros. The catastrophe and its ensuing casualties were mostly caused by an absence of serious commitment at the top, and a lack of strategic planning on the ground. A lack of resources from the beginning meant that men did not have enough transport, anti-aircraft guns, ammunition or air cover. The only anti-aircraft guns were Italian, the only British contribution being 12 Bofors guns. Douglas 'Roger' Wright who served with the SBS on Leros declared,

> We the British, for reasons only known by the hierarchy, put a brigade of infantry on the Isle of Leros with no ack-ack or air cover, knowing full well that they would be over-run within weeks. The Jerry battered us with air raids, they soon attacked us with a large force, mostly Paras, within days we surrendered, three hundred British were killed and about 1,000 Jerry. It seemed madness to us, this happened at the end of 1943.[16]

The Allies' trust in Italian support was also misplaced. Churchill had expected to use Italian forces on the islands as part of the Allied defence but his assumption was not to be borne out. Any idea that it was easy for the Italians to change sides with gusto so quickly can easily be dispelled from reports of those involved with them. Although some Italian gunners fought hard, other Italian soldiers no longer saw it as their war and simply wanted to go home. The difference in fighting spirit between the Italians appears to have been between those who came from the north of Italy and those who came from the south. Ashley Martin Greenwood, head of the Artillery Division of the LRDG, had been put in charge of the Italian gunners. He recalled how all their guns were out of calibration, and it was unsurprising they were missing their shots at enemy aircraft flying over them. He went round the gun emplacements and ensured they were aligned. The first Italian took his shot and just missed; they realigned, and he took another shot. It was a direct hit and the plane came down in smoke. A roar of cheering went up and Italians appeared from nowhere full of congratulations. They decided to throw a party and went back to one of their houses – it was well-furnished with carpets and was quite luxurious. Women came out of the background to join them and liquor was pulled out – such was their celebratory spirit. However, Greenwood said that although this was typical of the southern Italians, the northern gunners were much more hardened and better fighters.[17] One gunner officer, Capitano Cacciatori from the Italian battery, was much more stoic; he had joined Brigade HQ after his guns had been destroyed. When the Germans had begun to ascend Meraviglia, he charged down the hill at them throwing his hand grenades. When they were finished and his gun was empty, he continued throwing rocks at the enemy. He lost an arm and was wounded in the face, legs and side, but according to Anwyl 'made good progress later'.[18]

Another problem contributing to the confusion of the troops and officers, especially in the middle of the battle, was poor communications. Because of the mountainous terrain the radios did not work effectively. Furthermore, the signallers were overstretched, having neither enough trained operators nor sufficient wireless sets. Signal officer Reg Neep recalled,

We went there with radios which were heavy packs on your back but in that terrain they didn't work. So we had to resort to cable laying, you know, field telephones and of course, when the German paratroopers dropped on the island one of their duties was to look for cable and cut the cable and wait for some poor linesman to come along to repair it and he would get killed – we lost a lot of men in that predicament.[19]

The fact that many of the troops had not previously worked together or had been under their commanding officers only a few months prior to battle meant they were lacking in direction and confidence. On top of this, during the battle, many officers were killed, leaving platoons leaderless. As men fell in battle, soldiers from different regiments were hastily pulled together, some of whom had not worked together before; counter-attacks therefore had to be improvised on the spot as the battle moved forward. Even when they were in the same regiment, some companies came in piecemeal (as with the Royal West Kents) with new second-in-commands and unfamiliar commanding officers, which did nothing to help them cohere as a fighting unit. They were in battle alongside people they had not trained with. Some companies fared worse than others. Sid Bowden of Royal West Kents said,

I think my company had a right rough time. I remember a message came through that Captain Flood had been wounded [...] You see, the trouble was I was in headquarter company in Malta, and we were just drafted all over to the rest of the companies, when we got to Syria. It was to us, a muddle up. It was rough weather, they said, why our battalion couldn't get to us easier. I think it was about the third day [of the battle] before one company arrived. And you see, they were landed in the dark, they didn't know the area or nothing.

Another report suggested that the swapping of officers undermined moral. 'The shuffling of officers in six months had been remarkable. Apart from the HQ Company which had been commanded by the same officer since April, not one company had an officer who had been with them for six months.'[20]

How far Tilney can be held responsible for the debâcle is debatable. As Lieutenant Richard James pointed out,

Infantry battalion and the HQ were all in position when suddenly out of the air these parachutists start coming down and one fired at them, so did other companies. Again, if immediate responses had been made when they first fell, it might have been successful. But it's very very difficult to move troops about when any movement gets attacked from the air, and pretty unpleasantly, they had these parachuting bombs which explode on hitting the ground, the shrapnel goes out.[21]

The constant change of plans led to a waste of troops' energy in moving from one hill to another; Ted Johnson remembers having moved up Appetici, taking the gun emplacements, then being told to leave, only to be told to go back up the same mountain. Similar difficulties were experienced by troops on Rachi Ridge. Men were being sent down valleys and up mountains without due consideration of the time this took. They were moved out of positions which were then overridden in places they had hard won only the previous day.

Poor defence preparations with too much emphasis placed on covering the perimeter of the island instead of covering the centre heights left the battalion without strong means of resistance as the troops were spread too thinly. Some of the officers saw this as poor judgement on Tilney's part. Many believed that Maurice French had the proper strategic plan to hold the higher ground rather than disperse all the troops to cover the bays – but this strategy was overridden by Tilney.

Tilney's surrender of the island when overcome by the Germans at HQ was inexcusable, when the power should have been divested to whoever was next in line still in the field, and fighting could have continued. Lieutenant Ted Johnson said of Tilney, 'As he arrived we wondered how well equipped he would be as a Gunner to organise the fight which would be an infantry battle. It was to prove a classic mis-posting. The brigadier, and apparently his staff too, had neither the grasp of first principles of defence nor the tactical experience necessary.' Johnson attacked Tilney as not fit for the job. 'Maurice French could have done the job but his original defence plan was overturned by Tilney. Maurice, left to himself, would have held the island by his original plan, even with the Faughs alone, by sitting tight and shooting it out, and by his proven ability as a leader.'[22] Mistakes made included siting guns on top of hills unable to point down well enough to cover the beaches. Only 8 of 12 anti-tank guns covered beaches, and 12 Bofors were used against ground targets instead of air.

In fact, there appears to have been no clear line of order authorisation generally throughout the whole of the battle. Tilney, in particular, can be cited for ordering troops without going through their commanding officers. He not only made some bad decisions, he did not have the infantry experience of general command necessary for such an operation. He had been temporarily promoted to the role from command of an artillery regiment specifically for this venture. Sergeant Lieutenant Ambrose has pointed out, 'It does not seem that he had much knowledge of the principles of defence; it is clear that he had no grasp of infantry organisation or tactics.'[23] He added,

> One cannot avoid the impression that he was apt to make hurried decisions on insufficient information, and to vacillate and waver in their execution with consequent counter order and disorder. On more than one occasion he issued orders direct to companies and even platoons without informing their immediate superiors. Indeed, if he had followed the due process of the chain of command, he would have stepped down when captured rather than simply surrender the island.

It should have devolved to the next in the chain of command. Lieutenant Richard James of the Queen's Own Royal West Kents remembered, 'Many of the men felt quite disgusted with the surrender as they had given their all. This is why a lot of ill feeling was held – the commander-in-chief, the brigadier [Tilney] in Leros, surrendered the island when the Germans captured Meraviglia. I can't make comment on whether this was right or not.'[24] Even the Italian admiral, Mascherpa, was angry about Tilney's surrender and claimed the Italians would have kept going with their large force.

Clifford Clarke was even more dismissive of Tilney.

> We had a commander who wasn't an aggressive commander. To give you an idea, on the second night [13 November], I think it was, they had obviously come in with some force by then, but we could still deal with them so the idea was to go on company strength to in the middle of the night, about three o'clock in the morning [14th], and we were to arrive at the command post of the general before that time. I took my mobile platoon, others came from the Royal Irish Fusiliers to make up a composite company. We arrived all right, they'd issued out rum and all that sort of thing, and then we found that one platoon had gone to the wrong map reference over a mountain top away and couldn't get there in time. Now I and the others said to the commander that it doesn't

matter, we know this inside out we can deal with this, and he foolishly said no, I can't let you go with a reduced number, so we were sent back to our positions. Now this was disastrous. Tilney didn't know the island and had a defeatist attitude, he wasn't aggressive. If you had had 'Blood and Guts' Patton or someone, he would have dealt with it easily. The time to strike when paratroopers drop is immediately – they all landed in the wrong places, they hadn't got their kit with them.[25]

David Sutherland now in Turkey was informed of developments. He recalled, 'It appeared that even on the 15th the situation was in hand in spite of the terrific bombardment.'[26] Müller himself had thought the battle hung in the balance.[27] Clifford Clarke also believed most of the men thought they were winning and it was a poor decision that Tilney made to surrender – the men would have continued fighting. Captain Clarke recalled,

What he [Tilney] got from Cairo, I don't know. He came up there with an order. He would have to tell Cairo that he couldn't continue any longer. They took it that he decided he couldn't continue. In HQ there would be him and his staff officers, and they would be receiving information in, not from platoon level, from battalion and company level – he was the one who said his troops could not carry on any longer through tiredness, lack of ammunition and lack of reinforcement. Mine were well prepared to obey orders. If I'd have said, 'Come on, we are to set off,' they'd have come. We still had around 150 men I reckon, because everyone who strolled by, I pulled in. They were only too happy to join somewhere where there is some action, someone who will think for them and give them instructions.[28]

To make the point clear, most of the men believed the surrender should not have taken place. Although they were worn out with fatigue, they still thought they were in with a fighting chance, and German records would support the idea that the Germans thought they might lose the battle. Furthermore, Brigadier Tilney, once captured, had no authority over the troops. The chain of command automatically should have devolved to the next infantry officer, Colonel Iggulden, the commanding officer of the Buffs. He still had control of the north of the islands. Many men continued to fight in small areas with no communication, notably those on Mount Clidi. The main mitigating fact in reasoning why Tilney surrendered was the sheer amount of enemy artillery coming in. With the British troops running out of ammunition, and huge new enemy guns being set into place, there was a swing in the balance of the battle. Tilney must have thought there was no hope and more loss of life was pointless.

A problem with who was in charge of the overall operation added to the confusion. The Commanders-in-Chief Committee in Cairo made policy and major decisions, but naval operations were conducted by the Commander-in-Chief, Levant from his head-quarters. The latter was combined with No. 201 (Naval Co-operation) Group, RAF, at Alexandria. The army appointed a corps commander with a headquarters in Cairo, and the RAF an air vice marshal who, though himself in Cairo, had his operational headquarters in Cyprus. Finally, General Headquarters, Middle East and Headquarters, Royal Air Force, Middle East took over the direct control of operations.[29] If ever a coordination plan was set up to fail, this was it. This combination proved a disaster in practice.

The activities of the Raiding and Reconnaissance Forces merited special mention in the final reports. 'These forces were acting over the Southern-Aegean throughout the period of operations. They were the first to arrive and the last to leave, and carried out many daring and successful operations in enemy-occupied islands. There is no doubt that forces of this type, well-trained and led, can be of great value both for harassing the enemy and obtaining important intelligence.'[30] A mention must also be given to the submarine operations as, although not the main focus of this book, they provided admirable support. In common with all other forces operating in the Aegean during this period, the submarines were driven hard. Their patrols were largely carried out in narrow waters in close proximity to known or suspected minefields for long periods of time, mainly because they had to respond to local emergencies.[31] The determination of the First Submarine Flotilla managed, under these difficult conditions, to knock out three merchant ships, and 21 caiques and schooners. Supply submarines were severely challenged given the heavy air attacks at night making unloading impracticable at these times.[32] The naval forces engaged on these operations – cruisers, destroyers, submarines and coastal craft – and the small force of aircraft available to them all fought hard and did valiant work under particularly trying conditions. They achieved considerable success against the enemy and held off the attack on Leros for some time, but not without heavy casualties to British forces.[33]

The feeling of the men was best summed up by Captain Clifford Clarke who said bluntly, 'We could easily have knocked them [the Germans] off the island if it had not been for our terrible brigadier-general commanding officer who eventually surrendered to them.'[34] Tilney, of course, may have seen so many men losing their lives that he felt he could not bear to lose any more. As with all of the men, no doubt he did his best within the scope of his knowledge and experience. He may have felt the British position untenable, but nearly all the men I interviewed thought they could have won the Battle of Leros and were prepared to keep on fighting.

APPENDICES

Military Terminology

Unit name	Consists of	Approx. number of men	Commanded by
Army	2 or more corps	100,000–150,000	Field Marshal or General
Corps	2 or more divisions	25,000–50,000	General or Lieutenant General
Division	3 or more brigades or regiments	10,000–15,000	Lieutenant General or Major General
Brigade	3 or more battalions	1,500–3,500	Major General, brigadier or colonel
Regiment	2 or more battalions	1,000–2,000	Colonel
Battalion	4 or more companies	400–1,000	Lieutenant Colonel
Company	2 or more platoons	100–250	Captain or Major
Platoon (Troop)	2 or more squads	16–50	1st Lieutenant
Squad	2 or more sections	8–24	Sergeant
Section		4–12	Sergeant

Rank (officers)	Command	No. of men under command
General (Chief of General Staff)	Army	300,000
Lieutenant General (HQ)	Corps	60,000
Major General	Division	12,000
Brigadier (Field Officer)	Brigade	3,500
Colonel	Operational advisors	
Lieutenant Colonel	Battalion commanding officer (CO)	650–1000
Major	Battalion second in command	650–1000
Regimental Sergeant Major	Regiment	650
Squadron Sergeant Major	Regiment	650
Captain	Company	200
Staff Sergeant	Troop or platoon	120
Lieutenant or Second Lieutenant	Platoon	30–50
Sergeant	Troop or platoon (assists junior officers)	35
Corporal	Troops and equipment	12
Lance Corporal	Soldiers	4
Private	Lowest-ranking	0

Chronology

Date	Event	
1911–12	Italian–Libyan War	
1920	Treaty of Sèvres (between Allies and Turkey)	Turkey renounces claims in favour of Italy, but treaty was never ratified
1922	Ratification of Treaty of Lausanne	End of Greco–Turkish War
3 September 1939	Britain and France declare war on Germany	
10 June 1940	Italy joins the war on Germany's side	
July 1940	Special Boat Section founded	
22 July 1940	SOE established	
28 October 1940	Oxi Day	
28 February 1941	Operation Abstention	Allies try unsuccessfully to take Castelerizo
6 April 1941	Loss of mainland Greece to Germans	Germans invade via Bulgaria
20 May–1 June 1941	Battle of Crete	
1 June 1941	Surrender of Crete	
13 June 1942	Jellicoe raids Heraklion	
4–18 September	Sutherland and Allott raid Rhodes	
12 September 1942	Greek Sacred Squadron formed	
14–24 January 1943	Casablanca Conference, Morocco	
1 April 1943	SAS splits into the Special Raiding Squadron and the Special Boat Squadron	Jellicoe takes over command of the SBS
July 1943	Allied landing in Sicily	
17–24 August 1943	Quadrant Conference in Quebec	
8 September 1943	Italian capitulation	Rush by the British to claim the Dodecanese islands

Date	Event	
9 September 1943	Jellicoe dropped into Rhodes	
11 September 1943	Surrender of Rhodes	Hitler orders all Italian officers resisting to be shot on sight
12 September 1943	Castelerizo liberated by the Allies	
13 September 1943	Jellicoe liberates Kos	
14 September 1943	Milner Barry and Sutherland visit Kalymnos and Samos	
15 September 1943	British garrison on Kos	
24 September 1943	Germans land on Corfu and take over within 3 days	
26 September1943	*Intrepid* and *Olga* sunk	First enemy raid in Portolago
2 October 1943	Prendergast, Sutherland and Milner Barry in conference with Turnbull on Leros	
3 October 1943	Kos invaded by enemy	
4 October 1943	Fall of Kos at 12.00 hours. British resistance ceased	Rescue operations begin
5 November 1943	Brigadier Robert Tilney arrives in Leros	
12 November 1943	Invasion of Leros at dawn	Battle lasts 4 days
16 November 1943	Leros surrendered at 17.00 hours	Allied escapes begin
14 October 1944	Liberation of Athens	
29 April 1945	Surrender of German troops in Italy	Hitler commits suicide
7 May 1945	Surrender of all German forces	
8 May 1945	Victory in Europe	
15 August 1945	Japanese surrender	

Medals Awarded*

(*This list of medal awards and those killed in action is by no means definitive and merely reflects on those I have managed to collate who are mentioned in the book.)

Lieutenant Colonel John Richard Easonsmith was awarded the Military Cross and a Distinguished Service Order. He was killed in action leading his men into an attack in Platanos

Lord George Jellicoe had already won his DSO in 1942 for his part in a raid on Heraklion airfield, Crete, and would also be awarded a Military Cross for his later actions on Rhodes in December 1943

David Lloyd Owen won the Distinguished Service Order MC and DSO in 1945

Anders Lassen was awarded the Military Cross and Two Bars (effectively three MCs). He continued to carry out raids on Simi, Santorini and Paros. He was killed on the night of 8/9 April 1945, carrying out an attack on Lake Comacchio, and was posthumously awarded the Victoria Cross for his bravery

Lieutenant Colonel David Stirling was awarded a DSO.

Colonel David Sutherland was awarded the MC for his raid on Crete in September 1942.

Military Cross Awarded To:

Lieutenant Robert Austin Ardill

Georges Roger Pierre Bergé of the Free French army won the MC for his part in the Cretan raid in 1942 with Jellicoe, and ended up in Colditz with David Stirling

Lieutenant Clifford A.L. Clarke

Captain J.W. Hoare

Lieutenant Richard Austin 'Jimmy' James

Lieutenant Edward 'Ted' Johnson

John Richard Olivey MC plus bar

Lieutenant E.J. Ransley gained the Military Cross for leading the battle on Leros as the enemy landed

Lieutenant Tom J. West

Military Medals To:

'Drummer' Brown (Royal West Kents)

Lieutenant Corporal R. Cunningham

Captain H.W. Dougall

Marine John Duggan received the Military Medal for his part in the raid on Crete with David Sutherland

Fusilier J. Lyn

Fusilier J. McNeiff for his bravery having dealt effectively with three German officers and two soldiers hidden in a house on Leros

Fusilier M. Nee

Sergeant N. Findlay Distinguished Conduct Medal (mentioned by Frank Smith)

Mentioned in Despatches

Sergeant J.B. Doyle

Fusilier Elliot

Sergeant T. Fagan

Lieutenant Colonel Maurice French

Fusilier Gurren

Fusilier J. Hardy

Sergeant Hogan

Lieutenant Hugh Gore-Booth
Regimental Sergeant Major (RSM) M.D. Johnson
Fusilier J. Justice
Fusilier E. Law
Fusilier B. Lynn
Lieutenant Corporal McGee
Fusilier J. McKeever
Sergeant D.P. O'Connell
Fusilier R.J. Power
Corporal Proctor
Fusilier H. Rushton
Major William Shepherd
RSM Trainor

SOLDIERS BURIED IN LEROS CEMETERY

Name	Rank	Service Number	Date of Death	Age	Regiment/ Service	Service Country	Grave/Memorial Reference
ACOTT, JOHN THOMAS EMERICK	Private	2032649	15/11/1943	30	Queen's Own Royal West Kent Regiment	United Kingdom	3. B. 5.
ALLAN, DAVID THOMAS CHRISTIAN	Private	5959169	16/11/1943	33	The Buffs (Royal East Kent Regiment)	United Kingdom	2. A. 7.
ASHDOWN, CHARLES GEORGE HUBERT	Private	6287711	16/11/1943	26	The Buffs (Royal East Kent Regiment)	United Kingdom	2. A. 5.
ASPINALL, EDWARD HENRY	Lance Sergeant	3713000	24/11/1943	24	King's Own Royal Regiment (Lancaster)	United Kingdom	4. B. 10.
BAKER, FREDERICK LOUVAINE	Lance Corporal	2385113	15/11/1943	28	Royal Corps of Signals	United Kingdom	1. A. 8.
BANCROFT, JOHN	Bombardier	71141	05/10/1943	24	Royal Artillery	United Kingdom	4. B. 11.
BISHOP, CRESWELL	Private	5442465	16/11/1943	27	King's Own Royal Regiment (Lancaster)	United Kingdom	1. C. 3.
BLYTH, CECIL JOHN	Captain	95579	16/11/1943	23	King's Own Royal Regiment (Lancaster)	United Kingdom	2. C. 10.

Continued

Name	Rank	Service No.	Date	Age	Regiment	Country	Grave
BORROWDALE, PETER STANISLAUS	Trooper	7939136	14/11/1943	21	Royal Tank Regiment, RAC	United Kingdom	1. A. 11.
BROWN, HARRY	Gunner	1510639	25/11/1943	25	Royal Artillery	United Kingdom	4. B. 8.
BURNETT, THOMAS ALEXANDER	Gunner	897652	14/11/1943	25	Royal Artillery	United Kingdom	2. B. 8.
CHUTER, JOHN	Private	6344386	16/11/1943	24	Queen's Own Royal West Kent Regiment	United Kingdom	3. B. 7.
CLARK, B.E.H.	Lieutenant	42772V	12/11/1943	22	Cape Town Highlanders, SA Forces	South Africa	3. B. 6.
COLEMAN, FREDERICK THOMAS WALTER	Lance Corporal	6288418	13/11/1943	25	The Buffs (Royal East Kent Regiment)	United Kingdom	3. A. 5.
CONSTABLE, ALFRED WILLIAM	Gunner	1753241	11/11/1943		Royal Artillery	United Kingdom	3. A. 9.
COOPER, ARTHUR ROBERT	Corporal	6287435	13/11/1943	28	The Buffs (Royal East Kent Regiment)	United Kingdom	2. B. 10.
COWELL, ERNEST CHARLES	Corporal	5954469	12/11/1943	26	The Buffs (Royal East Kent Regiment)	United Kingdom	2. A. 10.
CRAIG, ROY JAMES	Lance Corporal	6288828	14/11/1943	24	The Buffs (Royal East Kent Regiment)	United Kingdom	3. B. 11.

Name	Rank	Service Number	Date of Death	Age	Regiment/ Service	Service Country	Grave/Memorial Reference
CREASEY, GEORGE EDWARD	Gunner		26/09/1943	38	Royal Navy	United Kingdom	Coll. grave 4. C. 4-9.
CRUDDAS, JAMES WILLAME	Fusilier	4458970	12/11/1943	24	Royal Irish Fusiliers	United Kingdom	4. B. 7.
DARTNELL, GEORGE WILLIAM	Private	6292397	14/11/1943	30	The Buffs (Royal East Kent Regiment)	United Kingdom	3. A. 3.
DE SAULLES, DOUGLAS	Private	2181400	14/11/1943	26	King's Own Royal Regiment (Lancaster)	United Kingdom	Sp. Mem. 'C'. 2. B. 5.
DIXON, ISAAC	Private	3913783	12/11/1943	34	King's Own Royal Regiment (Lancaster)	United Kingdom	1. A. 3.
DIXON, RICHARD HAROLD	Major	62606	16/11/1943	29	Cheshire Regiment	United Kingdom	4. D. 5.
DOUGLAS, ROBERT	Gunner	1795168	16/11/1943	22	Royal Artillery	United Kingdom	4. D. 6.
DOYLE, JAMES	Gunner	1830483	12/11/1943	23	Royal Artillery	United Kingdom	2. B. 6.
DUNCAN, CHARLES SPENCE	Captain	126691	16/11/1943	28	Royal Artillery	United Kingdom	3. C. 6.

Continued

Name	Rank	Service No.	Date	Age	Regiment	Country	Grave Ref.
DUXBURY, GORDON HINSHELWOOD	Major	76561	13/11/1943	34	Lancashire Fusiliers	United Kingdom	4. A. 5.
EASONSMITH, JOHN RICHARD	Lieutenant Colonel	140546	16/11/1943	34	Royal Tank Regiment, RAC	United Kingdom	3. B. 3.
EGALTON, HENRY ALFRED	Private	13019018	13/11/1943	35	Essex Regiment	United Kingdom	1. D. 5.
ELLIOTT, THOMAS ANDREW	Fusilier	6977686	16/11/1943	33	Royal Irish Fusiliers	United Kingdom	1. C. 5.
ENDERSBY, ERNEST JOHN	Sergeant	5954543	13/11/1943	26	The Buffs (Royal East Kent Regiment)	United Kingdom	1. D. 2.
FLOYD, WILLIAM RONALD	Private	6095123	14/11/1943	23	Queen's Own Royal West Kent Regiment	United Kingdom	1. A. 1.
FOSBRAEY, JOHN EDWARD	Corporal	6284597	13/11/1943	30	The Buffs (Royal East Kent Regiment)	United Kingdom	1. D. 1.
FRENCH, MAURICE	Lieutenant Colonel	23812	14/11/1943	40	Royal Irish Fusiliers	United Kingdom	3. D. 9.
GARNHAM, JAMES CHARLES HANLEY	Leading Airman	FX.80213	26/11/1940	20	Royal Navy	United Kingdom	2. C. 1.
GIBBINS, JAMES EDWARD	Corporal	6757848	16/11/1943	28	Queen's Own Royal West Kent Regiment	United Kingdom	3. B. 4.

Name	Rank	Service Number	Date of Death	Age	Regiment/ Service	Service Country	Grave/Memorial Reference
GIBLETT, HERBERT JAMES	Private	4076179	12/11/1943	32	King's Own Royal Regiment (Lancaster)	United Kingdom	Sp. Mem. 'C'. 1. C. 8.
GINN, DESMOND PATRICK ROPER	Lieutenant	130069	12/11/1943	26	The Loyal Regiment (North Lancashire)	United Kingdom	2. A. 6.
GORE-BOOTH, HUGH	Lieutenant	130758	11/11/1943	33	Royal Irish Fusiliers	United Kingdom	3. D. 1.
GREEN, JOHN NORMAN	Able Seaman	C/JX 416214	26/09/1943	19	Royal Navy	United Kingdom	Coll. grave 4. C. 4-9.
GREENLAND, STANLEY EDWARD	Lance Sergeant	5438065	14/11/1943	25	King's Own Royal Regiment (Lancaster)	United Kingdom	3. B. 8.
GRUNSHAW, HENRY	Corporal	6025894	16/11/1943	32	Durham Light Infantry	United Kingdom	1. D. 8.
GUEST, GORDON CARDO	Lieutenant	174156	14/11/1943	25	King's Own Royal Regiment (Lancaster)	United Kingdom	3. A. 7.
HALL, HENRY JOSEPH	Private	3712867	16/11/1943	26	King's Own Royal Regiment (Lancaster)	United Kingdom	3. C. 8.

Continued

Name	Rank	Service No.	Date	Age	Regiment	Country	Grave Ref.
HAMILTON, RICHARD WILLIAM VESEY	Lieutenant		26/11/1940	25	Royal Navy	United Kingdom	2. C. 3.
HAMMOND, ARTHUR EDWARD JAMES	Private	6288453	18/11/1943	23	The Buffs (Royal East Kent Regiment)	United Kingdom	1. B. 3.
HANKS, HARRY JAMES	Private	5954558	14/11/1943	28	The Buffs (Royal East Kent Regiment)	United Kingdom	3. A. 1.
HARDY, NORMAN WILLIAM	Lance Corporal	3909148	16/11/1943	22	King's Own Royal Regiment (Lancaster)	United Kingdom	2. A. 1.
HARLAND, ERNEST STAYMAN	Private	4394840	16/11/1943	29	The Buffs (Royal East Kent Regiment)	United Kingdom	1. B. 11.
HEATON, HENRY	Private	6093620	14/11/1943	23	The Buffs (Royal East Kent Regiment)	United Kingdom	1. B. 7.
HEWETT, GORDON HARRY	Private	6344076	16/11/1943	23	Queen's Own Royal West Kent Regiment	United Kingdom	2. D. 2.
HEWETT, VICTOR HERBERT	Lieutenant	174476	16/11/1943	24	Queen's Own Royal West Kent Regiment	United Kingdom	Sp. Mem. 'C'. 1. A. 2.
HINES, STANLEY FRENCH	Private	5442618	15/11/1943	29	King's Own Royal Regiment (Lancaster)	United Kingdom	Sp. Mem. 'C'. 2. B. 7.

Name	Rank	Service Number	Date of Death	Age	Regiment/ Service	Service Country	Grave/Memorial Reference
HOLE, ERNEST ARTHUR	Major	90574	14/11/1943	33	The Buffs (Royal East Kent Regiment)	United Kingdom	3. A. 2.
HOLT, DESMOND CAMPBELL	Captain	65566	17/11/1943	28	Royal Artillery	United Kingdom	3. C. 7.
IRELAND, DAVID WILLIAM	Corporal	3961554	13/11/1943	27	King's Own Royal Regiment (Lancaster)	United Kingdom	3. A. 8.
JOHNSON, GEORGE	Private	5889929	16/11/1943	30	Northampton-shire Regiment	United Kingdom	3. C. 10.
JOHNSON, JOHN McCARTHY	Lieutenant	179743	12/11/1943	22	King's Own Royal Regiment (Lancaster)	United Kingdom	Sp. Mem. 'C'. 1. A. 4.
JOY, DANIEL	Sergeant	3712858	16/11/1943	25	King's Own Royal Regiment (Lancaster)	United Kingdom	1. A. 5.
KANE, FRANCIS BENEDICT	Fusilier	6979036	12/11/1943	28	Royal Irish Fusiliers	United Kingdom	Sp. Mem. 'C'. 1. C. 10.
KENNEDY, PATRICK	Fusilier	7043197	12/10/1943	29	Royal Irish Fusiliers	United Kingdom	Sp. Mem. 'C'. 4. B. 4.
KERR, THOMAS DAVID	Fusilier	6976531	14/11/1943	32	Royal Irish Fusiliers	United Kingdom	Sp. Mem. 'C'. 2. B. 2.

Continued

Name	Rank	Service No.	Date	Age	Regiment	Country	Grave
KNOX, CHESTER DWANE	Pilot Officer	J/88478	03/07/1944		Royal Canadian Air Force	Canadian	Coll. grave 2. C. 4–6.
LAYTON, LESLIE JOHN SAUNDERS	Able Seaman	C/JX 130727	26/09/1943	31	Royal Navy	United Kingdom	Coll. grave 4. C. 4–9.
LITTLE, STANLEY EDWARD	Private	10548025	13/01/1946	24	Royal Army Ordnance Corps	United Kingdom	4. D. 11.
McCONAGHIE, JOSEPH	Fusilier	6978527	11/11/1943	25	Royal Irish Fusiliers	United Kingdom	3. A. 10.
MacDONALD, BRYAN GEORGE GHISLAIN	Captain	138961	12/11/1943	33	Royal Irish Fusiliers	United Kingdom	Sp. Mem. 'C'. 1. C. 9.
McFARLAND, SAMUEL	Fusilier	6978507	12/11/1943	26	Royal Irish Fusiliers	United Kingdom	4. B. 9.
McILWAINE, HAROLD	Fusilier	6978716	16/11/1943	23	Royal Irish Fusiliers	United Kingdom	4. A. 3.
McMASTER, JOHN McCAIG	Flight Sergeant	1344310	03/07/1944	31	Royal Air Force Volunteer Reserve	United Kingdom	Coll. grave 2. C. 4–6.
MARTIN, FRED ARTHUR	Private	6292476	14/11/1943		The Buffs (Royal East Kent Regiment)	United Kingdom	Coll. grave 4. A. 1.
MAXWELL, RODERICK LEIGHTON POTTER	Captain	103030	12/11/1943	31	Wiltshire Regiment	United Kingdom	Sp. Mem. 'C'. 4. A. 7.
MEAD, GWILYM LEONARD	Lance Corporal	5676703	14/11/1943	27	The Buffs (Royal East Kent Regiment)	United Kingdom	1. B. 2.

Name	Rank	Service Number	Date of Death	Age	Regiment/ Service	Service Country	Grave/Memorial Reference
MITCHEM, ROY ALBERT JAMES	Private	6094576	16/11/1943	26	Queen's Own Royal West Kent Regiment	United Kingdom	2. D. 11.
MODERWELL, KENNETH JOSEPH ANDREW	Flying Officer	J/16878	03/07/1944		Royal Canadian Air Force	Canada	2. C. 8.
MOORE, FRANCIS	Private	4978223	12/11/1943	25	Queen's Own Royal West Kent Regiment	United Kingdom	Sp. Mem. 'C'. 1. C. 11.
MOORE, PERCY JOHN	Sergeant	1503140	13/11/1943	25	Royal Artillery	United Kingdom	4. B. 3.
MORGAN, FREDERICK WILLIAM	Private	3914718	17/11/1943		King's Own Royal Regiment (Lancaster)	United Kingdom	3. A. 6.
MORGAN, THOMAS LEONARD	Second Lieutenant	307384	23/11/1943	23	The Buffs (Royal East Kent Regiment)	United Kingdom	1. B. 8.
NEWBY, HORACE WILLIAM	Private	6287758	13/11/1943	28	The Buffs (Royal East Kent Regiment)	United Kingdom	2. D. 5.

Continued

Name	Rank	Service No.	Date of Death	Age	Regiment	Country	Grave Reference
NORRIS, RICHARD	Lieutenant	138226	16/11/1943	26	Bedfordshire and Hertfordshire Regiment	United Kingdom	2. C. 11.
O'CONNELL, DANIEL JOSEPH	Sergeant	6979444	12/11/1943		Royal Irish Fusiliers	United Kingdom	3. C. 11.
OELOFSE, LOUIS JOHANNES NEL	Rifleman	6857918	18/11/1943	26	King's Royal Rifle Corps	United Kingdom	1. B. 4.
PAPE, JOSEPH EDWARD	Lance Sergeant	3853855	18/11/1943	31	King's Own Royal Regiment (Lancaster)	United Kingdom	3. A. 11.
PERT, FREDERICK ROLAND OLIVER	Chief Petty Officer	C/J 37976	26/09/1943	45	Royal Navy	United Kingdom	Coll. grave 4. C. 4-9.
PHELAN, PATRICK JOSEPH	Lance Sergeant	6978897	16/11/1943	21	Royal Irish Fusiliers	United Kingdom	2. D. 4.
PHIPPS, ALAN	Lieutenant		16/11/1943		Royal Navy	United Kingdom	3. C. 4.
PILCHER, JOHN MATHEW	Corporal	6140853	14/11/1943	28	Queen's Own Royal West Kent Regiment	United Kingdom	4. A. 11.
POLLARD, ALBERT	Lance Sergeant	1503170	13/11/1943	25	Royal Artillery	United Kingdom	2. B. 4.
PRICE, ALBERT HENRY PROBERT	Lance Corporal	3909234	16/11/1943	25	King's Own Royal Regiment (Lancaster)	United Kingdom	1. B. 5.
PRYNNE, HERBERT JAMES JOE	Private	5442368	16/11/1943	28	King's Own Royal Regiment (Lancaster)	United Kingdom	1. C. 6.

Name	Rank	Service Number	Date of Death	Age	Regiment/ Service	Service Country	Grave/Memorial Reference
REDFERN, ALAN GARDINER	Captain	291976	12/11/1943	37	King's Royal Rifle Corps	United Kingdom	3. C. 9.
REDMAN, HENRY JOHN	Private	3910341	12/11/1943	29	King's Own Royal Regiment (Lancaster)	United Kingdom	Sp. Mem. 'C'. 4. A. 4.
REEVES, NORMAN PHILIP	Lieutenant	245295	13/11/1943	20	The Buffs (Royal East Kent Regiment)	United Kingdom	2. A. 2.
RICHARDSON, ARTHUR EDWIN	Private	5959709	16/11/1943	37	The Buffs (Royal East Kent Regiment)	United Kingdom	2. A. 4.
ROBINSON, MAURICE FRANCIS	Captain	137938	12/11/1943	25	Royal Irish Fusiliers	United Kingdom	4. B. 1.
ROCHE, ROBERT DAVID	Private	4398188	13/11/1943	34	The Buffs (Royal East Kent Regiment)	United Kingdom	1. D. 4.
ROELOFSEN, JOHN ERIC OTTO	Captain	73410	12/11/1943	25	Green Howards (Yorkshire Regiment)	United Kingdom	2. B. 11.
ROWE, NORMAN HENRY	Able Seaman	D/JX 150642	13/10/1943	22	Royal Navy	United Kingdom	3. C. 2.

Continued

Name	Rank	Service Number	Date	Age	Regiment	Country	Grave
SAUNDERS, SYDNEY JOHN	Sergeant	1610621	03/07/1944	22	Royal Air Force Volunteer Reserve	United Kingdom	Coll. grave 2 C. 4-6.
SENNECK, JOHN	Lance Corporal	3712949	12/11/1943	25	King's Own Royal Regiment (Lancaster)	United Kingdom	1. C. 7.
SEXTON, OSBORNE	Corporal	3913030	16/11/1943	31	King's Own Royal Regiment (Lancaster)	United Kingdom	2. B. 3.
SHIELLS, JOHN ROY	Private	3779836	14/11/1943	31	King's Own Royal Regiment (Lancaster)	United Kingdom	3. B. 9.
SMITH, AUGUSTUS WILLIAM	Able Seaman	C/JX393277	28/10/1943	20	Royal Navy	United Kingdom	3. C. 1.
SOMMERWILL, HOBEN CHARLES	Private	4398215	16/11/1943	34	Green Howards (Yorkshire Regiment)	United Kingdom	1. D. 3.
SPOONER, FREDERICK CHARLES	Warrant Officer Class II	6339148	15/11/1943	35	Queen's Own Royal West Kent Regiment	United Kingdom	4. B. 2.
STEDMAN, PERCY HARRY	Private	6288507	15/11/1943	25	The Buffs (Royal East Kent Regiment)	United Kingdom	1. B. 9.
STEWART, PATRICK	Fusilier	4459933	16/11/1943	25	Royal Irish Fusiliers	United Kingdom	1. A. 6.

Name	Rank	Service Number	Date of Death	Age	Regiment/ Service	Service Country	Grave/Memorial Reference
STOREY, JAMES HENRY	Flight Sergeant	1099164	03/07/1944	34	Royal Air Force Volunteer Reserve	United Kingdom	2. C. 7.
STOTER, EDWARD JAMES	Private	6344585	11/11/1943	22	Queen's Own Royal West Kent Regiment	United Kingdom	Sp. Mem. 'C'. 2. D. 7.
STREETLY, JOHN	Private	2935025	16/11/1943	23	King's Own Royal Regiment (Lancaster)	United Kingdom	4. D. 7.
STRETCH, ARTHUR	Private	3716938	16/11/1943	31	King's Own Royal Regiment (Lancaster)	United Kingdom	1. D. 10.
TAYLOR, JOHN RICHARD	Corporal	5378845	16/11/1943	34	The Buffs (Royal East Kent Regiment)	United Kingdom	Coll. grave 4. A. 1.
THWAITES, EDWARD LIONEL	Major	118448	17/11/1943	22	Royal Artillery	United Kingdom	1. B. 6.
TODMAN, H.A.	Signaller	SR/598851V	23/11/1943	25	South African Corps of Signals	South Africa	Sp. Mem. 'C'. 1. A. 7.
TORRANCE, ROBERT FERGUSON	Sergeant	1371239	03/07/1944	23	Royal Air Force Volunteer Reserve	United Kingdom	Coll. grave 2. C. 4-6.

Continued

Name	Rank	Service No.	Date	Age	Regiment/Unit	Country	Grave Reference
TRINDER, ALFRED REGINALD	Private	6287440	13/11/1943	29	The Buffs (Royal East Kent Regiment)	United Kingdom	1. D. 7.
TURNER, JOSEPH	Seaman	LT/JX 198963	13/11/1943	22	Royal Naval Patrol Service	United Kingdom	1. B. 1.
WAFER, JOHN	Private	3913396	16/11/1943	31	King's Own Royal Regiment (Lancaster)	United Kingdom	2. B. 1.
WEEKES, JOHN RICHARD BORRODELL	Midshipman (A)		26/11/1940	20	Royal Navy	United Kingdom	2. C. 2.
WELBURN, JOHN RAYMOND	Sergeant	6288524	14/11/1943	25	The Buffs (Royal East Kent Regiment)	United Kingdom	3. C. 3.
WHEELDON, HAROLD	Signalman	2048644	09/10/1943	25	Royal Corps of Signals	United Kingdom	Sp. Mem. 'C'. 4. D. 3.
WHORLOW, FRED WILLIAM	Private	6288525	17/11/1943	25	The Buffs (Royal East Kent Regiment)	United Kingdom	Sp. Mem. 'C'. 2. D. 6.
WILSON, LEONARD	Signalman	2352280	09/06/1945		Royal Corps of Signals	United Kingdom	2. C. 9.
WOODWARD, JOHN	Private	3781131	13/11/1943	34	King's Own Royal Regiment (Lancaster)	United Kingdom	2. A. 3.
WRIGHT, ALBERT EDWARD	Ordinary Seaman	C/JX 407407	26/09/1943	35	Royal Navy	United Kingdom	Coll. grave 4. C. 4-9.

Men in the Battle of Leros Cemetery

Not all those killed were buried in Leros Cemetery.

Captain Derek John Platagenet Thirkell-White was killed in action on 14 November 1943 on Leros. His name is on the Athens Memorial Roll. He died on Searchlight Hill along with Captain C.J. Blyth (in Leros Cemetery), his second-in-command, while leading King's Own in battle. Captains H.P.J.M. Burke and J. McG. Mathieson were also killed in this encounter.

Major G.H. Duxbury was killed in action defending Clidi. Captain R.L.P. Maxwell was also killed while leading a patrol on Clidi. Other King's Own who were killed in action on Leros include D.R. Humm, F.B. King, J.H. Thorp; Lieutenants B.G.G. Macdonald, D.B. Steward, D.P. Ginn, F.B. Lawson, G.E.R. Brewer and J.M.C. Johnson. Wounded: Majors M.R. Lonsdale and I.B. Cunningham, Lieutenants A. Burgess, A.A. Porter and W. Middleton. Wounded and missing: Major W.P.T. Tilly; Lieutenant P.R.H. Buckland and Second Lieutenant J.D. Brown. Missing: Lieutenant Colonel S.A.F.S. Egerton; Major M.P. Huthwaite; Captains A.J. Hands and A.J. MacKenzie; Lieutenants S.J. Griffin, D.M.D. Broster, G.M. Harvey, R. King, S.L.M.B. Constable, D.C. Williams and Lieutenants (Q.M.) W.G. Spier and Edwin Wallace Glenn.

Of the LRDG, those killed on Leros include: Medical Orderly Ken Foley, J.T. Bowler, S. Federman, P. Wheeldon, H.L. Mallett, Rifleman L. Oelofse and A.J. Penhall.

Notes

Chapter 1   In the Beginning

1. Winston Churchill in a speech in Parliament, 24 April 1941.
2. Peter E. Smith and Edwin R. Walker, *War in the Aegean: The Campaign for the Eastern Mediterranean in World War II* (Mechanicsburg, PA, Stackpole Books, 2008), p. 9.
3. Martin Gilbert, *Winston S. Churchill: Finest Hour, 1939–1941* (London, Heinemann, 1983), p. 898.
4. Gerhard Schreiber, Bernd Stegemann and Detlef Vogel (eds), *Germany and the Second World War, 1939–1941, Vol. III* (London, Oxford University Press, 1995), pp. 530–1.
5. Anthony Beevor, *Crete: The Battle and the Resistance* (London, Penguin, 1991), p. 60.
6. John Parker, *SBS: The Inside Story of the Special Boat Service* (London, Headline, 1997), p. 12.
7. Courtney has been described thus: 'Naturally indifferent to authority, he was a wild, adventurous man of 40, who between the wars, had been a professional big-game hunter and gold prospector in East Africa.' Parker, *SBS*, p. 11.
8. Ibid., pp. 13, 34.
9. Dobrski Papers File 1/3, King's College Archives. One of the men with whom Jellicoe was to work during his drop into Rhodes was Lt Col. Julian Antony Dolbey known as Dolbey, supposedly a Polish count. This training manual was amongst his papers.
10. Ibid., File 1/3, 1–44, Rf Code GB00099 KCLMA.
11. Ibid., File 1/3.
12. J.P. interview with Lord the Earl George Jellicoe (hereafter George Jellicoe).
13. J.P. interview with George Jellicoe.
14. David Sutherland, *He Who Dares. Recollections of Service in the SAS, SBS and MI5* (London, Leo Cooper, 1998), p. 68.

15. Sutherland tells of his Rhodes adventure in his memoir, *He Who Dares*, pp. 71–91. It was made into a film *They Who Dare* (1953), with Dirk Bogarde in his role and Denholm Elliot as Duggan.
16. J.P. interview with Nikos Pyrovolikos. The Greeks were from all over the islands, from Samos, Kalymnos, Ikaria and Korthi. Three of them were Mikalis Provataris, Yiannis Stambirakis, Mikalis Karabis.
17. Sutherland, *He Who Dares*, p. 99.
18. SBS War Diary, 7 April 1943, WO218/98, PRO.
19. Sutherland would continue his raids on enemy installations on Aegean islands north of Rhodes in early 1944. He was parachuted into Albania in October 1944 to join men of his 'S' Detachment operating with local partisans against the withdrawing German army. On his return, still only 24, Sutherland became a lieutenant colonel, and succeeded Jellicoe as commander of the SBS.
20. Lorna Almonds Windmill, *A British Achilles: The Story of George 2nd Earl Jellicoe* (Barnsley, Pen and Sword, 2005), p. 52.
21. Sutherland, *He Who Dares*, p. 99.
22. Quoted in Gavin Mortimer, *The SBS in World War II* (Oxford, Osprey Publishing, 2013), p. 35.
23. J.P. interview with George Jellicoe; Sutherland, *He Who Dares*, p. 101.

Chapter 2   The Italian Capitulation

1. Dolbey to Jellicoe before he jumped from the aircraft into Rhodes. J.P. interview with George Jellicoe.
2. *The Times*, 7 September 1943. Also on the extent of the famine on the island of Syros, see Sheila Lecoeur, *Mussolini's Greek Island: Fascism and the Italian Occupation of Syros in World War II* (London, I.B.Tauris, 2015).
3. See 'Operations in the Dodecanese Islands, September–November 1943 (Royal Air Force Centre for Air Power Studies, n.d.), footnote 2, p. 9.
4. Peter E. Smith and Edwin R. Walker, *War in the Aegean: The Campaign for the Eastern Mediterranean in World War II* (Mechanicsburg, PA, Stackpole Books, 2008), pp. 33–4.
5. J.P. interview with George Jellicoe.
6. Dobrski Papers, File 12, King's College Archives.
7. Ibid., File 3/1–7.
8. Churchill, *The Second World War. Vol. V: Closing the Ring* (London, Cassell, 1952), p. 181.
9. Despatch of Vice-Supplement Sir Algernon U. Willis, Commander-in-Chief Levant, 'Naval Operations in the Aegean Between the 7th September and 28th November 1943', dated 27 December 1943, reproduced in the *London Gazette*, 8 October 1948. www.ibiblio.org/hyperwar/UN/UK/LondonGazette/38426.pdf. Accessed 16 December 2015.
10. Quadrant Conference Papers and Minutes of the Meeting, 1943, p. 253: www.znaci.net/00002/336.pdf. Accessed 30 September 2016;

Michael Howard, *Grand Strategy, Vol. IV: August 1942–September 1943* (London, Her Majesty's Stationery Office, 1972), p. 685.

11. 19 August 1943, Premier 3/3/7, PRO.

12. Mike Morgan, *Sting of the Scorpion: The Inside Story of the Long Range Desert Group* (Stroud, Sutton Publishing, 2000), p. 120.

13. Smith and Walker, *War in the Aegean*, p. 40.

14. Churchill, *The Second World War, Vol. V*, pp. 181–2.

15. Ibid., p. 102.

16. J.P. interview with George Jellicoe.

17. J.P. interview with George Jellicoe.

18. Dobrski Papers, File 13.

19. J.P. interview with George Jellicoe.

20. J.P. interview with George Jellicoe.

21. J.P. interview with George Jellicoe.

22. Dobrski, File 13.

23. Lorna Almonds Windmill, *A British Achilles: The Story of George 2nd Earl Jellicoe* (Barnsley, Pen and Sword, 2005).

24. J.P. interview with George Jellicoe.

25. J.P. interview with George Jellicoe.

26. Smith and Walker, *War in the Aegean*, p. 52.

27. Jellicoe, Sound Archive, Catalogue no. 26767, Imperial War Museum.

28. Quoting Gen. Wilson's despatches in John Grehan and Martin Mace, *Operations in North Africa and the Middle East 1942–1944* (Barnsley, Pen and Sword, 2015), pp. 197, 201.

29. Smith and Walker, *War in the Aegean*, p. 56.

30. As anticipated, on 17 October 1943 Castelorizo would be bombed for the first time by six Stukas which were supported by two escort planes. The island was again heavily bombed on 18 October 1943 at 10.00 a.m. by 12 Junkers 88s. Serious damage was caused to a number of residences, with loss of life and injuries to soldiers and inhabitants. Taken from www.empirepatrol.com/theodyssey.htm. Accessed 28 October 2016.

31. David Sutherland, *He Who Dares. Recollection of Service in the SAS, SBS and MI5* (Barnsley, Leo Cooper, 1998), pp. 115–16.

32. Ibid., p. 117.

33. Leonard Marsland Gander, *Long Road to Leros* (London, MacDonald, 1945), p. 164.

34. Walter Milner-Barry cat.no. 16753, IWM.

35. J.P. interview with George Jellicoe.

36. They were followed by motor launches which landed parties of SBS and SAS By 13 September, FFS *La Moqueuse, Commandant Domine*, HMIS *Sutlej* and HHMS *Koundritotis* had landed 350 troops and stores in Castelorizo; 'Admiralty War Diaries of World War II, Levant Command – September to November 1943', transcribed by Don Kindell: www.naval-history.net/xDKWD-Levant1943d.htm. Accessed 28 December 2015.

37. Windmill, *A British Achilles*, p. 82.

38. There is some discrepancy whether the Commander of the Raiding Forces Middle East, Colonel Turnbull, was there or not. Jellicoe's biographer, Laura Almonds Windmill, says he had been briefly on the island having arrived from Cyprus on Castelorizo on 10 September, but had gone by the time Jellicoe arrived. Sutherland recalls he was at the meeting when Jellicoe described his eventful adventure in Rhodes: ibid., p. 82; Sutherland, *He Who Dares*, p. 117. The likelihood (since he was there) is that Sutherland's recollections are correct and Turnbull was at the meeting.

39. J.P. interview with George Jellicoe.

40. Sutherland, *He Who Dares*, p. 118.

41. J.P. interview with George Jellicoe.

42. Churchill, *The Second World War, Vol. V*, p. 184.

43. Sutherland, *He Who Dares*, p. 119.

44. *Daily Telegraph*, 23 September 1943.

45. J.P. interview with George Jellicoe.

46. Jeffrey Holland, *The Aegean Mission, Allied Operation in the Dodecanese, 1943* (London and New York, Greenwood Press, 1988), p. 127.

47. PREM 3/3/1–7, p.17.PRO.

48. Smith and Walker, *War in the Aegean*, p. 43.

49. Ibid., p. 57.

50. Supplement to *London Gazette*, 8 October 1948; Smith and Walker, *War in the Aegean*, p. 43.

51. G.W. Read, *A Story of an Independent Command in the Aegean 1943–45; Raiding Forces and the Levant Schooner Flotilla. No 1 Public Relations Service*, GHQ MEF, July 1943, p. 15.

52. 'Admiralty War Diaries of World War II, Levant Command – September to November 1943'. Transcribed by Don Kindell: www.naval-history.net/xDKWD-Levant1943d.htm. Accessed 28 December 2015.

53. Admiralty War Diaries.

54. Ramseyer and Anderson returned to Kos where a detachment of SBS unit was ordered to Simi and occupied the island in early hours of 18 September; the two officers returned to Cairo leaving Colonel Kenyon and Major C.F. Blagden in charge of Kos. Admiralty War Diaries.

55. Admiralty War Diaries.

Chapter 3   Troops to Leros

1. John Norman Cowell, 'King's Own: WW2 People's War', www.bbc.co.uk/history/ww2peopleswar/about/siteinformation.shtml. Accessed 21 October 2016.

2. Lt Ambrose's Report on '2nd Battalion, The Royal Irish Fusiliers, Leros, November 1943', Royal Irish Fusiliers Museum, Armagh, and author's copy.

3. The main references for the LRDG are R.L. Kay, *Long Range Desert Group in the Mediterranean* (Wellington, New Zealand, War History Branch of Internal Affairs, 1950; reprint Merriam Press, 2012); Major-General David Lloyd Owen, *The Long Range Desert Group 1940–1945: Providence Their Guide* (Barnsley, Leo Cooper, 2003); and Mike Morgan, *Sting of the Scorpion: The Inside Story of the Long Range Desert Group* (Stroud, Sutton Publishing, 2000).

4. Lloyd Owen, *The Long Range Desert Group*, p. 4.

5. Ibid., p. 127.

6. Morgan, *Sting of the Scorpion*, p. 82.

7. Capt. R.P. 'Doc' Lawson, quote in ibid., p. 117.

8. Lloyd Owen, *The Long Range Desert Group*, p. 129.

9. Ibid.

10. Ibid., p. 130.

11. Ibid., p. 131.

12. Ibid.

13. According to Lloyd Owen's memoirs, this was dusk of 14 September, yet only a couple of days before, Jellicoe says he had enjoyed a fine welcome. Ibid., p. 133.

14. Ibid., p. 134.

15. J.P. interview with Ted Johnson.

16. J.P. interview with Ted Johnson.

17. J.P. interview with Ted Johnson.

18. J.P. interview with Ted Johnson.

19. Raymond Williams, *The Long Road from Leros* (privately printed, 1983), p. 6.

20. J.P. interview with Ted Johnson.

21. J.P. interview with Ted Johnson.

22. J.P. interview with Ted Johnson.

23. Copy of letter from Tom Massey Lynch to Amanda Moreno, previous curator to RIF Museum, in author's possession.

24. J.P. interview with Ted Johnson.

25. J.P. interview with Ted Johnson.

26. J.P. interview with Ted Johnson.

27. J.P. interview with Ted Johnson.

28. J.P. interview with Ted Johnson.

29. J.P. interview with Vic Kenchington.

30. J.P. interview Vic Kenchington.

31. Jack Harte, *Limits of Endurance* (Dublin, Liberties Press, 2007), p. 103.

32. Ibid., p. 105.

33. Ibid., p. 107.

34. Ibid.

35. Leonard Marsland Gander, *Long Road to Leros* (London, MacDonald, 1945), p. 179.

36. J.P. interview with Paddy McCrystal.

37. J.P. interview with Paddy McCrystal.
38. J.P. interview with Paddy McCrystal.
39. J.P. interview with Paddy McCrystal.
40. www.naval-history.net/xDKWD-Levant1943d.htm. Accessed 31 May 2016.
41. Admiralty War Diaries.
42. Reg Neep, 'The Long March 1943–5', typewritten MS.
43. J.P. interview with Reg Neep.
44. Neep, 'The Long March 1943–5'.
45. J.P. interview with Ted Johnson.
46. *Daily Telegraph*, 23 September 1943.
47. Premier 3/3/7, PRO.

Chapter 4   Digging In

1. J.P. interview with George Hatcher.
2. J.P. interview with George Hatcher.
3. J.P. interview with Clifford Clarke.
4. J.P. interview with Clifford Clarke.
5. J.P. interview with Paddy McCrystal.
6. J.P. interview with Sid Bowden.
7. J.P. interview with Sid Bowden.
8. J.P. interview with George Hatcher.
9. J.P. interview with Clifford Clarke.
10. Supplement to *London Gazette*, 1948,.
11. Raymond Williams, *The Long Road from Leros* (privately printed, 1983), p. 9.
12. J.P. interview with Dimitris Tsaloumas. He went on to become a well-known poet both in Leros and in Australia, to where he emigrated.
13. Jack Harte, *Limits of Endurance* (Dublin, Liberties Press, 2007), p. 104.
14. J.P. interview with Richard James.
15. He had just spent three days on Castelorizo in great celebration. While there, Jellicoe had been aboard the *Tewfik*, having just come back from his drop into Rhodes, along with David Sutherland and a detachment of SBS. Grech and the squadron leader would swim out to Jellicoe's boat at gin time to share a tipple. Once in Leros, he seemed to be having a good time as he was always late to bed after evenings of alcohol. He was there when the *Queen Olga* and *Intrepid* were bombed and the Italian naval barracks flattened. He was involved in recovering the bodies in the seaplane, and bringing them ashore. He said, 'This was my first experience of destruction and death on such a scale.' Adrian Seligman, *War in the Islands* (Stroud, Sutton Publishing, 1996), pp. 59–65.
16. Ibid.
17. Quoted from the *Oberkommando der Wehrmacht* (Diary of the Wehrmacht High Command) in Peter C. Smith and Edwin R. Walker, *War in the*

Aegean: The Campaign for the Eastern Mediterranean in World War II (Mechanicsburg, PA, Stackpole Books, 1974), p. 40.

18. Ibid., p. 41.
19. This was on 25 September 1943, but the Germans were already well advanced in Rhodes. Ibid., p. 45.
20. Ibid., p. 81.
21. Geoffrey B. Mason, 'HMS *Faulknor*, destroyer', *Service Histories of Royal Navy Warships in World War II* (2003), www.naval-history.net/xGM-Chrono-10DD-22F-HMS_Faulknor.htm. Accessed 5 February 2011.
22. *Queen Olga* was a Greek destroyer which had served with the Royal Hellenic Navy, and was one of its distinguished ships. It had been used to transport members of the LRDG to the island. The ships mounted four 45-calibre 4.7-inch (120-mm) Mark IX guns in single mounts. For anti-aircraft defence, they had two quadruple Mark I mounts for the 0.5-inch Vickers Mark III machine gun. The I-class was fitted with two above-water quintuple-torpedo tube mounts for 21-inch (533-mm) torpedoes. One depth charge rack and two throwers were fitted; 16 depth charges were originally carried, but this increased to 35 shortly after the war began. M.J. Whitley, *Destroyers of World War Two: An International Encyclopedia* (Annapolis, MD, Naval Institute Press).
23. J.P. interview with Georgious Papadopoulos, 23 May 2002. His father was Manolis Papadopoulos.
24. J.P. interview with Ted Johnson.
25. Admiralty War Diaries.
26. Notes sent to me by Peter Colman in November 2005.
27. J.S. Guard, *Improvise and Dare: War in the Aegean 1943–45* (Lewes, The Book Guild, 1997), p. 90.
28. J.P. interview with Ted Johnson.
29. Admiralty War Diaries.
30. J.P. interview with Ted Johnson.
31. J.P. interview with Ted Johnson.
32. Supplement to *London Gazette*, 1948.
33. Premier 3/3/7, PRO.
34. Admiralty War Diaries.
35. Ibid.

Chapter 5   Fall of Kos

1. Premier 3/3/7, PRO.
2. David Sutherland, *He Who Dares. Recollections of Service in the SAS, SBS and MI5* (Barnsley, Leo Cooper, 1998).
3. David Lloyd Owen, *The Long Range Desert Group 1940–1945: Providence their Guide* (Barnsley, Leo Cooper, 1980), p. 134.
4. Sutherland, *He Who Dares*, p. 124.

5. Lloyd Owen, *The Long Range Desert Group*, p. 135.
6. Ibid., p. 135.
7. J.P. interview with George Jellicoe.
8. R.L. Kay, *Long Range Desert Group in the Mediterranean* (Wellington, New Zealand, War History Branch of Internal Affairs, 1950; reprint Merriam Press, 2012), p. 37.
9. Owen, *The Long Range Desert Group*, p. 135.
10. Admiralty Air Diary.
11. Premier 3/3/7, PRO.
12. Ibid., 3 October 1943.
13. Stephen E. Ambrose, *The Supreme Commander: The War Years of Dwight D. Eisenhower* (New York, Anchor Books, 1970), p. 285.
14. Premier 3/3/7, PRO 3 October 1943.
15. Milner-Barry, IWM, cat. no. 16753.
16. Sutherland, *He Who Dares*, p. 127.
17. Leonard Marsland Gander, *Long Road to Leros* (London, MacDonald, 1945), p. 155.
18. Charles T. O'Reilly, *Forgotten Battles: Italy's War of Liberation, 1943–1945* (Lexington, MD, Lexington Books, 2001), p. 98.
19. Gavin Mortimer, *The SBS in World War II* (Oxford, Osprey Publishing, 2013), p. 100.
20. Lloyd Owen, *The Long Range Desert Group*, p. 136.
21. Ibid.
22. 5 October 1943, Premier 3/3/7, PRO.
23. 7 October 1943, Premier 3/3/7, PRO.
24. Winston Churchill, *The Second World War. Vol. V: Closing the Ring* (London, Cassell, 1952), pp. 186–7.
25. Ibid., p. 187.
26. Ibid., p. 194.
27. Ibid., pp. 194–5.
28. Ibid., p. 195.
29. Ibid., p. 196.
30. Lt Ambrose's Report on '2nd Battalion, The Royal Irish Fusiliers, Leros, November 1943', Royal Irish Fusiliers Museum, and author's copy.
31. Kay, *Long Range Desert Group in the Mediterranean*, p. 40.
32. Supplement to *London Gazette*, 1948.
33. Adrian Seligman, *War in the Islands* (Stroud, Sutton Publishing, 1996), p. 66.
34. Sutherland, *He Who Dares*, p. 130.
35. Ibid., p. 128.
36. Ibid.
37. Ibid., p. 129.
38. Kay, *Long Range Desert Group in the Mediterranean*, p. 46.
39. Lloyd Owen, *The Long Range Desert Group*, p. 142.

40. Cdr Mercer of *Pathfinder* wrote to authors Peter C. Smith & Edwin R. Walker, *War in the Aegean: The Campaign for the Eastern Mediterranean in World War II* (Mechanicsburg, PA, Stackpole Books, 1974), p. 160.

41. 'Admiralty War Diaries of World War II, Levant Command – September to November 1943', transcribed by Don Kindell: www.naval-history.net/xDKWD-Levant1943d.htm. Accessed 28 December 2015. The *Carlisle* had been damaged beyond repair when she was hit on 9 October 1943 by German Ju 87 dive bombers which also sank HMS *Panther*.

42. Supplement to *London Gazette*, 1948.

43. Captain Taprell Dorling Taffrail, *Western Mediterranean, 1942–45* (London, Hodder & Stoughton, 1947).

44. Admiralty War Diaries.

45. HMSs *Jervis, Penn, Pathfinder, Petard Eclipse, Fury, Dulverton, Beaufort* and *Belvoir* were major ships assisting in transporting troops, supplies and bombardment of the enemy. For a fuller examination of the war at sea in the Aegean, see Admiralty War Diaries; and Lew Lind, *Battle of the Wine Dark Sea. The Aegean Campaign 1943–1945* (Kenthurst, NSW, Kangaroo Press, 1994).

46. Admiralty War Diaries; Supplement to *London Gazette*, 1948.

47. J.P interview with Nikos Pyrovolikos.

Chapter 6   Making Preparations

1. Jimmy James's typewritten MS of his recollections given to me by himself.

2. J.P. interview with Sid Bowden.

3. J.P. interview with Clifford Clarke.

4. Typed MS of memoirs given to me by Jimmy James.

5. J.P. interview with Major E.W. Tassell.

6. J.P. interview with Major E.W. Tassell.

7. The Memoirs of Stanley Norman Froud of Buffs, Record no: 2001-08-5, The Army Museum.

8. J.P. interview with Clifford Clarke.

9. Leonard Marsland Gander, *Long Road to Leros* (London, MacDonald, 1945), p. 184.

10. Rev. Reginald Anwyl, Account of The Battle of Leros 1943, King's College, p. 72.

11. J.P. interview with Clifford Clarke.

12. J.P. interview with Clifford Clarke.

13. J.P. interview with Clifford Clarke.

14. The Greek Sacred Squadron was in Samos (but not in Leros) working closely with the British army under Kristos Tsigantis: J.P. interview with George Jellicoe.

15. Jack Harte was warned by his fellow pilferer that the padre had spotted them.

16. Jack Harte, *Limits of Endurance* (Dublin, Liberties Press, 2007), p. 109.
17. Raymond Williams, *The Long Road from Leros* (privately printed, 1983), p. 7.
18. J.P. interview with Vic Kenchington.
19. J.P. interview with Vic Kenchington.
20. Guard, p. 93: WO 201/2308; ADM 199/2521, PRO.
21. J.P. interview with Reg Neep.
22. J.P. interview with Paddy McCrystal.
23. J.P. interview with Clifford Clarke.
24. J.P. interview with Clifford Clarke.
25. J.P. interview with George Hatcher.
26. J.P. interview with Tassos Kanaris.
27. J.P. interview with Nikolas Drakos.
28. J.P. interview with Thespina Taxhliambori.
29. J.P. interview with Peter George Koulianus.
30. J.P. interview with Peter George Koulianus.
31. J.P. interview with Peter George Koulianus.
32. One of the pilots dropping supplies into Leros was the courageous Squadron Leader Hugh 'Jimmy' James; see his obituary in *The Telegraph*, 14 January 2015.
33. Peter C. Smith & Edwin R. Walker, *War in the Aegean: The Campaign for the Eastern Mediterranean in World War II* (Mechanicsburg, PA, Stackpole Books, 1974), pp. 163–4.
34. A despatch was submitted to this effect to the Lords Commissioners of the Admiralty by Vice-Admiral Sir Algernon U. Willis, Commander-in-Chief, Levant; published in Supplement to *London Gazette*, 5 October 1948.
35. J.P. interview with Don Bush.
36. J.P. interview with Don Bush.
37. J.P. interview with Don Bush.
38. J.P. interview with Don Bush.
39. J.P. interview with Don Bush.
40. J.P. interview with Don Bush.
41. J.P. interview with Don Bush.
42. Admiralty War Diaries.
43. Admiralty War Diaries.
44. Admiralty War Diaries.
45. Smith and Walker, *War in the Aegean*, p. 161.
46. Admiralty War Diaries.
47. Major D. Rollo, 'Regimental History (1LAA regiment 1943)' for serial 12501 (Royal Artillery Historical Trust, 1998).
48. Admiralty War Diaries.
49. Admiralty War Diaries.
50. The Memoirs of Stanley Norman Froud of Buffs, Record no: 2001-08-5, The Army Museum.

51. http://www.naval-history.net/xGM-Chrono-10DD-21E-HMS_Eclipse.htm
    Among them was 26-year-old Edwin Wallace Glenn, 4th Battalion. He is
    remembered on the Margate War Memorial. Admiralty War Diaries.
52. www.bbc.co.uk/history/ww2peopleswar/stories/03/a4104703.shtml
    Accessed 4 July 2016.
53. The Memoirs of Stanley Norman Froud of Buffs, Record no: 2001-08-5,
    The Army Museum.
54. www.iwm.org.uk/collections/item/object/6957.
55. Seligman, *War in the Islands*, p. 68.
56. J.P. interview with Ted Johnson.
57. Admiralty War Diaries.
58. Admiralty War Diaries.
59. Admiralty War Diaries.
60. J.P. interview with Clifford Clarke.
61. J.P. interview with Clifford Clarke.
62. Supplement to *London Gazette*, 8/11 October 1948.
63. Churchill, *The Second World War. Vol. V: Closing the Ring* (London, Cassell,
    1952), p. 279.
64. Lt Ambrose's Report on '2nd Battalion, The Royal Irish Fusiliers, Leros,
    November 1943', Royal Irish Fusiliers Museum, and author's copy.
65. Supplement to *London Gazette*, 8/11 October 1948.
66. Churchill, *The Second World War. Vol. V*, p. 196.

Chapter 7   Waiting Under Bombs

1. J.P. interview with Ted Johnson.
2. Reginald Anwyl, Account of The Battle of Leros 1943, King's College
   Archives.
3. Ibid.
4. J.P. interview with Ted Johnson.
5. Anwyl, Account of The Battle of Leros 1943.
6. Ibid., p. 66.
7. Ibid., p. 67.
8. Ibid.
9. Jeffrey Holland, *The Aegean Mission: Allied Operation in the Dodecanese,
   1943* (London and New York, Greenwood Press, 1988), p. 128.
10. J.P. interview with Major E.W. Tassell.
11. www.ww2incolor.com/forum/showthread.php/8848-Battle-for-Leros
    Accesssed 11 March 2016.
12. Battalion Headquarters Commanding Officer Lt Col. Egerton was
    accompanied by Maj. M.P. Huthwaite as second-in-command, Adjutant
    Capt. A.J. Mackenzie, Intelligence Officer Lt S.J. Griffin and Regimental
    Signals Officer Lt M.B. Constable. HQ Company was commanded by Maj.
    I.B. Cunningham with Capt. J.A. Thorpe second-in-command command-
    ing the Anti-Tank Platoon. Capt. R. King was troop commander supported

by Lieutenants Harvey and Lawson. Motor Transport Platoon was commanded by Lt G.E.R. Brewer. Capt. D.J.P. Thirkell-White commanded A Company with Capt. Blythe as his second-in-command supported by Lieutenants Porter, Broster and Burgess. Maj. W. Tilly commanded C Company, with Capt. D.R. Humm as his second-in-command and platoon officers Lieutenants Brown, Horne and Ginn. D Company was commanded by Maj. Lonsdale, with Capt. H.J.P. Burke as his second-in-command, with platoon officers Lieutenants P.R.H. Buckland, D.C. Williams and I. Matheison. King's Own Report, www.kingsownmuseum.com/ww2-1ko-leros-01.htm. Accessed 5 October 2016.

13. Ibid.

14. Leonard Marsland Gander, *Long Road to Leros* (London, MacDonald, 1945), p. 158.

15. Ibid., p. 160.

16. J.P. interview with Sid Bowden.

17. J.P. interview with Sid Bowden.

18. Clifford Clark's account in *The Echo, Queen's Own Regimental Magazine*, March 1998, p. 11.

19. J.P. interview with Richard James.

20. J.P. interview with Richard James.

21. J.P. interview with Richard James.

22. 'Admiralty War Diaries of World War II, Levant Command – September to November 1943'. Transcribed by Don Kindell: www.naval-history.net/xDKWD-Levant1943d.htm Accessed 28 December 2015.

23. Supplement to *London Gazette*, 1948.

24. Ibid.

25. Ibid.

26. See David Bruhn, *Wooden Ships and Iron Men: US Navy's Coastal and Motor Minesweepers, 1941–1953* (Cirencester, Heritage Books, 2005); and www.naval-history.net/WW2Ships-BYMS72.htm.

27. A.U. Willis, Vice-Admiral, Commander-in-Chief, Report of Naval Operations in the Aegean between the 7 September 1943 and 28 November 1943, believes that the capture of BYMS 72 at Kalymnos on the night of 11/12 November seriously hampered the activities at sea; see Bruhn, *Wooden Ships and Iron Men*.

28. PRO, ADM 199/1040.

29. Adrian Seligman, *War in the Islands* (Stroud, Sutton Publishing, 1996), pp. 68–70.

30. Ibid.

31. Ibid., p. 70.

32. David Sutherland, *He Who Dares. Recollections of Service in the SAS, SBS and MI5* (Barnsley, Leo Cooper, 1998) p. 130.

33. OKW Diary reports, see Peter C. Smith and Edwin R. Walker, *War in the Aegean: The Campaign for the Eastern Mediterranean in World War II* (Mechanicsburg, PA, Stackpole Books, 1974), p. 176.

34. Royal Artillery Historical Trust, printed 9 March 1998, compiled by Major D. Rollo (1LAA regiment 1943) in Regimental History for serial 12501.

35. Taken from German war diary; Smith and Walker, *War in the Aegean*, p. 210.

36. J.S. Guard, *Improvise and Dare: War in the Aegean 1943–45* (Lewes, The Book Guild, 1997), p. 130.

37. Supplement to *London Gazette*, 1948.

38. Ibid.

39. Holland, *The Aegean Mission*, pp. 125–40. See his chapter on the Battle of Leros.

40. According to Holland, 2nd Battalion, Royal Irish Fusiliers were the largest group, with about 570; followed by 1st Battalion King's Own Royal Regiment (Lancaster) about 450 men; 4th Battalion Buffs (Royal East Kent Regiment) around 360 men; 2nd Battalion, Queen's Own Royal West Kent Regiment came in smaller groups at different times. Estimates vary slightly: see note 42.

41. www.ww2incolor.com/forum/showthread.php/8848-Battle-for-Leros Accessed 11 March 2016.

42. The breakdown according to Stanley Froud was 2nd Royal Irish Rifles plus B Company of the 2nd Royal West Kents with 500 men; 1st King's Own with 450 men; 1st Light AA Regiment, Royal Artillery three batteries with 250 men; a detachment of sappers and miners from the 9th Field Company, Madras; 50 men with a few 25-pounders found on Samos; 50 RIASC men; 70 men from the RAOC; 100 RAMC personnel; 100 or so men of the LRDG and SBS; 4th Royal East Kents (The Buffs) with 360 men – A Company, which had been so decimated when HMS *Eclipse* went down, had been added to the HQ Company. The Memoirs of Stanley Norman Froud of Buffs, Record no: 2001-08-5, The Army Museum.

43. J.P. interview with Richard James.

44. David Lloyd Owen, *The Long Range Desert Group 1940–1945: Providence Their Guide* (Barnsley, Leo Cooper, 2003), p. 142.

45. J.P. interview with Richard James.

46. J.P. interview with Richard James.

Chapter 8   The First Day of Battle

1. J.P. interview with George Hatcher.

2. Leonard Marsland Gander, *Long Road to Leros* (London, MacDonald, 1945), p. 176.

3. Also see Maitland Wilson, Dispatch: Middle East Operations 16 February 1943 to 8 January 1944; *Faugh-a-Ballagh*; *Lion and Rose* magazine; S.W. Roskill, *The War at Sea* (London, Imperial War Museum, 1994); Brigadier Tilney, 'After Action Report to the War Office', 16 April 1947, Imperial War Museum.

4. J.S. Guard, *Improvise and Dare: War in the Aegean 1943–45* (Lewes, The Book Guild, 1997), p. 134.

5. Gander, *Long Road to Leros*, p. 178.

6. Ibid., p. 181.

7. Some historical reports have asserted that no enemy aircraft was sighted before 7.30 a.m. that day. See, e.g., Jeffrey Holland, *The Aegean Mission: Allied Operation in the Dodecanese, 1943* (London and New York, Greenwood Press, 1988), p. 129.

8. Brigadier Tilney's Report of Operation on Leros, 12–16 November 1943, LRDG, 11/4.

9. See Gander, *Long Road to Leros*.

10. Peter C. Smith and Edwin R. Walker, *War in the Aegean: The Campaign for the Eastern Mediterranean in World War II* (Mechanicsburg, PA, Stackpole Books, 1974), quoting from OKW Diaries; although Air 41/53 quoting Luftwaffe records states 135 bomber sorties.

11. Royal Air Force Centre, 'Operations in the Dodecanese Islands, September–November 1943 (London, Royal Air Force Centre for Air Power Studies, n.d.), p. 45. This book gives a comprehensive outline of the activities of the RAF throughout this period.

12. Rev. Reginald Anwyl, Account of The Battle of Leros 1943, p. 68, King's College Archives.

13. Ibid., p. 69.

14. Ibid.

15. Ibid., p. 67.

16. Ted Johnson's POW Log Book.

17. Ibid.

18. German forces at Kos and Kalymnos before the Battle of Leros included four F-boats, 13 I-boats, five auxiliary naval craft and a number of caiques, all loaded with troops and equipment.

19. Supplement to *London Gazette*, 8 October 1948.

20. Ibid.; Holland, *Aegean Mission*, pp. 127–32.

21. These were named after each of their commanding officers: Anthony Rogers, *Churchill's Folly* (London, Cassell, 2003), p. 116. Rogers supplies information from the German side of the battle.

22. Landing was at a point between Pasta di Sopra and Pasta di Sotto further round from Palma Bay. This is according to the map of the Geographical Section of General Staff, 1943.

23. Lt C.H.J. Morgan (Buffs), Wartime Log, Record No. 2001-07-525, The Army Museum; also see Supplement to the *London Gazette*, 13 November 1946.

24. 'Admiralty War Diaries of World War II, Levant Command – September to November 1943'. Transcribed by Don Kindell: www.naval-history.net/xDKWD-Levant1943d.htm. Accessed 28 December 2015.

24. Gander, *Long Road to Leros*, p. 180.

25. C.R.B. Knight, *Historical Records of the Buffs 1919–1948* (London, Gale & Polden, 1905–51); Peter Schenck, 'The Battle for Leros', *After the Battle*,

No. 90, p. 19; Pauline Bevan, *Travels with a Leros Veteran* (privately published, 2000), p. 172.

26. Gander's account more or less accords with the Admiralty War Diaries which state that two landing craft were sunk and two damaged in the first assault. Gander, *Long Road to Leros*, p. 180; 'Admiralty War Diaries'.

27. About 500 according to Smith and Walker, *War in the Aegean*, p. 212; Royal Air Force Centre, 'Operations in the Dodecanese', p. 46; Morgan, Wartime Log.

28. A small enemy landing craft was sighted creeping into Alinda. However, because of an earlier accident when a young Royal Naval Volunteer Reserve lieutenant had mistakenly been fired upon by Italian batteries while trying to thwart enemy landing craft, having been mistaken as an enemy boat, the batteries had been told to be more careful. Since most small motor launches were easy targets for German dive-bombers most of them did not hang around Leros during the day but would go off and seek safe havens on the coast of Turkey or other small inlets elsewhere. The Italian gunners had therefore taken him as an enemy. The small boat now crept forward, with the gunners only shooting at the last minute. A rowing boat was then spotted. Since all Greek fishermen had left for the mainland or were in the caves sheltering, it must have been a German. The gunners seem to have missed him. Admiralty 234/364; Admiralty 199/2521, PRO.

29. See Captain Olivey's account in LRDG 11/3, IWM.

30. Mike Morgan, *Sting of the Scorpion* (Stroud, Sutton Publishing, 2000), p. 130.

31. Colonel Cowper, 'The King's Own – The Story of a Royal Regiment', http://leros2002.bravepages.com/leros_war2.html Accessed 17 April 2015.

32. www.ww2incolor.com/forum/showthread.php/8848-Battle-for-Leros Accessed 11 March 2016.

33. Captain J.R. Olivey, 'Report on Operations in Leros', 1 June 1944, LRDG 11/3, IWM.

34. Col. J.M. Cowper *The King's Own: The Story of a Royal Regiment* (Aldershot, Gale & Polden, 1957), Vol. III.

35. The King's Own who were sent to fight up Mount Clidi came under the direction of the Buffs, having lost most of their officers. Some of them took orders from the LRDG there, including Pte Lemuel Bevan of C Company. Bevan, *Travels with a Leros Veteran*, p. 8. Pte Bevan had been transported on HMS *Phoebe*, with his company disembarking on smaller vessels to get ashore.

36. Ibid., p. 21.

37. Ibid., p. 24.

38. Cowper, 'The King's Own'.

39. Smith and Walker, *War in the Aegean*, p. 213.

40. Bevan, *Travels with a Leros Veteran*, pp. 133–5.

41. Ibid., p. 133.

42. www.ww2incolor.com/forum/showthread.php/8848-Battle-for-Leros Accessed 11 March 2016.

43. LRDG 2/1, 'Operations in Aegean 11th Sept 1943 to 30th November 1943', IWM.

44. Ibid.; Lt Pavlides, Operations in Leros 10–16 November 1943, LRDG 2/1. See Tilney's After Action Report, LRDG, David Lloyd Owen's Papers, 11/4, IWM; and Captain Olivey, 'Story in Dodecanese', LRDG, 11/3. See Bevan, *Travels with a Leros Veteran*, p. 134.

45. Schenck says it was 11 a.m. before the RIFs counter-attacked, but this would seem a rather tardy response; Schenck, 'The Battle for Leros', p. 21.

46. Gander, *Long Road to Leros*, p. 181.

47. Smith and Walker, *War in the Aegean*, p. 214. See Gander, *Long Road to Leros*; *Faugh-a-Ballagh*; *Lion and Rose* magazine.

48. J.P. Interview with Lt Ted Johnson.

49. Edward B.W. Johnson, *Island Prize, 1943* (Banbury, Kemble Press, 1992), p. 47.

50. Ibid., p. 47.

51. Jack Harte, Limits of Endurance (Dublin, Liberties Press, 2007), pp. 122–3.

52. E.B.W Johnson, *Island Prize*, p. 48.

53. www.ww2incolor.com/forum/showthread.php/8848-Battle-for-Leros Accessed 11 March 2016.

54. Gander, *Long Road to Leros*, p. 181.

55. Harte, *Limits of Endurance*, p. 126.

56. J.P. interview with Ted Johnson.

57. Johnson, *Island Prize*, p. 51.

58. J.P. interview with Vic Kenchington.

59. Accounts differ about the timing of these events, which is not unusual given the stressful situation. In my interview with Vic Kenchington, he stated, 'At about 1 o'clock that same day about 50 troop carriers landed on the narrowest point with their troops, the Brandenburgers, the elite of the German army.' Brig. Tilney's post-battle report stated parachutists dropped at 2 p.m., although others such as Don Coventry say 3 p.m. Lt Morgan with Buffs believed the first airborne parachutist attack was at 4.30 p.m. with 700 parachutists dropped from a height of about 200 ft. He estimated that about 50 troop-carrying aircraft were used, with 15 or so in each plane. Also there are widely differing estimates of the numbers of parachutists dropped, at anything between 50 and 700. Churchill states 600 parachutists (Winston Churchill, *The Second World War. Vol. V: Closing the Ring* (London, Cassell, 1952), p. 196). Lt Morgan reckoned 700 parachutists were dropped from a height of about 200 ft. Peter Schenck believes there were 470 German parachutists dropped from 400 ft (Schenk, 'The Battle for Leros'). There is also variation as to how many drops were made that day; in my interviews with them, both George Hatcher and Jellicoe believed there were two drops. See James Lucas, *Storming Eagles* (London, Arms and Armour, 1988); and Peter

Darman, *Surprise Attack: Lightning Strikes of the World's Elite Forces* (London, Brown Books, 1993). Also see www.ww2incolor.com/forum/showthread. php/8848-Battle-for-Leros Accessed 11 March 2016.

60. The enemy intention was to drop at dawn on 12 November, but they were turned back after a few minutes as the situation of the troops on the landing crafts was unclear. Some hours later they dropped on ridge between Gourna and Alinda bays. They carried belts of Spandau ammunition.

61. www.ww2incolor.com/forum/showthread.php/8848-Battle-for-Leros Accessed 11 March 2016; see also Schenk, 'Battle for Leros'.

62. Gander, *Long Road to Leros*, p. 186.

63. Ibid.

64. Ibid., p. 187.

65. Anwyl, Account of The Battle of Leros 1943, p. 71.

66. Ibid., p. 72.

67. J.P. interview with George Hatcher.

68. J.P. interview with George Hatcher.

69. R.L. Kay, *Long Range Desert Group in the Mediterranean* (Wellington, New Zealand, War History Branch of Internal Affairs, 1950; reprint Merriam Press, 2012).

70. J.P. interview with Paddy McCrystal.

71. J.P. interview with Reg Neep.

72. J.P. interview with Peter George Koulianus.

73. J.P. interview with George Hatcher.

74. Corporal Reg Neep, 'The Long March 1943–5', typewritten MS given to J.P. by Reg Neep.

Chapter 9   Central Collision

1. The Commanding Officer to Lt John Browne and his troops; Lt C.J.H. Morgan, 'Wartime Log', Record No 2001-07-525, p. 18. The National Army Museum.

2. Jeffrey Holland, *The Aegean Mission: Allied Operation in the Dodecanese, 1943* (London and New York, Greenwood Press, 1988), pp. 127–13.

3. 'Admiralty War Diaries of World War II, Levant Command – September to November 1943'. Transcribed by Don Kindell: www.naval-history.net/ xDKWD-Levant1943d.htm. Accessed 28 December 2015.

4. J.P. interview with Sid Bowden.

5. J.P. interview with Sid Bowden.

6. J.P. interview with Sid Bowden.

7. J.P. interview with Sid Bowden.

8. J.P. interview with George Hatcher.

9. J.P. interview with Clifford Clarke.

10. J.P. interview with Clifford Clarke.

11. J.P. interview with Clifford Clarke.

12. J.P. interview with Clifford Clarke.

13. J.P. interview with George Jellicoe.

14. Sgt George Hatcher of the Royal West Kents believed there were two parachute landings, one in the morning and one in the afternoon. J.P. Interview with George Hatcher.

15. J.P. interview with George Jellicoe.

16. *LRDG Newsletter* No. 49 (1993). Also see http://rhodesianafricanrifles.co.uk/alan-gardiner-redfern-mbe-%C2%B7-november-11-1943 Accessed 10 October 1943.

17. *LRDG Newsletter* No. 49 (1993).

18. J.P. interview with Ted Johnson.

19. Mike Morgan, *Sting of the Scorpion: The Inside Story of the Long Range Desert Group* (Stroud, Sutton Publishing, 2000), p. 135.

20. William Moss's memoirs: www.kingsownmuseum.plus.com/ww2-1ko-leros-moss.htm Accessed 18 October 2001. Also at https://familysearch.org/photos/artifacts/18562819 Accessed 13 July 2016.

21. Ibid.

22. Ibid.

23. www.kingsownmuseum.plus.com/ww2-1ko-leros-moss.htm Accessed 25 February 2016.

24. William Moss's memoirs.

25. http://ww2today.com/12th-november-1943-german-paratroopers-attack-island-of-leros Accessed 17 February 2016.

26. J.P. interview with Richard James.

27. J.P. interview with Richard James.

28. Brig. R.A.G. Tilney, 'After Action Report to the War Office', 16 April 1947, Imperial War Museum.

29. David Lloyd Owen, *The Long Range Desert Group*, p. 142.

30. www.kingsownmuseum.plus.com/ww2-1ko-leros-01.htm Accessed 17 May 2016.

31. www.ww2incolor.com/forum/showthread.php/8848-Battle-for-Leros Accessed 11 March 2016.

32. Leonard Marsland Gander, *Long Road to Leros* (London, MacDonald, 1945), p. 189.

33. Ibid., p. 190.

34. The *Dulverton* was a Type II Hunter class destroyer of the Royal Navy and played an important part in the war. 'Admiralty War Diaries of World War II, Levant Command – September to November 1943'. Transcribed by Don Kindell: www.naval-history.net/xDKWD-Levant1943d.htm Accessed 28 December 2015.

35. John English, *The Hunts: A History of the Design, Development and Careers of the 86 Destroyers of This Class Built for the Royal and Allied Navies during World War II* (Kendal, World Ship Society, 1987). J.J. College and Ben Warlow, *Ships of the Royal Navy: The Complete Record of all Fighting Ships of the Royal Navy* (rev. edn.) (London, Chatham Publishing, 2006).

36. J.P. interview with Don Bush; also from notes on 'Don Bush's Account' written by himself.
37. J.P. interview with Don Bush; also from notes on 'Don Bush's Account' written by himself.
38. J.P. interview with Don Bush.
39. J.P. interview with Don Bush.
40. College and Warlow, *Ships of the Royal Navy*; Smith and Walker, *War in the Aegean*, p. 220, state 3 officers and 103 rankings were lost.
41. www.naval-history.net/xGM-Chrono-10DE-Dulverton.htm.

Chapter 10   And the Fight Goes On

1. For Churchill's statement, see Leonard Marsland Gander, *Long Road to Leros* (London, MacDonald, 1945), p. 175.
2. Peter Schenck, 'The Battle for Leros', *After the Battle*, No. 90, p. 21.
3. Colonel Cowper, Account of the Battle of Leros. http://www.ww2incolor. com/forum/showthread.php/8848-Battle-for-Leros. Accessed 11 March 2016; Peter C. Smith and Edwin R. Walker, *War in the Aegean: The Campaign for the Eastern Mediterranean in World War II* (Mechanicsburg, PA, Stackpole Books, 1974), p. 221.
4. Schenck, 'Battle for Leros', p. 30.
5. Gander, *Long Road to Leros*, p. 149.
6. Ibid.; and J.P. interview with Jellicoe.
7. Ibid., p. 192.
8. J.P. interview with E.W. Tassell.
9. Anthony Rogers, *Churchill's Folly* (London, Cassell, 2003), p. 148.
10. According to one report, the Beaufighters had a 'no flying over Leros' zone, the thinking being that they would have no chance against the strength of the enemy airforce: 50 per cent of Beaufighters were lost in the Aegean operations; J.S. Guard, *Improvise and Dare: War in the Aegean 1943–45* (Lewes, The Book Guild, 1997), pp. 104–105.
11. Air 41/53, PRO; also see 'Operation in the Dodecanese', Air Ministry, p. 46.
12. 'Operation in the Dodecanese', p. 47.
13. Jeffrey Holland, *The Aegean Mission, Allied Operation in the Dodecanese, 1943* (London and New York, Greenwood Press, 1988), p. 131.
14. J.P. interview with Ted Johnson.
15. This account concurs with the author's interview with Lt Ted Johnson (see previous chapter); and Pauline Bevan's findings (*Travels with a Leros Veteran* (privately published, 2000), p. 172).
16. The Küstenjäger had been reinforced by a Pionierlandungsboot containing the men from II/Gren. Reg. 440 who had failed to land at Palma Bay earlier. According to Schenck they had come from Brindisi (Schenck, 'The Battle for Leros', p. 21).

17. Edward B.W. Johnson, *Island Prize: Leros, 1943* (Banbury, Kemble Press, 1992),p. 55.
18. This was the night of 13/14 November.
19. Holland, *The Aegean Mission*, pp. 127–39. Smith and Walker say the Allied bombardment took place between 0045 and 0100 (*War in the* Aegean, p. 224); but Ted Johnson says it never materialised (*Island Prize*, p. 62).
20. See Brig. R.A.G. Tilney, Report of Operation on Leros, 12–16 November 1943, IWM.
21. Johnson, *Island Prize*, p. 56.
22. Account by Second Lt Pavilides LRDG on Operation in Leros 10–16 November 1943, IWM, LRDG 2/1.
23. Lt Ambrose's Report.
24. Ibid.
25. The account of this is remarkably confused. Tilney in his report writes that he instructed French to provide a plan with three companies of King's Own under command of King's Own commanding officer. He reported he was dismayed to hear French would lead the attack himself as he was 'unable to locate' the CO. Lt Ambrose's Report, RIFS Museum, Armagh; author's private papers; Tilney's War report TNA, Kew.
26. Ardill's account written for Ted Johnson.
27. Holland, *The Aegean Mission*, pp. 127–39.
28. Johnson, *Island Prize*, p. 62.
29. Quoted ibid., p. 63.
30. This is the clearest account. However, accounts of which companies were supposedly allocated to Lt French that afternoon are contradictory. Rogers states 'three companies of King's Own' comprising A, D and HQ companies: Bevan states 'a total of four RIF and KORR companies'; Holland states, 'The plan was that B and C Companies of his [French's own regiment, the Faughs], HQ reserve and a company of King's Own would be involved.' Anthony Rogers, *Churchill's Folly* (London, Cassell, 2003), p. 154; Bevan, *Travels with a Leros Veteran*, p. 175. According to the regimental magazine, the *Lion and the Dragon*, A Company reached the top and, after their withdrawal, D Company held the crest.
31. King's Own Report.
32. Holland, *The Aegean Mission*, p. 131.
33. Colonel Cowper, 'The King's Own – The Story of a Royal Regiment'. http://leros2002.bravepages.com/leros_war2.html Accessed 17 April 2015.
34. Jack Harte, *Limits of Endurance* (Dublin, Liberties Press, 2007), pp. 128–9.
35. Gavin Mortimer, *The SBS in World War II* (Oxford, Osprey Publishing, 2013), p. 109.
36. A company of Royal Irish Fusiliers (less one platoon) was holding positions south of Alinda, and another platoon (Jack Harte's from D Company) was holding position on Castle Hill. B Company was overlooking Pandeli, but handed over to King's Own in order to take

part in the attack. C Company was exhausted, having been sent up Appetici and then down again and up to Rachi where they had had their original position. There was little left of D Company, only the odd standing soldier linked up to B Company of Royal West Kents on Rachi Ridge above Gourna. Holland, *The Aegean Mission*, pp. 127–39; Ted Johnson states that the attack was set for 8 a.m. but put back half an hour (*Island Prize*, p. 56).

37. Holland, *The Aegean Mission*, pp. 127–39.
38. Johnson, *Island Prize*, p. 56.
39. Ibid.
40. Ibid.
41. Ibid.
42. Ted Johnson's Diary.
43. Johnson, *Island Prize*, pp. 57–62.
44. Clifford Clarke, *The Echo*, September 1997.
45. R.L. Kay, *Long Range Desert Group in the Mediterranean* (Wellington, New Zealand, War History Branch of Internal Affairs, 1950); reprint Merriam Press, 2012).
46. Raymond Williams, *The Long Road from Leros* (privately printed, 1983), p. 25.
47. A company of Royal Irish Fusiliers still had Platoon 9 at Castle Hill, and Platoons 7 and 8 above Alinda on Rachi. D Company at Germano was in contact with Platoon 11 of B Company Queen's Own Royal West Kents. The Royal Irish Fusiliers had two weak platoons in A Company; one and a half platoons in C Company; and D Company was now virtually non-existent. Those up on the Castle positions were out of food, apart from a few hard biscuits. A member of the LRDG had managed to get through to them with a small supply of water.
    See Gander, *Long Road to Leros*, and Faugh-a-Ballagh.
48. He returned to Point 320 where the Buffs were commanding the rest of the LRDG men – Second Lt Cross's T2 Patrol, Captain Alan Denniff's Y Patrol and Captain Saxton's T1 Patrol. Captain John Olivey, *Long Range Desert Group Story in the Dodecanese Islands* (LRDG 11/13, IWM).
49. Bevan found an LRDG account that Clidi was lost on the morning of the 13th; and a report that they were still fighting at midnight that same day: Bevan, *Travels with a Leros Veteran*, p. 176. See LRDG report.
50. Schenck, 'Battle for Leros', p. 30.
51. Mike Morgan, *Sting of the Scorpion* (Stroud, Sutton Publishing, 2000), pp. 141–2.
52. Smith and Walker, *War in the Aegean*, p. 227.
53. Ibid., pp. 222–3; *Faugh-a-Ballagh*.
54. *Bury Times*, 29 December 1987.
55. Second Lt White, 'Report on Operations in Leros', 14 December 1943, LRDG papers, IWM.
56. Colonel Cowper, Account of the Battle of Leros.

57. Pte Goodman, Maj. V.G. Bourne's batman, reported 73 prisoners taken, but accounts of numbers vary; Rogers, *Churchill's Folly*, p. 269, fn. 6; Schenck, 'Battle for Leros', p. 31.

58. Johnson, *Island Prize*, p. 68.

Chapter 11 Tired, Hungry and Lost

1. Reg kept his memories of this operation and his other war experiences to himself for 40-odd years. He told me, 'I was very successful in forgetting everything. I didn't belong to any reunion people [...] Reg Talbot and I were the only survivors of our special unit on Leros. We were a signal section at the King's Own Royal Headquarters. The only survivors of our little unit.' J.P. interview with Reg Neep.

2. Jack Harte, *Limits of Endurance* (Dublin, Liberties Press, 2007), p. 28.

3. Ibid., pp. 138–49.

4. LRDG Papers 2/1 'Operations in Aegean'. IWM.

5. Rev. Reginald Anwyl, Account of the Battle of Leros 1943, p. 77, King's College Archives.

6. Ibid., p. 76.

7. Ibid.

8. Ibid.

9. Ibid.

10. J.P. interview with Paddy McCrystal.

11. John Browne, *Recollections of Island Warfare* (privately printed, no date), p. 87.

12. Colonel Cowper, 'The King's Own – The Story of a Royal Regiment'; http://leros2002.bravepages.com/leros_war2.html Accessed 17 April 2015.

13. J.P. interview with Clifford Clarke.

14. J.P. interview with Clifford Clarke.

15. J.P. interview with Clifford Clarke.

16. J.P. interview with E.W. Tassell.

17. J.P. interview with E.W. Tassell.

18. J.P. interview with Peter Anthony Barham.

19. J.P. interview with Peter Anthony Barham.

20. J.P. interview with Peter Anthony Barham.

21. Edward B.W. Johnson, *Island Prize: Leros, 1943* (Banbury, Kemble Press, 1992), pp. 66–7.

22. Ibid., p. 67.

23. Raymond Williams, *The Long Road from Leros* (privately printed, 1983), p. 11.

24. J.P. interview with Clifford Clarke.

25. J.P. interview with Paddy McCrystal.

26. J.P. interview with Ted Johnson.

27. J.P. interview with Ted Johnson.

28. J.P. interview with Ted Johnson.

29. Harte, *Limits of Endurance*, p. 114.
30. J.P. interview with Vic Kenchington.
31. www.wartimememoriesproject.com/ww2/allied/battalion.php?pid=1066.
32. Diary of Maj. W.S. Shepherd, RIF Museum, Armagh.
33. Anwyl, Account of The Battle of Leros 1943, p. 68.
34. Ibid., p. 73.
35. Ibid., p. 75.
36. Ibid.
37. J.P. interview with E.W. Tassell.
38. J.P. interview with E.W. Tassell.
39. Williams, *The Long Road from Leros*, p. 27.
40. J.P. interview with Ted Johnson.
41. J.P. interview with Ted Johnson.
42. J.P. interview with Clifford Clarke.
43. Browne, *Recollections*, p. 84.
44. Ibid., p. 85.
45. Brigadier R. Tilney, RAG Report of Operation on Leros, 12–16 November 1943.
46. However, although the writer of this report was on Leros from 5 to 11 November, Hall was not there for the battle so was not witness to the events. H.R. Hall, 'HQ Aegean Report on Operations', quoted in Lt Ambrose's Report on '2nd Battalion, The Royal Irish Fusiliers, Leros, November 1943', RIF Museum, and author's copy.
47. J.P. interview with Clifford Clarke.
48. J.P. interview with George Hatcher.
49. Pauline Bevan, *Travels with a Leros Veteran* (privately published, 2000), p. 179.
50. J.P. interview with Peter Anthony Barham.
51. J.P. interview with Peter Anthony Barham.
52. J.P. interview with Richard James.
53. J.P. interview with Richard James.
54. J.P. interview with Richard James.
55. J.P. interview with Richard James.
56. Browne, *Recollections*, p. 87.
57. Ibid., pp. 86–7.
58. HMS *Belvoir* transferred her troops to MTBs and BYMS for passage to Leros. While withdrawing to Pharlah Bay to lie up, she engaged at dawn an F-lighter loaded with troops off Alinda Bay and left it on fire and sinking. Rogers, *Churchill's Folly*, pp. 169–70: 'Admiralty War Diaries of World War II, Levant Command – September to November 1943'. Transcribed by Don Kindell: www.naval-history.net/xDKWD-Levant1943d.htm Accessed 28 December 2015.
59. Browne, *Recollections*, pp. 85–6.
60. Leonard Marsland Gander, *Long Road to Leros* (London, MacDonald, 1945), pp. 205–6.

61. HMSs *Fury* and *Exmoor* and ORP *KRAKOWIAK* would arrive to take the place of *Belvoir* and *Echo*. Supplement to *London Gazette*, 1948.
62. J.P. interview with Sid Bowden.
63. J.P. interview with Sid Bowden.
64. J.P. interview with Sid Bowden.
65. J.P. interview with Sid Bowden.
66. J.P. interview with Sid Bowden.
67. J.P. interview with George Hatcher.
68. J.P. interview with Peter Anthony Barham.
69. J.P. interview with Peter Anthony Barham.
70. Captain R.A. James, *The 2nd Battalion The Royal West Kents Regiment on the Island of Samos Sept–November 1943*, LRDG, IWM; Lt Colonel Robert Butler, *Nine Lives through Laughing Eyes* (Lymington, Invicta Publications, 1993), p. 120. Colonel B. Tarleton, *The 2nd Battalion: The Royal West Kent Regiment on the Island of Leros November 1943*, LRDG 11/5, IWM; Lesley Frank Ramseyer (Royal Navy), *Report of Proceedings during and after the invasion of Leros, 12 November to 4 December 1943*, LRDG, IWM. Rogers, *Churchill's Folly*, pp. 178–9.
71. Browne, *Recollections*, p. 89.
72. Ibid., p. 88.
73. Ibid., p. 90.
74. Ibid.
75. Butler, *Nine Lives*, p. 120.
76. Tarleton, *The 2nd Battalion*; Bevan, *Travels with a Leros Veteran*, p. 181.
77. *The Telegraph*, Obituary, 1 November 2008.

Chapter 12   Final Day of the Battle

1. Note to author from Ewart William Tassell.
2. He was later buried in the Leros military cemetery.
3. www.dailymail.co.uk/news/article-3769741.
4. Pauline Bevan, *Travels with a Leros Veteran* (privately published, 2000), p. 184.
5. Peter Schenck, 'The Battle for Leros', *After the Battle*, No. 90, p. 33.
6. Colonel B. Tarleton, *The 2nd Battalion. The Royal West Kent Regiment on the Island of Leros November 1943*, LRDG 11/5, IWM.
7. Report by Colonel Guy L. Prendergast on his Escape from Leros. IWM LRDG 5/3.
8. Lt P.A. Mould, The Story of my Adventures following the Capitulation of Leros Island. IWM: LRDG 5/4.
9. Again, there is discrepancy about the timing (although the actual capture and overtaking of the tunnel, and the official declaration of surrender differed). Gavin Mortimer, *The SBS in World War II* (Oxford, Osprey Publishing, 2013), says the Germans had captured Tilney at 15.00 hours (p. 110); Anthony Rogers, *Churchill's Folly* (London, Cassell, 2003), states

16.30 (p. 208). Peter C. Smith and Edwin R. Walker, *War in the Aegean: The Campaign for the Eastern Mediterranean in World War II* (Mechanicsburg, PA, Stackpole Books, 1974), say a German swastika was flying over the HQ by 17.30 (p. 243); Lt Ambrose of RIFs states the surrender was at 18.00 hours (Lt Ambrose's Report on '2nd Battalion, The Royal Irish Fusiliers, Leros, November 1943', Royal Irish Fusiliers Museum, and author's copy).

10. 'Signals in and out of Leros', LRDG 2/3, IWM.
11. Smith and Walker, *War in the Aegean*, p. 240.
12. Schenck, 'The Battle for Leros', p. 35.
13. Tarleton, *The 2nd Battalion. The Royal West Kents Regiment.*
14. Report by Colonel Guy L. Prendergast on his Escape from Leros. IWM LRDG 5/3.
15. Ibid.
16. Mike Morgan, *Sting of the Scorpion* (Stroud, Sutton Publishing, 2000).
17. Schenck, 'The Battle for Leros', p. 33.
18. Edward B.W. Johnson, *Island Prize: Leros, 1943* (Banbury, Kemble Press, 1992), pp. 69–70.
19. Ibid.
20. Ibid., pp. 70–1.
21. J.P. interview with Ted Johnson.
22. Rogers, *Churchill's Folly*, p. 199.
23. Schenck, 'The Battle for Leros', p. 33.
24. J.P. interview with E.W. Tassell.
25. Rogers, *Churchill's Folly*, p. 199.
26. Lt Commander Ramseyer, *Report of Proceedings during and after Invasion of Leros, 12th November–4th December, 1943.*
27. J.P. interview with E.W. Tassell.
28. J.P. interview with E.W. Tassell.
29. Ramseyer, *Report of Proceedings during and after Invasion of Leros.*
30. Smith and Walker, *War in the Aegean*, p. 243.
31. Bevan, *Travels with a Leros* Veteran, p. 184.
32. Tarleton. *The 2nd Battalion. The Royal West Kent Regiment.*
33. BBC War Stories: www.bbc.co.uk/ww2peopleswar/stories/03/a4104703.shtml.
34. www.bbc.co.uk/history/ww2peopleswar/stories/03/a4104703.shtml Accessed 28 May 2016.
35. Cowper, Col. J.M., *The King's Own: The Story of a Royal Regiment* (Aldershot, Gale & Polden, 1957), Vol. III.
36. Rev. Reginald Anwyl, Account of The Battle of Leros 1943, King's College Archives, p. 90.
37. Ibid., p. 79.
38. Ibid., p. 80.
39. Ibid.
40. Ibid., p. 81.
41. Ibid., p. 82.

42. Quoted in The Memoirs of Stanley Norman Froud of Buffs, Record No. 2001-08-5, National Army Museum.
43. Morgan, *Sting of the Scorpion*, p. 122.
44. Winston Churchill, *The Second World War. Vol. V: Closing the Ring* (London, Cassell, 1952), pp. 196–8. Commander of the British naval forces in the Mediterranean Admiral Andrew Cunningham stated, 'The enemy succeeded in landing on Leros on November 12th, and on the 16th the slender British garrison was forced to surrender after nearly five days of continuous bombing and hard fighting. Leros was by way of being an Italian naval base; but neither the Italian troops, not their coast defence or anti-aircraft batteries, made any substantial contribution to the defence.' This was challenged by some of the British and Italian forces. Charles T. O'Reilly, *Forgotten Battles: Italy's War of Liberation, 1943–1945* (Lexington Books, MD, Lexington Books, 2001), p. 98.
45. Churchill, *The Second World War. Vol. V*, p. 198.
46. Ibid., p. 199.
47. Ibid., p. 293.
48. J.P. interview with Paddy McCrystal.
49. J.P. interview with Paddy McCrystal.
50. J.P. interview with Paddy McCrystal.

Chapter 13   Surrender or Escape

1. The commanding officer to Lt John Browne and his troops; Lt C.J.H. Morgan, 'Wartime Log', Record No. 2001-07-525, p. 18, National Army Museum.
2. The Memoirs of Stanley Norman Froud of Buffs, Record No. 2001-08-5, National Army Museum.
3. J.P. interview with Reg Neep.
4. J.P. interview with Peter Anthony Barham.
5. J.P. interview with Peter Anthony Barham.
6. Edward B.W. Johnson, *Island Prize: Leros, 1943* (Banbury, Kemble Press, 1992).
7. Reg Neep, 'The Long March 1943–5', typewritten MS.
8. This was on 20 November; ibid.
9. Ibid.
10. Jack Harte, *To the Limits of Endurance* (Dublin, Liberties Press, 2007), p. 155. He mentions other friends taken as POWs including George Mullet, Walter Pancott, Davy Thompson, Bobby O'Neill, Andy Roy, Johnnie King, Tom Magee, Matt King, 'Pukie' Orr and 'Red Digger Dawson' McCormack, p. 157. Missing in Action were long-time friends of his: Gutrie Kane, Sab McMaster, Beaver Elliot and Polly McIllwaine, p. 158.
11. John Browne, *Recollections of Island Warfare* (privately printed, no date), p. 93.

12. Ibid., p. 94.
13. Ibid., p. 95.
14. *Faugh-a-Ballagh Gazette*, Vol. 43, No. 190, March 1957.
15. They were taken to POW Camp No. 4b at Mühlberg on the River Elbe and then to the naval POW camp Marlag und Milag Nord (M&MN) at Westertimke. All the POWs were interrogated upon arrival at M&MN in Lager 1, Dulag, which was used as a transit compound. http://www.naval-history.net/WW2Ships-BYMS72.htm Accessed 14 March 2016.
16. Browne, *Recollections of Island Warfare*, p. 95.
17. Ibid., p. 98.
18. Browne mentions who he could remember: a couple of Greek men called Jack and Constantine; an Italian called Tony; British soldiers named Hodges, Mole, McGuire, Donald Crower and Londres (a Greek who was to help them).
19. Browne, *Recollections of Island Warfare*.
20. Rev. Reginald Anwyl, Account of The Battle of Leros 1943, King's College Archives, p. 80.
21. Ibid., p. 85.
22. Ibid.
23. Ibid., p. 87.
24. Ibid., p. 89.
25. Ibid.
26. Ibid., p. 90.
27. Ibid., p. 91.
28. Ibid., p. 93.
29. Ibid.
30. Ibid., p. 94.
31. Ibid.
32. Ibid. p. 97.
33. Ibid., p. 95.
34. J.P. interview with Clifford Clarke.
35. J.P. interview with Clifford Clarke. Also see his articles in *The Echo*, March, June, September 1998.
36. J.P. interview with Clifford Clarke.
37. *The Echo*, March 1998, p. 13.
38. Ibid.
39. J.P. interview with Clifford Clarke.
40. Lt Clarke wrote a letter to me on 14 October 2002 stating 'George Hatcher was a highly respected NCO of B Platoon of B Company of the 2nd Battalion of the Queen's Own Royal West Kents.' He was commanded by Clarke who said, 'He was one of the nine that I specially picked to escape with me from the island after its surrender.'
41. J.P. interview with George Hatcher.
42. J.P. interview with George Hatcher.
43. J.P. interview with Clifford Clarke.

44. J.P. interview with Clifford Clarke.
45. J.P. interview with George Hatcher.
46. J.P. interview with Clifford Clarke.
47. J.P. interview with George Hatcher.
48. *The Echo*, March 1998, p. 15.
49. J.P. interview with Clifford Clarke.
50. *The Echo*, June 1998, p. 12.
51. J.P. interview with Clifford Clarke. Lt Clarke had recently searched for Stokes, but had failed to find him.
52. J.P. interview with George Hatcher.
53. *The Echo*, June 1998, p. 13.
54. J.P. interview with Clifford Clarke.
55. *The Echo*, June 1998, p. 14.
56. J.P. interview with George Hatcher.
57. J.P. interview with George Hatcher.
58. J.P. interview with Clifford Clarke.
59. *The Echo*, June 1998, p. 16.
60. J.P. interview with Clifford Clarke.
61. *The Echo*, September, 1998, p. 8.
62. J.P. interview with George Hatcher.

Chapter 14   The Rescue Parties

1. There are actually three islets: Leriko, Micro Glaronisis and Megalo Glaronisi.
2. Mike Morgan, *Sting of the Scorpion: The Inside Story of the Long Range Desert Group* (Stroud, Sutton Publishing, 2000), pp. 136–7.
3. Supplement to the *London Gazette*, 8 October, 1948.
4. Ibid. www.thegazette.co.uk/london/issue/38428/supplement/5391/data. pdf Accessed 22 September 2016.
5. Peter C. Smith and Edwin R. Walker, *War in the Aegean: The Campaign for the Eastern Mediterranean in World War II* (Mechanicsburg, PA, Stackpole Books, 1974), p. 245.
6. J.P. interview with George Jellicoe.
7. J.P. interview with George Jellicoe.
8. J.P. interview with George Jellicoe.
9. J.P. interview with George Jellicoe.
10. J.P. interview with George Jellicoe.
11. C.W.M. Ritchie from his account written in captivity; see Anthony Rogers, *Churchill's Folly* (London, Cassell, 2003), p. 195.
12. J.P. interview with George Jellicoe.
13. J.P. interview with George Jellicoe.
14. J.P. interview with George Jellicoe.

15. Interview with Ashley Martin Greenwood. Interview Catalogue, IWM, www.iwm.org.uk/collections/item/object/80009875 Accessed 27 November 2016.

16. According to Greenwood, Mold's dysentery eventually got the better of him and he had to return to hospital. www.iwm.org.uk/collections/item/object/80009875.

17. Morgan, *Sting of the Scorpion*, p. 134.

18. J.P. interview with Sid Bowden.

19. J.P. interview with Sid Bowden.

20. J.P. interview with Sid Bowden.

21. J.P. interview with Don Bush.

22. J.P. interview with Vic Kenchington.

23. www.wartimememoriesproject.com/ww2/allied/battalion.php?pid=1066.

24. Smith and Walker, *War in the Aegean*, p. 246.

25. Ibid.

26. Morgan, *Sting of the Scorpion*, p. 143.

27. David Lloyd Owen, *The Long Range Desert Group 1940–1945: Providence Their Guide* (Barnsley, Leo Cooper, 2003), p. 144.

28. J.P. interview with E.W. Tassell.

29. J.P. interview with E.W. Tassell.

30. www.gutenberg.us/articles/queen's_own_royal_west_kent_regiment Accessed 16 March 2016.

31. Smith and Walker, *War in the Aegean*, p. 246.

32. Ibid., p. 247. Sgt Finley escaped Leros and arrived in Belfast; he was awarded the DCM (London Gazette, 2 May 1944). http://www.ww2incolor.com/forum/showthread.php/8848-Battle-for-Leros Accessed 11 March 2016.

33. David Sutherland, *He Who Dares: Recollections of Service in the SAS, SBS and MI5* (Barnsley, Leo Cooper, 1998), p. 131.

34. J.P. interview with Don Bush.

Chapter 15   Prisoners of War

1. OKW (Oberkommando der Wehrmacht (Wehrmacht High Command)) Diary. Frank Smith believes 80 per cent of men taken on Leros were Italians.

2. J.P. interview with Richard James.

3. J.P. interview with Richard James.

4. J.P. interview with Richard James.

5. J.P. interview with Clifford Clarke.

6. After he returned home, he went to Cambridge University, did a degree, joined the Home Office, and became deputy under-secretary of state at the Home Office. The Telegraph Online. Accessed 9 June 2016.

7. Frank Smith recorded the daily rituals in his log book and in a diary after his capture by the enemy, information which he shared with me as well as giving an interview.

8. Frank Smith's Diary Notes, p. 4.

9. Ibid., p. 7.

10. Frank Smith's Log Book.

11. Diary of Major W.S. Shepherd, RIF Museum, Armagh.

12. Maurice McMulkin was also with the 2nd Batallion RIF and in the Drums and Pipes as a drummer, ending up in Stalag XI-A.

13. *Faugh-a-Ballagh* (the Regimental Gazette of the Royal Irish Fusiliers), Vol. 37, No. 163, November 1947, p. 239.

14. J.P. interview with Paddy McCrystal.

15. Frank Smith's Log Book.

16. *Faugh-a-Ballagh,* Vol. 37, No 163, November 1947, p. 240.

17. Bob King, 'For You the War is Over'. Typed MS, author's copy.

18. *Faugh-a-Ballagh*, Vol. 37, No. 162, February 1947, p. 161.

19. J.P. interview with Clifford Clarke.

20. J.P. interview with Reg Neep.

21. Frank Smith's Log Book.

22. J.P. interview with E.W. Tassell.

23. *Faugh-a-Ballagh*, Vol. 37, No. 162, February 1947, p. 161.

24. J.P. interview with Reg Neep.

25. Reg Neep, 'The Long March 1943–5', typewritten MS.

26. Frank Smith's Log Book.

27. Ibid.

28. Ibid.

29. Ibid.

30. J.P. interview with Paddy McCrystal.

31. Neep, 'The Long March 1943–5'.

32. Frank Smith's Log Book.

33. J.P. interview with Paddy McCrystal.

34. Neep, 'The Long March 1943–5'.

35. Ibid.

36. Ibid.

37. *Faugh-a-Ballagh*, Vol. 37, No 163, November 1947, p. 241.

38. Ibid.

39. Ibid.

40. Mike Morgan, *Sting of the Scorpion: The Inside Story of the Long Range Desert Group* (Stroud, Sutton Publishing, 2000), p. 127.

Chapter 16   The German POW Camps

1. Reg Neep, 'The Long March 1943–5', typewritten MS.

2. Ibid.

3. Ted kept a record of his time in the camp in a 'Wartime Log for British Prisoners', a gift from the War Prisoners Aid of the YMCA in Geneva, Switzerland. He wrote 'Most of this piece of scrap was written in Germany in the winter of 1944 when things were not so comfortable, hence the jumble of work and subjects' – indicating that his mental health had deteriorated due to lack of nourishment and poor conditions. He records himself as POW No. 1820 VIIIF. Ted was kind enough to photocopy his complete Log Book, which I have now donated to the Imperial War Museum.

4. Ted Johnson, BBC website. www.webarchive.org.uk/wayback/archive/20060522120000/http://www.bbc.co.uk/ww2peopleswar/stories/98/a5836098.html. Accessed 5 November 2016.

5. Jimmy James's typewritten MS of his recollections given to me by himself.

6. Copy of telegram now in possession of the author, given by Lt Jimmy James.

7. Reg Neep, 'The Long March 1943–5'.

8. Ted Johnson, BBC website.

9. Ibid.

10. J.P. interview with Paddy McCrystal.

11. J.P. interview with Paddy McCrystal.

12. Pauline Bevan, *Travels with a Leros Veteran* (privately published, 2000), pp. 34–5.

13. Ibid., p. 36.

14. Neep, 'The Long March 1943–5'.

15. Ibid.

16. Ibid.

17. *Faugh-a-Ballagh*, Vol. 37, No 162, February 1947, p. 161.

18. Ibid.

19. Ibid.

20. Ibid., p. 162.

21. Ibid.

22. Neep, 'The Long March 1943–5'.

23. Frank Smith's Log Book.

24. Ibid.

25. Ibid.

26. J.P. interview with Ted Johnson.

27. Frank Smith's Log Book.

28. Ibid.

29. Ibid.

30. 'Mother's Cooking was his Dream' by Pitt Clark interviewing Lt Gordon Emeric Horner for *Sunday Chronicle* in 1945. After liberation and his return home, Horner was responsible for some evocative drawings of times in Oflag 79 Brunswick after he was captured in 1942 in Italy. In Ted Johnson's collection of cuttings.

31. Frank Smith's Log Book.

32. Captain Richard Austen James, 'Wartime Log', 14/2/1, IWM.

33. Bob King was with Signal Officer Maurice Constable when they heard of the surrender. Luckily, Constable knew that if he flashed a Morse signal at night, they would be picked up by a submarine. Unfortunately, the navy had already sustained heavy losses, with six destroyers and three submarines sunk, along with ten smaller ships and ten ships badly damaged. Unable to get off the island, they 'gave themselves up so as not to imperil the locals who has suffered a great deal'. Bob King, 'For You the War is Over', typed MS author's copy given to me by Ted Johnson.

34. Ibid., p. 5.

35. Ibid., p. 6.

36. Ted Johnson's POW Log Book.

37. Frank Smith's Log Book.

38. Clifford Clarke told me that the men in the POW camps had thought, '"There must be loads of children in England much worse off than us, what shall we do, lets form a boys' club." So they all put chits in for the tune of £13,000 which was a vast sum of money then. And when they came back, every bit was honoured, and they opened the Brunswick Boys Club, and the Duke of Edinburgh opened it, just after the war. It's still going today, and all of those men became trustees, and eventually I became a trustee – they invited me to, although I wasn't a prisoner of war – all the rest were. I am still a vice-president of that, and it's a wonderful club in Fulham. It's a tough area. It takes about 300 youngsters off the streets every night.' J.P. interview with Clifford Clarke.

39. Frank Smith's Log Book.

40. Ted Johnson's POW Log Book.

41. An article taken from Ted Johnson's collection of cuttings from the *Daily Telegraph* entitled 'Courage in Captivity Saved the Men of Oflag 79', not dated.

42. Neep, 'The Long March 1943–5'.

43. Ibid.

44. Ted Johnson, BBC website.

45. Frank Smith's Log Book, 20 March 1944.

46. Ted Johnson, BBC website.

47. 'Courage in Captivity Saved the Men of Oflag 79' (*Daily Telegraph* cutting).

48. Neep, 'The Long March 1943–5'.

49. Ibid.

50. King, 'For You the War is Over', p. 6.

51. 'Mother's Cooking was his Dream'.

52. King, 'For You the War is Over', p. 5.

53. Neep, 'The Long March 1943–5'.

54. Ibid.

55. Ibid.

56. Ibid.

57. J.P. interview with Paddy McCrystal.

58. J.P. interview with Ted Johnson.

59. King, 'For You the War is Over', p. 6.
60. 'Mother's Cooking was his Dream'.
    Ibid.
61. King, 'For You the War is Over', p. 6.
62. Ibid., p. 7.
63. Ibid.
64. Ted Johnson, BBC website.

Chapter 17   Aftermath Considerations

1. *The Spectator*, 19 November 1943.
2. J.P. interview with Sid Bowden.
3. J.P. interview with George Hatcher.
4. *The Spectator*, 19 November, 1943.
5. J.P. interview with George Jellicoe.
6. Charles T. O'Reilly, *Forgotten Battles: Italy's War of Liberation, 1943–1945* (Lexington, MD, Lexington Books, 2001), pp. 98–9.
7. See fn. 118 of Ian Gooderson, 'Shoestring Strategy: The British Campaign in the Aegean, 1943', *Journal of Strategic Studies*, Vol. 25, No. 3 (Sept. 2002), pp. 1–36.
8. O'Reilly, *Forgotten Battles*, pp. 98–9.
9. Ibid.
10. They were executed for refusing to swear allegiance to Mussolini and the *Repubblica Sociale Italiana* (Italian Social Republic) in the north of Italy.
11. Commander-in-Chief Levant's Remarks, Conclusion Section 30–40, 39, pp. 34–5.
12. Supplement to *London Gazette*, 8/11 October 1948. In fact, the Germans had been building up forces and tank divisions on Rhodes after Mussolini was first deposed in July 1943. They suspected the Italians would change sides and were ready to act way before September 1943. Campioni was weak, but even if the Italians had resisted on Rhodes they might well have lost in the end.
13. Ibid.
14. Ibid.
15. J.P. interview with Clifford Clarke.
16. Douglas 'Roger' Wright, Record No. 2005-05-44, The Army Museum. There is obviously some discrepancy in numbers according to the references.
17. Ashley Martin Greenwood interview, Record No. 10094, IWM.
18. PRO: AIR 20/5465.
19. J.P. interview with Reg Neep.
20. Lt Ambrose's Report on '2nd Battalion, The Royal Irish Fusiliers, Leros, November 1943', Irish Fusiliers Museum, and author's copy.
21. J.P. interview with Richard James.

22. Edward B.W. Johnson, *Island Prize: Leros, 1943* (Banbury, Kemble Press, 1992), pp. 36–7.
23. Lt Ambrose, 2nd Battalion The Royal Irish Fusiliers Report for Leros November 1943, Royal Irish Fusiliers Museum, Armagh; author's copy.
24. J.P. interview with Richard James.
25. J.P. interview with Clifford Clarke.
26. David Sutherland scrapbook, SAS Archives, quoted in Gavin Mortimer, *The SBS in World War II* (Oxford, Osprey Publishing, 2013), p. 109.
27. As seen by his comment at the end of Chapter Ten.
28. J.P. interview with Clifford Clarke.
29. Supplement to *London Gazette*, 8/11 October 1948.
30. Ibid.
31. Ibid.
32. Ibid.
33. Ibid.
34. J.P. interview with Clifford Clarke.

Bibliography

Interviewees

Peter Anthony Barham, Queen's Own Royal West Kents
Sydney Bowden, Queen's Own Royal West Kents
Don Bush, Royal Navy
Clifford Clarke, Queen's Own Royal West Kents
Nikos Drakos, Leros civilian
George Hatcher, Queen's Own Royal West Kents
Richard James, Queen's Own Royal West Kents
George Jellicoe, Special Boat Squadron
Ted Johnson, Royal Irish Fusilier
Victor Richard 'Taffy' Kenchington, Royal Irish Fusilier
Peter George Koulianus, Leros civilian
Patrick 'Paddy' McCrystal, Royal Irish Fusilier
Reginald Neep, King's Own
George Papadopoulos, Leros civilian
Nikos Pyrovolikos, Special Boat Squadron
Frank Smith, Royal Irish Fusilier
Ewart William Tassell, Royal East Kents (The Buffs)
Thespina Taxhliambori, Leros civilian
Dimitri Tsaloumas, Leros civilian

Primary sources

Newspapers and journals
After the Battle, No. 90, 1995
Bury Times
Daily Telegraph
The Echo, March, June, September 1998

Faugh-a-Ballagh, Vol. 37, No. 162, February 1947; No. 163, November 1947
Faugh-a-Ballagh Gazette, Vol. 43, No. 190, March 1957
Gooderson, Ian, 'Shoestring Strategy: The British Campaign in the
    Aegean, 1943', *Journal of Strategic Studies*, Vol. 25, No. 3 (September
    2002), pp. 1–36
Lion and Rose
London Gazette, 2 May 1944
LRDG [Long Range Desert Group] *Newsletter*, No. 49 (1993)
Parliamentary Papers, London
The Spectator, 19 November 1943
Supplement to *London Gazette*, 8/11 October 1948
The Times

Public Record Office (PRO), London
Admiralty 199/1040, PRO, The National Archives, Kew
Admiralty 199/2521, PRO
Admiralty 234/364, PRO
Air 20/5465, PRO
Air 41/53, PRO
Premier 3/3/1, PRO
Premier 3/3/7, PRO
SBS [Special Boat Service] War Diary, 7 April 1943
War Office 201/2308, PRO
War Office 218/98, PRO

King's College London
Anwyl, Rev. Reginald, Account of The Battle of Leros, 1943
Dobrski Papers

Imperial War Museum (IWM)
Barry, Walter Milner, Sound Archive 16753
Greenwood, Ashley Martin, Interview, Sound Archive, Record No. 10094
James, Captain R.A., *The 2nd Battalion The Royal West Kents Regiment on the
    Island of Samos Sept–November 1943*, LRDG
James, Captain Richard Austen, 'Wartime Log', 14/2/1
Jellicoe, Lord George, Sound Archive 26767, Imperial War Museum
LRDG Papers, 'Operations in Aegean 11th Sept 1943 to 30th November 1943',
    2/1
LRDG 2/3
Mould, Lt P.A., *The Story of my Adventures following the Capitulation of Leros
    Island*, LRDG 5/L
Olivey, Captain John, *Long Range Desert Group Story in the Dodecanese Islands*,
    LRDG 11/13

Pavlides, Lt, Operations in Leros 10–16 November 1943, LRDG 2/1
Prendergast, Report by Colonel Guy L. Prendergast on his Escape from Leros, LRDG 5/3
Ramseyer, Lt Commander, *Report of Proceedings during and after Invasion of Leros, 12th November–4th December, 1943*, LRDG Papers
Sutherland, David, scrapbook, SAS Archives
Tarleton, Colonel B., *The 2nd Battalion. The Royal West Kent Regiment on the Island of Leros November 1943*, LRDG 11/5
Tilney, Brigadier R.A.G., Report of Operation on Leros, 12–16 November 1943
Tilney, Brigadier R.A.G., 'After Action Report to the War Office', 16 April 1947
White, Second Lt, Report on Operations in Leros, 14 December 1943, LRDG papers

National Army Museum, London
Froud, The Memoirs of Stanley Norman Froud of Buffs, Record No. 2001-08-5
Morgan, Lt C.J.H. (Buffs), Wartime Log, Record No. 2001-07-525
Douglas 'Roger' Wright, Record No. 2005-05-44

Royal Irish Fusiliers (RIF) Museum, Armagh
Lt Ambrose's Report on '2nd Battalion, The Royal Irish Fusiliers, Leros, November 1943', RIF Museum, and author's copy
Copy of letter from Tom Massey Lynch to Amanda Moreno, previous curator to RIF Museum, in author's possession
Shepherd, Major W.S., Diary

Online resources
http://leros2002.bravepages.com/leros_war2.html
http://rhodesianafricanrifles.co.uk/alan-gardiner-redfern-mbe-%C2%B7-november-11-1943
http://ww2today.com/12th-november-1943-german-paratroopers-attack-island-of-leros
http://www.bbc.co.uk/ww2peopleswar/stories/98/a5836098.html http://www.bbc.co.uk/history/ww2peopleswar/about/siteinformation.shtml
http://www.bbc.co.uk/history/ww2peopleswar/stories/03/a4104703.shtml
http://www.empirepatrol.com/theodyssey.htm Accessed 28/10/16
http://www.gutenberg.us/articles/queen's_own_royal_west_kent_regiment
http://www.ibiblio.org/hyperwar/UN/UK/LondonGazette/38426.pdf. Accessed 16 December 2016
http://www.kingsownmuseum.com/ww2-1ko-leros-01.htm
http://www.kingsownmuseum.plus.com/ww2-1ko-leros-moss.htm
http://www.naval-history.net/WW2Ships-BYMS72.htm
http://www.naval-history.net/xDKWD-Levant1943d.htm. Admiral War Diaries
http://www.naval-history.net/xGM-Chrono-10DD-22F-HMS_Faulknor.htm

http://www.naval-history.net/xGM-Chrono-10DE-Dulverton.htm
https://www.thegazette.co.uk/london/issue/38428/supplement/5391/data.pdf
http://www.wartimememoriesproject.com/ww2/allied/battalion.php?pid=1066
http://www.webarchive.org.uk/wayback/archive/20060522120000
http://www.ww2incolor.com/forum/showthread.php/8848-Battle-for-Leros
http://www.znaci.net/00002/336.pdf
http://www.bbc.co.uk/ww2peopleswar/stories/03/a4104703.shtml

Author's resources

Lt Ardill's account written for Ted Johnson, in author's possession
Pitt Clark, 'Mother's Cooking was his Dream', *Sunday Chronicle*, 1945.
An article taken from Ted Johnson's collection of cuttings
Notes sent to me by Peter Colman in November 2005
Jimmy James's typewritten MS of his recollections given to me by himself
Copy of telegram now in possession of the author, given to her by Lt Jimmy
James
Ted Johnson's Diary
Ted Johnson's POW Log Book
An article taken from Ted Johnson's collection of cuttings from the *Daily
Telegraph* entitled 'Courage in Captivity Saved the Men of Oflag 79', n.d.
Bob King, 'For You the War is Over', typed MS author's copy given to me by
Ted Johnson
Reg Neep, 'The Long March 1943–5' typewritten MS
Frank Smith's Diary Notes
Frank Smith's Log Book

Secondary Sources

Anthony Beevor, *Crete: The Battle and the Resistance* (London, Penguin, 1991),
p. 60.
Ambrose, Stephen E., *The Supreme Commander: The War Years of Dwight
D. Eisenhower* (New York, Anchor Books, 1970).
Bevan, Pauline, *Travels with a Leros Veteran* (privately published, 2000).
Brescia, Maurizio, *Mussolini's Navy: A Reference Guide to the Regia Marina 1930–
1945* (Barnsley, Seaforth Publishing, 2012).
Browne, John, *Recollections of Island Warfare* (privately printed, no date).
Bruhn, David, *Wooden Ships and Iron Men: US Navy's Coastal and Motor
Minesweepers, 1941–1953* (Cirencester, Heritage Books, 2005).
Butler, Lt Colonel Robert, *Nine Lives through Laughing Eyes* (Lymington, Invicta,
1993).
Churchill, Winston, *The Second World War. Vol. V: Closing the Ring* (London,
Cassell, 1952).
College, J.J. & Ben Warlow, *Ships of the Royal Navy: The Complete Record of All
Fighting Ships of the Royal Navy* (London, Greenhill, 2003).

Cowper, Col. J.M., *The King's Own: The Story of a Royal Regiment* (Aldershot, Gale & Polden, 1957), Vol. III.

Darman, Peter, *Surprise Attack: Lightning Strikes of the World's Elite Forces* (London, Brown Books, 1993).

English, John, *The Hunts: A History of the Design, Development and Careers of the 86 Destroyers of this Class Built for the Royal and Allied Navies during World War II* (Kendal, World Ship Society, 1987).

Gander, Leonard Marsland, *Long Road to Leros* (London, MacDonald, 1945).

Gilbert, Martin, *Winston S. Churchill: Finest Hour, 1939–1941* (London, Heinemann, 1983).

Grehan, John and Martin Mace, *Operations in North Africa and the Middle East 1942–1944* (Barnsley, Pen and Sword, 2015).

Guard, J.S., *Improvise and Dare: War in the Aegean 1943–45* (Lewes, The Book Guild, 1997).

Harte, Jack, *Limits of Endurance* (Dublin, Liberties Press, 2007).

Holland, Jeffrey, *The Aegean Mission: Allied Operation in the Dodecanese, 1943* (London and New York, Greenwood Press, 1988).

Howard, Michael, *Grand Strategy, Vol. IV: August 1942–September 1943* (London, Her Majesty's Stationery Office, 1972).

Johnson, Edward B.W., *Island Prize: Leros, 1943* (Banbury, Kemble Press, 1992).

Kay, R.L., *Long Range Desert Group in the Mediterranean* (Wellington, New Zealand, War History Branch of Internal Affairs, 1950; reprint Merriam Press, 2012).

Knight, C.R.B., *Historical Records of the Buffs 1919–1948* (London, Gale & Polden, 1905–51).

Lecoeur, Sheila, *Mussolini's Greek Island: Fascism and the Italian Occupation of Syros in World War II* (London, I.B.Tauris, 2015).

Lind, Lew, *Battle of the Wine Dark Sea: The Aegean Campaign 1943–1945* (Kenthurst, NSW, Kangaroo Press, 1994).

Lloyd Owen, David, *The Long Range Desert Group 1940–1945: Providence Their Guide* (Barnsley, Leo Cooper, 2003).

Lucas, James, *Storming Eagles* (London, Arms and Armour, 1988).

Morgan, Mike, *Sting of the Scorpion: The Inside Story of the Long Range Desert Group* (Stroud, Sutton Publishing, 2000).

Mortimer, Gavin, *The SBS in World War II* (Oxford, Osprey Publishing, 2013).

O'Reilly, Charles T., *Forgotten Battles: Italy's War of Liberation, 1943–1945* (Lexington, MD, Lexington Books, 2001).

Paget, Julian, *Second to None: The History of the Coldstream Guards, 1650–2000* (Barnsley, Leo Cooper, 2000).

Parish, Michael Woodbine, *Aegean Adventures 1940–1943* (Lewes, The Book Guild, 1993).

Parker, John, *SBS: The Inside Story of the Special Boat Service* (London, Headline, 1997).

Pitt, Barry, *Special Boat Squadron in the Mediterranean* (London, Century, 1983).

Read, G.W., *A Story of an Independent Command in the Aegean 1943–45; Raiding Forces and the Levant Schooner Flotilla. No 1 Public Relations Service* (GHQ MEF, July 1943).

Rogers, Anthony, *Churchill's Folly* (London, Cassell, 2003).

Rollo, Major D., 1LAA regiment 1943, Regimental History for serial 12501 (Royal Artillery Historical Trust, 1998).

Roskill, S.W., *The War at Sea* (London, Imperial War Museum, 1994).

Royal Air Force Centre, 'Operations in the Dodecanese Islands, September–November 1943 (Royal Air Force Centre for Air Power Studies, n.d.).

Schenck, Peter 'The Battle for Leros', *After the Battle*, No. 90.

Schreiber, Gerhard, Bernd Stegemann and Detlef Vogel (eds), *Germany and the Second World War, 1939–1941*, Vol. III (London, Oxford University Press, 1995).

Seligman, Adrian, *War in the Islands* (Stroud, Sutton Publishing, 1996).

Smith, Peter C. and Edwin R. Walker, *War in the Aegean: The Campaign for the Eastern Mediterranean in World War II* (Mechanicsburg, PA, Stackpole Books, 1974).

Sutherland, David, *He Who Dares: Recollections of Service in the SAS, SBS and MI5* (Barnsley, Leo Cooper, 1998).

Taffrail, Captain Taprell Dorling, *Western Mediterranean, 1942–45* (London, Hodder & Stoughton, 1947).

Whitley, M.J., *Destroyers of World War Two: An International Encyclopedia* (Annapolis, MD, Naval Institute Press, 1988).

Williams, Raymond, *The Long Road from Leros* (privately printed, 1983).

Windmill, Lorna Almonds, *A British Achilles: The Story of George 2nd Earl Jellicoe* (Barnsley, Pen and Sword, 2005).

Index

PLATE 1 Platanos Square, Leros

PLATE 2   Inhabitants of Leros

PLATE 3   Leros town with the Castle above

PLATE 4   Alinda Bay looking north

PLATE 5   Caique used by Special Boat Squadron (SBS)

PLATE 6 A panoramic view overlooking Agia Marina to the left, and Platanos to the right, from the back of the Church of Evangalismos

PLATE 7 Castelorizo

PLATE 8   George Jellicoe, SBS

PLATE 9   David Lloyd Owen, Long Range Desert Group (LRDG)

PLATE 10   Anders Lassen, SBS

PLATE 11   Lieutenant Colonel David Stirling

PLATE 12   Jake Easonsmith, LRDG

PLATE 13   Leonard Marsland Gander, war correspondent

PLATE 14 Guy Prendergast, LRDG

PLATE 15 Jellicoe's SBS after a successful raid in the Aegean

PLATE 16   George Hatcher, Queen's Own Royal West Kents

PLATE 17   Clifford Clarke, Queen's Own Royal West Kents

PLATE 18   Frank Smith, Royal Irish Fusilier

PLATE 19   Paddy McCrystal, Royal Irish Fusilier

PLATE 20 Lieutenant Richard 'Jimmy' James, Royal West Kents

PLATE 21   Don Bush (right), Royal Navy

PLATE 22   Sid Bowden, Queen's Own Royal West Kents

PLATE 23 Peter Antony Barham (left), Royal West Kents, with his friend 'Aggie' Aldridge who was killed in action on Leros

PLATE 24   Ted Johnson (right), Royal Irish Fusiliers, with Peter Craig, the year before the Battle of Tobruk

PLATE 25   Ted Johnson on-board a ship going to Malta

PLATE 26   British officers are received at Portolago, Leros, by Italian commander, 20 September 1943. Brigadier Brittorious saluted Italian Admiral Mascherpa

PLATE 27   Officers of Royal Irish Fusiliers. Ted Johnson second from left, back row. Reverend Anwyl front row, first left

PLATE 28 Commanding Officer of 1st Special Boat Squadron Lieutenant Colonel Lord Jellicoe (left), with Captain Chevilier an officer of the Greek Sacred Squadron on the bridge at Tewfik, HQ Boat

PLATE 29 Captain Alan Redfern. Killed in action on Leros

PLATE 30   Meeting of Brigadier Brittorious (middle) with Admiral Mascherpa on right of photograph, IWM, E4297

PLATE 31   British and Italian officers after luncheon together on 22 September 1943. Third from left is Admiral Mascherpa, next to him Brigadier Brittorious, Commander Borghi (chief of staff, in white), Brigadier Turnbull, Lieutenant Colonel Livolsi (OC Infantry Battalion), behind him George Jellicoe of SBS

PLATE 32 General Paget being welcomed by the Mayor of Leros

PLATE 33 Carriage assemblies for 40-mm anti-aircraft guns strapped to the casings of the submarine HMS *Severn* at Beirut, 18 October 1943, about to be taken to Leros

PLATE 34   Soldiers taking a break

PLATE 35   Stretcher-bearers carry a wounded soldier to makeshift hospital

PLATE 36   German paratroopers escort Italian POWs, 15 November 1943, IWM HU67411

PLATE 37   Tilney (left) with German officer after surrender

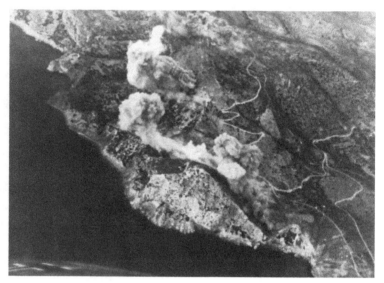

PLATE 38   German air raid on Leros, 12 November 1943

PLATE 39   Enemy bombs fall on Leros

PLATE 40   After the surrender. Paratroopers' assembly point, Alinda

PLATE 41   Enemy bombs fall on the outskirts of Portolago, Leros, 1943

PLATE 42　A photograph taken covertly at Stalag VIIA at Moosburg, showing British POWs talking to new inmates captured on the Greek island of Leros

PLATE 43 A German soldier inspects the remnants of a British coastal gun destroyed by an air raid by German Ju 87 Stuka dive bombers, December 1943

PLATE 44   Agia Marina today, looking toward Alinda

PLATE 45   Battlement emplacement

PLATE 46   One of the many tunnels used for storage and living quarters

PLATE 47   Another army tunnel

PLATE 48   Leros cemetery

www.ingramcontent.com/pod-product-compliance
Ingram Content Group UK Ltd.
Pitfield, Milton Keynes, MK11 3LW, UK
UKHW020731280225
455688UK00012B/594